For The best of
spirits!

C B Tayh

"All old houses wherein men have lived and died
Are haunted houses. Through the open doors
The harmless phantoms on their errands glide
With feet that make no sound upon the floors."
—Longfellow

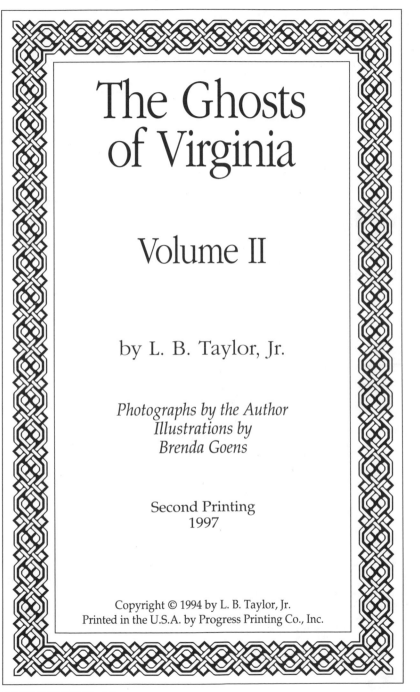

The Ghosts of Virginia

Volume II

by L. B. Taylor, Jr.

Photographs by the Author
Illustrations by
Brenda Goens

Second Printing
1997

ISBN 0-9628271-4-2

Contents

SOUTHWESTERN VIRGINIA

Author's Note

I had no intention of writing this book. When I completed "The Ghosts of Virginia" in 1993 — all 120,000 words of it — I was convinced that I had all but exhausted the ghostly material in the commonwealth. After all, there were something like 95 separate incidents in the book. What more could there be? My files were bare. But I was wrong. Dead wrong!

It all happened by accident. Brenda Goens, the artist whose fine illustrations adorn these pages, and I went to Roanoke over the holidays in 1993 to visit her relatives. We more or less got snowbound in the city, and consequently I spent several days in the Virginiana Room of the Roanoke Public Library. The more I dug, the more I found. Here, buried in county histories and special bicentennial publications, and in ancient scrapbooks, were the leads to dozens of "new" ghost stories. Here were the notorious "Black Sisters" of Christiansburg. I had been looking for documentation on them for years! Here were legendary Indians and Indian fighters of the valleys. Here I became literally entranced with Samuel Kercheval's "History of the Valley," written in the 1830s. It, too, held clues to mystic events. Here was a wealth of information on supernatural occurrences and superstitions of the mountain people of southwest Virginia.

I was hooked. I wrote hard through the months of January and February, when snow, sleet and ice made it difficult to leave the house. The chapters began piling up. When the weather permitted, I ransacked the library archives at Williamsburg, the College of William and Mary, Richmond, Charlottesville, the Alderman at the University of Virginia, Harrisonburg, Winchester, Fairfax and others along the way. I interviewed gracious Virginians at points from Clarksville and Chatham in the southern part of the state to Weyer's Cave and Covington in the west, to Alexandria and Fairfax in the north.

I gathered data on ghosts, poltergeists, devils, angels, witches and even a couple of Virginia vampires! People wrote or called me about such famous haunted mansions as: Hewitt in Urbanna; Avenel in Bedford; Prestwould in Mecklenburg County; and Vaucluse in Fairfax County. I drove hundreds of miles — from the Northern Neck to the mountains bordering West Virginia, and from Leesburg to Danville. In the Virginia State Library in

Richmond, I sorted through hundreds of papers written in the depression-era 1930s and early 1940s by writers who combed the state interviewing ordinary people in a government-sponsored project. Among these yellowed handwritten and typed drafts were original folklorian tales, including some precious haunts which had been passed down by families generation to generation.

I am deeply indebted to the Blue Ridge Institute at Ferrum College for allowing me access to some historic files dating back to the 1930s and 1940s, and including material written by Works Progress Administration (WPA) writers. A great amount of authentic Virginia lore was recorded under this program. Among the collection of James Taylor Adams were more than 200 ghost legends, most in the Southwestern part of the commonwealth. I have included a number of these in a special section of this book, through the courtesy and permission of Clinch Valley College and the Blue Ridge Institute.

I heard other stories and accounts of actual experiences at a number of the talks I gave and at craft shows I participated in. Some of these, such as "The Terrible Crash That Wasn't," collected at the Newport News Fall Festival, led to colorful chapters for this book.

Why? Why would I subject myself to the rigors and loneliness of research and writing a second book on Virginia ghosts when I have hardly begun to market my first one? Obviously not for money. Certainly, a fringe reason would be the recognition. Writers love recognition. But even more important, I think, as I have often said, is the fact that the recording of ghost stories, encounters, and legends helps preserve a part of our common-wealth's heritage; a part that is being obliterated in the glare of modern-day television and the computer-electronic age. In a way I felt compelled to continue writing about Virginia's supernatural history. My only real surprise has been that there was so much fresh material I hadn't found before. And here, let me thank the many people who wrote and called me, encouraging me to "keep writing." It helped make the effort worthwhile.

Among the many letters I have received, I was particularly pleased with the following. Mrs. Bertha Story of Hopewell wrote me, "Thank you for giving our son, Tim, many hours of enjoyment from reading your books. You really sparked his imagination." From Coral Springs, Florida, Mrs. Isabel Arismendi said, "I would like to thank you for sending us 'The Ghosts of Richmond.' I'm very happy because now my 11-year-old son, Frederico, is reading a lot more." And from 14-year-old Parker Perry of Newport News: "As a born Virginian I can enjoy and respect each story. Your books let me look at history in a way that gets me interested." That makes all the long hours in the musty stacks of town and county libraries, and all the days staring at the blank computer screen worthwhile.

That is also why I enjoy speaking to groups across the state, especially to library associations and to school children. Our kids are eager to learn about our past when it is presented in an interesting manner. And are they sharp! They ask some of the best questions! They ask not only about ghosts, but about how I gathered the material, and how I wrote and published it. A lot has been said in recent years about the sad deterioration of our school systems, but when I face a group of 30 or 40, or 100 fresh-faced students, I don't see that. I see a keen desire to hear and ask and learn. And I always come away impressed and refreshed, feeling they gave as much or more to me as I did to them.

One of the most pleasurable experiences I had last year came from a phone call I got at home one night. "This is the Today Show calling," the voice said. "We would like to film you telling a ghost story for a Halloween segment we're doing." Sure, I answered, thinking one of my friends was playing a trick on me. Turns out it was the Today Show. Producer Eric Hill and a photography team flew down, and we filmed segments at Westover and Berkeley Plantations in Charles City County, and at the Edgar Allan Poe Museum in Richmond. We spent 12 hours in all. They wanted me at Westover at six in the morning to film the fog rolling in off the James River. I told of the spectral return of Miss Evelyn Byrd at Westover, who died in 1737 of a broken heart at age 29, and this was the piece the show aired October 29, 1993. It was fun.

* * * * *

I received a letter about a year ago from a young man named Gary Boze of Richmond. He had read my book, "The Ghosts of Tidewater," and was fascinated about the chapter of the multiple haunts of a place called "Old House Woods," in Mathews County, bordering the Chesapeake Bay. He said he wanted to go out there and see for himself, so I gave him directions.

A few months later I talked to Gary again. He was helpful in gathering information about the chapter in this book on Virginia vampires. Gary said he and his wife and their young child drove out to the Mathews area one day looking for the ghostly woods.

"I'm not sure if we ever found them or not, but a very strange and scary thing did happen to us that day," he said.

"We were walking around when I got this real creepy feeling. I didn't see anything, but it was weird. Then, suddenly, we were literally attacked by a huge swarm of horseflies." It sounded like a scene out of "The Amityville Horror." "These weren't just ordinary horseflies," he continued. "They were the largest horseflies I had ever seen. They were gigantic. They were the size of a quarter! We ran back to the car, and it took me several minutes to get all of them out of the car.

"We took off, and then noticed — and I'm not exaggerating — the horseflies followed us down the road. We thought we had lost them when we drove around a vacant field, but then we saw them again. They had cut across the field. I know this is hard to believe, but they followed us for six miles! My wife got really spooked, and I have to admit I was pretty scared, too."

* * * * *

Included in my first book on Virginia ghosts was a chapter on the famous McChesney farm in Augusta County, where, in 1825, a succession of strange psychic occurrences took place, including barrages of rocks sailing about inside the house, hurled by unseen hands. The phenomena seemed to swirl around a young slave girl named Maria, and was never explained. The McChesneys literally were driven from their home by this "evil force."

Charlie Witten of Roanoke, a descendent of the McChesneys, called me one night to add to the initial account. She said her grandmother and great aunt, who later were in the house, reported that chairs would be inexplicably broken, china cracked apparently of its own accord, and heavy furniture would be mysteriously rearranged. "Succeeding owners have told of sounds they couldn't explain, and were so frightened in the house they wouldn't talk about it," Charlie said.

"I was never comfortable when I visited there. You got an eerie feeling at the entrance to the master bedroom, in the dining room, and near the old slave quarters. My brother and I felt things we weren't supposed to feel." And so it appears that although little Maria has been gone for nearly 160 years, either her spirit, or someone else's, still is actively creating haunting manifestations at McChesney's farm.

* * * * *

In "Volume I" of "The Ghosts of Virginia," I covered the Wythe House in Colonial Williamsburg, where there is a legend that the jealous Lady Skipwith, miffed at an incident which took place at a fancy ball, raced to the Wythe House where she was staying, losing a slipper along the way. Her ghost is said to be heard ascending the stairs. What was curious about this is that the master of the house, George Wythe, one of the most brilliant yet least known of our founding fathers, did not himself return in spirit form. He had just cause since he died a tragic death, being poisoned by a greedy nephew.

I said at the time that there were no reports of Wythe's return. However, since that book was published I have come across an account which contradicts this. William Oliver Stevens wrote "Old Williamsburg," which came out in 1938. He found another ghost at the house, which he toured at the time. He called Wythe "one of the great legal lights of early Virginia and his home was a resort of distinguished visitors even before the revolution." He noted that George Washington used this house as his headquarters at the out-set of the Yorktown campaign.

Here is what Stevens said about the "extra" ghost: "Unhappily, Chancellor Wythe was poisoned by a villainous nephew to whom he had bequeathed a large amount of his estate. The murder was committed in Richmond, but the old gentleman's ghost came back to haunt his old house in Williamsburg where it felt more at home. Regularly, on the eighth of June, the anniversary of his murder, George Wythe emerges from the closet of his bedroom and lays a *chilly hand* on the face of whoever is sleeping therein. There is a story that the subsequent owner, instead of being disturbed by this ghostly tenant, used this room for his unwelcome guests. He con-trived to invite them to come for the first fortnight in June. They never tarried after the morning of June 9, and never returned!"

Just as this book was going to press, I got a call from a young lady in Seattle, Washington, named Vickie Galloway. She told me she and a friend had taken the Williamsburg ghost tour (based on my book) in May 1994 during a vacation, and that she was so enamored with the legend of Lady Skipwith, the ghost of the famous Wythe House in Colonial Williamsburg, that she decided to visit the house the next day.

She took a photograph of the stairway inside the house where the ghost of Lady Skipwith is said to appear from time to time. Very excitedly, Vickie then told me that when she had the photos processed, *Lady Skipwith's ghost appeared on the stairs!* Would I be interested in seeing a copy of the print, she asked. Would I?!!!

Here is the photo she sent. In her letter, Vickie said she and her friend toured the Wythe House May 19, 1994. "I took pictures to illustrate the story of Lady Ann for anyone who would listen to my vacation travelog," she wrote. "As a last thought, I took the enclosed photo looking down the stairs from the upstairs landing. When I got the pictures back from the developer there was Lady Ann! In case anyone asks, I was using 100 ASA, Fuji film and a Ricoh point and shoot 35mm camera.

"I'm really anxious to hear your reaction to my photo. Both Carol (her friend) and I have become very fond of her."

I have to admit, it is one of the most fascinating photos I have seen. Judge for yourself.

* * * * *

Lady Skipwith's ghost(?) on the Wythe House stairs!

In the first volume of "The Ghosts of Virginia," there was a chapter on Monticello and a report of a mysterious "humming" sometimes heard on the grounds. It was noted that the Man himself, Thomas Jefferson, liked to hum as he strolled about his magnificent estate. That was about the extent of the psychic phenomena that was uncovered at the mansion near Charlottesville.

However, one evening in March 1994, I received an intriguing phone call from a young lady named Jennifer Wilson who lives in Fairfax. She had just read the chapter described above, and felt compelled to call. "I thought you might be interested in the experiences I had at Monticello," she said. It seems that in the summer of 1992, Jennifer, grieving over the deaths of some close friends and relatives, began taking a series of weekend trips to take her mind off the losses. She toured Jefferson's home in June of that year.

"I really don't know quite how to explain it," she began. "I was out on the terrace and walked over to the little Honeymoon Cottage and went up to peer into the window. There was no one else around at the time, when I suddenly felt a frigid chill. This was Charlottesville in the middle of June and I was freezing! As I leaned over to look through the window, the door began rattling

Gravesite of Thomas Jefferson

violently. There was no wind. I looked around to see if anyone was doing it and there wasn't anyone. I had the strangest feeling that there was a presence there. It was a little scary. I had a camera, and I took a picture through the window.

"A little later I walked down to Jefferson's grave site and the feeling of a presence was so overwhelming there, I had to leave." When Jennifer had her photos developed, she was stunned when she looked at the shot taken through the window at the cottage. There, on the left side of the picture, was a large "blob." "I showed it to my mother and she said, 'oh, that's just part of the curtains.' But there were no curtains!"

About a year later, in July 1993, Jennifer went back to Monticello, this time with her mother. Again, she felt the strong sensation of a presence. It seemed to follow her throughout the main house. Outside, she decided to walk about the grounds, and left her mother sitting on the edge of the terrace. When she returned, her mother appeared visibly shaken. "She had felt the same sensation I had," Jennifer said. "She wanted to leave immediately."

Had not her mother confirmed her feelings, Jennifer said she would have chalked her experiences up to a vivid imagination and the fact that she was emotionally overwrought at the time. "Now, I really don't know what to make of it all," she said. "It sort of clashes with my religious beliefs, but on the other hand, I believe I have a modest psychic ability. I can remember once before, while touring Civil War battle sites in the Winchester area, having a similar feeling that there were presences all around me."

When asked if she knew of any possible reason a spirit or spirits might make themselves felt to her at Monticello, Jennifer said, "I'm not really sure. But I have done some genealogy work and it may be that Alex Garrett is one of my ancestors." Alex Garrett was Jefferson's lawyer!

* * * * *

One of the most interesting letters I have received since the publication of the first Ghosts of Virginia, was from 70-year-old Ed Barr of Dale City, Virginia. "Enclosed," he said, "you will find 'ghost slides' to add to your personal picture collection." One slide was of a spectral "pair of legs" in a room at Woodlawn Plantation, adjacent to Mount Vernon. The second slide portrayed a phantom woman at a quilt show held at the Westminster Historical Society in Maryland.

Apparitional Legs at Woodlawn

At Woodlawn, Ed took a picture of a "piano bench" in the music room in 1972. It looked more like a footstool to me. Ed didn't know about the apparitional feet until three years afterward, when he was showing the slide on a screen to a lady. They were viewing shots of needlework. The lady asked whose feet were in the photo, and Ed noticed them for the first time. The silhouetted image of one foot, from the shoe halfway up the calf can be seen directly under the third leg of a small table above the center of the piano bench. It appears to be the left leg. The right leg, barely discernible in a large print from the slide, is a stride to the right of the left leg.

The photo was included in Judy McElhaney's book, "Ghost Stories of Woodlawn Plantation." The book said it appeared to be leggings and buckle shoes from the 1700s, and one person even suggested it might have been the legs of George Washington. There are some unconfirmed legends that his ghost has been seen riding a horse around Woodlawn. Ed leans more toward the supposition that the shoes are those of a lady, and that they are more likely from an era after 1850, and possibly around 1900. I tend to agree.

In the second slide, taken at the quilt show in 1975, Ed says when he took it, it was late in the day, about 4:45 p.m., and the show was about to close. "There was hardly anyone in the building at the time," he says, "and I was trying to get a good view of a piano at the end of the aisle with a beautiful quilt draped over it. When I snapped the shutter the aisle was perfectly clear! There was no one there. In fact, when I got the slides developed I was upset, because the piano was blocked out. And then I saw the image of the woman with half of her head missing. I was astounded! "It looks as if she has no hair, but actually, if you look at the original slide, she is wearing a cloth hat. This was popular in the 1920s. The cloth coat she is wearing, I think, also dates from that era." Ed points out that if one looks closely on the left side of the woman's coat, part of it is transparent!

The obvious question concerning both photos is could they be double exposed? Ed says, emphatically, no. "I used a Minolta SRT 101 for both shots. After each frame the shutter locks. You cannot take another photo until you advance the film. There is no way to recock the shutter without advancing the film. It is therefore impossible to get a double exposure. I've been taking slides for over 30 years, and I have shown these two to experts. They all believe the pictures are genuine. I can't explain them, but the images are there. If they are not ghosts, what are they?"

Ed Barr's "Headless" Lady

I have a photo story of my own to add. When I was in Danville to cover the "The Recurring Wreck of Old 97" chapter — the account of one of the most famous train wrecks in Virginia and U.S. history, and the eerie events which have happened at the site ever since, I walked to the scene just off highway 58. I took a photo looking down into the gorge where the train plunged more than 60 years ago. When the picture was developed there was a strange white blob in it. At first, I thought it might just be a reflection off the water below. But on closer examination I decided it wasn't a reflection. I don't know what it is!

Mysterious Phenomena in Danville

* * * * *

Wherever I speak, the most often asked question I get is "have I seen a ghost?" The answer is no. It certainly isn't because I haven't tried. I have gone to scores of haunted houses and even stayed in some overnight, but nothing has appeared. I believe that some people are more sensitive than others, and the manifestations of otherworldly subjects are experienced only by these relatively few.

I have been scared out of my wits, however, on more than one occasion. The one I remember best happened when I visited "Old Mansion," a 300-plus-year-old house in Bowling Green a few years ago. In asking directions to the house, several people told me they wouldn't go near the place. It was dark when I drove down the 300-yard-long entrance way. Pitch black! There were no lights. When I parked and got out of the car, I couldn't see my hand in front of my face. And then, as I stood up, I felt something pound hard against my chest! I was knocked backward a step or two. I was terrified. I could feel the hair on the back of my neck stand up. But then, as my eyesight adjusted to the blackness, I could make out the outline of a large dog. It was the house owner's dog and he had just given me a friendly welcome to "Old Mansion" by jumping up and thumping me with his front paws.

I'm not sure I could stand a spectral greeting!

Anyway, it all has been great fun. I have enjoyed the research, the discoveries, the tours of historic homes, and the genuine hospitality of Virginians all over the commonwealth.

Enjoy!

SHAKESPEARE: ODE TO THE GHOST OF HAMLET'S FATHER
I am thy father's spirit,
Doom'd for a certain term to walk the night.
And for the day confin'd to fast in fires,
Till the foul crimes done in my days of nature
Are burnt and purg'd way. But that I am forbid
To tell the secrets of my prison-house,
I could a tale unfold whose lightest word
Would harrow up thy soul, freeze thy young blood,
Make thy two eyes like stars start from their spheres,
And each particular hair to stand on end,
Like quills upon the fearful porpentine.

Introduction

The national newspaper, "U.S.A. Today," confirmed it. A year or so ago, they ran a map of the United States showing sites where hauntings had taken place. Virginia led the country. But the number of reported hauntings — 69 — barely scratches the surface. There are literally hundreds of ghosts in the commonwealth.

Why? Maybe Philip Goodwilling of St. Louis, considered one of America's foremost ghost hunters, summed it up best when he said there are so many hauntings in Virginia, "because there were so many tragic and traumatic things happening there, from Revolutionary War times through the Civil War. You have such battlefields that tend to leave plenty of psychic imprints. Not to mention the great minds that Virginia has provided for governmental leadership. Virginia has got to be very much haunted." Another writer has added that the state has so many spirits "because the rolling hills south of Washington, dotted as they are with magnificent manor houses, many of them dating back to colonial days, seem to (provide) the kind of atmosphere ghosts prefer … Virginia … is very much like England in many respects. Even the ghosts, such as they are, that continue a shadowy existence in some of the estates and plantation houses, are similar in their habits to those found in English stately homes… Even though the plantations that were once the life blood of these houses are no longer in existence, the houses themselves continue to flourish because the Virginians have a keen sense of history and tradition."

Curiously enough, one possible reason so many ghosts frequent the rustic houses and manor homes of Virginia is the preponderance of boxwoods on the grounds, some dating back two centuries or more. According to one author, writing in the October 1928 issue of "The Black Swan" magazine, "The majority of old houses of Virginia have boxwood planted on their lawns, and it has been said that an atmosphere conducive to its growth is also favorable to psychic phenomena."

Ghosts, of course, have been discussed and debated for thousands of years. Legends of apparitions are recorded in cuneiform on clay tablets that date back to a period of at least 4,000 years. The earliest accounts show that the belief in the apparitions of disembodied spirits was common among the ancient people of Babylonia. Sumerians who dwelt in the valleys of the Euphrates, commonly believed that apparitions of the dead visited the earth.

The ancient Greeks talked of hauntings in considerable detail. For example:

Pliny the Younger told the story of a house in Athens, Greece, in which no one would live because it was believed to be haunted. A number of tenants had moved in, and just as abruptly moved out, declaring they heard eerie sounds of rattling chains in the dead of night.

The philosopher Athenadorous, apparently harboring no fears of the supernatural, moved into the house. On his first night there, he sent his servants to bed and set himself down with his writing materials to do some work. For some time, all was still. Then Athenadorous heard a distinct sound — the rattling of chains. He shut this out of his mind, and continued his writing without lifting his eyes up toward the source of the noise.

The sounds, however, grew louder and closer. They seemed to enter the room and come up behind him. Finally, he looked around and "beheld the figure of an old man, lean, haggard, and dirty, with dishevelled hair, and a long beard, who held up his finger and beckoned him." Incredibly, Athenadorous waved the apparition off and went back to his work. Then, the figure advanced and "shook his chains over the philosopher's head," who, on looking up, saw him beckoning as before. This time, the Greek arose and followed. The apparition walked slowly, as if obstructed by his chains. He led Athenadorous to a certain spot in the court, which separated the two divisions of the ancient house. And then he vanished.

The next day, the philosopher recommended that authorities dig at the spot where the figure disappeared. They did, and found the skeleton of a human body encircled with chains! Once the remains were removed and properly reburied, the haunted house was no longer disturbed.

* * * * *

What are ghosts? The only real definitive and indisputable answer is, simply, no one knows.

Experts have tried to define ghosts for centuries:

* Ghosts are the disembodied spirits or energy that manifests itself over a period of time, generally in one place.

* Ghosts are the souls of the dead.

* A ghost is the surviving emotional memory of someone who

has died traumatically, and usually tragically, but is unaware of his or her death.

* A ghost is a person who has died and "missed the bus" going to where they should go. They're stuck.

* Apparitions are the super-normal manifestations of people, animals, objects and spirits. Most apparitions are of living people or animals who are too distant to be perceived by normal senses. Apparitions of the dead are also called ghosts.

Andrew Mackenzie, an author and authority on the subject, says: "Instead of describing a 'ghost' as a dead person permitted to communicate with the living, let us define it as a manifestation of persistent personal energy, or as an indication that some kind of force is being exercised after death which is in some way connected with a person previously known on earth."

The fact is, despite extensive study since the late 19th century, science still knows precious little about the nature of ghosts. Studies have shown, however, that in most cases, spirits appear for specific reasons:

* To communicate a crisis or death.
* To provide a warning.
* To comfort the grieving.
* To convey needed information.
* To fulfill a mission left undone on earth.
* To ask the living for help or understanding. This is especially true of ghosts of people murdered or killed in battles, and also of those who have been improperly buried, or whose burial places have been desecrated.

Most ghostly manifestations feature noises, unusual smells, extreme cold, and the displacement of objects. Other phenomena include visual images, tactile sensations, voices, and the apparent psycho-kinetic movement of objects. While the most common perceived image of a ghost is a filmy apparition, in actuality, visual images are seen only in a small percentage of reported cases. Such figures are always clothed, and most often appear in period costume.

The term "haunt" comes from the same root as "home," and refers to the occupation of houses by the spirits of deceased people and animals who lived there. Other haunted sites seem to be places merely frequented or liked by the deceased, or places where violent death has occurred. Some haunts are continual; others are active only on certain dates that correspond to the deaths, or major events in the lives of the dead.

Are ghosts real? That question has remained unanswered through the ages. It is, ultimately, up to each individual to decide. A Gallop poll reported that 14 percent of Americans said they have had a ghostly experience. Certainly, most all instances of reported supernatural happenings can be explained by scientific or rational means. But not all! As psychic expert Hans Holzer once said, "There are theories, but no proof, as to why (hauntings) happen. But that the incidence of such happenings exceeds the laws of probability, and that their number establishes that there is something to investigate, is beyond dispute."

Regardless of one's personal feelings, there is, unquestionably, an innate longing in human nature to "pierce the veil" which hides the future after death. Thus, the origin and nature of ghosts have popularly appealed to mankind at all times and in all places, and will doubtless continue to do so until the craving to know something of the unseen world is satisfied.

It is not the author's intent to make readers either believers or disbelievers. I will only say that I deeply believe in the sincerity of the people I have interviewed; that they genuinely believe they have had experiences and encounters that cannot be explained by normal means. My real intent is to present these incidents as they have been described in the hopes that the effort might preserve a small portion of Virginia's anecdotal history. I hope the chapters will be, in a small way, interesting and educational, and, in a larger way, entertaining.

* * * * *

Now, a final word on organization. Organization of such a book, in a clear, concise and cohesive manner, is difficult. Where does one begin? For this second volume of "The Ghosts of Virginia," I have chosen to commence the ethereal journey in the Northern Neck with a chapter on the extraordinary Christ Church in Lancaster County. From there, the route leads through Urbanna, and the Fredericksburg area to northern Virginia, then across to the upper Shenandoah Valley. We then move south through the valley into the central part of the state, and then go all the way down to the southwestern tip. We cross the southern boundary to Danville and move back up to the greater Richmond-Petersburg region, and wind up in the Williamsburg-Tidewater section, ending, appropriately enough, in Virginia Beach, home of the legendary psychic, Edgar Cayce.

The spectral road is interrupted with periodic detours to allow coverage of collections of chapters. These include specific sections on such subjects as: Legends of Unrequited Love; Spectral Vignettes, or shorter pieces; Gambling Ghosts; Monsters; Indian Spirits; and a five-part series on the ghosts surrounding the Lincoln assassination conspiracy.

I hope you will find this somewhat circuitous haunting highway as interesting to travel as I did. It is designed so you may stop over at any point, and pick up again without missing a single apparition. Enjoy!

"And their eyes were opened and they recognized him, and he vanished from their sight."
St. Luke 24:31

"Then a spirit passed before my face; the hair of my flesh stood up."
Job

Is Christ Church An American Stonehenge?

(Lancaster County)

lthough he was possibly the most powerful man in the Virginia colony during his time — a dynamic, charismatic and arrogant individual who was viewed with a mixture of respect, awe and fear — his celebrity has not survived the centuries nearly as well as that of many of his early 18th century contemporaries. In fact, it is probable that relatively few Virginians today can even tell you who he was, where he lived, or what he did. Yet, during the first three decades of the 1700s no man stood taller or cast a greater shadow.

Such was the living legend of Robert "King" Carter of Corotoman. Next to the Fairfax family in Northern Virginia, he was the colony's largest landlord. At the time of his death in 1732, he left an estate of 300,000 acres, about 1,000 slaves, and 10,000 pounds sterling, a princely sum in that day.

Carter used a brilliant talent as a shrewd businessman and a highly effective, if sometimes harsh, executive to parlay a lifetime of wheeling and dealing into a huge fortune. In his day tobacco was the chief crop and his ships regularly plied the Rappahannock and Corotoman Rivers carrying it to European markets. On return trips he brought in "all sorts" of merchandise, necessities and luxuries needed in farming and home life. For his personal use he is said to have imported rum from Jamaica by the hogshead, brandy and wines from France by the hundreds of gallons, and once placed a single order for 2,000 bottles of ale. His lifestyle was, in a word, flamboyant.

He struck an imposing if somewhat less than attractive figure. One historian described him as being a "plump-faced man of middle height, with alert, probing brown eyes. An aquiline nose drew the features to a prowlike convergence, appropriate to one who made such indomitable progress through life." He was, too, a deadly serious man, for it has been written that nowhere in all the records and papers covering his life does a single "flash of humor appear."

He was born in the Northern Neck in 1663 and quickly rose to prominence and wealth by serving as agent for Lord Fairfax and as proprietor for all the land lying between the Potomac and Rappahannock Rivers. During his lifetime he served in almost every important post in the colonial government, including President of the colony. He was prolific in other ways, also. He fathered four daughters and one son by his first wife, and five daughters and five sons by his second wife. And he was lavish in accommodating his offspring, building majestic mansions for them ranging from historic Sabine Hall in Lancaster County to the magnificent Carter's Grove near Williamsburg. Among Carter's descendents were: seven governors of Virginia; three signers of the Declaration of Independence; two Presidents of the United States, William Henry Harrison and Benjamin Harrison; and Robert E. Lee.

He also built his own church. It stands today in the tiny community of Weems, near Kilmarnock, in Lancaster County, on the site of an earlier church completed in 1670. Some believed he wanted to erect a church superior to Bruton Parish in Williamsburg. More likely, he financed the construction to protect the grave site of his father and four of his father's five wives. Work began on the Christ Church sometime around 1730, and it probably wasn't completed until 1734 or early 1735, although some say it could have been in use as early as 1732, coincidentally the year Robert "King" Carter died.

How much satisfaction he got out of this philanthropic venture is not recorded. However, he was buried by the east wall of the new church beside his two wives. There, today, one can read the elegant wording on his tomb: "Here lies buried Robert Carter, Esq., an honourable man, who by noble endowments and pure morals gave lustre to his gentle birth... Possessed of ample wealth, blamelessly acquired, he built and endowed, at his own expense, this sacred edifice — a signal monument to his piety toward God... Entertaining his friends kindly, he was neither a prodigal nor a parsimonious host.

"At length, full of honours and of years, when he had well performed all the duties of an exemplary life, he departed from this world on the 9th day of August, 1732, in the 69th year of his age.

"The unhappy lament their lost comforter, the widows their lost protector, and the orphans their lost father."

The marble and limestone tombs have been restored. The handsome slabs are replicas of the originals which were all but destroyed by vandals. The tombs are decorated with cherubic heads and acanthus leaves. Curiously, Carter's tomb has a skull and crossbones at its eastern end.

King Carter did not just build a church. He built an architectural gem of legendary proportions. It is acknowledged to be the best-preserved colonial church in Virginia, and is a registered national historic landmark. The National Geographic Society has called it "an imposing mausoleum-like brick structure built in the form of a Greek cross."

The Virginia Landmarks Register says "The ensemble is the epitome of colonial Virginia design and craftsmanship. Enhanced by its quiet rural setting, Christ Church is without peer among Virginia's colonial churches in the quality of its architecture and state of preservation... The exterior is set off by its beautiful brickwork, especially the exquisitely crafted molded-brick doorways, the finest of their type in the nation. Inside, the church retains its original pews and stone pavers. The architectural highlights of the interior are the handsomely trimmed pulpit and the walnut afterpiece."

Outside, bricks fired on the property more than 250 years ago still burnish orange, red and gray on the three-foot-thick walls. Roof pitches produce a pagoda-like effect. Inside, the flagstones were brought by ship from England. Sunlight shimmers through 12 tall, narrow windows and the oval "ox dyes" in each of the three gabled ends. A staircase curls around a three-deck pulpit with a walnut sounding board that carries a voice perfectly to all areas of the cross-shaped structure.

Impressive as all that is in itself, it pales in comparison to a remarkable discovery made in 1988 by a man named Stephen Stewart. A retired sporting goods buyer for a store in New Jersey, and a collector of antique clocks, Stewart now lives near the church. He visited the church on March 30th of that year and saw

Christ Church

something that literally changed his life. "I tripped over a sunbeam and woke up a sleeping giant," he says.

On that day Stewart noticed that above the altar, the gold lettering of the Ten Commandments was aglow. A sunbeam from the oval window in the west wall was trained on the Decalogue "like a spotlight." He wondered if the beam of light would find its way to the cross in the church by Easter. He came back to check. Day by day, as the afternoon sun moved higher in the sky, the beam approached the cross. Finally, at 5:13 p.m. on Easter day, April 3, the beam landed squarely on the altar, capturing the cross in its glare.

This enthralled Stewart, and began an obsessive investigation that has continued ever since. He began studying other aspects of the church's unique architecture, and his findings over the years have convinced him Christ Church is a veritable calendar, designed, he says, "in harmony with the universe as a tribute to God. It is a time machine, no question about it. The whole building is a building of numbers. It's inundated with calendric, solar and lunar numbers."

His findings lend impressive evidence to such a claim. Consider the following:

* The sunbeam from the west oval window strikes the altar twice a year, 14 days after the vernal equinox, a day on which Easter sometimes falls, and 14 days before the autumnal equinox.

* Sunbeams from the oval window in the west and south wings land precisely on the tombstone of David Miles, an early county justice, at the intersection of the church's two aisles in the very center of the building. This happens four times a year on the "cross quarter" days between each of the four seasons.

* Shadows from the eaves on the west-facing wing plot a calibrated course on the western walls of both the north and south wings that count the days from spring to summer and back to fall. The shadows move one row of bricks a day. There are 94 days between spring and summer, and 94 between summer and fall. There are precisely 94 bricks between the building's water table and cornice! Coincidentally, there are 94 characters in the epitaph on David Miles' tomb.

* There are 188 brick dentils above the church's west entrance. There are 188 days from the first day of spring to the first day of fall.

* The cruciform church has 12 walls and 12 windows. There are 12 numbers on a watch.

* There are 26 pews in the church. Twice 26 is 52, the number of weeks in a year.

* There are 208 dentils carved in the wooden sounding board over the pulpit. Dividing that by four yields 52,

* From front to rear there are exactly as many dentils as there are days in the year.

* Along the sides there are 104 dentils, twice the number of weeks in a year.

* There are 938 dentils at the cornice, a sum equal to twice the number of days in a year plus four times the number of weeks.

* The west door has 26 panels, one half the number of weeks in a year.

* A water table around the exterior of the building is made from 417 bricks — equal to the number of days in a year plus the number of weeks.

* For eight hours each day, Stewart claims, the church also acts as a sundial, casting an exact shadow on the north lawn.

Can all of this be dismissed as accident, as coincidence? "How could that many things happen in one building and just be chance," asks P. L. Anderson, a Danville builder of colonial-style structures. "The strongest arguments are your eyes. The first time I saw the church I was struck by its extraordinary height. The architect had to have a great familiarity with astronomy and trigonometry to figure out these dimensions."

Anderson added that whoever designed the church had to coordinate three dimensions to make its west oval capture the sun during the Easter season. These coordinates were the height of the oval window, the length of the oval window from the cross at the altar, and the angle of the sun. For the window to capture the sun at the times that it does, the building has to be about three and a half degrees west of a true east-west alignment. No other alignment, experts say, would produce the observed solar phenomena.

Stewart, Anderson and others who have researched the phenomena agree that whoever designed the church really knew what they were doing. It was not done by happenstance. Who then was the brilliant designer of this incredible structure, which has been called by some an American Stonehenge?

That is a question that is hotly debated, for it remains a puzzling mystery. There are no records to indicate who designed Christ Church, or why it was so constructed. Stewart, Anderson, and a growing number of others who have analyzed the church's unusual architecture believe they know. They suggest it was designed by the legendary Christopher Wren, who grew up near Stonehenge in England, and had a lifelong fascination with astronomy!

Stewart says, "Wren was first an astronomer. Second, he was an architect. Learned men at the time were deeply involved with the heavens. The more you get into it, it's inconceivable that he would have built anything that was not to do with astronomy."

This thesis has one essential flaw, however. Christopher Wren died in 1723. Christ Church construction did not start until 1732, nine years later. Stewart and others, however, offer the view that Carter may have commissioned Wren to draw up the plans for the church before his death, or Wren plans could have been used without his permission. This is supported by Dr. Alan Gowans, chairman of the division of Art History at the University of Victoria, British Columbia. In his book, "King Carter's Church," he minutely compared the plans and details of Christ Church with the generally accepted Wren design of ancient Farley Church, and feels assured that the two buildings had the same architect — Christopher Wren. He said Christ Church, in its provincial simplicity, is "Wren stripped to the essence." (It is interesting to note that

Tombstone at Christ Church

Farley Church had a circular window over its main entrance door virtually identical to the one at Christ Church.)

Church officials, somewhat perplexed by the curious findings and speculations of the past few years, have said, simply, "Whether a plan from Wren's collection or other 'style book' sent from England was adapted by Robert Carter for his use, and whether or not a master builder came from England for the special purpose of building the church, are not recorded."

And so the mystery remains. Was the Christ Church designed to be a living calendar? And if so, why? Was it, as Stewart has speculated, built in harmony with the universe as a tribute to God? And was it designed by Wren or some other genius of the times? We may never know the answers.

But that is not all that is intriguing about this haunting church. There is, too, a genuine ghost story connected with it. It was first recorded, more than 60 years ago, by Margaret DuPont Lee in her classic book, "Virginia Ghosts." It concerns the Reverend John Bell, who is believed to be the first Episcopal minister at Christ Church. When Mrs. Lee wrote about the church, in 1930, it was in a sad state of neglect and deterioration. (It has since been painstakingly restored to original glory by the Foundation for Historic Christ Church.) "One finds," Mrs. Lee wrote, "woodland and undergrowth on two sides; here and there great walnut trees, nuts pressed into the earth by the feet of slaves felling their giant forbears; these trees living today in pulpit, table and panelling within this splendid relic of a bygone age. Beneath her shadows, here and there among the trees, interesting inscriptions may be deciphered on old stones, and a number of graves are within a crumbling wall."

The Reverend Bell's daughter, it is written, was engaged to a young planter named Carter. It is not specified if he was a relative of King Carter. Her fiance, however, was killed in a fight with Indians on the day before the wedding. The girl, Mrs. Lee said, "pined and died."

Perhaps sensing she did not have long to live in this world, she had asked her father to bury her on the glebe beneath a certain old poplar tree, where she had often met with her lover. When she died, though, Reverend Bell laid her body to rest in the Christ Church courtyard.

This apparently did not set well with the young lady's spirit. She is said to have returned "again and again" at night to plead to the minister and remind him of his promise to fulfill her last wish. The reverend, "wearied by the continued haunting," gave in and had her body reinterred under the poplar tree. Her apparition never appeared again. Sometime after this, the grave began to sink and a pond sprang up "covering the place of her burial."

* * * * *

(Author's note: There is one curious footnote that may involve Christ Church. I am not certain, because the historic reference is to the "Church at Currotoman," which could mean Corotoman. It was reported in a book published many years ago covering the reminiscences of Mrs. Sally McCarty Pleasants. It is titled "Old Virginia Days and Ways."

In the book, Mrs. Pleasants refers to an incident involving a young man named Townsend Dade. The time is not specified, although it probably occurred in the second half of the 18th century. Dade brashly boasted one day that he was not afraid of anything dead or alive. He was promptly challenged by his friends to go to "the old haunted Church at Currotoman," and write his name in the parish register. The church then was in a sad state of repair.

Mrs. Pleasants says Dade accepted the challenge and, "with a bottle of ink in one hand and a lighted candle stuck in his cap, he strode off through the woods whistling merrily." His friends waited for him till "long after cockcrow," but he did not return. When he was still missing a day or two later, they went to the authorities and reported him missing. At the church, searchers found fresh footprints in the "ancient dust of the aisle," and there, on the yellowed page of the old register, "was a large capital 'T,' followed by a long scrawl that trailed to the foot of the page. It appeared that if Dade indeed had signed the book, something must have terrified him at the precise instant he did. To add to this supposition, the ink bottle had been overturned and the ink was dried on the floor!

The mystery festered for several weeks. Then one day Townsend Dade returned to the area from "parts unknown." He seemed to be a changed man. There was no more boastfulness in his countenance, and friends noticed a white lock on his temple. They were convinced he had witnessed some sort of spectral phenomena, but "no persuasion could induce him to tell what he saw at midnight in the ruined chapel of Currotoman!")

C H A P T E R 2

Is Hewick Virginia's Most Haunted House?

(Urbanna, Middlesex County)

(Author's note: The letter immediately intrigued me. "I have believed in ghosts all my life and I've had lots of encounters," wrote Mrs. Evelyn Edwards of Urbanna, the town of the famous oyster festival on the Rappahannock River near its entrance to the Chesapeake Bay. "I'm sending you a picture of a truly haunted house. My husband, children and I lived there 21 years. When I tell people I'm afraid of ghosts, they don't believe me. They say anyone who lived in *that* house isn't afraid of the Devil himself!")

he house Mrs. Edwards sent a picture of was Hewick, an ivy-covered brick mansion that is reputed to be more than 300 years old, and is located just off state highway 227 a few miles north of the town of Urbanna. The house is believed to have been built in 1678 for Christopher Robinson who came to Virginia from England about 1666. Says historian Julia Jarvis, who wrote about the celebrated Robinson family: "He (Christopher) must have been a man of ability, for he soon built a home beside a little off-shoot of the Rappahannock still called Robinson's Creek." At his death in 1693, "he left a great many acres of land because he had early been granted permission to bring into the colony both white settlers and Negroes, which meant that he acquired extra tracts of land for his colonizing efforts."

The name Hewick apparently came from the Robinson ancestral home in Yorkshire, England. One early description of Hewick says it was located "amid beautiful trees, with a lane leading to the house lined by 60 Lombardy poplars on each side and with beautiful lawns bordered by the popular boxwood." It also was said to be "a village unto itself," complete with blacksmith, carpenter, cobbler and butcher shops to take care of the plantation's needs. Slave quarters were near the river where there also were docks for loading shipments of tobacco for England. On the thousands of acres Hewick once encompassed were lavish gardens and orchards, a family burying ground, and a spring and springhouse. The separate building which served as the kitchen had a fireplace so wide, "that almost the entire trunk of an ordinary tree could be put across its andirons," and so deep that there were several compartments with iron doors built in the brick walls at either side used as warming ovens.

The main house itself is built of Flemish bond brick two feet thick, with stone steps and stone window sills. The parlor fireplace originally was five feet wide. Right of the entrance hall is the high-ceilinged parlor, and to the left is the dining room. The staircase rises against the left wall to a platform which crosses the back and continues up the right wall. Upstairs are two huge bedrooms and a smaller room over the front entrance.

It is written that when Christopher Robinson and his two sisters first came to America they "immediately took as their right their place in the well-established and exclusive aristocracy of Virginia." Robinson served as Middlesex County clerk, as coroner, and as a member of the House of Burgesses. According to historical accounts, many of the most prominent names in the colony — Wormeleys, Beverleys, and Braxtons, among others — regularly gathered at Hewick to "discuss the affairs of the nation they were helping to build." These were some of the leaders "who first placed the name of Virginia on the maps of all the civilized world and laid the foundation for her greatness."

Hewick also apparently is a house that veritably crackles with ghostly eminences. No less than seven separate spirits are believed to haunt the mansion. In one book on historic houses in Virginia there is a paragraph on this phenomenon: "Many old homes have their ghosts, and Hewick is no exception. There is 'The lady in Pink' who appears every seven years... Another ghostly visitor is the big man dressed in black. Scents of perfume and tobacco pervade the house and cemetery. Music boxes play and a spinning wheel turns."

"It's all true, every bit of it," says Evelyn Edwards, who lived there from 1957 until 1978, the last four years by herself. Now 71-years-young and living in Urbanna, the sprightly Evelyn professes to have personally experienced just about everything that has been written about the spectral activity.

"When we first moved in, the house hadn't been lived in for a number of years and it already had a reputation as being haunted," Evelyn says. "There had been squatters there, but it was in an awful state of repair. But Ernie, my husband, knew I liked big old houses, so he arranged for us to live there. We were so busy at first working on fixing Hewick up that we didn't notice anything. Then one day even before we moved in, something strange happened. My collie dog ran off and then stopped dead in his tracks and went into a frenzy. It looked as if he was circling around someone or something, but my mother and I couldn't see anything. Then it appeared as if whatever it was was approaching us, and we suddenly got a real chilled feeling. We got in the car and left."

Later, Evelyn says, her mother dreamed of the scene and said she plainly saw a big man dressed in a black suit, and that was what had upset the dog. "We didn't learn until much later that one of the legends of the house was the ghost of a man in a black suit!"

Shortly after the Edwards moved in, they held a Thanksgiving dinner for about 20 relatives and friends. There was only one bathroom in the house, upstairs. "I went up the backstairs to go to the bathroom after everything had settled down, and as I looked up, there was a man standing at the top of the stairs," Evelyn says. "I didn't think anything about it at the time," but later I realized it wasn't anyone I recognized. In fact, I don't even think it was a real person. The thought sent chills through me."

Over the next 21 years, scores of otherworldly incidents occurred at Hewick, witnessed not only by Evelyn, but by her husband, her children, and others. Following is an excerpted account of some of them. "One night my son was in his bed upstairs when he heard someone calling his name," Evelyn begins. "He answered and looked up and saw a man dressed in black standing in the room. My son hid under the covers.

"Another evening, everyone had gone to bed and I was getting ready to when I heard a girl singing. The sound was coming from the north bedroom, but when I entered it the singing stopped and there was no one there. Exactly seven years later I heard a girl laughing when I was in the house by myself. It scared me so bad I ran down the stairs. I read somewhere that a ghost returns every seven years."

Was this the girl or lady in pink that had been previously described? Evelyn thinks it was. "One day," she continues, "my husband's foreman came to the house when we were gone somewhere. Later, he told us he had met a girl going out of Hewick. He said he didn't recognize her, but that she was dressed in a long pink gown of another era, and that her hair was in 'red rivulets!' I told him it was our ghost. Then around Christmas that year, my daughter heard an upstairs door open when no one was upstairs. She saw a girl going down the stairs with a pink dress on and red hair. My daughter just stood looking at her until she vanished.

"Once my youngest grandson, who was about seven at the time, came to spend the night with us. The next morning he came downstairs and was going to the kitchen to get some oatmeal. He stopped in the hall like he was rooted to the floor and stared into the kitchen. I asked him what was the matter, and he turned and said he saw a little boy go in there. When we went in, there was no one there."

Evelyn says one of the most prevalent manifestations was the fragrance of flowers — always when there were no fresh flowers in the house. "It seemed like you could always smell them, and usually in two places. One was at the old family cemetery, and the other was at the front door. We never could find an explanation for it. For example, one night my son and his wife came over to spend the weekend. I got up early the next morning. It was still dark, but I noticed a light on in my son's room. He said he kept it on all night. He couldn't sleep because there was a ghost there. He had smelled fresh flowers.

"Another time, George (her son) was sleeping when he felt something tapping him on the shoulder. At first he thought it was his wife, but he looked over and she was asleep. He then looked up and said he saw two red looking lights. He said it was like two shining eyes staring at him. He woke his wife and screamed 'something's in here.' He was literally too scared to get out of bed."

Evelyn's sister came over with her daughter one day to use the Edwards' set of encyclopedias. "I told them the books were in the other room and to go ahead in and get them. They went in once, then went back a second time. When they came out of the room my sister said, 'there's something in there.' I just smiled. Then they went in again and this time they came out running and their backs were arched. They said there was a ghost in that room and he was trying to grab them. I just laughed and said if the ghost was not

Hewick

chasing them it would be chasing me. They didn't think that was very funny. I guess it wasn't, but I couldn't help it."

One day Evelyn was polishing the floor and the closet door was open. "I tried to close it, but for the life of me I couldn't budge it. I went on polishing. Then, as I finished, something grabbed that closet door and slammed it shut. This happened a number of times, doors would just open and shut by themselves. There was the incident with the threshold between the front hall and the dining room. It was worn bare. We were putting in new sills and repairing the threshold. One night my husband and his three brothers-in-law were sitting in the dining room and the door to the dining room slammed shut. I mean slammed! The men just sat there looking at it. One of them said it must have been the wind. Well, my husband got up, walked over and struck a match over the threshold, and the match flame *never flickered!*"

At one time the Edwards had a little antique shop, and they stored many of the antiques in the basement at Hewick. "I never could stay in the basement very long," Evelyn says. "I always had this eerie feeling that someone else was there. I can't really explain it, it was like a presence. There was an old spinning wheel that sat by the door. When I went down to the basement one day, the spinning wheel was just flying at a high velocity, spinning around as hard as it could spin. When I looked at it, it stopped abruptly."

On another occasion, Evelyn, in the house alone, was going up the stairs when she heard a music box in the bedroom playing. "It used to play 'Oh What A Beautiful Morning'," she says. "The box had a string on it about a foot long and a ball at the end of the string. You played the box by pulling the ball down, and as it played, the string would slowly wind up toward the box. But when I went into the bedroom, the song was playing and the *string wasn't moving. It never moved through the whole song!*"

Then there was the episode with the piano. Says Evelyn: "It used to play by itself at least once a week. We never could figure out what caused it. There was never a soul in the living room where it sat. Finally, we got rid of it. We set it out in the yard to be picked up. And after that, would you believe it, we heard the piano playing out in the yard."

Evelyn says the movements of the Hewick ghosts were not necessarily restricted to the house, either. "We would encounter them in the lane outside. If you walked in the lane, you would always have the feeling that someone was walking behind you. We believed it was the girl dressed in pink. I remember one time one of the neighbor boys, Clinton, came over and asked me if he could hunt squirrels on our property. I said sure. But he never came. I asked him why, and he said his little brother wouldn't come with him because he saw a ghost in the road."

Evelyn says the common manifestations of spirits, such as footsteps, were so plentiful at Hewick that no one thought much about them anymore. "We used to hear someone walking around in the attic all the time. We'd go up to look at first, but there was never anyone there. A visitor once remarked that it was probably a rat. I laughed and said rats don't walk like people do. It was definitely the footsteps of a person, or of a person's ghost. We would also hear someone coming up the stairs at night, but they never got to the top. Our dog must have heard the sound one night because it got to the landing and went crazy. It barked and barked, and its hair bristled, and then we could feel a gush of frigid air coming up from the stairs. The dog backed into our bedroom and wouldn't come out. Ghosts can scare a dog to death.

"That didn't bother us near as much as what would happen on the couch did. Apparently, the ghost liked the couch. I recall one time my son-in-law was sitting there and he said something sat down beside him. He said whatever it was must have taken its shoes off, because he said he smelled 'stinking feet.' It happened to me, too. It sat down beside me one time so close I couldn't even move. Oh, yes, sometimes the ghost would get physical. It grabbed hold of my leg once as I was walking through the dining room. Grabbed hold of my calf. I just stood there for a minute or two and then it let go. Another time I was laying in the bed and it pinned my arms above me. I screamed 'turn me loose,' and it did. They say take a Bible in a room and the ghost won't come in. I put a Bible in my bedroom after that."

Apparently, the spirit or spirits got upset with Evelyn once about reading in bed. She was reading a newspaper once and fell asleep with the paper laying on top of her. When she awoke she couldn't find the paper anywhere. "I looked and looked, and I just couldn't find it. It was a mystery. Someone said a mouse might have done it. I said that mouse would have to have been as big as a beaver. Sometime later, I was looking for an old picture frame that we had put behind the headboard of the bed, and there, crammed behind the frame, was the newspaper. You tell me how it got there!"

A number of other curious things happened at Hewick while the Edwards lived there. One Christmas, Evelyn was wrapping and sorting presents, when she noticed she was missing one package containing some bedroom slippers. "I couldn't find it anywhere, never did. The next April that package suddenly reappeared on my bed upstairs. No one else in the house knew anything about it.

"Every year my husband would decorate a big tree outside with lights. He did it every year for about 25 years, and then he got sick with cancer, and the year before he died, he couldn't get out to decorate the tree. Someone called me one night and said they didn't think we were going to light the tree that year, but they were glad that we did. I said we didn't know anything about it. When I went outside to look, the tree was fully lit from top to bottom. Now, who did that?"

The thing that scared Evelyn the most took place after there had been a number of break-ins in the area. She had put extra hooks on both sides of each door, so that they could be latched from the inside or out. "I heard the hook on my bedroom door going back and forth one night," she says. "Then I heard footsteps, and no one else was supposed to be in the house. I jumped out of bed and ran out into the hall. The hook on the other side of the door was just swinging away. My dog wouldn't move. I ran out of the house and spent that night at my sister's house!"

Evelyn says she always heard that one ghost was that of Christopher Robinson. She adds that she had heard tales of a man named Ross who lived nearby in the Cedar Park region, which was at one time part of the 3,000-acre Hewick Plantation. "The story that I heard was that this man named Ross once was afraid he was going to lose his money sometime around the Civil War. So he took some iron pots filled with gold, and had his slaves carry them off into the woods with him. Then, he supposedly shot the slaves so no one would know where the money was hidden. I can remember when I was a child and we used to walk in the woods in that area, we always got a creepy feeling that someone was following us."

While Evelyn doesn't know exactly who the ghost or ghosts are at Hewick, she says the family once bought an Ouija board and asked the board who was haunting the house. "The board said there were seven ghosts there. It said they were Christopher Robinson, his wife, Agatha, and one of their children. But the board didn't say who the other four ghosts were. It scared us real bad. All I can say is don't make fun of an Ouija board." She also says a psychic once came and went through the house and said there were ghosts in every room.

Evelyn says that after the Jones family moved out of Hewick, another couple and their daughter and son-in-law moved in. It was about 1928. The younger man apparently drank to excess, and in time his wife and her parents moved out, leaving him there alone. He reportedly often went on drinking sprees that lasted for days at a time. "Then, he seemed to disappear," recalls Evelyn. "No one saw him for about two weeks, but not too much was thought of it, because everyone knew he would go on binges. But then one day, right after a blizzard we had one winter, some hunters found him in the yard, halfway between the house and the outhouse. He was frozen to death."

Evelyn says that since that time, she has had a strong sensation of the young man's presence at Hewick. "He was a heavy smoker, too," she says, and his cigarette and whiskey smells pervaded the dining room, back hall and kitchen. You could hear him scratch at the back door, and whenever we had snow or sleet, we could hear his pitiful moans from the back yard. When I first moved into the house, there was a picture of him and his wife in the living room. I swear that whenever I went into that room, his eyes would follow me. We had to take the picture down."

According to Evelyn, there was a house known as Pine Tree, that stood up the hill on land that was once part of the Hewick

Plantation. It had been built around 1812. When a family moved out of the house in the late 1960s, they left behind a lot of old furniture and told Evelyn and her sister they were welcome to anything they wanted.

"We went over and looked around," says Evelyn. "There were beds, dressers, wash stands, trunks, a roll-top desk, some tables and chairs and other things. We picked out a few things we wanted, and came back a few days later with a pickup truck to get them. Upstairs, we heard some heavy panting, and it sounded like someone was running up the stairs toward us, but we never saw anyone. We thought maybe someone doesn't want us taking any of the furniture. So we left, and came back again later with my sister's dog, a large collie. When he got to the base of the stairs, however, he froze. His back stiffened and he wouldn't move. We heard something at the top of the stairs, but we couldn't see anything, so we left again."

Eventually, Evelyn and her sister were able to take some items. One was a cradle. She cleaned it up and placed it upstairs in the hall at Hewick. "One night, my husband and I were startled to hear what sounded like a baby waking up. It came from the cradle. We jumped up to look, but didn't see anything. This happened a number of times, so we finally put the cradle in the south bedroom.

Cemetery at Hewick

"My youngest daughter was pregnant at the time and she asked if she could borrow the cradle. I said 'sure,' but I didn't tell her about hearing the sounds. I got a call from her a few days later and she said she was returning the cradle," Evelyn says. "I asked her what was wrong, and she said she and her husband kept hearing a baby crying in it. She asked me if I had heard any such sounds, and all I could do was chuckle.

"Then one day my sister's son, Fred, came over to take some photos of antique furniture for a class project he was doing. I told him to be sure and take a picture of the cradle. When he came back downstairs to the kitchen, he was visibly shaken. He said he had heard a baby whimpering in the cradle. I had placed a boy doll in the cradle, and Fred also said that he swore the doll had *grinned* at him! I couldn't help but smile myself. I had seen the same grin. It was a sinister grin."

After Evelyn moved out of the house in 1978, she said several people moved in, but didn't stay long. Perhaps the ghostly activities were too much for them. Hewick fell into disrepair and weeds and thick underbrush surrounded it. In the mid-1980s a couple then living in California, came to the rescue. Ed and Helen Battleson were visiting relatives in Virginia, when, by chance, they learned that the house was on the market. This was a rare coincidence — that they should find this out while vacationing, plus the fact that Ed was a direct descendent of the founding Robinsons.

The Battlesons decided to put in a bid on Hewick. This led through a long series of negotiations to their eventual purchase of the house. They have restored it with meticulous and loving care. "It was deteriorating at a pretty rapid pace when we got it," Ed says. "The grounds were so overgrown that we couldn't find the old family cemetery, although we knew it was somewhere near the house. They began clearing the land, and found the graveyard about 100 yards to the rear and right of the back door.

Both Ed and Helen had heard the stories of past hauntings. "I never really thought much about it," says Helen, "but I have to admit that there have been times when, as I was walking towards the cemetery, it seemed like I would see something there. It was like a flash of a vision, something moving about among the tombstones. I would have to rub my eyes, and when I looked again there was nothing there."

They both say they have smelled the scent of sweet tobacco at Hewick, generally in the area of the front hall. "We do know from research, that this was an area of the state where sweet tobacco was grown in the colonial days," Ed says. "We know the odor wasn't caused by either one of us or anyone else living. It was like pipe tobacco." Helen adds that while she hasn't personally seen or felt anything out of the ordinary in the house, her mother has. During a visit once she heard a girl giggling in an upstairs bedroom when no one was there. Could this have been the mysterious "Lady in Pink," returning after another seven years had passed?

The Battlesons, who deal in antiques in the nearby town of Saluda, have furnished their home with period pieces, and have opened it up to tours, and as a bed and breakfast inn. "Anyone interested in history would enjoy a stay here," Ed notes.

Is Hewick Virginia's most haunted house? If not, believes Evelyn Edwards, it certainly should be near the top of the list. "Everything I said is the truth," she says. "I lived there. It happened."

There is one extraordinary footnote to include. Back when Ed and Helen Battleson were first considering offering a bid on the house, Ed had a vivid, and, as it turned out, prophetic dream. In the dream he and Helen were at Hewick and he walked up to a front window and peered inside. (At the time the house was completely empty, and this window was virtually obscured by brush, but in the dream it was not.) Inside, Ed saw about six people, men and women, all dressed in colonial costume of the early 1700s period. Some were seated on a couch in the room.

After they bought the house, and Ed walked into this room for the first time, *it was exactly as he had envisioned it in his dream!* "It was incredible," he says. "It was really as if I had been there before. Not only that, but when Helen furnished the room she put in a couch in the exact spot that I had seen a couch when I had looked through the window in my dream. And at that time I hadn't even told Helen about my dream!"

(Author's note: Sadly, Evelyn Edwards died as this book was being finalized. May her spirit rest in peace.)

Good and Evil Spirits at Bladensfield

(Richmond County)

here is considerable conjecture as to just when a venerable old house called Bladensfield, in Richmond County about 20 miles from Tappahannock, was built. In a paper written for the Northern Neck of Virginia Historical Magazine several years ago, Catherine L. Milsted, who once lived in the house, said, "There is a local Richmond County tradition that a house was built sometime prior to 1700, on the Bladensfield property by Nicholas Rochester of Westmoreland County for a Captain John Jenkins. Jenkins had been granted 1,000 acres by Virginia's Governor, Richard Bennett, in 1653, for bringing 20 new settlers to Virginia."

In her book, "The Children of Bladensfield," published in 1978, Evelyn D. Ward said, "According to the 'Guide Book of the Northern Neck' the house was built about the year 1690, by Nicholas Rochester of the family of Rochesters who founded the city of Rochester in New York." Mrs. Ward also called Bladensfield "one of the very old places in Virginia. One of the two oldest that he knew of, was the surmise of our State Historian and Director of Archeology when he visited it. Other experts have confirmed his testimony."

Yet, the Virginia Landmarks Register says, "This weather-boarded old Northern Neck plantation house, on land that was once the property of Robert ("King") Carter, probably was built in the third quarter of the 18th century by Carter's grandson, Robert ("Councillor") Carter.

Catherine Milsted adds, "It is very probable that the present house was built over and around the original one by a Carter. It became known as Councillor Carter's quarter, 'Billingsgate.' The name 'Bladensfield' was given to the property after Councillor Carter's marriage to Frances Tasker, daughter of Benjamin Tasker and Anne Bladen of Maryland." To this, Evelyn Ward adds, "Tradition says the place was for a time the home of George Eskridge, guardian of Mary Ball, George Washington's mother."

Whatever, there is agreement that, in its original form, the house was a two-story, five-bay structure with a center passage. It is also agreed that in 1790, Bladensfield was deeded to Benjamin Tasker's daughter, Anne Tasker Carter, and her husband, John Peck, the Princeton scholar who followed Philip Fithian in 1774, as tutor of the Carter children at neighboring Nomini Hall.

The house passed from Peck descendents to the Reverend William Norvell Ward, rector of the Cople, North Farnham and Lunenberg Parishes, either in 1842 or 1847, depending upon which source you select. Ward enlarged the house and made it into a female academy. The doors have "H L" hinges designed to "keep the witches out." There is also an "Indian peep-hole" in the facing of the rear door.

Peck family members lie buried in the old Peck graveyard below the garden. In writing a memoir of the house and the times in the mid-18th century, Mrs. Ward said, "When you stand in the south door and look down the garden walk, you see the handsome group of the graveyard trees. It looked very lovely this spring with the dogwood and the yellow sassafras blooming among the dark pines and cedars. It is carpeted with periwinkles. We used to look at them, but never pulled them. Mamma wouldn't let us. 'They were for the poor dead people,' she said.

"Very quiet the graves looked, lying in the sunshine, but the servants used to tell us stories of the ghosts of the people buried there; how they came out at night and walked about their old haunts." Mrs. Ward noted that the servants had recalled that Mr. Peck, in particular, had been a hard drinker and "a very severe master." One beloved servant named "Old Uncle Armistead Jackson," used to tell the children about Peck's sightings. He said that "a great many of the colored people" saw his ghost in the studio where Peck did his drinking and kept his accounts. His apparition would be seen "in the late hours of the night, and always a flame of burning sulfur blazed up from his bosom." The servants were convinced Peck had gone to "the bad places" because he had worked his people so hard in life. Those who claimed to see him, said he was chained, and that he "rattled his chains angrily."

Mrs. Ward's favorite ghost story was of "Miss Alice," the beautiful daughter of John Peck. She had been the last one buried in the graveyard, and her rosebush still bloomed in the garden. She had fallen in love with a handsome young man who was addicted to gambling and horse racing. Alice refused to marry him until he reformed. She went on a trip to the mountains, "from which she returned ill with the fever that brought her death." Her lover returned and it was said she died as he held her trying to tell her something. Thereafter, her spirit was often seen wandering about, the servants said, because she had died before hearing what her young man had been trying to tell her.

Alice's presence was most often felt in her upstairs bedroom. Once, years after her departure, a clergyman named Temple visited the house and spent the night in her bedroom. He told Mrs. Ward's mother, "Madam, I could not sleep in that room." Yet, he said he would not have missed the experience for anything. Some believed he had been her young lover.

Aunt Amy Fauntleroy, a very old colored woman, told the Wards that when she had been a little girl at Bladensfield, the ghosts had become so troublesome that the house owners at the time decided to have them "laid." This apparently meant some sort of exorcism. Aunt Amy said a Baptist preacher was called in. He came into the hall from the back of the house, "wearing his coat inside out and upside down, and read verses of the Bible going from the bottom line to the top!" The servants all gathered and observed this strange action with their eyes open and their mouths agape. It must have been at least partially successful, however, because Aunt Amy said that after "the laying," the ghosts weren't as bad.

Still, Mrs. Ward, in her memoir, noted that at least some remnants of the spirits remained at Bladensfield during her childhood there. She noted, "Mamma did not like us to hear these stories. She told us not to believe them. We thought we didn't; only we loved to play about Miss Alice and make believe in the daytime. When twilight began to make the far corners of the halls and stairways dim and mysterious, we used to go running noiselessly to where the grown people were, looking backward as we went with a feeling that something not of earth was behind us."

Kindred Spirits at Kenmore

(Fredericksburg)

One of the truly unsung heroes of the American Revolutionary War was an aristocratic gentleman not necessarily noted for his physical appearance but more so for his courtly bearing and great dignity. Though his name may be unfamiliar to high school history students, he was a close and respected associate of such noble patriots as Edmund Pendleton, Francis Lightfoot Lee, Richard Henry Lee, George Wythe and many others. He also was a lifelong intimate friend and brother-in-law of George Washington. His name was Fielding Lewis.

Born in Gloucester County in 1725, Lewis moved north to the Fredericksburg area as a young man, where it is said his natural leadership abilities and distinguished connections quickly won him a position of prominence in the community. Biographers have described him as an efficient man of affairs with polished manners who was widely recognized as a gentleman of wealth and integrity.

Perhaps his greatest measurable contribution to the cause of American freedom was the sacrifice of his personal wealth — and possibly of his health as well — to launch and operate a gun manufactory during the war, which provided arms for the colonial troops. He literally threw everything he had, materially, physically and otherwise, into keeping this factory going during the darkest years of the fighting. And when the war ended with no proper compensation, as promised, from the Continental Congress, Lewis went broke. With less patriotic creditors pressing him, he suffered serious lung trouble — then called consumption — and died after a lingering illness in December 1781.

Among his other notable accomplishments was the building of a mansion and estate in Fredericksburg which came to be known as Kenmore. After his first wife died in February 1750, Lewis married Betty Washington, the only sister of the first President of the United States, in May of that year. Shortly after that he reportedly asked his new brother-in-law to advise him in the selection of a favorable site for the home he proposed to build. The site was chosen near the corner of what is now Lewis Street and Washington Avenue, on a green slope which fell away towards the Rappahannock River. The grounds then were surrounded by orchards and woods full of gum, hickory and red, white and black oak trees.

Construction of the house began in 1752 and evolved into what architects consider to be one of the most beautiful colonial mansions in America. The walls of the elegantly simple exterior of Kenmore are two feet thick, fashioned of Flemish bond brick. Inside is an exceptionally elaborate interior containing what the Virginia Landmarks Register calls "the finest 18th century plasterwork and chimneypieces in the country."

Following Fielding Lewis' death in 1781, Betty Lewis maintained the 1,100 acre estate, raising her three youngest sons, for 15 years before moving to a farm south of town. The mansion passed through the ownership of several families during the 19th century and into the 20th, and after suffering relatively little damage through the Civil War, fell on hard times by the 1920s. When plans were announced to subdivide the property and dismantle the great house, a movement began to save it. This led to the formation of the Kenmore Association and fostered a nationwide preservation effort which, as any visitor to the site today will readily attest, has been highly successful.

It is now a museum open to the public, complete with period furniture, a beautifully restored garden, a gift shop, and a kitchen dependency in which old fashioned gingerbread is served. The recipe is said to be the same as that used by Mary Ball Washington, George Washington's mother. There are many special exhibits illustrating the history of Kenmore and the colonial period, and the Association calls it a house that "belongs to the nation."

It also has been said that when in the mansion one becomes conscious of the "brooding presence" of Fielding Lewis. And there are many people — both tourists and Association employees and

Kenmore

volunteers alike — who have sworn they have seen and heard the ghost of this refined gentleman at Kenmore. The most common manifestation is the sound of his heavy tread in an upstairs bedroom as he paces back and forth.

He has been sighted a number of times, too, and the descriptions vary little. Often in broad daylight, witnesses have reported seeing a man with a "worried expression" on his face dressed in clothes of the Revolutionary War period. Some have claimed to have seen him poring over a sheaf of papers, which they have speculated were the bills of creditors he could not pay.

At times, the Kenmore Association hostesses have tried to discourage the stories of psychic experiences in the house, saying, appropriately, that the beauty and history of Kenmore are far more interesting. Still, the legends persist. Door knobs turn when no one is at the door. Doors have stuck shut for days at a time, but when a carpenter is called, they mysteriously open. Guests have felt inexplicable cold drafts "blowing on their heads" in the dead of summer. A visitor standing in the Betty Washington Lewis chamber with two friends in the 1920s remarked, "I think this is a haunted room." As she did, to their astonishment, they heard a "click" and the wardrobe door slowly swung open.

In October 1971 — just five days before Halloween — an "official" seance was held at Kenmore. It was requested by Adi-Kent Thomas Jeffrey, a Pennsylvania writer and psychic investigator. The session was conducted by a woman named Grace Walker of Yardley, Pennsylvania, a member of the International General Assembly of Spiritualists, and a self-described "born clairvoyant." Mrs. Jeffrey apparently had asked for such a meeting a year after she had observed closet doors in the house swinging open and shut by themselves.

Among those present, aside from Mrs. Jeffrey and Ms. Walker, were then-Kenmore director, Col. Robert Burhans, Susie Hallberg, then-director of the Fredericksburg Information Center, two friends of Mrs. Jeffrey, three members of a Washington radio station there to record the event, and a newspaper reporter. Also present were two Kenmore hostesses, Ann Cunningham and Claire Barnard.

Mrs. Walker said the "vibrations were good" in the children's room, but she felt "utter confusion and sadness" there, so the seance instead was held in the master bedroom where the doors supposedly swung open and shut on occasion. The participants were then seated in a circle and asked to place their feet on the floor, to uncross their arms, and to relax and be silent. The Lord's Prayer was recited.

Mrs. Walker sat on a folding chair with her hands on her lap, the palms turned upward. Her eyes were half closed. After some initial conversation with members of the circle, she said she envisioned the spirit of an older man, "tired and weary of life." He was dressed in a collarless shirt and his hair was "threaded with gray." She placed the time of his "era" as being shortly after the Revolutionary War.

Immediately, the other members of the party thought of Kenmore's master, Fielding Lewis, who probably was at his most troubled period at that time, worn down with physical illness and the heavy burden of his debts. The medium said the man she was "communicating with" from the beyond was "not very pleasant and was inclined to be snappish." Indeed, Lewis was known to be a no-nonsense man of business who exhibited little humor in his affairs. Mrs. Walker added that this "soul" had appeared to her because he did not rest at peace; he was unhappy and was doomed to "always wander."

Beyond this, she indicated that there was a second spirit in the house responsible for the swinging doors. She said it was a young man who caused this manifestation periodically, more as a prank than anything else, "just to let you know he is present and around the house." During the seance a door was shut to see if it would open, but nothing happened. Mrs. Jeffrey explained this inactivity by saying psychic phenomena rarely happened "on command." With that, the seance closed, conclusively or inconclusively, depending upon your point of view.

Twenty years later, Ann Cunningham says she hasn't seen anything happen at Kenmore. "I guess you can't see what didn't happen," she acknowledges. "I think I'm just too practical a person." Yet she admitted there were many tales of "things" occurring in the house. "There is a lot of hearsay," says another hostess who asked not to be identified by name. "People hear things here. We've found beds puffed up. Lights flicker at times and windows sometimes seem to open by themselves.

"I did hear one story," the hostess continued, "about a lady who once stayed here as a guest with her mother. They were in a front bedroom, and each night they would hear footsteps, so they would get up and close the door. The next morning when they awoke the door would be wide open. So one night they pushed a heavy table across the room and shoved it against the door. They said the next morning the table was back where it had been the night before and the door was open again." On another occasion, a student at Mary Washington College claimed she got a "ghostly image" in photos she took at the house.

One person who has had a number of psychic encounters at Kenmore over the past few years is a young lady named Evelyn Kealey, a volunteer who works on the archeological digs that take place on the mansions's grounds. "I definitely think I have more psychic powers than the average person," she says. "That may explain why I was the only one who saw some of the things I did."

Several of the "occurrences" take place around Labor Day and in the fall and winter, when Evelyn and her associates spend a lot of time in the basement sifting through, cleaning and cataloguing the artifacts found in the diggings. These have included animal bones and teeth, apothecary weights, Civil War buttons, shards of 18th century ceramic and glass, nails and other items. "I've said the more they dig, the more it will stir up the restless spirits," she laughs. She may be right.

Evelyn says some of the more common manifestations have

included "someone fooling with the light. You have to flip the lights on and off or trip the circuit box," she points out. "The lights have gone out for no reason on more than one occasion, and no one working in the basement was anywhere near the switch. We joke about it. We just say it's Fielding. We think he likes to play pranks sometimes just to let us know he's around.

"Sometimes he, or it, locks the door to the basement. Again, you would have to latch it, or lock it with a key, and sometimes when we try to get through the door, it's like someone is holding it, and then all of a sudden it releases." On another occasion, Evelyn set a pail of silty water down to open the door. She was taking it outside to dump the water which had been used to wash off the artifacts. She opened the door and turned back to get the pail only to find that it had been "knocked over" by unseen hands or feet, and the water spilled down the stairs. "I had to clean it up," she says. "I wasn't very happy with Fielding about that."

Evelyn also has seen two apparitions in the basement, although

Fielding Lewis

she doesn't know if it was the same entity or two different ones. "Once, I saw a big willowy outline of a person move from one room to another. It had a cloudy, billowy shape. I had had the feeling that day that something was going to happen. I don't know why but I did. There was not a whole lot of shape to what I saw, but it definitely was moving. Shortly after that, the lights went out."

The second sighting proved to be more frightening. "It was about four in the afternoon in the fall, and I was taking a bucket of water out to empty it. I felt very strange. I was getting spooked out. As I got to the area I call 'mortuary wall,' I stopped. Against the wall I saw a dark outline. This is the darkest part of the basement, but I saw a tall figure that I estimated to be about six feet tall, draped with a cape around its shoulders.

"It was just standing there looking at me. I assumed it was a man, possibly a military officer in some kind of uniform. I could see the outline of his head, neck and shoulders, but when I looked down, I couldn't see any boots or footwear.

"I just stood there. I froze. I was stunned. I could feel goose bumps. I know there was no way what I was looking at was mortal! Nor could it have been my shadow. The sun doesn't get to this part of the basement. When I couldn't see his feet or legs, a thought struck me that maybe they had been amputated. Kenmore had been used as a hospital during the Civil War and I had a theory that when any soldiers died, they stacked them up against this particular wall, because it is the coolest place in the entire house in the summer.

"Anyway, I stood there for what seemed like an eternity. I guess it was only a few seconds. Then I went outside and dumped the water and when I came in again, the figure was gone. It was very eerie. No one else has seen anything like it, but as I said, I believe I am more psychically sensitive than most. I can tell you this, though. There are people who work here who won't come into the basement. They are afraid. It doesn't really bother me in that respect. I know there is some kind of presence down there. But I say it adds character."

Another person who has had unusual experiences at Kenmore — although he doesn't claim to be psychically sensitive in the least — is Ed Patton, who worked at the mansion as a part-time security guard for more than 15 years. Ed, now retired, is 83, but he remembers his encounters as if they happened yesterday, although he is in no way afraid of ghosts.

"Actually, there were three separate things that happened to me at different times, and I can't really explain any of them," Ed says. "One was the night I got a call at home from the police at two in the morning saying that a burglar alarm had been set off at Kenmore and that I should go check it out. Well, when I got there I didn't see anything out of the ordinary, but when I got up on the second floor and was walking down the hall, checking things out, a very strange thing occurred.

"I heard someone, or something, calling out my name. I heard it three times. It said, 'Eddie, Eddie, Eddie.' It was very distinct. I know I wasn't imagining it. I looked up and down the hall and in the nearby rooms. I saw nothing. Then I looked out the windows onto the grounds. There was no one there. It never happened again, only that once."

Ed continued his story: "The second time, I was outside the house at night and looked down toward the gate. There was a lady there. She had on a veil, which I thought was a little odd. It looked like a mosquito net to me. I watched as she crossed the brick walkway, and when she got to the other side — well, the thing is, and I don't know quite how to explain it — she never got to the other side! She disappeared right in front of me. I never figured that out."

Ed says that many times when he was in the basement of the mansion he heard footsteps on the floor above, when no one should have been in the house. Every time that he went to investigate, he found nothing amiss. "Sometimes, these things can play on your imagination, you know what I mean," he notes. "But I never made a big deal out of it. It never scared me. I always thought I was safer in the house with a ghost than I was out in the streets with a crowd."

The third specific episode at Kenmore took place one night when Ed was alone in the gift shop, eating a sandwich. To most people, this particular manifestation might have been the scariest of all — as the scene has been done and redone in chiller movies — but Ed, as usual, took it in stride. "I was just sitting there minding my own business, when I heard this screeching noise," he recalls. "Sounded a little like what a mouse would make. I turned around to the door where it was coming from and saw that the door knob was turning. It was turning real slow like, and making a slight screeching sound. Now this was one time I know I wasn't imagining things. I was sitting right there and I saw it. After I watched it for a minute or two, I got up and opened the door. There was no one on the other side. You explain it. I can't."

Fielding Lewis was not known to have had a sharp sense of humor during his lifetime. He is better remembered as a brooder, a worrier, and those who have claimed to have seen his apparition say that's the way he appeared to them. But maybe he did have a lighter side, too, and maybe that could account for some of the more prankish manifestations which have taken place over the years — and still occur — at historic Kenmore.

The Survival (?) of John Wilkes Booth

(Caroline County)

(Author's note: In my book, "The Ghosts of Fredericksburg," I included a chapter on the legends, ghostly and otherwise, surrounding John Wilkes Booth, the man who killed Abraham Lincoln. In a further review of this intriguing case, one which encourages lively debate and controversy to this day, I discovered considerable evidence of supernatural events involving several other prominent "players." They include: Mary Surratt, suspected but never proven to be a member of the conspirators; Judge Joseph Holt, who sentenced Lincoln assassination perpetrators to death by hanging; Dr. Samuel Mudd, the physician who attended to Booth's broken leg and was subsequently accused of being a member or supporter of the plot; and Lincoln himself, perhaps the most haunted of all.

While some of these events crossed the Virginia state line into Washington, DC, and southern Maryland, I included them in order to provide a full picture of one of the most famous, or infamous, incidents in American history, and the multiple accounts of psychic phenomena which surrounded the participants in it.)

t has been written that when he was a school boy, he once had his palm read by a Gypsy who told him he had a "bad hand, full of sorrow and trouble." The fortune teller said that he would "break hearts, but they'll be nothing to you. You'll die young, and leave many to mourn you. You'll make a bad end... Young sir, I've never seen a worse hand, and I wish I hadn't seen it, but if I were a girl, I'd follow you through the world for your handsome face."

The Gypsy was talking about the palm of John Wilkes Booth, the ill-fated assassin of Abraham Lincoln.

With the possible exception of the assassination and the ensuing storm of controversy which engulfed the death of John F. Kennedy, there is, arguably, no chain of historic events so shrouded in mystique and myth greater than that associated with Booth following his shooting of Lincoln at Ford's Theater in Washington.

While it has been only a generation since Kennedy's death, the confusion and contention which cloaked Booth's death — or alleged death — in a farmer's barn four miles from Port Royal, Virginia, just south of Fredericksburg, has lasted for more than 125 years and still rages today! The questions still are asked. Was Booth shot by a Yankee soldier, or did he kill himself? Was it Booth who was trapped in the burning barn, or was it someone portraying the handsome actor? Did he somehow escape the cordon of soldiers tracking him through the Virginia countryside to live out his life, as many believe, first in San Francisco and later in London? Why did the U.S. Government rush his body out of Caroline County and secretly bury it? Was this all part of a massive coverup to hide a much broader conspiracy against Lincoln and members of his cabinet?

Why was Booth's diary impounded by Secretary of War Stanton for two years after Booth's death? And why, after it finally was released, were 18 pages missing? Why were Booth's co-conspirators so cruelly treated before their trial, each shackled to a 75-pound iron ball, with his head encased in heavy canvas padded an inch thick with cotton, with one small hole for eating through, no opening for eyes or ears, and laced so tightly around the neck that speech was impossible?

Such questions were fanned for decades after his supposed death by countless reports of sightings of Booth all over this country and in Europe. As one writer put it early in this century, "Booth's ghost, a will-o'-the-wisp, has stalked the Republic, no witness sufficiently impartial and free from suspicion having been found to swear that he looked upon the disputed corpse and knew it either to be or not to be J. Wilkes Booth."

Millions of words have been written about Booth's life and death. Many authors, including immediate members of his family, have sworn that it was not Booth who was killed in Richard Garrett's barn in the early morning hours of April 26, 1865. But if not Booth, who was it, and what happened to the one-time matinee idol?

Adding to the deep mystery are scores of strange facts and happenings:

* Booth's alcoholic father claimed to have had "ghostly experiences."

* The ghost of Mary Surratt, said to have been one of Booth's co-conspirators in the assassination plot, and the first woman ever executed for murder in the United States, haunts the Surratt House and Tavern near Washington.

* The Sergeant who claimed to have shot and killed Booth was described as being a crazy man "who talked directly to God."

* Many of the main characters involved in the Booth story reportedly died strange and mysterious deaths.

* And, 20-odd years ago, a simple Midwestern farm boy, under professional hypnosis, claimed to have been John Wilkes Booth in a past life. What made this story of reincarnation unusual was that this young man recited obscure details of Booth's life that he had no way of knowing anything about. He also said that, in fact, he had not died on the porch steps of the Garrett farmhouse!

Many of the circumstances of Booth's escape are well known and are fairly unchallenged. After shooting Lincoln in his box at Ford's Theater, Booth, a fairly athletic young man of 27, leaped upon the stage. However, a spur in his boot snagged a draped flag and he fell awkwardly, breaking a bone in his lower left leg. He nevertheless managed to escape by horseback with another young man, named Davy Herold. They stopped at Mary Surratt's tavern around midnight, bolted down some whiskey, and rode on. At dawn the next morning Dr. Samuel Mudd treated Booth's leg, patching it in pasteboard splints. They slept in Mudd's house until near evening. Booth shaved of his trademark mustache, and he and Herold rode off.

For the next 12 days they eluded trackers on a winding route that took them through part of southern Maryland and into Virginia. Eventually, they shot their horses, and on April 24, 1865, crossed the Rappahannock River on a ferry with three Confederate soldiers returning from the war. A short time later Booth and Herold arrived at the Garrett farm, pretending to be soldiers on their way home.

Suspicious of the visitors from the start, Garrett's sons mistakenly believed Booth and Herold were horse thieves, and they locked them in their tobacco barn. Tipped off to their whereabouts, a troop of 26 Union soldiers rode hard from Bowling Green, 13 miles away, and surrounded the Garrett farm at about two in the morning. They encircled the barn and demanded that the fugitives come out and surrender. Herold did, but Booth, playing the actor to the hilt, shouted tragedian speeches, and threatened to fight the troops with his crutch if he had to. In an effort to smoke him out, the soldiers set fire to the barn.

The objective was to take Booth alive, but as the flames began consuming the barn, an inexplicable thing happened. A single shot rang out, striking Booth in the back of the skull, oddly at virtually the same spot Booth's bullet had entered Lincoln's head. At first, soldiers who dragged Booth out, had thought he had shot himself, but then a sergeant named Boston Corbett, a former hat cleaner known as the "Mad Hatter," admitted that he had pulled the trigger of his pistol, felling Booth. When he was asked why, Corbett said, "God Almighty directed me."

Barely alive, Booth was taken to the porch of the Garrett farmhouse where his bleeding head rested on a pillow in the lap of Lucinda Holloway, a spinster relative of the Garretts. He died shortly afterwards, and she cut off a lock of his dark, curly hair, which according to a 1977 newspaper article, can still be seen at the Caroline County Historical Museum. Old time area residents said that for years afterward whenever it rained the bloodstains could still be seen on the porch. In fact, souvenir hunters so haunted the farm that the Garretts finally had to remove the boards and refloor the porch.

One of the many who claimed to have seen Booth, if indeed the man lying in Lucinda Holloway's lap was Booth, was William B. Lightfoot, a native of Port Royal who had just returned from Appomattox a few days earlier. Years later, in an interview, he told of seeing something he could never explain. "There was always one queer thing about the barn," he said. "The center post, against which Booth was leaning just before they shot him, didn't burn. Next day everything was burned up but it. It stood up there, sir, all blackened but still sound, mightily strangely, in all the ashes."

Equally extraordinary, was the highly secretive manner in which Booth's body was literally whisked from the Garrett porch, rushed back to the Washington area, and buried. The corpse was rolled into a blanket and loaded onto a cart commandeered from a black neighbor named Ned Freeman. He was ordered to drive it northward at break-neck speed. The king bolt on a wheel snapped en route causing the front end to fall, sending the dead man's body lurching forward in the red-soaked blanket. As Freeman worked on the broken bolt, blood dripped on his hands, sending him tumbling backwards screeching, "It's the blood of a murderer — it will never wash off!" Another wagon was appropriated and Freeman left his cart by the side of the road, never to use it again.

At the Potomac River, Herold and the body were transferred to the ironclad Montauk. Ironically, because of all the mystery arising from this curious action, rumors began circulating all over Washington that the body aboard ship in the middle of the river was not Booth. As dense crowds gathered on the bank, Booth's body next was lowered into a skiff and placed into a makeshift coffin — a gun-box. As the skiff drifted downstream, the crowds of spectators on the shore followed, "splashing through the shallows" to keep pace. Under the disguise of darkness, the boat turned into the great swamp behind Geeseborough Point, and the spectators could follow no further, because this area was a swampy morass into which worn out horses and mules were thrown.

At midnight the weird sojourn continued. Oarsmen rowed stealthily upstream to the old penitentiary building, where a hole had been chopped in the masonry to allow them to enter. Here, on the grounds where Mary Surratt and three other Lincoln conspirators later were hanged, Booth's body, now reposed in a white-pine casket, was buried under a warehouse floor. Everyone involved in this bizarre ritual was sworn by sacred oath never to disclose what they had seen or done, and the entrance door was bolted.

Is it any wonder, under such fantastically abnormal circumstances, that the enormous wellspring of myth and lore about Booth's death was born? It began immediately. Many believed his body had been weighted and tossed into the swamp. Grotesquely, fishermen said the body had been dissected and its parts, heavily shotted, were dropped overboard from the skiff. One newspaper reported: "Out of the darkness Booth's body will never return. In the darkness like his great crime, may it remain forever; impassable, invisible, nondescript, condemned to that worse than damnation — annihilation. The river-bottom may ooze about it, laden with great shot and drowning manacles. The fishes may swim around it or the daisies grown white above it; but we shall never know."

Soon, the myth swept across the nation that all the secrecy surrounding the burial had been maintained to hide the fact that the wrong man had been shot; that Booth had escaped. From the great groundswell of rumor came scores of reports of "Booth sightings." While the government, in the worst traditions of Watergate, stonewalled, and refused to comment, suspicion throbbed to hysteria proportions. Booth was allegedly seen in the South, in Illinois, in Canada, and on ships bound for Mexico and South America. By mid-year 1865, the staid Richmond Examiner reported in its columns, "we know Booth escaped."

One of Booth's nieces once told a news service that there were "stories" in the family of her uncle's survival after the assassination, one of which told of Booth meeting his mother in San Francisco in 1866 in which he told her how he escaped. His mother told several members of the family she had "visited" with her son.

Booth's granddaughter, Izola Forrester, wrote a book about her famous ancestor, "This One Mad Act." In it, she proclaimed

John Wilkes Booth

that older residents in a certain area of the Telegraph Hill section of San Francisco shunned a "badly dilapidating" house they considered to be haunted by the spirit of Booth. She added that newspaper accounts published a year after the end of the Civil War mentioned a "mysterious stranger" who roamed about only after dark at this house and was described as being aloof, handsome and cloaked.

Adding to the fury, which continued to burn for years afterward, was a sequence of inexplicable occurrences quickly caressed by the superstitious. Mary Todd Lincoln, it was pointed out, died pitifully after years of insanity. Little Tad Lincoln died before reaching manhood. Major Rathbone and Miss Harris, guests in the Lincoln box at Ford's Theater on the fateful night, were caught in "the evil spell," when the Major later killed himself and Miss Harris after they were married. There were reports that all nine Union officers on the commission that had tried and condemned Mary Surratt and three others in the conspiracy, had died violent deaths, "most of them driven to suicide by remorse for having hanged an innocent woman." While at least this story proved to be fiction, Captain Willie Jett, a Confederate officer who had helped Booth on his flight, was said to have perished miserably.

Louis Weichmann, a chief government witness in the trial against Mrs. Surratt and the others, reportedly lived in fear of being avenged by either an escaped John Wilkes Booth or his ghost. Whether this is true or not is uncertain, but historians have said that when he died in 1902, "he was old and broken far beyond his 60 years."

In the years from the end of the Civil War even into the early 20th century, dozens of men stepped forward and claimed to have been Lincoln's slayer. Most were dismissed as lunatics, but the myth was kept alive, at times bordering on the ludicrous. One man in Texas who claimed to be Booth killed himself, whereupon his body was mummified and exhibited across the South and Southwest for ten to 25 cents a look.

In the late 1870s a rumor ran rampant through Richmond that John Wilkes Booth was alive and well in that city and preaching sermons every Sunday! An author, writing in "The Black Swan" magazine in June 1928, told of this belief, passed on to him by his father, when he was but a lad of eight. The man many thought to be Booth was the Reverend Dr. J. G. Armstrong, who came to Richmond in 1878 to be rector of Monumental Episcopal Church.

He was a man of "impressive presence," and a pulpit orator of "transcendent ability." The close resemblance between Armstrong and Booth "lay not alone in similarity of feature." The minister limped in the same leg which the actor broke in making his exit from Ford's Theater in Washington. Further, it was noted that Dr. Armstrong had a small scar on his neck "identical with a similar mark imprinted upon the neck of Booth."

Each man was impressive in appearance, in gesture, and in general deportment. Both wore their hair unusually long. Both men's hair was "very dark, throwing into bolder relief features as clean cut as a cameo." To add to the mystique, Armstrong frequently carried a long cape, or cloak. The effect of this garment, "hanging loosely from his shoulders, was in a sense theatric, and added emphasis to an already striking presence. He dressed in the deepest black."

Dr. Armstrong left Richmond in 1884 to accept another position "further south," but the rumors persisted. They were additionally fanned by a woman living in Richmond at the time; an English actress named Sally Partington. She steadfastly maintained, until her death, that Booth was never captured. She "never wearied" of telling the story how, while playing with a Mrs. DeBarr in a theater in St. Louis shortly after the Civil War, that Mrs. DeBarr "drew her" into a room and produced a letter she said was from Booth. "Who will now claim that John Wilkes Booth is dead?" Mrs. DeBarr told Miss Partington. "Behold the evidence of his living hand. I tell you that this letter is from him!"

Mrs. DeBarr then showed the letter to her friend. It was postmarked Australia, and the writer told how he was operating a business establishment in his "far away retreat." Miss Partington claimed that Mrs. DeBarr was in "constant communication" with Booth, and that Booth had explained to her in his letters how he had effected his escape, pawned his wife's diamond ring to a sea captain, and sailed from Norfolk in a three-masted schooner for Australia!

Still more questions and clues concerning Booth's fate arose following an episode on the network television program "Unsolved Mysteries," which included interviews with historical experts who have specialized in the Lincoln conspiracy and its aftermath. There was strong evidence that Booth was not the man shot in the Garrett barn. During part of his escape journey through northern Virginia, Booth was said to be hiding in the back of a covered wagon. Sympathizers got word to him that Union troops were nearby, and the assassin, with the help of friends, scrambled out of the wagon and hid in the woods. In the process, he lost his wallet and his personal papers.

Later, he sent a friend back to retrieve his effects and told him he would meet him at the barn. Booth arrived early, however, and again was tipped off that captors were near. He fled. So, the experts said on television, it was the friend, carrying Booth's identification papers on him, who was trapped in the barn with David Herald. In fact, when Herald came out of the barn to surrender, it was reported that he told Union troops that the man in the barn, the man Boston Corbett shot and apparently killed, was not Booth!

There was more. Lieutenant William C. Allen, assigned to the military secret service, was at the farm when they brought the body out of the barn. He saw it, and said it was not Booth because Booth had jet black hair, and this man had reddish-sandy colored hair. His statement was corroborated by two other soldiers, one who had known Booth! This man said that he knew at once the body wasn't that of Booth, because there was no injured leg. Officers told Allen and the two soldiers to keep their thoughts to themselves, and to treat the whole affair as top secret. They were to discuss it with no one. Ever!

Then there was the observation of one of the doctors who performed an autopsy on the body believed to be Booth's. His name was Dr. John F. May. He, too, felt the corpse bore little resemblance to Booth, also noting that the man had sandy hair and was freckled. He had once removed a tumor from Booth's neck and said Booth had no freckles. He was told to keep quiet. Additionally, the experts pointed out that no photographs were taken of the body. This was strange, because if it was, in fact, Booth who had been slain, the government would have photographed the body and publicized the photo across the country in an effort to quell the hysteria which arose among the public in the wake of Lincoln's killing. To the contrary, the government moved swiftly to close the book on the case and seal all documents regarding it.

And, finally there was an incident involving a man named John St. Helen, who, in 1877, thought he was dying. As he lay on his bed in a midwest state, he confessed to a friend of his that he actually was John Wilkes Booth. The friend was skeptical until St. Helen began to pour out, in great detail, the story of the assassination and escape; details only Booth could have known. Was St. Helen in reality Booth? A number of historians think this is a possibility. St. Helen took his own life by drinking poison in January 1903. Some time later, hearing of the possible St. Helen-

Booth connection, doctors examined his body. They found a scar over the right eyebrow, a damaged thumb, and a right leg that had once been broken — all physically identifying characteristics of Booth!

Lastly, there is the incredible story of Dr. Dell Leonardi a hypnotist of Kansas City, who wrote a book in 1975 titled "The Reincarnation of John Wilkes Booth," based on 73 hours of taped conversations with a young man named "Wesley." Under hypnosis — or in regression as the psychics say — he said he had been Booth in a past life. Dr. Leonardi, after painstakingly checking Wesley's comments about his former life against historical fact, came to believe that the young man indeed had lived before as the notorious assassin.

Wesley's story, as reported in book excerpts and reviews published in the mid-1970s, was that, as Booth, he had evaded his pursuers and had not been shot at Garrett's farm in 1865. He had, instead, fled to San Francisco and later lived in England where he continued his acting career, dying years later of a natural death in Calais, France.

"I have talked with the infamous John Wilkes Booth," Dr. Leonardi said. "I believe that to be a fact."

In her book, Dr. Leonardi asked was it reincarnation or was it "an entity" (Booth's ghost?) who claimed Wesley's body during hypnotic trance? She believed it to be reincarnation. Nevertheless, the question arose.

And so, it seems, the haunting mystery continues. The questions remain. In Caroline County there is an historic marker in the median strip of Route 301. It reads: "This is the Garrett place where John Wilkes Booth, assassin of Lincoln, was cornered by Union soldiers and killed April 26, 1865."

But was he?

* * * * *

THE CRUEL FATE OF MARY SURRATT

 ossibly the most pathetic figure in the Lincoln assassination aftermath was a solemn faced woman of 42 who appeared much older at the time; understandable considering the suffering, grief, and, many think, injustice she endured. Her name was Mary Jenkins Surratt, the accused co-conspirator of John Wilkes Booth. As a young girl she was sent to Alexandria to be educated by the Sisters of Charity. She became a "relentless" Roman Catholic, and developed what was described as an "abiding kinship" with the Southern secessionist movement. She married at 17, and operated, with her husband, a tavern and inn in what is now Clinton, Maryland.

When her husband died in 1862, she leased the tavern to a former Washington policeman, John Lloyd, and moved to a boarding house in the Capitol city. It was here that her "association" with Booth developed. It was here that she was accused of conspiring with Booth and others regarding the assassination of Lincoln — a charge that has triggered heated debate for 130 years. Many experts believe Mary Surratt had little or nothing to do with the plot and became the victim of a frenzied witchhunt in the aftermath of the President's death.

Be that as it may, what happened was that at midnight on April 14, 1865, the evening Lincoln had been shot at Ford's Theater, Mrs. Surratt was summarily rousted out of her bed and hauled off to jail without even being allowed a change of clothes. She protested her innocence to no avail. The government had made up its mind to force justice through, post haste, in an effort to calm the country. At the speedy trial, Mary was found guilty solely on the testimony of John Lloyd, who said she had told him to expect at the tavern he rented, "travelers to arrive on the night of April 14, and to provide them with supplies, including field glass and guns she had hidden in the house." The fact that Lloyd was a drunk and an unreliable witness was totally dismissed. The other evidence against her was superficially circumstantial. Tenants at her boarding house on H Street said she had met there regularly with Booth and the conspirators.

Flimsy as the case was, Mary was swiftly convicted by a military court "bent on vengeance and in satisfying a bloody national mood." She was sentenced to hang in the old District penitentiary, now Fort Leslie McNair, on the Anacostia River. It would be, perhaps, the most famous hanging in American history. No woman in the U.S. had ever been hanged before.

The date was July 7, 1865. Mary was barely able to walk when she was led to the scaffold outside the prison building — the "combined effects of debilitating fear and the shackles around her ankles." She practically had to be carried up the steps to the platform. From there she could see her own coffin below and a freshly dug hole in the ground waiting for her. She is said to have begged her executioners "Don't let me fall," seconds before the floor dropped from beneath her.

In an article published in the Washington Post in 1991, Michael Farquhar wrote, "It is said that a person who dies violently under the shadow of unresolved circumstances is remanded to a certain purgatory — a disturbed spirit in the realm of the living — waiting for a time when the truth behind his (or her) death is revealed. Mary Surratt qualifies as a ghost of exceeding prominence, as her innocence, or at least the degree of her guilt, remains stubbornly debated well beyond a century after her death. And, it is said, her spirit is restless."

Indeed, that seems to be somewhat of an understatement. Since that time, from shortly after her death to the present, the ghost of Mary Surratt has been seen and felt in three different places: the site of her hanging at Fort McNair; her old boarding house on H Street in Washington; and at the tavern in Clinton, Maryland! It is highly unusual, if not unprecedented, for a spirit to haunt more than one location. Yet there have been persistent reports of her reappearance at all three places.

Her wraith was said to frequent the boarding house almost immediately after her death. In a book titled, "Myths after Lincoln," by Lloyd Lewis, published in 1929, the author said Mary's apparition was seen within days of her death. Hearing of this, crowds gathered outside the house daily. Mrs. Surratt's daughter sold the house for a "bargain" $4,600, but the purchaser was driven away within six weeks because "his nervous system was reputedly shattered by what he had seen and heard." The Boston Post noted how other tenants came and went in "swift succession, swearing that in the dead of night, Mrs. Surratt walked the hallways clad in her robe of death."

Others who have lived in the house, or have visited it over the years have told of hearing "ominous sounds," such as mumblings, and muffled whispers coming through the walls at night. Some have even said they have heard the voices of the conspirators again going over details of the assassination. The occasional creaking of floor boards on the second floor, when no one is there, has been explained as the specter of Mary, "doomed to an eternity of pacing" until her name is cleared.

Her presence, however, may be even stronger at the site of her hanging. For example, there is an inexplicable appearance, directly beneath her gallows, of a single boxwood tree that "seemingly grew of its own accord." It has been claimed that this is her way of continuing to attract attention to prove her innocence. Another eerie and unexplained possible manifestation some years ago was the path that mysteriously appeared through a foot of snow; a path two feet wide, right down to the bare grass, maybe 300 yards long! According to Erik Swanson, a young honor guard officer at Fort McNair, the path "just appeared" in the snow; no shovel dug it. "There are no pipes or anything else below it," Swanson said at the time. "Nothing to explain it."

The path of bare ground, incidentally, covered precisely the route Mary Surratt was forced to take from the jail where she had been held to the gallows where she was hanged!

There have been many more strange occurrences here. In 1977, an army lieutenant saw "the apparition of a stout, middle-aged woman, dressed in black, seemingly floating through the hallways" of an officer's quarters. Others have heard voices and felt the sensation of being touched by "unseen hands." A major's wife said she, too, had seen a "woman in a long, dark dress floating around." She told psychic investigators it was Mary Surratt!

In the late 1980s, the Army Times did a feature on the subject. It quoted an Army Captain, Dave Osborne, who swore he heard Mary weeping and begging for help outside his window in the pre-dawn hours on Lincoln's birthday in 1989. "It started off softly crying, 'Help me, help me'," he said. "Then she began screaming, 'Oh no, help me, help me'!" He ran outside, but no one was there.

In yet another account, recorded in 1989, "Former residents of Quarters 20 at Fort McNair have reported objects moving supernaturally, drumming sounds at night, and shrieking voices outside where the Lincoln conspirators were executed." Mary Surratt was held prisoner in a first-floor apartment there! Four years earlier first lieutenant Anthony Plana said he heard "the noises of a large crow" outside of Quarters 20. He could find no source for them. Hammering, sawing, and other noises have also been heard. Several years before this, Major Bob Tonnelli and his wife brought psychics into the quarters to study the phenomena. Pool balls and flower pots had supposedly been tossed about in their apartment. Whispering voices called out to Tonnelli and his wife, and once "a bedroom unexplainably burst into flames!"

The legend of Mary's hauntings extends into Prince George's County, Maryland, the site of the old tavern in Clinton, now the Surratt museum. Her specter has been sighted there on occasion "in her sweeping long black dress and tight bun in her hair." One person who has experienced Mary's "return" is Laurie Verge, his-

Mary Surratt

torian for the Maryland-National Capital Park and Planning Commission. She used to hold meetings in the Clinton building. "When I was there at night," she recalled, "I got a very eerie uneasy feeling. The hair on my neck would stand on end. I can't explain it."

One night some years ago, Laurie and four others were meeting in a room on the second floor when they heard the front door open. This was followed by "loud thudding footsteps, the kind that might be made by clodhopper 19th century woman's boots, a *big* woman's boots, pacing the hall, stopping in the middle of the house. Ever so cautiously, Laurie and the others crept down the stairs, but saw no one.

Joan Chaconas, a facility aide at the state-owned Surratt House museum in Clinton, told the Associated Press that she once found daisies — Mary's favorite flower — hanging from the door knob of the house. They had been left by a woman who said she had "communicated" with the spirit of Mary via an Ouija board. The woman said Mary told her she would return one night to her old home. Intrigued, Joan later gathered a group of spiritualists, including the woman who had left the flowers, and they waited one night to see if there would be a spectral appearance. Nothing was seen, but one woman cried out that "something had touched her." Joan Chaconas also said that there is a portrait of Mary in the house, facing the stairs. She called it a "creepy" portrait, with eyes that "reflect a certain unhappiness." She added that the picture's eyes "follow you everywhere you go!"

And so it appears that the sad and chagrined spirit of Mary Surratt is bound to remain restlessly wandering from Fort McNair to H Street in Washington to the old tavern in Clinton, Maryland, in a continuous quest to seek understanding and redemption.

* * * * *

THE MAN WITH NO HEART!

et another ghostly chapter in the Booth-Surratt saga is that of Judge Advocate General Joseph Holt. He served as the U.S. government prosecutor in the trial which sent Mary to the gallows. He had insisted on the death penalty for her, and Surratt supporters say he hid from President Andrew Johnson the fact that the military commission's recommendation in the case had been to impose a life imprisonment sentence in deference to Mary's age and sex. Johnson said he never saw the recommendation.

Holt has been described as "taciturn, vindictive and ill-mannered." He also was said to be a man who "has no heart." Yet Holt became somewhat of a tragic figure himself in the aftermath of the hanging. Newspaper articles of the period say he became a recluse, and withdrew into the privacy of his home, which was only a few blocks from the old brick capitol prison where Mary had been incarcerated. One reporter said his house "was decaying, with bars on the windows and shades that never permitted the sun's rays inside."

By the 1880s, his eccentricities had become well known, and children crossed the street rather than pass by his shuttered house with its "overgrowth of weeds and tangled vines." Neighbors said "his irrevocable decision weighed heavily upon him" and he was thought to spend endless hours poring over the trial transcripts. He spent his remaining years in almost total solitude, and after he died, the new owners of the house tried to make it cheerful but, as one writer put it, "the presence of the departed 'man with no heart' is said to have chilled more than one room." For years afterward, mysterious footsteps could be heard pacing back and forth across the library in an upstairs room. People said it was Judge Holt forever questioning his harsh treatment of Mary Surratt.

Even after the old house was torn down, there were accounts of sightings of Holt, "clad in his midnight blue Union uniform, with the cape pulled tightly about him" walking toward the old brick capitol. As Mary sought vindication, the Judge sought forgiveness.

* * * * *

THE REDEMPTION OF DR. SAMUEL MUDD

ary Surratt was not the only victim of the Lincoln conspiracy. Another person, whom many feel was wrongly accused and punished in the questionable justice which was meted out in the days and weeks after the President died was Dr. Samuel Mudd who lived at a farmhouse in Charles County, Maryland, near Beantown. His legacy is to have become a prominent figure in one of the most controversial episodes in American history. Whether or not he was implicated in even the slightest way in the assassination plot has been heatedly argued for more than a century and a quarter and to this day has not been satisfactorily answered. It is a question that not only figuratively haunts historians, but also literally spooks his old farmhouse!

Dr. Mudd's life, and his reputation, was dramatically and inexorably shattered at about 4 o'clock on the morning of April 15, 1865, with a knock at his door. He opened it to face David Herold and John Wilkes Booth, who had broken his leg in the leap from Lincoln's box to the stage floor at Ford's theater the previous evening. Dr. Mudd set Booth's leg and fed and sheltered the two fugitives until mid-afternoon when they rode off to destiny at the Garrett Farm in Virginia. Whether or not Mudd knew of Booth's deed the previous evening has been the subject of raging debates ever since.

Regardless of his guilt or innocence, he was summarily taken into custody several days later, subsequently tried and convicted of having been a part of the conspiracy, and sentenced to life imprisonment at Fort Jefferson on Dry Tortugas Island, Florida. Outgoing President Andrew Johnson pardoned him four years later, and he returned to his home, although it has been written that he died a broken man in 1883, never able, in his lifetime, to clear his name.

Apparently, from the beyond, he is still trying! According to Trish Gallagher, in her interesting book, "Ghosts and Haunted Houses of Maryland," published in 1988, the ghost of Samuel Mudd periodically is seen by his youngest granddaughter, Louise Mudd Arehart; a woman who has laboriously fought to vindicate him. She also has successfully restored and preserved the circa 1830 family farmhouse, which, in 1974, was listed on the National Register of Historic Places.

Mrs. Arehart told author Gallagher that in the late 1960s she began experiencing a series of strange happenings at the house. It began with phantom knockings at the front door and footsteps up the stairs and down the hall. Eventually, she began catching glimpses of an apparitional man dressed in black trousers and vest, with a white shirt, "its sleeves rolled up to the elbows." The visions lasted but a few seconds at a time before vanishing. In time, Mrs. Arehart began to realize that the figure was, in reality, her grandfather, Dr. Mudd, and that he was appearing to her for a specific reason. He was, she felt, upset that the farmhouse had fallen into disrepair, and he made it known to her that she should do something about it.

She did. She has spent the past 25 years spearheading an effort at complete restoration. The Mudd House today is open to the public as a site of national historic significance. Even more satisfying has been the paralleling effort to clear the Doctor's name; an effort that resulted in former President Jimmy Carter publicly proclaiming belief in Dr. Mudd's innocence. His spirit, at last, could now rest in peace.

THE MOST TROUBLED SPIRIT OF ALL

nd, finally, there are the ghostly legends surrounding the victim of the Booth assassination, Abraham Lincoln himself. In one of the most famous instances of precognition ever recorded, Lincoln is said to have envisioned his death in a dream. It was a recurring dream which so disturbed him that he looked for answers in his Bible. "I turned to other passages, and seemed to encounter a dream of a vision wherever I looked," he said. "I kept on turning the leaves of the old book, and everywhere my eye fell upon passages recording matters strangely in keeping with my own thoughts — supernatural visitation, dreams, visions, etc."

At one point, Lincoln detailed his dream to his wife, Mary Todd Lincoln. He did it in a deliberate slow and sad countenance. "About ten days ago," he said, "I retired late. I soon began to dream. There seemed to be a death-like stillness about me. Then I heard subdued sobs, as if a number of people were weeping. I thought I left my bed and wandered downstairs. There, the silence was broken by the same pitiful sobbing, but the mourners were invisible. I went from room to room; no living person was in sight, but the same mournful sounds of distress met me as I passed along."

Lincoln continued: "It was light in all the rooms; every object was familiar to me; but where were all the people who were grieving as if their hearts would break? I was puzzled and alarmed. What could be the meaning of all this? Determined to find the cause of a state of things so mysterious and so shocking, I kept on until I arrived at the East Room (of the White House), which I entered. Before me was a catafalque, on which rested a corpse wrapped in funeral vestments. Around it were stationed soldiers who were acting as guards; and there was a throng of people, some gazing mournfully upon the corpse, whose face was covered, others weeping pitifully.

" 'Who is dead in the White House?' I demanded of one of the soldiers. 'The President,' was the answer. 'He was killed by an assassin.' Then came a loud burst of grief from the crowd, which awoke me from my dream. I slept no more that night; and although it was only a dream, I have been strangely annoyed by it ever since."

Following Lincoln's death, Mrs. Lincoln was distraught with horror, and it is said her first coherent exclamation, was, "His dream was prophetic."

It has been documented that on the night before the assassination, Lincoln had another dream, "so troubling" that he related it the following morning at a cabinet meeting. "I had a warning dream again last night," he said. "It related to water. I seemed to be in a singular and indescribable vessel that was moving with great rapidity toward a dark and indefinite shore."

Later that day Lincoln told his bodyguard, W. H. Crook, that he had dreamed for three nights running that he would be assassinated. Crook begged the President not to go to the theater, but Lincoln said that he must go because he had promised Mrs. Lincoln. Was Lincoln psychic? Many think so. One strong indication might have occurred that evening as he was leaving for the theater. Normally, he said "good night" to Crook on such occasions. This night, however, he said "good bye!"

Lincoln's ghost, too, has been reported to have reappeared over the past 130 years. At Fort Monroe, Virginia, for example, there have been numerous sightings of the President's figure in a splendid old plantation-style house facing the east sallyport known as Old Quarters Number One. He has been seen, appropriately enough, in the Lincoln Room, clad in a dressing gown standing by the fireplace "appearing to be deep in thought."

But it is in the Lincoln Room of the White House in Washington where his best known "reappearances" have occurred. In fact, "his ghost there is probably the most famous and most written-about spirit in American history. To be sure, no one had more cause to return as a lamentable specter as did this man whose life was so entwined with tragedy.

He lost his mother when he was only four years old. His first sweetheart, Ann Rutledge, died at an early age of typhoid. His sons, Edward and Willie died in childhood. Willie's death, especially, had a profound impact on Lincoln. There are newspaper accounts that he often visited his gravesite, and on at least two occasions, had the crypt opened so he could view his son. He allegedly sat there for hours and wept. There was, too, his long-troubled relationship with Mary Todd.

Additionally, there are references to Lincoln's interest in spiritualism, and to his wife's more fervent feelings about the supernatural. One encyclopedia writeup noted that Lincoln believed in dreams, and "other enigmatic signs and portents." It is known that a number of seances were held in the White House during Lincoln's term. At one session, the President is said to have asked a congressman to sit on a piano that was being levitated by a spiritualist. His added weight made no difference at the piano rose and fell on command.

A National Geographic News Bulletin reported that medium J. B. Conklin supposedly once received a telepathic message from Senator Edward D. Baker for Lincoln. Baker had been a close friend (see chapter on the Battle of Ball's Bluff), but at the time the message was received, he had been dead for two months!

The list of those who have claimed to have seen Lincoln's ghost in the White House reads like a celebrity Who's Who. Theodore Roosevelt once said, "I see him (Lincoln) in the different rooms and in the halls. I think of him all the time." Grace Coolidge, wife of President Calvin Coolidge, told a newspaper reporter she saw Lincoln dressed "in black, with a stole draped across his shoulders to ward off the drafts and chills of Washington's night air." Eleanor Roosevelt, wife of President Franklin D. Roosevelt, admitted she felt Lincoln's "presence" in the house. One of her staff members told of passing the Lincoln bedroom one day and seeing a "lanky figure" sitting on the bed pulling on his boots. She screamed and ran downstairs as fast as she could! The Washington Star once observed that a White House valet also ran screaming from the house, claiming that he had seen Lincoln's apparition.

In one widely circulated encounter, Queen Wilhelmina of the Netherlands was visiting the White House and was spending the night in the Rose Room. She heard a knock at the door late at night, got up from bed and opened the door, to see a vision of Lincoln, his "large frame taking up most of the doorway." She fainted. When she revived, the figure was gone. She later recounted this to guests at a cocktail party. Sir Winston Churchill often slept in the Lincoln bedroom when he visited Washington, although it was said he never felt comfortable there. Frequently, he would move across the hall in the middle of the night.

President Harry Truman, as no-nonsense a person as ever resided in the White House, once told his press secretary, James Haggerty, that he often felt Lincoln's presence. He said he was awakened one night in the early morning hours by two distinct knocks at the door to his bedroom. When he got up to investigate, there was no one there, although he felt a sudden chill, and heard "footsteps trailing off down the corridor."

Lady Bird Johnson also told of a "Lincolnesque visitation" one evening as she sat watching a television special on Lincoln's death. She later told her press secretary that she felt "compelled by someone" to look at the mantel in the room. There, she saw a small plaque she had never noticed before. She felt "ill at ease" as she walked over to read it. It told of the importance of that room to Lincoln.

A number of servants in the White House said they had encountered the great man's spirit in the halls and rooms as they went about their work. Many witnesses also said they glimpsed Lincoln's apparition peering out of the office in the Oval Room. All of this caused Washington Post reporter, Jacqueline Lawrence, to write: "The most troubled spirit of 1600 Pennsylvania Avenue is Abraham Lincoln, who during his own lifetime claimed to receive regular visits from his two dead sons."

And, lastly, there is this chilling footnote to Lincoln's untimely death, and to those who may or may not have been involved. In July 1865, on the eve of Mary Surratt's execution, her daughter, Anna, forced her way inside the White House grounds and made it to the front door. She pleaded desperately for her mother's release. It has been written that on the anniversary of that occasion, some have seen Anna's spirit banging on the front door in an otherworldly plea for mercy.

So, it seems, the incredible spiritual happenings involving John Wilkes Booth, Mary Surratt, Judge Joseph Holt, Dr. Samuel Mudd, and Abraham Lincoln himself, live on, perhaps to eternity!

The Ghost Who Warned of a Fiery Death

(Springfield)

airfax Herald news item — Stafford County, July 31, 1964: "The cottage called Concord, built in the 18th century overlooking Aquia Creek, was saved from destruction by fire years ago by a ghost who came equipped with an axe. When the chimney caught fire, the friendly apparition appeared, ran with his axe to the second floor and knocked out the burning wall. The owner of the house, cheered by this aid, set to work on the first floor and together they saved the house. Thanks to the efforts of man and spook, the house still stands with a new chimney."

News Item 2 — The Journal Messenger, Manassas, October 30, 1985: "(Connie) Minnick, (whose family owns the house, in Nokesville) says that the ghost, whose name is Ruth, protects the house, and twice has prevented the house from fire. In one instance, a burning log from the fireplace rolled out onto the floor when no one was there, but it didn't catch anything on fire.

"In the second incident, 'the attic caught on fire and, although it was a very dry summer, it didn't burn nearly as much as it should have, but just stopped when it got to the second floor. We expected the house to go up in flames,' Minnick said. She said that Ruth's ghost had been credited with saving the house on those two occasions."

* * * * *

Did a ghost try to warn a Springfield couple that a devastating fire would sweep through their house in late June 1982, killing both husband and wife? According to the couple and other witnesses, a "supernatural entity" made its presence known several times over a period of months in a vain effort to alert Gary and Epi Belofsky of pending doom. In retrospect, it was as if the specter was trying to scare the Belofskys out of the house they had moved into, with another roommate, in March 1981.

Almost from the beginning, a series of frightening manifestations took place. Epi first told neighbors and later newspaper reporters that a number of objects, including antiques and glass figurines broke mysteriously, and the house gutters sometimes "rattled furiously." Epi was terribly shaken one day when, as she described it, someone unseen pulled the rug out from under her feet on the upper landing, sending her cascading down the stairs. It certainly did appear as if some evil force were trying to get rid of the house occupants.

Then one night Epi dreamed of a "slender woman with reddish brown hair." A housemate named Cindy awoke from a nap one day and reported seeing a figure that matched the one Epi had envisioned. Epi wondered if this woman was connected with the haunting activity in any way. She began checking around. After asking neighbors and consulting with a parapsychologist, she learned that a woman named Mary Conlon had committed suicide in the house nine years earlier. Mary was 46 years old at the time and had become despondent over "marital problems." She hanged herself in the basement, beneath the kitchen. Wallace Dean, a county fireman was one who got the call after Mary's body had been found. He still remembers getting "quite an eerie feeling" when he saw her hanging from the rafters. "Maybe it was the angle at which she was hanging," dean said, "but it was a shock, and it gave me an eerie, funny, strange type of feeling."

Thus it was Mary, Gary and Epi came to believe, who was making all the fuss. But they didn't know why. Meanwhile, the occurrences continued. Epi told one of her neighbors, Lorraine Maslow, about another fearful experience she had. She had been taking a shower one day when the bathroom door inexplicably opened not once, but three times! Each time she got out of the shower to close the door. No one else was in the house.

A second housemate, a man named Davies, then told of a harrowing incident he witnessed. He was alone in the house one morning when he heard what he said "sounded like a bull or an elephant in a tin can factory." He searched the house from top to bottom, but found no cause. The dogs were soundly sleeping. He attributed it to Mary's ghost.

Parapsychologist James McClenon visited the house and said the activity represented a typical poltergeist case. He wrote an article based on the occurrences for the Journal of the Psychical Research Foundation.

But the real omen of coming tragedy centered around the kitchen sink. On at least three occasions, Gary, Epi and Cindy all saw smoke rising from the sink, "for which no explanation could be found." This happened twice after reporters had telephoned to interview Epi about the ghost. Epi felt that "Mary" didn't like publicity. "I think she just wants to be left in peace to roam the house," Epi said, apparently not reading the signals as signs of warning.

A few days later, in the early hours of a Sunday morning, a fire broke out and raged through the house. Gary was burned to death downstairs, in what appeared to be an attempt to save some kittens. Epi died upstairs from smoke inhalation. There was some mystery as to why they didn't make an attempt to jump out of a window. Curiously, firefighter Dan Bickham, who as shift commander, answered the call when the fire broke out, had also been at the scene nine years earlier when Mary Conlon's body had been found. "It just seems odd that I was there nine years ago, and here I am again," he said, pointing out that it was only because he had switched shifts with another fireman that he was on call that day. "There's just a lot of coincidences with this whole thing," he added. "It's really weird and it kind of makes you wonder."

The Fairfax Journal reported at the time: "Fire investigators who are aware of the ghost stories associated with the house have been unable to determine the cause of the fire and say they may never know." Was the spirit of Mary Conlon desperately trying to warn Gary and Epi Belofsky that danger lurked in the house where she had taken her life? Were her loud manifestations attempts to drive them away to safety? Did Mary cause the fire, or did she just have a premonition of it?

These are all questions that parapsychologist McClenon says may never be answered. "These (poltergeist) cases do have a potential to start fire," he said in a newspaper interview. "I don't dismiss this possibility. But I will tell you, you will never know. As long as you live, you will never know!"

CHAPTER 7

The Phantom Diners at Ash Grove

(Fairfax County)

strain of eccentricity must have run through at least a part of the Fairfax family in colonial days. The Fairfaxes were reputed to be one of the, if not the, wealthiest clans in the colony with land holdings that at one time covered fully one fourth of the commonwealth, including everything between the Potomac and the Rappahannock Rivers, and stretching across the Allegheny Mountains. Certainly one of the most colorful of this noble clan was the Lord Fairfax born in England in 1690. He was described as "a man of eccentric turn of mind, of great private worth, generous and hospitable. He had been accustomed to the best society, to which his rank entitled him, in England."

He came to the new country sometime around the middle of the 18th century and built his home, Greenway Court, across the Blue Ridge Mountains in the Shenandoah Valley, a few miles south of Winchester. Here, he lived in comparative seclusion, "often amusing himself with hunting, but chiefly devoted to the care of his estate, to acts of benevolence among his tenants; a friend of liberty, honored for his uprightness, esteemed for the amenity of his manners, and his practical virtues."

According to Henry Howe, in his "Historical Collections of Virginia," published in 1847, "His Lordship" was a "dark, swarthy man, several inches over six feet in height, and of a gigantic frame and personal strength. He lived the life of a bachelor," and "when in the humor, he was generous — giving away whole farms to his tenants, and simply demanding for rent some trifle, for instance, a present of a turkey for his Christmas dinner."

Howe says the Lord was passionately fond of hunting and greatly enjoyed the "pleasures of the chase." When on these expeditions, he made it a rule that he who got the fox, cut off his tail and held it up, should share in the jollification which was to follow, free of expense. As soon as a fox was started, the young men of the company usually dashed after him with great impetuosity, while Fairfax leisurely waited behind with a favorite servant who was familiar with the water courses, and of a quick ear to discover the course of the fox. Following his directions, his lordship would start after the game, and, in most instances, secure the prize, and stick the tail of the fox in his hat in triumph."

Lord Fairfax died at the advanced age of 92 in 1782, and was buried at Winchester under the communion table of the old Episcopal church. Because he was a life-long bachelor (it is said that he was "crossed in love" and came to Virginia to bury himself and his pique), and because of his imposing size and sometimes odd behavior, particularly for a lord, rumors and superstitions seemed to swirl around him. These were enhanced some years after his death when servants on his plantation, excavating ground near his house, unearthed a small fortune in cob-like square coins called joes and half-joes. Lord Fairfax is said to have secreted them there. They also found, under a shelving rock nine feet from the surface, a human skeleton of gigantic proportions!

Lord Fairfax also built a wing to a house, really a small hunting lodge, at a site in Fairfax County, about 12 miles from Washington. After his death, one of the descendents, Thomas Fairfax, the ninth lord of the line, built a magnificent home here in 1790 called Ash Grove. Unfortunately, time and fires have claimed the other Fairfax mansions, including Greenway Court, Belvoir, Towlston, and Mount Eagle. Like so many other old Virginia places, Ash Grove was named for an older Fairfax home in England.

The main building is three stories tall, unusual for that day. The wide entrance hall is flanked by large rooms on either side. There is hand carving on the impressive stairway, which is finished with a mahogany rail, and the mantels are hand carved in the dignified fluted designs of the period. The house is surrounded by large graded lawns and adorned with 15-foot-high hedges of lilac. In the spring, masses of blooms — snowballs, daffodils,

peonies, Madonna lilies, fleur-de-lis, and abundant Fairfax roses —
fill the house and grounds with fragrance.

Gigantic oaks tower over Ash Grove. At the foot of the hill, on
which the house stands in "quiet dignity," is an old willow,
brought as a slip by Commodore Jones from the willow that
droops over Napoleon's grave at St. Helena.

Whatever myths, legends and speculations the original Lord
Fairfax spawned were perpetuated and embellished at Ash Grove
by the even stranger behavior of Thomas Fairfax, and, in part, by
some curious architectural details of the house itself. All of this in
time built to a genuine tradition that Ash Grove, indeed, was
haunted.

For example, for no known reason, two false doors in the
house lead nowhere. Monks' cupboards are found in several of the
chimneys. They are not, as one historian phrased it, "really secret
cupboards, but are so rare, so unexpected as to approach secret
places in mystery." There is, too, a small wine cellar under the old
dining room closet, reached through a trap door over which a piece
of furniture "was always artfully drawn." It is said that most of the
servants never knew of this subterranean closet, thus when a rare
wine mysteriously appeared on the table, which they knew had
not come from the household stores, they were astonished.

Adding to the mystique, one woman who lived at Ash Grove
for many years, "according to authentic tradition," practiced "her
gift of second sight." She was, in other words, an early psychic,
and her exploits no doubt "did much to give Ash Grove the eerie
reputation which, for long, it held among the slaves of the earlier
day and the freed men of the later period."

In an article in the William and Mary Quarterly, published
more than 20 years ago, author Caroline Baldwin Sherman said,
"many were the weird tales that were told of it (Ash Grove). Most
of the Negroes of the neighborhood, and not a few of the white
neighbors firmly believed it was haunted. Certainly, many were
the weird noises that it gave forth in the dead of night..."

Many of these noises, of course, could be explained by "old
latches, loose windows and crumbled foundations that admitted to
the interstices of the walls enterprising flying squirrels that made
merry in their strange domains during the long nights." Yet not all
of the noises could be so rationally explained. Often, there were
footsteps overhead from unseen and unfound sources, and lights
sometimes inexplicably appeared in upstairs windows when it was
known the entire family was away.

But perhaps the greatest single source of Ash Grove's haunted repute was Thomas Fairfax himself. As author Sherman put it, "The unusual personality of Thomas, ninth lord, who built and long occupied the house, undoubtedly had much to do with its atmosphere of mystery. Characterized by almost Spartan simplicity, he was yet reserved and almost austere in his demeanor."

Generous to a fault, like the Lord Fairfax of Greenway Court, he freed all his slaves and spent much time and money in the effort to make them self-supporting. Heir to an old and honored title, highly prized by his father, he discarded it and never allowed it to be used with his name.

Most mystifying, however, were Thomases' weird experiments and his even more extraordinary behavior at times. He would spend hours on end in a well-equipped "shop," more likely a laboratory, absorbed in a variety of experiments all considered strange at best by the servants and others in the house. He was, to them, the Doctor Frankenstein of his day. When, for example, he hand fashioned the first pair of lightning rods seen in Northern Virginia, which, he said, would protect Ash Grove against lightning strikes and the dangers of fire, some believed this "savored of witchcraft, or of Satan."

He assembled an assortment of chemicals and weird (for the time) apparatus, including a chemical bath tank, and experimented in galvanism, magnetism and higher mechanics among other things. His equipment was described by neighbors as "Mr. Thomas Fairfax's spiritual things." In this manner, he "inspired many tales that his great dignity forbore to explain."

But the events that most fostered the widely held belief that Ash Grove housed otherworldly spirits, were Thomases' periodic "ghostly dinners." It is said that on certain dates he "caused to be prepared and set forth with great ceremony (such dinners) for the spirits of his forefathers." Places were set at a large table for numbers of spectral guests. Fairfax would then "withdraw to distant places," and the dinners would somehow magically disappear, as if eaten by unseen diners!

Thomas Fairfax died and was buried in the family cemetery at Ash Grove in 1843. Twelve years later, his remains were dug up and replaced beside those of his wife at Ivy Hill Cemetery near Alexandria. It was only then, it is said, that the psychic manifestations at his old house came to rest.

More Apparitions in Old Alexandria

(Alexandria)

(Author's note: In my first volume of "The Ghosts of Virginia," I included a chapter on "Apparitions Aplenty in Old Alexandria." It covered Gadsby's Tavern, Red Hill, Culross, the Stamp Collector from Beyond, and The Vanishing Pitt Street Ghost. From additional research, especially at the Lloyd House Library on North Washington Street, and from letters and calls I received, I have come across considerable additional material. Alexandria, my home when I was a small child, apparently abounds in ghosts. I quote magazine writer Marjorie J. Seng: "The Northern Virginia area — particularly the seaport town of Alexandria, founded in 1749 and inhabited by many of our country's notables — has a history replete with ghost tales, folklore and stories of things that go bump in the night."

In turn, Seng quotes Ruth Lincoln Kaye, genealogist and author of "Legends and Folk Tales of Old Alexandria, Virginia:" "You can't go a single block in Old Town without someone telling you about a ghost story. And I don't mean just creakings, either!"

In fact, at one time a ghost hunting society was formed in the city. From the December 22, 1897, issue of the Alexandria Gazette comes this report: "The fad of ghost hunting has extended to this city, and a number of ladies and gentlemen of the Third Ward are organizing an "Occultorium" to make a thorough story of ghosts and their habits. Among the early purposes of the occultorium is a visit to the graveyards at midnight."

I was delighted to find one otherworldly account in an old

house on North Alfred Street. When I was about eight or nine years old and living in Alexandria (Mount Vernon school area), I occasionally used to visit my grandmother on Friday or Saturday and spend the night. She lived in an old two-story building at 522 South Alfred. The building may have dated to the 18th century, and probably is no longer there, since my visits were in the 1940s!

I would hop on a bus and ride downtown, getting off in the area of King Street. It would usually be dark as I walked the several blocks through some of the poorer neighborhoods of the town. In those days, however, there was no fear of muggings or shootings. Besides, I never had more than a quarter or so on me. My grandmother's house had to be one of the creepiest structures in existence. I recently conferred with my cousin, Jane Ward, about this and she concurred. We have shared memories of long, darkened halls filled with scary shadows.

One of my earliest remembrances as a child four years old was being alone in the master bedroom when my Aunt Offa died. And then there were the shutters. Wooden shutters. They would be fastened across the windows when I slept by myself in the front downstairs bedroom. Many were the nights when I lay awake endless hours terrified by the procession of nocturnal sounds on the other side of those shutters. I was convinced a ghoulish assortment of ghosts and other dark creatures were seeking devilish ways to gain entrance. Consequently, I most often slept with the covers pulled tightly over my head.

The reported instance of spectral phenomena on Alfred Street was at 105 on the north end some years ago. This was an 18th century building and it occurred one evening past midnight. A young man who lived there was climbing up the stairs to his apartment on the third floor. Halfway up the first flight he was "suddenly conscious of a blast of cold air." He said it hit him like "a malevolent force" that followed him up the steps and along the upper hall. It enveloped him until he got to the flight to the third floor, which, it might be added, he reached in a great hurry. He looked back, searching for a possible explanation, but found nothing. Then, "as suddenly as it had materialized, the freezing air dissipated."

Disturbed by the chilling event, he told others in the house what had happened. They said that a century earlier a skeleton had been found behind a boarded-up fireplace in the house, and it could be the spirit of this person who returned to haunt the premises. The reason the specter did not go farther than the second floor, it was explained, was that the third floor had been added sometime after the skeleton had been found.

Now that I have confessed, herewith are some additional ghosts who still abide in and around the Old Town:)

* * * * *

THE VANISHING VISION AT VAUCLUSE

One of the best known accounts was first told to me by Harold and Roxie Weitzen, long-time residents in Northern Virginia. It has been well documented in a number of publications, including Margaret DuPont Lee's book, "Virginia Ghosts," and Ruth Lincoln Kaye's "Legends and Folk Tales of Old Alexandria, Virginia," among others. Vaucluse was a home dating to the 18th century, a spacious brick mansion which stood on a hill offering a commanding view of surrounding area. For decades it was owned and occupied by the Fairfax family. A part of the estate of George Mason of Gunston Hall on the Potomac was bought from the Vaucluse tract. Sadly, the house was torn down by General George McClellan's troops during the Civil War.

The first report of haunting activity at Vaucluse preceded this by perhaps as much as three quarters of a century. It was told by one of the Fairfaxes, who was then master of the house. He was standing in the drawing room, called the Long Room, one day when he glanced into the pier mirror and saw over his shoulder, a Negro woman, who, he said, "gazed into his face appealingly." He recognized her as a servant he had sent to his son's home at Ash Grove (see separate chapter on this manor home). He turned to ask why she had come back, but, to his astonishment, there was no one there! Two days later he received a message that the faithful old servant had died at the very hour that he had seen her in his mirror!

In 1862, before Vaucluse was destroyed, Federal pickets were said to be stationed everywhere about. At the time, one of the mistresses of the house was Constance Cary, of the Cary family of Ampthill on the James River. She was allegedly a beautiful Southern belle whose sweetheart had joined the Confederate army. One night as he snuck through the ravine toward the house in hopes of seeing Miss Constance, he was shot and killed by a picket.

63

He fell beside the main spring, "whence a few stone steps up the hillside would have brought him to his love." He lies buried where he fell, near the spring.

But, as Mrs. Lee wrote in 1930, "the spirit of the brave young lover — perchance seeking once more his heart's desire, as on that fateful evening — or maybe just to revisit the scene of his last earthly experience, keeps ever in the minds of the youth of today the knowledge that he long years ago risked his life both to save his state and to see the girl he loved."

As Mrs. Lee added, "For years the land desolated by the fortunes of war was neglected... All that remains of that chapter in its history and of the once beautiful old garden are the hardy daffodils and narcissi, blooming here and there on the hillside in the spring sunshine; the thread of living water surging over the pebbles as old, and the ghost of the unlucky lover, visible on moonlight nights, lying at full length among the ferns, violets and periwinkle beside the spring."

In the intervening years even up to this day, a number of people have reported seeing the prone image of the young soldier, reposing peacefully in his gray uniform, "his breast stained with a dark red, his youthful face turned upward to the leafy roof of the interlacing poplars." The vision appears vividly for a few seconds to those who gaze upon it, and then it fades from their sight. Among those who have witnessed this phenomenon are the daughter of Harold and Roxie Weitzen, Jessica Handy, and her friend, Patricia Corvelli. "It must have been about 25 years ago or so when they saw him," says Harold. "They were about nine or ten at the time, and they both told of seeing the exact same thing, the young man lying there in his uniform. And then, just as suddenly he was gone."

* * * * *

THE VANISHING BUILDING AT SPRING GARDENS

There is an old house at 414 Franklin Street that, 200 years ago, was known as the Spring Garden Inn. It was said to have been frequented at the time by George Washington and other Revolutionary War soldiers. In 1798, Washington reviewed his troops here, including a group of young boys who called themselves the "Black Cockades." It apparently was a popular tavern and oysterhouse in its day, standing not far from the King's Highway, and was also frequented by travellers and townspeople as well as military men. Besides its "good food," it featured beautiful gardens of boxwood, arbors of wisteria, and "quantities" of spring and summer flowers, which incidentally gave it its name. It was, says one historian, "a happy place, it was also given to music and dancing, and many a gay banquet was held here in the old days."

Early this century, when Spring Gardens had been turned into a private residence, three sisters lived there. As they dined each evening, they said they were constantly aware that someone or something was "with them" in the room. They felt the sensation of "being observed." Then, on several occasions, they reported seeing who this "uninvited guest was." It was a man dressed in Revolutionary war clothing!

One night he walked past them *through* a sturdy, six-paneled door! Dumbfounded, two of the ladies nevertheless summoned the courage to follow the spirit outside. It was a moonlit evening, and the sisters clearly saw the specter enter a brick building *that wasn't there!* The next morning they went over to the area where they had seen the ghost walk to, and found, in the ground, the foundations of a brick building which had once stood there long ago. This was further confirmed by an examination of old city maps which indicated such a structure had stood at the spot where the women had seen their vision. Psychic experts would probably say the apparition of the soldier returned either to complete a mission unfulfilled in life, or maybe just to be prankish.

But the appearance of a building long demolished defies most known theories of psychic phenomena.

* * * * *

APPARITIONS FROM THE ARCHIVES

It appears from published reports that ghostly activity in Old Alexandria peaked during the last two or three decades of the 19th century. This is attested to by the large number of news accounts in the Alexandria Gazette during that period. An assortment of these clippings has been assembled by T. Michael Miller, author, and director of the

Lloyd House Library, and others. A few brief excerpts follow:

October 10, 1872: "For some nights past the guards at the jail have been hearing strange sounds, the cause of which are as yet unexplained, and the belief is beginning to be entertained among them that some of the persons confined there for murder are to be hung, and that their spirits have commenced to walk the earth already. The sounds resemble those made by rolling ten pins, and doors, which are shut and mysteriously opened."

* * * * *

September 8, 1874: "A veritable ghost now haunts that portion First Ward known as Tunnel Town. Upon several late occasions, towards the witching hour of night, it has been seen by the fear-oppressed eyes of belated denizens of that locality, as they home-ward wended their weary way, engaged in tricks fantastical. It appears in the questionable shape of a beautiful girl, dressed all in white, and of full, voluptuous, but not o'er grown bulk; the phantom whose frolic grace arms the admiration as well as excites the fears of the superstitious beholder, and, when approached by those of younger and bolder blood, who would clutch it and speak to it, flies like a guilty thing upon a fearful summons."

* * * * *

April 13, 1875: "Hardly had the amazement caused by such a remarkable occurrence (a pitcher broken by unseen hands at Godfrey Kreig's restaurant, 32 North Royal Street) subsided before a glass lamp-chimney, sitting on a shelf in the house, had fallen to pieces in the same mysterious manner, rapidly followed by the unaccountable breaking of the demijohn of whiskey. Mr. Kreig, alarmed by this series of inexplicable breakages, and deeming them ominous of some dire impending fate, retired to his sitting room and bemoaned the misfortune he felt certain would befall him." (Shortly thereafter his daughter was severely scalded by a pan full of boiling lard.)

* * * * *

August 23, 1881: "The residents of Vinegar Hill, (500 South Patrick Street), are much agitated over an alleged appearance of a ghost in the neighborhood, which is reported to roam the hill at midnight on a pure white horse. Mrs. John Verdon, it is said, went to her window about 12 o'clock Sunday night last, and upon look-ing out saw a strange looking man, tall, with long hair, standing erect on a white horse. This man, who was bare footed, had around him a bespangled blanket, which sparkled with a dazzling brilliancy. Mrs. Verdon, when she saw this wonderful sight, screamed, and her little daughter, who came to the rescue, testifies that she saw the ghost ride off. Mrs. Verdon was so frightened by the apparition that she is now seriously ill."

*　*　*　*　*

July 20, 1885: "It was twelve midnight, that lonely hour when graveyards yawn, and lunar's gibbous form had just sunk behind the western hills, when this gentleman, with a box of fried oysters under each arm, started from the Opera House restaurant for his home. He had arrived at the southwest corner of Prince and Pitt Streets, intending to pass over the square opposite St. Paul's Church, when directly in front of him there suddenly appeared the irrepressible figure he oft had heard of — not in sable habiliments, however, but snowy white.

"Mr. W. claims to be no believer in ghosts, hobgoblins, fairies or spirits, so he determined to catch up with and carefully survey whoever or whatever it was that glided — not walked — so stealthily before him. Accordingly, he accelerated his gait to the utmost to overtake the specter, but despite his every exertion he could get no nearer than five feet of the apparition.

"He smoked up vigorously on a cigar he had in his mouth, for the purpose of shedding as much light on the scene as possible, when in the twinkling of an eye, the spook vanished as suddenly as a ring of smoke or a burst soap bubble! At this denouement, our hero, sultry as the weather was, felt a cold chill meandering down the spinal column which soon eventuated in a tremor throughout the frame. His disbelief in visitants from the unseen world is not so strong now as formerly."

*　*　*　*　*

April 18, 1888: "Though scientific people have urged various theories in explanation of specters or apparitions, and notwithstanding the belief in ghosts grows less as the years of this century glide by, occasionally people of undoubtedly well balanced minds undergo experiences hard to explain and which serve to increase the credulity of those who believe in the supernatural. Some months ago one of our citizens living on North Washington Street, in a fit of despondency, placed a pistol to his head and thus ended his earthly career. The family having later vacated the premises, the house was rented by a gentleman from Washington, but the gentleman and his family had not been long in their new house before curious noises, the origin of which it seemed impossible to ascertain, began to be heard, and the belief that the house was haunted soon manifested itself among the inmates. This belief was strengthened about 100 percent, night before last by the appearance from the spirit world of the former tenant. The gentleman and his wife, positively affirm that they saw the deceased, and yesterday the family moved out, saying they would not pass another night in the house for the price of it."

* * * * *

April 17, 1897: "There is a rumor among the colored people of the First Ward that the spirit of Clem Dorsey who last week attempted to kill his wife at their home on Gibbon Street, and then committed suicide by cutting his throat in a neighboring alley, has returned to the earth; that his ghost walks by night, and, what is worse, that it carries a razor — presumably for use in case he meets some of those whom he fancied injured him."

* * * * *

THE TIDY HOUSEKEEPER HAUNT

Extraordinary is the word used to described the unnerving experience about a quarter of a century ago of a young man who lived in an old house at 708 Wolfe Street known locally as "The Blue Door." The building has been described as "rather gnarled, with a forbidding air about." It is back some distance from the street and is guarded by a cast iron fence. "A dark and scary sight it surely is," said Eric Segal, in his 1976 pamphlet on "Alexandria Ghosts."

On one particular night the young man was alone and sound asleep when he was rudely awakened by a "sharp shaking" on his shoulder. He awoke to see a wrinkled old woman standing beside his bed. She appeared to be angry, an assumption soon confirmed by her declaration. "Get out of my bed," she ordered. "Get out immediately." Visibly shaken, the young man readily complied, leaped out of bed, bounced down the stairs and ran out the front door. He spent the better part of the night trying to clear his head of the terrifying spectacle he had witnessed.

He walked the streets for hours finally convincing himself that he either had been dreaming, or had suffered an hallucination. He went back to the house and opened the door. He stood there for a few seconds, and when he saw and heard nothing, he started back up the stairs to his second floor bedroom, chiding himself for his cowardice. But as he entered the room, he shrieked in horror. His bed had been neatly made up! According to legend, he raced back down the stairs and went outside, *never again to open the blue door!*

CHAPTER 9

The Tell-Tale Heart – For Real!

(Alexandria)

In Edgar Allan Poe's classic short story, "The Tell-Tale Heart," a young man living in an old house with an aged gentleman, is driven to near-madness by the older man's evil, vulture-like eye, "a pale blue eye, with a film over it. "Whenever it fell upon me," Poe wrote, "my blood ran cold; and so by degrees — very gradually — I made up my mind to take the life of the old man, and thus rid myself of the eye forever."

Thus, for several days the younger man plotted his crime. He stood at the older man's bedroom door for hours one night, waiting for him to go to sleep, when, there came to his ears, "a low, dull, quick sound, such as a watch makes when enveloped in cotton. I knew *that* sound well, too. It was the beating of the old man's heart... the hellish tattoo of the heart increased. It grew quicker and quicker, and louder and louder every instant.

"So strange a noise as this excited me to uncontrollable terror." At this point the young man leaped into the room. The old man screamed once, and then was dragged to the floor and the heavy bed was pulled on top of him. He suffocated. "Yes, he was stone, stone dead. I placed my hand upon the heart and held it there many minutes. There was no pulsation... His eye would trouble me no more."

The young man then dismembered the corpse, cutting off the head, the arms and the legs. He next took up three planks from the flooring of the chamber, and deposited the body parts "between the scantlings." He replaced the boards and praised himself for his clever concealment. Not even a drop of blood showed. He had washed everything clean in a bathtub.

It was now four a.m., and just then, the front door bell rang. The young man opened the door to three officers of the police. They told him they had heard a report of a scream from a neighbor and came to check it out. The young man said the sound had been caused by him. He had had a nightmare. But they were welcome to search the house. The old master, he said, was away on a trip.

Eventually, they all wound up in the old man's bedroom. So confident was the young man that he had thoroughly hidden the body, that he invited them to sit down in the room and rest. He himself pulled up a chair and sat directly over the three boards he had taken up.

After some time, as the officers continued chatting, the young man's head began to ache. "I fancied a ringing in my ears ... it continued and it became more distinct ... at length I found that the noise was *not* within my ears... It was a low dull, quick sound — much like a sound as a watch makes when enveloped in cotton. I gasped for breath, and yet the officers heard it not." The young man grew horrified. "I foamed — I raved — I swore! ... but the noise grew rose above it all and continually increased. It grew louder — louder — *louder!*" At last, the young man's consuming guilt and encompassing madness took command. He could stand it no more. "I felt I must scream or die ... I admit the deed!" he finally stammered ... "tear up the planks! — here, here! — it is the beating of his hideous heart!"

Is it possible that a real-life tell-tale heart beat in Alexandria? Yes, say some. It occurred many years ago at an old house at 210 Gibbons Street. There is on file at the Lloyd House Library on North Washington Street a letter from a woman who wishes to remain unidentified. In the letter, the woman says she got a call in January 1977, from a man named Erich Kanin. He and his family had at one time lived in the house on Gibbons Street, and apparently were seeking information about the place, which at one time belonged to relatives of the woman who wrote the letter.

She said that Kanin told her that on one night in October (year unspecified), at 11:30 p.m., "they (Kanin and his wife) first became aware of a pulsating noise in the large front room which they used as a den. (It had formerly been a bedroom.) It continued to occur, and they tried to tape the noise, but it only caused a static sound on their machine. Since they intended to buy the house, they had plumbers, electricians, etc., in to check out structural problems, but everything was sound. They also tried bringing their cat into the room, but it would not stay. It would arch (it back) and hiss. Friends of the Kanins' also observed this. It went on until mid-December, when the Kanins awakened (one night) in their bedroom.

"As he explained," the woman's letter continued, "this was the first time that he felt frightened, since the pulsating was in the bedroom. The cat usually slept in the bedroom, but he was long gone. He said the pulsating usually stopped at dawn, and his wife felt that whatever it was, it was not a wholesome presence. So they left the house and took an apartment on North Pitt Street."

The mystery was never solved. The woman tried to find some background information from her relatives, but was unsuccessful. She wrote to Kanin to tell him this, but never heard from him again. She did say that when Kanin talked to her, he said the noise sounded exactly "like a pulsating heart."

The Wandering Haunts of Windover Heights

(Vienna)

I n the endless sea of look-alike condomini-
ums, tract homes and townhouses which
ring Washington, Windover Heights, virtually hidden on Walnut
Lane in Vienna, Virginia, stands like a lost beacon harkening back
to an era of architectural elegance that belonged to another time. It
has been described as having the appearance of a country manor,
elegant in its grandeur, although by plantation standards, it is not a
particularly large house. Depending upon whether or not you
count the bathrooms, there are roughly 15 to 20 rooms overall,
including a walled off area that conceals a secret passageway and a
narrow staircase leading upstairs.

The present house was built sometime between 1865 and 1869
(there are varying accounts) by a man named Captain Harmon L.
Salisbury, who had commanded the 16th regiment of U.S. Colored
Infantry during the Civil War. Some of his troops, in fact, came to
work for him on the dairy farm and in the orchards he operated in
the years after the war.

Windover Heights was built upon the foundations of a much
earlier building, Huntington House, which was believed to have
been destroyed by fire either during the Civil War or immediately
afterward. A barn and a cupola add further charisma to the property. If ever a house was a candidate for the presence of supernatural spirits, this would be it.

In addition to the secret passageway inside, it is said that tunnels once ran from the basement to the barn. Whether these were dug in Salisbury's day, or date further back is not clear, although the likelihood is that they may have been installed as an escape route from any invasion of Union soldiers. There is a report that the original Huntington House on the site was "riddled with bullets" during the fighting in the 1860s before it was destroyed by fire.

No one knows for sure just how many bodies are buried on the grounds. There are at least five: the wife of Captain Salsbury and two of her children; and a former slave and his daughter. It is not inconceivable that there may be a number of others, possibly former slaves and servants, and perhaps fallen soldiers from both the North and the South, unidentified victims of the fierce fighting that was waged through the area.

Beyond this, there are a number of suspected dark tragedies which took place either at Windover Heights, or its predecessor, Huntington House. There is no firm documentation on this — early records have been lost or consumed by fire — but it is strongly felt that there has been at least one murder-suicide here, possibly a second murder, and a terrible accident which killed yet another person.

Consequently, the house, over the past century and a quarter, harbored a reputation as being haunted by as many as five separate spirits! They ranged all the way from a benevolent feminine ghost who said she was there to watch over resident children — to a vindictive phantom whose purpose was to drive people away from the home. Others who lingered there included victims seeking exposure of their ill-fated demise, and their attackers, seeking forgiveness.

The haunting manifestations at Windover Heights reached their zenith during the mid to late 1960s after Mrs. Lucy Dickey and her five children moved into the house. So prominent were the incidents of psychic phenomena during this period that renowned parapsychologist Hans Holzer, possibly the best known ghost expert in the country, was called in twice to interpret the eerie events. Each time he brought with him a different, psychically-sensitive medium, and each, without knowing the background of the case, came up with similar conclusions.

Following is a general summary of some of the manifestations based on several published accounts which have appeared in recent years, including Holzer's own detailed report in his book, "The Ghosts That Walk in Washington." When Mrs. Dickey moved in, in the mid-1960s, she was already fully aware of the house's reputation. The hauntings had been mentioned to her by real estate agents, and also by the previous owners, Dean and Jean Vanderhoff, who had lived there for several years. They had experienced such occurrences as: garage doors banging at night; a mystery woman talking in the kitchen; and loud crashes and banging in the kitchen. At one point, Mrs. Vanderhoff thought she heard all of her china being smashed to pieces in the kitchen. Yet each time she and her husband investigated, nothing was found, not even a tiny chip of broken glass or china.

It didn't take the spirits long to show themselves once Mrs. Dickey and her family arrived. The children were the first to sense "strange things," which their mother at first dismissed. Then one night Mrs. Dickey herself heard the sound of loud footsteps pacing back and forth. They seemed to be coming from a part of a wall which had been sealed up years ago. This had at one time been an entrance to a secret passageway which led to a narrow staircase going upstairs. The footsteps continued for about 10 minutes, and then abruptly ceased. All the children were in bed asleep and no one else was in the house.

Not long after that, Mrs. Dickey awoke from a terrible dream and was shocked to see what she said was the shadow of a head high up on the wall. She could make out a fuzzy kind of head and neck, but it was not distinguishable enough to determine if it was male or female. A cold chill seemed to envelop the room, and she screamed. But when a daughter arrived, the apparitional head vanished.

Mrs. Dickey, who was apparently somewhat "sensitive" herself, decided to see if she could find out who the spirits were by asking questions on an Ouija board. The names "Martha" and "Morgan" appeared. They may have been the children of Sarah Salisbury, wife of the builder and first owner of the house. It was suspected that they were buried somewhere on the grounds. Mrs. Dickey said "Martha" revealed that she was the one who had been seen as the head on the wall, and that she had manifested herself in that way to alert Mrs. Dickey that one of her children had fallen out of bed. "Martha" made it known that she was back in the house to help out; that she realized Mrs. Dickey had a big job on her hands keeping up the house and raising five children.

The events continued. When Mrs. Dickey took some stones from the yard to help enlarge a terrace, all hell broke loose. Loud noises and midnight bangings occurred. Another session on the Ouija board indicated that "Morgan" was not happy with the changes being made.

Windover Heights

As the ghostly noises continued, a young woman named Nancy Camp visited the house and she and Mrs. Dickey asked more questions on the Ouija board. This time a new presence revealed itself as "Adam." He said he had been killed in the house and he "needed help." His apparition then appeared only to Nancy. Terrified, she knocked Mrs. Dickey over backwards, the board went flying in the air, and Nancy ran from the room.

The next incident involved a scary crisis premonition. One hot summer night in June 1967, Mrs. Dickey was having difficulty getting to sleep. She got up and went to one of her daughter's bedrooms because it was breezier. There, she heard the distinct sounds of someone "crying, whimpering and moaning." She checked everywhere in the house, even looking in on her dogs, but found no mortal cause. Then the phone rang. It was her 18-year-old daughter. She and another girl, a friend, had been in a bad automobile accident, and the friend was seriously injured. She was crying, whimpering and moaning!

The strange sightings and sounds were not limited to the Dickeys alone. A number of house guests and visitors also reported seeing and hearing inexplicable things, including a "shadowy woman in white," the figure of a man walking about, and a "slim dark-haired woman in a red robe." A friend named Pat Hughes said she saw an apparition which looked a lot like Lucy Dickey — a figure of a woman, tall and thin in a red robe, with "something like a shawl collar." The Dickey children saw grayish, wispy images. Young Douglas Dickey once observed such an apparition for "three to five minutes," an unusually long time for a spirit to remain observable. Normally, apparitions are only sighted for a second or two. One day a beautiful gold ring, fitted with three red rubies, mysteriously showed up in the house. No one knew where it came from, who it belonged to, or why it appeared.

On and on, the incidents continued. One evening 11 people were in the house and they were having an Ouija board session, when all of a sudden they heard what sounded like a "large horse" clomping across the front porch. They got up and ran to the windows, but saw nothing! Later, a maid told Mrs. Dickey that years earlier her uncle had ridden across the porch, his horse reared and threw him into a tree, killing him instantly!

The psychic expert Hans Holzer visited the house in 1968, and the Dickeys briefed him on all the happenings they had experienced. Young Joyce Dickey, for instance, told of the time she was in the cellar when she saw a coat "swinging" on its own. She opened a door and saw a man's "faint figure" walking away from her. Family members also said they had observed a "coiled head with mannish features" on the porch. They said the head looked like it was coiled in a lot of wires. No explanation was ever forwarded for this phenomenon.

The footsteps were heard again and again. One morning at 3 a.m., Mrs. Dickey was awakened by the thudding of heavy steps which seemed to be going up the narrow staircase in the secret passageway leading upstairs. She went to her daughter's bedroom upstairs, but she was sound asleep. The children told of several occasions where they felt sharp temperature drops in rooms, and thought someone or something was there with them although they couldn't see anything. One child heard the sounds of water dripping one night. The drip slowly increased in intensity until it sounded like a waterfall was cascading at the back entrance to the house. Yet not even a drop of moisture was found.

The Dickeys held a seance which seemed to greatly disturb the spirits. This caused more loud banging in the kitchen, and the sounds of something being dragged across the basement floor; something like a sack of potatoes. All of this caused the Dickey dogs to "go crazy." Holzer believed the psychic phenomena to be genuine, and that it was being created by multiple spirits. He also felt that most of the activity seemed to be centered around the secret passageway and its staircase.

A year later he came back with a medium who said she experienced a variety of clairvoyant impressions at Windover Heights. She said she talked to one spirit who must have lived in the first house on the site in the early 1800s, because, according to her, he believed Thomas Jefferson was still President of the United States! She also claimed to have seen the "slim woman" the Dickeys and others had earlier observed, and she saw a man who had hanged himself in the house. She envisioned a terrible tragedy in the past in which a man had killed another man and then hanged himself. She also "saw" ghosts who had been slaves or servants. One of them allegedly "told" her he was buried in the yard, but his daughter was still in the house and he had to free her — to get her out "to the other side." He said he was the one who caused all the loud noises in the kitchen, in an attempt to scare Mrs. Dickey and her family out of the house. There also was some indication that one of the spirits might have been that of Captain Salisbury.

Holzer concluded that there was no rational explanation for all of the many manifestations — the apparitions and the noises. He believed, too, that so many things happened because Mrs. Dickey was open to such phenomena; that the spirits could reveal themselves to her.

After Holzer left, Mrs. Dickey related another frightening encounter. A group of her children's friends were at the house for a party. One young man went upstairs to a bathroom. He turned around to see a man staring at him. He said the man was dressed in a white, full-sleeved shirt, with baggy, knicker-type pants. Deeply shaken, the young man ran down the stairs to tell the others. He had no previous knowledge of the house's haunting reputation.

A year or so later, Mrs. Dickey put the house up for sale. At her request, Holzer sent a second medium to Windover Heights. He, too, had not been told of the spirits there. He confirmed the first medium's findings. He said a man had killed his wife's lover in the passageway with an andiron, and then hanged himself. He also sensed much violence in the fireplace area, possibly including another murder, and he believed all the mayhem which had taken place had put a curse on the site. However, by coaxing the ghosts out into the open to "tell their stories" at last, they had thus been put to rest, and now could leave the premises.

After that, and after Mrs. Dickey and her family moved out, all has been relatively quiet at Windover Heights.

CHAPTER 11

A Sampling of Spectral Vignettes

* * * * *

THE BOGEY OF CRADOCK MARSH
(Eastern Shore)

ne of the earliest ghosts, or rather ghostly creatures, reported on the Eastern Shore, is believed to have begun its hauntings in the 17th century. It was (and apparently still is) known as "The Bogey of Cradock Marsh," and was recalled in Jennings Cropper Wise's book, "Ye Kingdome of Accawmack," published in 1911.

"This bogey, whatever it may be, whether man or beast," Wise wrote, "has been sought by armed hunting parties for several centuries. By day and by torchlight, its trail of foot-tracks has been followed only to be lost as the weird cry of 'Yahoo! Yahoo!' resounds through the dismal wastes of marsh to warn the curious of the futility of their quest, and to make the blood of the half-hearted searchers run cold."

Wise also told of a "headless man, who for centuries has exacted toll at 'Taylor's Bridge' until stingy travelers refuse to pass that way at night! It is said that he never demands more than four-pence-half-penny, and that those who refuse to pay him invariably come to grief."

Additionally, Wise referred to some possible spectral intrigue involving the legendary pirates who once frequented the Eastern

Shore. He whetted the curiosity when he wrote, "Then there are the ancient traditions growing out of the pirates' occupation of Parramore' Beach, Revell's Island, Hog Island, and Rogues' Island; the latter so named from the character of its early tenants. For a true appreciation of these charming old tales, one must visit the country and hear the old folks and the Negroes recount them before a winter's fire, as the gale howls and shrieks through the ancient pines and flurries the sand against the window panes; or one must lie out upon the deck of a fishing craft, anchored in some remote inlet among the sea islands, and listen to the weather-worn sailors tell their tales of mystery, as the tide swishes along the reedy shores and the weird voices of night whisper among the rushes of the neighboring marsh."

* * * * *

THE LADY AND THE PIRATE
(Eastern Shore)

(Author's note: Tantalizing is too weak a word to describe the feeling of hearing an intriguing ghost lead, and then not being able to track it down. Such was the case in the summer of 1993 when I was autographing books at the Norfolk Pirate's Festival. Someone told me to get in touch with a local dentist named Dr. Bagley Walker, and ask him about the ghost in his house on the Eastern Shore. The person said the ghost's name was "Goldie," and that she was the sweetheart of Blackbeard the notorious pirate. (Wouldn't you be intrigued?)

Sometime later I called Dr. Bagley. He chuckled at first, then acknowledged that there was something to the rumor, but he didn't have the details. "Yes," he said, "I bought a place called Currituck Farm a few years ago on the Eastern Shore. It is in the Exmore area. The house was about 100 or so years old then, and was on the Currituck Creek. The lady I bought it from said that the ghost of a woman named Goldie made its presence known from time to time in the house, and that Goldie had been the girl friend of a pirate. She didn't say it was Blackbeard, just a pirate."

"As you may know," Dr. Walker continued, "The Eastern Shore is full of legends about buried treasure left by pirates, especially in the north end of the state, so I suppose it was not uncommon for the house to have a resident spirit. I never did learn anymore about her, other than she apparently stayed around the house waiting for her lover to return. I never saw any apparition of anything. About the only thing I can remember out of the ordinary was that once, when I was away, the lights in the house came on. That was the only experience I had while I lived there." Dr. Bagley now lives in another house, on Pungoteague Creek. And Goldie, whoever she was, must have moved on to another sphere to reunite with the pirate who disappeared.)

* * * * *

THE HAUNTED OAK TREE IN ARLINGTON

There long has been a legend in Arlington that a towering old oak tree which leaned over Glebe Road near Little Falls Road in Arlington was reputed to have been haunted by the spirit of a spy who was hanged from it shortly after the beginning of the Civil War. This reputation has been enhanced by the addition of the story of a second spirit tied to the tree. This has been covered in various newspaper accounts, and in Eleanor Lee Templeman's book, "Arlington Heritage."

As Mrs. Templeman writes: "On an extremely cold moonlight night, a man on horseback had great difficulty getting his suddenly terrified mount to approach the tree. As they neared it, a man rose from the shadows and staggered down the road. Thinking it might be an inebriated neighbor in need of help, the rider called without response and was unable to overtake the figure at a gallop. When the man disappeared around a bend, the rider became terrified at the thought that he must have been chasing a ghost! Still upset by the harrowing experience of the night before, he rode back early next morning and found the frozen body of a man clutching a liquor bottle at the base of the tree."

* * * * *

GERMAN MYSTICS IN THE SHENANDOAH VALLEY
(Near Berryville)

Among the thousands of settlers who migrated west to the great Shenandoah area in the middle of the 18th century was a small band of German mystics and sabbatarians, whose odd living conditions and rather bizarre religious and other practices caused considerable concern among their neighbors. The history of these practices had caused these people much suffering and persecution in Europe, and even in Pennsylvania, where they first settled before moving south.

As a result, they contributed to their own widely-misunderstood reputation by settling as far away from civilization as they safely could, and keeping so much to themselves that they were commonly labeled as recluses and hermits. Here, in these pockets of isolation, they formed "mystical brotherhoods." Among other things, they were convinced that the world was about to end, and that their purpose was to await Judgement Day in the wilderness, where they expected to "find a closer communion with the Divine Spirit in complete seclusion from the world."

They led monastic-style lives, and many observed strict celibacy. One early account of them in Virginia stated that they "are an odd set of people, who make it a matter of religion not to shave their beards, lie on beds, or eat flesh." They were also said to seek "the quiet life of esoteric meditation," and often, for considerable periods of time, subsisted solely on bread, water and salt.

Little wonder these people, commonly called "Dunkards," aroused suspicion and sometimes fear in the minds of their superstitious-minded brother settlers. In an article written 30 years ago in the Virginia Magazine of History and Biography, author Klaus Wust reported that certain practices of the mystics "aroused the displeasure of their neighbors. Fire exorcism was one of these activities which outsiders found disquieting in the strange mixture of religion and cabalistic elements." Also, "much unrest was stirred in the country by a number of spiritual manifestations."

The most spectacular of these, said Wust, involved a woman named Elizabeth Beeler, the third wife of Christopher Beeler, who had a farm near Berryville in Clarke County. There, in 1760, the strange happenings commenced. On the night of January 10th, Elizabeth was said to have been visited by a spirit who told her where to look for concealed money "if she be good to her stepchildren." She found the money at the spot indicated by the ghost. The spiritual visitations continued for a time "almost every night." Finally, two spirits appeared, says Wust, "claiming to be those of Beeler's first and second wives."

They commanded Elizabeth to return to Pennsylvania to have further spectral sessions at the "twelfth hour of the night." Thus, the Beelers hastily left their farm in Virginia never to return, while the settlers in the Shenandoah "felt doubtlessly relieved by their departure." By 1764, most or all of the mysterious German sect had left the Old Dominion as well, leaving behind a curious legacy of intrigue and suspicion that lingers still.

* * * * *

THE CHARGE OF THE PHANTOM CAVALRY
(Loudoun County)

In a book called "Old Virginia Days and Ways — Reminiscences of Mrs. Sally McCarty Pleasants," there is a chapter on "Ghosts." The author says, "The isolation of the plantations, the environment of an ignorant and superstitious race, tales and traditions transplanted from the old world — all fostered a belief in the supernatural. Sometimes I have fancied that there might have been actual foundation for some of these stories and that ghosts did continue to manifest themselves in the South long after they had ceased to be welcome in more frequented parts of the earth. As rats, when driven from one place repair to another, so the poor discredited apparitions."

An apparent skeptic, Mrs. Pleasants, nevertheless, cited the following as an "absolutely authentic incident." "One winter night several years after the war (Civil War), two of our neighbors went coon-hunting. The moon shone bright, the air had a frosty stillness and the ground was frozen hard. The men bagged their game and were returning home about midnight when they distinctly heard a sound which had grown familiar during the years of conflict, the sound of *clanking sabers and of thudding hoofs*. So vivid was this impression, so certain were they that a squad of cavalry was coming down the road that, involuntarily, by a common impulse, they both stepped aside to let is pass. *It passed!* The invisible host went by, the rush of whose riding stirred their hair! Terror-stricken, they looked into each other's eyes and each murmured in a breath the one word, 'Yankees!' Then, as they told me in relating the experience, they took to their heels and ran home as fast as if the Yankees were really pursuing them."

* * * * *

AUNT ESTHER'S GHOSTLY PUMPKIN PIE
(Site Unknown)

(Author's note: The following anecdote was told to me by a young woman during a Christmas craft show in December 1993 at the Hampton Coliseum.)

Our Aunt Esther always seemed to find a way to mess up the pumpkin pie she baked each Thanksgiving. It invariably came out with a whole egg yoke in it. We always laughed. One year she died, and the first Thanksgiving after that, we were making a pumpkin pie, and, remembering Aunt Esther's problems, we literally 'beat the hell' out of the eggs! When the pie came out, we couldn't believe it. There was the whole yoke intact! We all just looked at each other in amazement. And then we said, almost in unison, 'Aunt Esther's back'!"

* * * * *

THE GHOST THAT SAVED A LIFE
(York County)

(Author's note: I frequently speak at elementary and middle schools, generally talking about writing careers or about Virginia's ghostly legends. Children seem fascinated by them, and always come up to me afterwards to relate experiences they have had or heard about. At the Yorktown Middle School recently, a young girl of about 12 or 13 told me of a spectral event which was told to her by her grandmother.

She said her grandmother was asleep in her house one morning about 8 o'clock when she felt the covers being pulled off her bed. She sat up and was startled by the sight of a white apparition in the form of an old woman. The spirit seemed to be beckoning to her. She got out of bed, put on her robe, and followed the filmy apparition down the stairs and out of the house. The figure led the girl's grandmother across the street to some railroad tracks.

There, sitting on the rail, was a little girl, about three or four years old. She seemed to be in a trance-like state, oblivious to her surroundings. Bearing down on the child was a freight train. The grandmother instinctively whisked the child from the tracks, saving her life. She then looked around. The ghost had disappeared!)

A MOST LOVING SPIRIT
(Williamsburg)

(Author's note: In January 1993, I got a phone call from a woman named Sybil Parr, in Davie, Florida. "I have read your books, and I have had an experience that I just have to tell you," she said in an excited voice. She had been a travel agent, and had taken a tour of Colonial Williamsburg in 1984 with a group of other agents. During a visit to the Palace, she had been "overwhelmed" by a supernatural presence. Following is what she told me.)

s soon as I entered the building, some being of some kind wrapped around me. I don't know how to explain it. It was inside me, all over me. It enveloped me. I was warm all over. It was the best feeling I ever had. This spirit, or whatever it was, loved me. I knew that. It was a fabulous experience.

"I am distantly related to the Adams family, and I asked one of the guides if the Adams had ever come there. But I had the strong sensation that whoever it was, it knew me. It kept holding me, caressing me. It was such a loving, warm feeling. Afterwards, I had to go back to the hotel. I couldn't continue on the tour. I was too shaken. The spirit had completely encased me.

"It had to be someone from my past. Maybe I was its wife in a past life. It felt like a man. It was like a reunion. I'm a Roman Catholic and I had never believed in reincarnation before, but I don't know how else to explain it. It loved me. The feeling lasted the whole time I was in the Palace, about 45 minutes. I never told anyone before. I thought they would think I was crazy, but I had to tell someone. I believe the spirit is still there. I hope to go back someday and see."

✳ ✳ ✳ ✳ ✳

TABLE TAPPING TERRORS
(Norfolk and Buckingham County)

(Author's note: In the second half of the 19th century and well into the early 1900s, a popular pursuit was the quest to communicate with departed spirits. This produced a worldwide rash of seances, often led by mediums who would allegedly lapse into a coma-like state and sometimes assume the spirit of the dead person being sought. Such sessions produced everything from levitating tables to voices and apparitions brought back from the beyond. The trouble was, many of the mediums were frauds, and used other than supernatural means to acquire the desired results, often gained at considerable expense to grief-stricken and emotional family members.

In this era, one popular, and less formal means of spirit communicating was through something known as table tapping. Something akin to the Ouija Board, this process involved participants to place their hands on a table, usually in a darkened setting, and hold a seance in which table movements, or tappings, would spell out spectral messages, often giving the names of deceased loved ones, and describing things they had left undone in mortal life.

Such was the setting in the following account which took place in 1938. While this incident occurred in Adairsville, Georgia, it involved a long-dead Civil War soldier from Norfolk, Virginia.)

In Adairville, Mrs. Alice Howard was hosting a table tapping attended by her in-laws and her 14-year-old daughter, when "Jack Kirby" was mysteriously spelled out. No one recognized the name. Then came a series of rappings saying, "My comrade and I were shot from the tree down by the railroad and were buried where we fell." This made sense, because Mrs. Howard and her guests knew that two Confederate soldiers had been buried in a shallow grave beside the Louisville and Nashville railroad tracks.

They asked who Kirby's comrade was. The table tapped out "T. W. Furrow, Norfolk, Virginia." Mrs. Howard was particularly moved, because, as others had, she long felt the soldiers had been improperly interred, and were "uncomfortable" in their graves. But nothing had been done over the years, because no one knew who the Confederates were.

A few years later, Mrs. Howard read an interview with a man who said he had helped bury the two men, and that a letter addressed to a "Tice W. Furrow," had been found on one of them. Subsequent research revealed that Furrow had been with the first company of the Fourth Virginia reserves. Again, years passed.

Then a descendent of Furrow's found a record of his ancestor's death in a Confederate Army casualty roster. It said he had been killed in the Adairsville area, and that Jack Kirby had been a neighbor and friend.

The U.S. government accepted this as proof of Furrow's identity, and he and Kirby were reburied, "away from the rumbling of passing trains." Furrow was given an official headstone, but because Kirby's identity could not be verified, he was not given a stone. Mrs. Howard and her friends of the Daughters of the American Revolution raised the money for a stone and placed it at his gravesite. The ceremony was held on May 15, 1974, and was attended by a large crowd. Taps were sounded and muskets ere fired. It was said that Mrs. Howard, then in her 80s, was especially pleased that the table tappings of 36 years earlier had at last produced such satisfying results.

*****

A second incident of table tapping apparently occurred at a house called Green Hill in Buckingham County, sometime during the second half of the 19th century. This one caused pandemonium among the participants. This was the home of Colonel John Cabell, a stern disciplinarian whose life seemed to change dramatically following a "visitation," sometime in the early 1800s, of three apparitional women. They confronted him in the parlor one evening, along with an "unearthly wind" which caused the pages of the family Bible to "turn rapidly." The Colonel became a "devout believer" on the spot. He died in 1815.

The table tapping session was attended by family members and friends decades later. Someone in the party asked for the spirits to "call up" Colonel Cabell. When there was no response after several attempts at this, the person called the colonel a "hot tempered, contrary man when living, and he is the same man when dead." Hardly had the words been uttered when the table — a large mahogany table with a heavy marble top — "rose up bodily high into the air, flinging the candles to the floor and crashing down again." The attendees, it was said, scrambled out of the room as fast as they could, never again to tempt the fates by further tappings.

*****

THE CLOCK THAT STRUCK DOOM!
(King and Queen County)

n the early 1800s the family of Thomas Gresham, once Commonwealth Attorney of Essex County, moved into a century old manor house called Woodlawn. Not to be confused with the better-known Woodlawn Plantation adjacent to Mount Vernon, this house was in King and Queen County, about 20 miles from Tappahanock. One of the family heirlooms was an old clock, set in an oblong case about four feet high and one-and-a-half feet wide. Its front contained a large mirror and paintings of houses and trees. Unfortunately, the clock did not survive the trip during the move and it never ran from the day the family moved into the house.

That is, it never ran until someone in the house was about to die! Its first striking signalled the death of a young family member stricken with consumption. The clock then stood silent for six years. When it struck again, a grandmother living at Woodlawn passed away within hours. Not long after that, as the ominous clock chimed a third time, the 12-year-old child of a servant was scalded to death in the kitchen. The clock became so feared, and "such a source of superstitious dread," that its works were removed and thrown into a woodshed, and the case was moved upstairs into what was known as "the haunted room!"

The Restless Casualties of Ball's Bluff

(Loudoun County)

t was Murphy's law carried to the extreme. Everything that could go wrong, did, and then some!

It was October 21, 1861. The Union army had amassed a large force on Harrison Island, in the middle of the Potomac River separating Maryland and Virginia. They had spotted Confederate troops a few hundred yards away, on the Virginia side, in the woods surrounding a point called Ball's Bluff, a few miles from Leesburg.

The orders from General Charles P. Stone, a distinguished Federal officer, graduate of West Point, and veteran of the Mexican War, had been somewhat vague to start with (as had Stone's orders from his commander.) Colonel Edward D. Baker had been told to advance his men across the river, scale the bluff, and move on toward Leesburg if conditions warranted. Baker had left his position as United States Senator from Oregon to join the Union army. Although he was a brilliant and energetic legislator, well admired and respected by his peers, his enthusiasm and unabashed zeal far outweighed his meager military experience.

And, so, on the night of October 20, he assembled his men for the crossing. This was complicated from the start by the fact that there were only two small boats available to ferry the men, and only about 30 at a time could be carried. Captain Francis J. Young, of Baker's staff, recalled the scene: "The river was swollen and the current rapid, and there was much labor and delay making use of the boats... The bank (at the base of Ball's Bluff) is a miry clay, and the heights almost precipitous (about 70 feet high), with fallen trees and rocks, making it very difficult to get up the artillery."

To this description, U.S. Colonel Milton Cogswell added: "Arrived at the landing opposite Harrison's Island, I found the greatest confusion existing. No one seemed to be in charge, nor any one superintending the passage of the troops, and no order was maintained in their crossing."

Further, the Union forces had no idea of the strength or location of the Confederates, or even if there were any troops there at all. One early report had it that a "row of tents" had been sighted by scouts, but once atop the bluff, this was determined to be a "row of trees" instead. The ground Colonel Baker and his men ascended to was open and vulnerable, and he was warned by more seasoned officers, that the surrounding woods offered a perfect cover for Southern infantry.

This and other suggestions went unheeded, and Baker decided on his own to launch a forward press. It was ill-advised. What followed was a tragic fiasco. The Confederates massed in the woods and began a furious onslaught. Union soldiers, trapped in the open, were backed to the edge of the bluff. Their artillery was rendered useless by sharpshooters who picked off the cannoneers as quickly as they took their places. Charging to the front to encourage his troops, Colonel Baker was killed.

By dusk, the Federal forces had been badly beaten, and were ordered to retreat in any way possible back across the river to Harrison's Island. They were told to toss their rifles into the water so they would not be confiscated. As the men scampered down the steep bluff they became ready targets for the advancing Rebels. About 35 or 40 men leaped onto an old barge that had been found, but in mid-stream it overturned and sank, and most of the unfortunate soldiers drowned. Others swam as best they could. Some made it, others were carried away by the swift currents.

More than 900 Union troops were killed in the disastrous movement, and many others were wounded or taken prisoner. The death of Colonel Baker shocked the young nation, and, eventually, and inexplicably, the blame for the ignominious defeat was placed on General Stone, although he actually had little to do with what went wrong. The following February he was placed under arrest and imprisoned at Fort Lafayette in New York Harbor. He was held there for five months, under guard, although no charges were ever filed against him! He finally was released, and later served credibly under General Ulysses Grant, although, some said, he was a broken man, his honor wrongfully tarnished.

Many of those who fell at Ball's Bluff are buried in a national cemetery there. It is from this graveyard that stories of strange happenings have emanated over the past 40 or more years; stories that have been told and retold by townspeople. The most prevalent account occurred sometime around 1950, when a group of teenagers drove out to the bluff one evening. As they walked around the perimeter of the otherwise deserted cemetery, they heard "terrible screams," from which no mortal source could be ascertained.

Frightened, they ran back to their car. The driver started it, but, mysteriously, it wouldn't move forward. The teens said it seemed as if some "unseen hands" were holding the car back. Amidst their panic, the force, or whatever it was, held them for several minutes, then suddenly released them. The car lurched forward and they sped to Leesburg, running both stop signs and red lights along the way. When they finally arrived home, still wondering what had happened, they got out and inspected the car. They found two huge gloved handprints of recently dried clay on each side of the trunk! As one chronicler of the event later noted, "It appeared that someone using these hands had been holding the car back."

One of the young men told his parents about the scary episode and showed them the handprints. His mother and father then got in their car and drove back to Ball's Bluff to investigate. It was a windless, moonlit night. All was quiet and eerily still. They heard no screams.

There are three grave sites outside the wall-enclosed cemetery. Two were believed to contain Federal soldiers, the other a Confederate. Beside this grave stood a small tree. Suddenly, the tree began to shake violently. Although there was no breeze at all, the small tree swayed back and forth, bending and dipping almost to the breaking point. No other tree in the area was so affected, not even a leaf elsewhere fluttered. The man and woman, shaken themselves, drove off without going nearer the site.

One might well speculate a number of supernatural sources for the extraordinary psychic occurrence. Would not Colonel Baker be justified in returning to the scene? Certainly, General Stone's spirit might be expected to assert itself in seeking vindication for his unwarranted punishment. Or might it well be one of the hundreds of Union soldiers who either were shot from ambush, or drowned in their desperate attempt to escape?

But, in time, local historians offered a more plausible explanation. They said, the grave over which the small tree shook so madly, was, in fact, not a grave at all. It rather was a marker signifying where a Virginia soldier had fallen. The word was this unidentified man's family had wanted him buried in the county's cemetery, but "because his religious faith frowned on participation in war," burial there was denied, and he was laid to rest elsewhere. And so, the belief persists that it was his spirit that psychically screamed and shook the tree, letting it be known that he would not be happy until he was buried with his fellow countrymen who died in the Battle of Ball's Bluff.

FOOTNOTE: Colonel Edward Baker, the brilliant young U.S. Senator who died tragically in the Battle of Ball's Bluff, has also made his ghostly presence known — but this time on the other side of the river. In Annington, Maryland, at seven miles distance from Ball's Bluff, within earshot of the muskets that fired during the fighting, there is a three story brick building on the promontory with the Potomac sweeping before it in a crescent, that is "the eternal home" of Baker.

His spirit has appeared there many times over the years to the James Caywood family. Both the Caywood daughters, Beth and Lin, recall often hearing, in the 1980s, the "stomp of the colonel's heavy military boots overhead in the house." Once, they said, Baker yelled down the stairs, calling someone's name, although the girls couldn't make it out. During house renovations one year, two workmen became alarmed when they ran into "an odd-looking guy in a Union uniform who just crossed the field in front of them and went into the woods."

Baker on the eve of the battle at Ball's Bluff is said to have boasted, "on the morrow I'll be in Leesburg or hell."

Nonpaying Guests at the Wayside Inn
(Middletown)

(Author's note: Middletown is on Route 11, just off Highway 81 a few miles south of Winchester and west of Front Royal. As early as 1766, the village was recognized as a clock making center, and its reputation increased as wooden-wheeled timepieces gave way to those with brass, which bowed in turn to elaborately patterned eight-day clocks. The same artisans fashioned watches and surveyors implements. One of them, Jacob Danner, constructed compasses of such mathematical precision that their reputation endures to this day. Middletown's streets today are lined with antique stores and other shops which sell Civil War relics. Down the road a short piece is Strasburg, the self-proclaimed "Antique Capital of Virginia." And, within a short distance (15 or 20 miles) is the famous and haunted Cedar Creek Battlefield, and the magnificent, and haunted, Belle Grove Plantation — both covered in Volume I of "The Ghosts of Virginia.")

n occasion, they serve pheasant at the old Wayside Inn in Middletown. When pheasant isn't on the menu, one can order everything from Virginia country ham to fresh caught trout and catfish with such side dishes as old fashioned spoon bread. The waitresses serve you in 18th century costumes, carrying on a tradition of feeding and housing tired travellers that dates back to 1797. In those days it was known as Wilkinson's Tavern, and when the valley pike was cut through

Wayside Inn

some years later, the tavern became a popular stagecoach stop, a relay station on "the old Black Bear Trail, where fresh horses were ready, and where "bounce-weary passengers could rest and refresh themselves."

According to an inn brochure, "In coaching days, a servant boy would be sent to the nearby hill to sight an expected stagecoach. When a cloud of dust appeared over the horizon, the servant waited anxiously, straining to sight the outline of the stagecoach, and then hurried back to the inn to report its approach. By the time the passengers arrived, delicious hot food would be waiting and they would dine and drink in comfort while the team of horses was being changed."

During the Civil War, soldiers from both the North and South marched and fought back and forth through Middletown so many times it confused townspeople as to just who was in command on any given day. The inn survived those treacherous times by "offering comfort to all who came." The name changed to Larrick's Hotel after the Civil War, and then again, later, to the Wayside Inn. Today there are 22 guest rooms and suites, "uniquely decorated with rare antiques, fine art, objets d'art, and an interesting potpourri of memorabilia." There are also four poster beds with canopies and cannonball and acorn carved details.

It was here, on May 24, 1862, that, according to a state highway historical marker in front of the inn, "Stonewall Jackson attacked Banks retreating from Strasburg and forced him to divide his army." For a time during this period, the inn was used as a hospital. Although there are no records of exactly how many men lost limbs or their lives in the vicinity, a number of Confederate and Union troops fell here, including one colonel whose stone marker sits just off the inn's front porch.

That undoubtedly is why witnesses — guests and hotel workers alike — have reported seeing the ghostly images of Civil War veterans "milling around" in the lobby on occasion. "Oh yes, that's what people tell me," says amiable Molly Clough who has worked at the inn for the past six years. "Some have said they have seen the figure outlines of soldiers dressed in Civil War uniforms; others have said they just felt something, you know, like a presence here.

"There are sounds, too," Molly adds. "Of course, you have to remember this is a drafty old house. It has been an inn since 1797, but the earliest part of the house, the old slave quarters, dates back to the 1740s. Old houses have a lot of creaks and groans. But I have to admit, I have heard footsteps right outside the front door when there was no one there. I never could explain that. Then you have to remember that this place was a hospital during the Civil War. A lot of young boys never left here alive. They weren't ready for that."

Molly is not the only employee to experience such manifestations. A co-worker who prefers not to be identified said she had seen "shadows pass by the front windows at night." She was told it was just the reflections from car lights going by, but she didn't believe this. "There weren't any cars going by," she exclaimed. "And there were no people outside either. It was pretty eerie."

The night auditor has had the most dramatic encounters. "She swears there's a ghost who talks to her when she works late at night here," Molly says. The auditor told one co-worker at the inn that she felt the breath of someone breathing on the back of her neck as she walked through the ancient slave quarter section of the building one evening. She was reportedly "pretty spooked" by it all. Molly adds that sometimes at night, she would be waiting for the night auditor to show up. "It was then that I heard the footsteps. At first I assumed it was the auditor, but when I got up to check, there was no one around. The odd part was that it was always at precisely 11:15 p.m. when I heard the footsteps."

Molly and others say that several guests have reported to them that they "felt something" in rooms 22 and 23. "They never said they saw anything, just that they felt a presence, like someone else was there. "There's nothing harmful about any of our ghosts," says Molly. "I think it kind of gives the place an added charm."

* * * * *

(Author's note: I had called and talked to Molly prior to visiting the Wayside Inn in February 1994. When I arrived there and walked into the lobby, she immediately asked if I felt anything. I had to admit I didn't, but I told her I was not sensitive to such things, as other people are, so she shouldn't be disappointed. Subsequently, I spent the night in room 22. Again, I sensed no spirits. Perhaps I was too tired from the journey from Williamsburg. It had been a long day. I can, however, vouch for the hospitality and the atmosphere at Wayside. It is delightful. And, too, the pheasant was delicious.")

CHAPTER 14

Weird Happenings at Wizard's Clip

(Jefferson County, West Virginia)

(Author's note: I am taking a little literary license here to
include the following unique episode, in that the site where this
most bizarre series of ghostly manifestations took place today lies
in Jefferson County, West Virginia. However, at the time the occurrences were experienced, and widely witnessed, the little town of
Middleway, north of 'Winchester, then was still a part of Virginia.
In psychic annals, this particular phenomenon has been written
about a number of times, in everything from popular newspapers
and magazines to scholarly journals. What is especially unusual
about what happened is that, although it occurred in the 18th century, it was attested to by scores of early pioneers and settlers,
many of whom travelled long distances to see for themselves. In
the many accounts, there are some conflicting dates and facts. I
have tried to reconcile them as best as possible and present a more
or less consensus version. Adding to the veracity of the legend was
the comment many years ago of the Reverend Alfred E. Smith, a
former editor of the Baltimore Catholic Review. He once called it,
"the truest ghost story ever told!")

ometime in 1790, Adam Livingston moved
with his family from Lancaster, Pennsyl-
vania, to the then-remote area of Jefferson County near the town of
Middleway, sometimes called Smithfield. It also was later referred

to as Clip, or as Wizard Clip. Livingston bought a 70-acre farm and began carving out a living in the wilderness.

On a "stormy and windswept" night four years later, a stranger knocked at Livingston's door and asked for refuge for the night from the storm. During the evening the man became seriously ill, and it appeared that he was dying. He asked his host if he could have a Catholic priest come to the house to administer the last rites. Livingston's wife, a devout Lutheran, told her husband she would not have a Catholic priest in her house, and anyway, the farmer didn't know where to find one in the first place.

Soon after — it is not clear whether it was that night or within the next couple of days — the stranger died, unshriven. Livingston arranged for the body to be placed in a crude coffin in his house to await burial. As was the custom in that day, he asked a neighbor, John Foster, to come over that evening to "sit up with the dead." That evening, the succession of strange happenings began. The two men lit several candles as darkness fell, but then stepped back in fright as "unseen" hands snuffed them out. They relit the candles several times and the same thing happened, although there was no wind or any other natural cause for the extinguishment. Foster was so shaken, he immediately left.

Following the burial the next afternoon, Livingston and his family returned home and built a roaring fire in their fireplace. Suddenly, and inexplicably, the fire flared up and "blazing logs leaped from the fireplace and whirled around the floor" in what has been described as a "weird dance." Showers of sparks and glowing embers cascaded over the hand-made rug, and Livingston and his wife jumped about stomping on them. Each time they returned a log to the fireplace, it mysteriously hopped out again "to resume its seemingly possessed dance." This continued through most of the night and then, just as suddenly, stopped. The Livingstons collapsed on the beds, physically, mentally, and emotionally exhausted.

The next night the perplexed farmer awoke, startled, to the sound a "thundering herd" of horses galloping around the house. He roused his wife and they looked outside. The moon was bright, but they saw nothing. Yet the sounds continued, off and on, for more than an hour, and the Livingstons spent another restless night.

As the days and weeks passed, the terrifying manifestations intensified. Inside the house, "showers of hot stones," appearing out of nowhere, sailed through the air ... dishes and cooking utensils were tossed about by unseen hands ... and heavy pieces of furniture moved across rooms on their own. At night, footsteps were heard, and flashes of what appeared to be ghostly apparitions materialized. Livingston's savings, a fairly large sum of money, disappeared from a locked chest in his bedroom.

Nor were the supernatural activities limited indoors. One day, the beleaguered Livingston walked down a road that passed by his

Wizard's Clip

house and was confronted by an irate man on a wagon. The man demanded to know why Livingston had "stretched a rope across the road," impeding traffic. Livingston thought the man was either crazy, or drunk. He saw no rope. Finally, the man leaped down from his wagon, took out a large hunting knife, and began slashing madly at the invisible rope. Another man in a wagon came up, and he, too, cursed the farmer demanding to know why he had put up a rope across the road. He also tried to cut it with a knife, and became frustrated at slicing through thin air. Livingston then suggested they get back in their wagons and drive *through* the phantom rope, which, to their amazement, they did. Word soon spread through the region that some *very* strange things were happening at the Livingston farm.

Many, in fact, began to believe that it was infested with demons; a conjecture fueled by the fact that Livingston's animals; including cattle, horses, and other stock began dying of unexplained causes. All of this, however, odd as it was, served merely as a prelude for what happened next.

Out of nowhere, an eerie clipping sound began to be heard. It was "like the sound made by an invisible pair of giant tailor's shears." And they were destructive shears! Wielded by "indiscernible hands," they cut crescent-shaped holes in the family clothes, in blankets and sheets, even in leather boots. This created an even greater stir in the community, and people came from miles around to catch a glimpse of the Devil at work. Many were not disappointed.

One woman who came to the farmhouse, upon leaving, discovered that the ghostly shears had cut half-moon shaped holes in her valuable Oriental shawl. Another lady who descended from Winchester, took the precaution of carefully wrapping her "handsome new cap' inside a silk handkerchief before entering the house. later, she found it had been "cut to ribbons." A skeptical man arrived one day in his new swallowtail coat, denounced the proceedings as a hoax, and then, as he departed, looked down and was shocked to see that the tails of his coat had been neatly snipped off!

One day three young men arrived and proclaimed they had come a long way to "face the Devil himself if he was the author of these things." They left the farmhouse abruptly when the hearthstone in the room in which they were sitting "arose from its place and whirled around the room"

On another occasion, a woman visiting Mrs. Livingston,

was strolling in the yard with her, admiring her fine flock of ducks. Suddenly, they heard the dreaded "snip snip" sound and looked on it total astonishment as one by one, each duck's head was clipped off by the diabolical sheers, and fell to the ground! It is recorded that other witnesses also saw this incredible sight.

And still they came. One was a local German tailor who said all the proclaimed occurrences were the result of stupid superstitions and wild imaginations. Then, he happened to pass by the bewitched farm one day carrying a package containing a suit he had made for a neighbor. He heard a loud, "clip clip" sound about his head, and, non-plussed, shouted at the unseen noise to "go for damn." When he arrived at the man's house he had made the suit for, he unwrapped the package and found the cloth, "full of crescent-shaped slits and utterly ruined!"

The weirdness had been going on for about three months when, one night, Livingston had a vivid dream. He envisioned himself climbing up a steep mountain. When he reached the top he saw a man dressed in clerical robes, and he heard a voice saying to him, "This is the man who can help you." He believed the dream to be an omen. He then began a fevered search to find the man in the robes. Eventually, he was led to a man named Richard McSherry, a Catholic. With McSherry's help, he met the Reverend Dennis Cahill, a Roman Catholic missionary priest. Livingston immediately recognized him as the man in his dreams! Overcome, he knelt to his knees and wept unashamedly.

With the corroborative testimony of others who knew of the demonic activities going on at his farm, Livingston was finally able to persuade the priest to help him. At first, the efforts of sprinkling holy water in the house seemed to have no effect; the clipping sounds continued unabated.

The next day, however, Father Cahill performed a mass in the very room where the stranger had died three months earlier. With this, the clipping ceased. As the priest was about to leave the house, one last otherworldly manifestation materialized. As the Father had "one foot over the doorsill and the other in the hall," the money that had disappeared from Livingston's chest earlier suddenly appeared between his feet!

And with that, the 90-day onslaught of hauntings halted as abruptly as they had began. Livingston was so overcome with deliverance from whatever evil spirit had plagued him and his family that he and his wife converted to Catholicism, and he subsequently deeded 34 acres of his farm, still known as Priest's Field, to the Catholic Church with the understanding that a chapel would be built there.

Today, no trace of the old Livingston house remains. Yet, the legend persists. On November 8, 1922, the Shepherdstown, West Virginia, Register ran the following notice: "A very interesting service was held last Thursday, All Souls Day, at the Priest's Field, near Middleway, Jefferson County, when Right Reverend Dennis O'Connell, Bishop of the Catholic Diocese of Richmond, Virginia, celebrated three masses for the repose of souls connected with a strange event in our local history."

And even today, the site where all this took place, and was verified by scores of witnesses, although officially known as Middleway, is often still referred to by oldtimers as Clip, or Wizard's Clip!

A Psychic Premonition in the Parlor

(Somewhere in the Shenandoah Valley)

(Author's note: Through the details of the following supernatural account have been lost in time, the legend has been faithfully passed down by members of the Donnely family, whose ancestors farmed in the valley during the 19th century. This experience was recorded by Elizabeth Proctor Biggs in her 1978 book, "Beyond the Limit of Our Sight," and in subsequent newspaper reports, and is hereby recounted.)

ridget Donnely and Gabriel Shenk had known each other since their childhood in the 1850s. They were married in 1863, but were soon separated by the war. A Confederate soldier, Gabriel was wounded in battle and sent to a military hospital near Staunton. It was there that he learned his young bride was pregnant. He was soon after returned to duty, was subsequently captured and taken to that most dreaded of Federal prisons, Fort Delaware. There, already in a weakened state from his previous wounds, he contracted small pox and lay "gravely ill."

All this was unbeknownst to Bridget and the Donnelys at the farm in Virginia. There, as she awaited the birth of her child, Bridget one day in June 1864, stood transfixed before the locked entrance to the parlor, a room that had been shut off and was unused during the war years. For some inexplicable reason, she felt compelled to enter the parlor where she and Gabriel had exchanged their vows. She got the key from her mother and entered. Once inside, she began crying, "her eyes shut tight against some yet unrevealed sorrow."

When she opened her eyes, they seemed drawn to an old marble-topped table which had served as the altar for her wedding. She perceived a faint glow coming from the table. She walked closer, and there she stared, unbelieving, at a pointed taper "fixed lightly on an exquisite saucer she had never before seen." The tiny flame burned steadily, *but no wax melted or ran down the taper!* (The family, for some unexpressed reason, always used the term taper, and never candle.) Bridget stared at the light perplexed. How could a taper be lighted in a room that no one had entered for some time? Who had put it there, and why? Why was the wax not melting? Where had the strange saucer come from? Bridget could not answer any of these questions, but she later said the atmosphere in the parlor felt "seemingly vibrant with a presence she could not see."

Trembling with emotion, she backed out of the room, told her mother of what she had seen, and they both reentered the parlor. Bridget's mother saw the burning taper, too, and felt "an unearthliness about her but nothing ominous; rather, the sense of 'smiling' somehow accompanied the rosy, slender flame." Again, the questions arose. No one else had access to the room. Together, the two women felt an instinctive chill as they left the parlor.

That afternoon, Bridget reentered the room. As author Biggs described it, "She opened the door upon a musty darkness no longer penetrated by the mystical glow of an uncannily burning taper in a fragile saucer. It was as if an invisible hand had removed all evidence of the scene, restoring the musty scent of total enclosure, every speck of finest dust, and the hollowness of solitude to the room." According to Donnely descendents, Bridget then whispered, "Goodbye. Goodbye," and left.

Ten days later word came from some Virginia prisoners recently released from Fort Delaware, that Gabriel had died of disease and neglect — on the exact day and time that Bridget had entered the parlor and witnessed the burning taper!

Upon hearing the news, Bridget was said to have shrieked from pent-up anxiety. She lifted her hands to her head and pressed her fingers into her scalp in utter anguish. That night she gave birth to a baby girl. Upon its scalp on each side, through the dark, silky hair, were the clear imprints of ten perfectly formed finger marks!

* * * * *

The child who was born that night in June 1864, grew up to be Mrs. Rebecca Kirkpatrick, a woman who 80 years later demonstrated "psychic qualities" similar to those which surrounded her birth. She was then, in the 1940s, spending the summer with her daughter, Hannah, at Hannah's home in the valley. Mrs. Kirkpatrick always read herself to sleep at night; the light in her bedroom stayed on until well past midnight. One evening, however, when Hannah and her husband came home at about 9:30 p.m., her mother's bedroom was dark.

Hannah went up to check. Her mother said she had been "distracted," and had not been able to concentrate. She then asked about Hannah's sister, Anna, who lived in Baltimore. Hannah said that as far as she know, Anna was fine. She had talked to her by phone recently.

Early the next morning, word came by telephone that Anna had died in her sleep the previous night. When Hannah approached her mother to tell her, Mrs. Kirkpatrick said, "I knew something had happened." She then told Hannah of an ethereal experience she had had the previous evening. She said she had been reading, when, at half past nine, she felt a distinct chill. She looked up and saw an apparition of Anna. She was standing at the foot of Mrs. Kirkpatrick's bed. She smiled, but said nothing. She was wearing, a gray dress with ruffles at the neck and wrists. "I know it sounds strange, but she held a deep red American Beauty rose, in her right hand," Mrs. Kirkpatrick said. "I started to call her name and she just vanished."

Hannah then told her mother than Anna had died in the night. At the funeral service, Mrs. Kirkpatrick viewed her deceased daughter in the casket. She was enshrouded in a *gray dress with ruffles at the neck and at the wrists*! Her right arm lay across the body, and cupped in her hand was *a deep red American Beauty rose*! Anna had died, the medical examiner estimated, at *9:30 the previous evening*!

The Happy Grave of Adam Kersh

(Rockingham County)

(Author's note: I have to admit I got a little excited a couple of years ago when I talked to Sherry Emerson, then working for the now-defunct Rockingham Magazine. I had asked her about ghosts in the greater Harrisonburg area. She didn't have any first-hand knowledge, she said, but she suggested that I contact a county historian named Andy McCaskey; that if anyone knew anything about regional haunts he would. Then she dropped the tantalizer. "Ask him about 'Adam's Curse,' " she said. That did sound intriguing didn't it?

In the press of getting my first book on "The Ghosts of Virginia" out, I didn't get around to calling Andy until about a year and a half later. He lives about halfway between Staunton and Harrisonburg in a beautiful rural area called Weyer's Cave. The name comes from a hunter named Bernard Weyer. In the year 1804 he was having a particularly difficult time with a wily ground hog, which, it has been recorded, "not only eluded all his efforts, but eventually succeeded in carrying off the traps which had been set for his capture." Enraged at the loss of his traps, Weyer made an "assault upon the domicile of the depredator, with spade and mattock." A few moments labor brought him to the ante-chamber of a "stupendous cavern" where he found his traps safely deposited.

This wonder of nature is now known as the Grand Caverns Grottoes and is open to the public. But for years it was called Weyer's Cave. Writing in the early 1800s, R. L. Cooke, quoted by historian Samuel Kercheval in this book on the history of the

Adam Kersh

Shenandoah Valley, said: "You visit the cave by the dim light of a few candles ... As successive portions of the cavern are presented to view, they produce successive and varied emotions. Now you are filled with delight at the beauty of the sparkling ceilings; again this feeling is mingled with admiration, as some object of more than ordinary beauty presents itself, and anon you are filled with awe at the magnitude of the immense chambers, the hollow reverberations of the lofty arches, and the profuse display of the operations on an omnipotent hand. Indistinctness of vision allows free scope to the imagination, and consequently greatly enhances your pleasure."

It is with such thoughts in mind that I visited Andy McCaskey and his wife, Vivian, at the home near the caverns in February 1994. He is a spry 78-year-old who has captured much of the area's colorful history in his writings, and he relates it to visitors and others in his lectures and on radio and television talk shows. He also is a human textbook on county lore.

At first I was a little disappointed that there was no "Adam's Curse." I had misunderstood Sherry Emerson. She had said "Adam *Kersh*." But Andy took over and told me Kersh's legend.)

ou don't have to believe it, of course," he started, "but it is something that has been handed down for some time, and there are people who claimed they witnessed 'Uncle Ad,' as he is known in these parts, in the act of doing what he does."

Adam Kersh was a cabinet maker of "marked ability," who was also a "gifted musician of some local renown. According to Andy, "He enjoyed his work and relaxed from his labors with his hobby of playing the fiddle." Kersh died in 1907, and was buried in the graveyard at Old St. Michael's Church in the Centreville-Bridgewater area near the Augusta-Rockingham County line.

Apparently, says Andy and others, Adam "isn't always content to stay in his grave." "He's what I call a cheerful ghost, a happy ghost," Andy points out. "This seems to disappoint some people because they believe all ghosts should be solemn and somber." Bridgewater wood sculptor John Heatwole was once quoted in the Harrisonburg Daily News-Record as recalling "two elderly men who pointed to the graveyard (of Adam Kersh) near their home and said matter-of-factly that Uncle Ad had been sighted more than once, usually on those starry nights when there's just a hint of a breeze in the top of the trees. 'He just sits on his tombstone and plays a tune,' the two men said."

Andy McCaskey has written about Kersh, too. "When the hushed breeze of evening is swishing through the treetops just right, Uncle Ad enters from some unseen portal and sits there on his unpretentious tombstone and plays a sprightly tune on his rosin-dusted fiddle!" "They tell me," Andy says, "it sounds forth as a toe-tapping melody, a bright tune for those who have a happy heart; a sad dirge for those of dour disposition."

The Cline House Manifestations

(New Hope)

ill Eakle was, for decades, a well-known history buff in the Harrisonburg area who loved to track down and then tell and retell a good ghost story. One of the reasons Will, who died in 1992 at age 75, had such a respect for the past was the fact that his ancestors helped settle the Shenandoah Valley region, first moving there in 1749.

"Oh, I know, Will was interested in ghosts and that sort of thing," says his brother, Frank, who now lives in Fairfax. "Personally, I don't believe in them. I have never seen a ghost and I never want to see one. But I know my father and grandfather used to talk about them once in a while. My father was one of the first radio hams in the state. He was on the wireless four years after Marconi invented it." Will's sister, Mary Fately, now living in Hampton, also recalls a few occasions where spectral phenomena were discussed. "I can remember, she says, "that when I was a little girl, we used to visit our grandparents on Sunday, and they used to talk about some of the hauntings. I never had much interest in it, but the subject used to fascinate Will."

One manifestation Will Eakle used to tell about involved the return of "an old black man" who perished in a fire at a tavern located on a flat stretch of the Valley Pike near the entrance to the Rockingham County Fairgrounds. This allegedly happened in the pre-Civil War era, and Will said that for years after the tragic death people travelling in that area on "dark, foggy nights" reported seeing the man standing at the edge of the road.

But the ghostly account Will most often talked about stemmed from personal knowledge. It concerns multiple appearances both at an abandoned building known locally as the Cline House, and also on the grounds of the old Finley Farm at New Hope, which is about 12 miles southeast of Harrisonburg. The battle of Piedmont in June 1864 was fought over part of this land, and according to long-held legend, apparitional soldiers can still be seen there on occasion, refighting the bloody skirmishes which took place 130 years ago! Or as Will once put it, "the fury is once again staged as regiments of specters march across the battlefield."

"I did hear that people used to see visions of the soldiers. I can remember my father and grandfather mentioning it," Frank says. He and his sister, Mary, also heard about the dark encounters which went on at the Cline House, which in ante-bellum days was part of the thriving Finley Farm. The farm was a huge, bustling operation said to have been "fueled by the labor of hundreds of slaves."

Mary Fately says when she was a child she heard stories that strange things happened at the Cline House because the Finleys had the reputation of having been mean to their slaves. Whippings and other harsh punishments were said to be common. Will, Frank and Mary's grandfather lived at the house at one time, and he said the hauntings were frequent and sometimes scary. The spirit or spirits apparently had an aversion to bolted doors, because locked doors were said to "fly open" from no observable cause.

But it was the moans and the rattling of chains which seemed to cause the most concern. Will's grandfather spoke of hearing such sounds in the dead of night, mostly emanating from the basement. The chains, particularly, drove fear into house residents, sounding as if shackled feet were shuffling about trying to free themselves from their rusty restraints. Occasionally, the sounds were accompanied by "apparitions floating through the rooms."

Little wonder then that Will said one night his grandfather and his great uncle "fled from the house in terror after the ghosts came out in full force."

C H A P T E R   1 8

The Lost Maid of Milton Hall

(Callaghan, Alleghany County)

(Author's note: I am indebted to Horton Beirne, editor and publisher of the Covington Virginian — a newspaper that has been in his family since 1914 — for the following chapter. Horton wrote a generous review of my first book on Virginia Ghosts, and intrigued me when he said, "I have thought about doing a short book on ghosts in Covington, Alleghany County and Bath County, but have not found the time." When I called him and told him I was anxious to include this colorful area in my "Volume II," he mentioned three possibilities. One was a house that had been built about 1730, in which "things were moved around all the time." The second involved a statue of a young girl in a Covington cemetery, which, people say, "cries at times." The third was about "The Lost Maid of Milton Hall," which follows.)

t is an incongruous site deep in the heart of the "springs and spa" mountain country six miles from Covington near the West Virginia border. There, comfortable amidst the natural splendor, sits a beautiful 120-year-old English manor home; a Gothic villa which was built in 1874. Says the Virginia Landmarks Register, "Nestled among the mountains in a remote corner of western Virginia, Milton Hall stands as an expression of the renewed British interest in New World real estate, in the years just after the Civil War... (It) was a late use of the Gothic Revival mode, illustrating the lingering popularity of the style among the British after it passed from fashion for rural residences in this country."

The 17-room building was built for William Wentworth Fitzwilliam Viscount Milton and his wife — Lord and Lady Milton for short. One might naturally wonder how the Lord and Lady found such well-concealed spot in the first place. In fact, Lady Milton's brother had fought for the Union in the Civil War and came upon the place. Actually, it wasn't that remote. The old Callaghan Tavern, which stood here for many years, was an important stage coach stop on the valley turnpike which ran all the way from the seaport at Norfolk, west into what is now West Virginia. It was the old Midland Trail over the mountains.

Lady Milton chose this particular place because of its marvelous healthy environment. Not only was the air brisk and fresh, but the famous White Sulphur Springs (now the home of Greenbrier) was just 15 or so miles away; Hot Springs (now the site of the Homestead) was 20 miles away; and even nearer was Sweet Chalybeate Springs. (A century ago this was one of the "hottest" spa resorts in the country.) Lady Milton felt such an environment would benefit her ailing husband, but, unfortunately, he died of tuberculosis three years after Milton Hall was erected.

Today, Milton Hall is a strikingly attractive Bed and Breakfast inn run by John and Veronica Eckert, who bought the property about four years ago. The retreat features spacious rooms with private baths and no less than 13 fireplaces. John and his wife say they have experienced no psychic phenomena in the house, but they have "heard the stories," that have circulated throughout the greater Covington area for generations.

"I've heard about the ghost from several persons," John says. One of those who told it to him was Robert McAllister, now living in the Galax area. Robert and his family lived at Milton Hall from 1928 until 1962. "I will say there were some strange things that happened when we lived there," he recalls. Some of them, however, could be easily explained by rational means. "Old houses do creak, and make noises when they settle," Robert says. "And then we had some vertical vents in the attic. They were about four feet long by six inches. If the light in the attic was left on at night and it was foggy outside, it would throw out a shadow in the shape of a cross. It was very eerie."

According to Robert, the ghostly legend associated with Milton Hall originated shortly after Lord and Lady Milton arrived in the area, sometime in the early 1870s. They brought along with them a

113

young Irish maid, a girl of about 12 or 13. The Lord and Lady then purchased the old Callaghan Inn, and moved in there to await the building of their vacation mansion.

It is not known exactly when — one account has it on New Year's Day 1871, the day they moved in — that the inn burned to the ground. Lord and Lady Milton escaped, but the young Irish maid perished in the flames. "The story we always heard was that she came back after Milton Hall was built, and showed up in the servants' quarters looking for her mistress," Robert McAllister says. He doesn't know why her spirit would do this, because the Hall wasn't even there when she died.

Still, over the years, through successions of owners, a variety of ghostly manifestations have occurred; events witnessed by a number of residents and guests. Robert suggested to the author that he try to locate a book written at least 50 or more years ago that covered an account of the ghost. "I can remember a woman who wanted to write about it," he says. "But my father didn't want to talk about it at the time. I think she eventually did publish something, but she had it in a different location, in the Winchester area I think."

* * * * *

(Author's note: After considerable research, I did find a chapter on the happenings in Margaret DuPont Lee's classic, "Virginia Ghosts," published in 1930. Curiously, she had for some reason placed this chapter in a section on the Winchester area.)

rs. Lee called the building "a commodious and comfortable dwelling, in the style of a typical Irish house." If the specter of the maid appeared to the Miltons, there is no record of it. "Her" first appearance apparently came some years later, possibly in the 1890s, after Milton Hall had been sold to a family named Doe. It was during this time that a young woman named Marie Swift lived in the house and was governess to Annie Doe, daughter of Colonel and Mrs. Doe.

One night she stayed downstairs reading after everyone else had retired. When the clock struck midnight, she put out her lamp and tip-toed up the stairs in the dark. As Mrs. Lee reported it, "Turning on the landing towards her room, a hand caught her skirt, holding it firmly for an instant!" Terrified, Marie finally tore herself loose and fled into her room in "almost a fainting condition." The next morning at breakfast when she related her experiences, she was told that others had felt the same thing.

Sometime later, Marie and little Annie Doe were asleep together in a bed when Annie began screaming hysterically. Marie rose up in bed, and both of them "*saw distinctly*" a woman standing at the foot of their bed who "stared fixedly at them, and then faded — vanished!" Marie later said she might have dismissed the apparition as a dream had not Annie seen the same figure.

"We always understood that she was a friendly ghost," says Robert McAllister. "I never saw her myself, but we did have visitors who said they saw or felt some sort of presence in the back of the house, where the old servants' quarters were. In fact we had a servant when we first moved into the house to help mother out. She stayed about two weeks and then abruptly left and never came back. She never did say why she left. She wouldn't talk about it."

Robert's sister, Harriet Loving of Richmond never saw the spirit either. "Oh, you hear a lot of sounds in an old house," she says. She did admit, however, that as a child at Milton Hall she was afraid to go by a certain closet. She couldn't explain why. "I think it was just a childhood fear," she laughs. "It was just a feeling."

Robert adds that a Mr. Rumpole, a previous owner, had said he once had a guest who saw "something" in one of the lower rooms. He also remembers that after the servants quarters had been converted into an apartment, a guest staying there reported hearing a "rustling sound" in the room one night. She awakened and turned on the light, but saw nothing. She said there was no breeze that evening so she couldn't explain the sound.

John Eckert, the present owner, says the Irish maid was buried in a grave about a mile and a half from Milton Hall. The consensus of thought is that it is her spirit which occasionally roams the halls and rooms of the manor seeking her mistress. As Mrs. Lee put it, "Hauntings can frequently be traced to a tragedy." It could well be that the maid, likely homesick and buried in unfamiliar ground, feels more comfortable in the familiar surroundings of an English-style country home.

CHAPTER 19

The Curse of Buck Hill Cavern

(Natural Bridge)

 wo centuries ago, a young girl named Alice Lewis was kidnapped by Indians who hid the child in "a secret palace." She was rescued by an alleged witch named "Mad" Mary Greenlee, although it is not specified whether or not psychic powers were used. Alice told of "mysterious passages, statues and flowers," she had seen in "this wonderful place," and, at the time, the early settlers in the valley thought that she had made all this up; that this was her fantasy.

Actually, she had been held captive in one of Virginia's marvelous caverns. In the generations since, everyone from Thomas Jefferson to historian Samuel Kercheval has raved about the grandeur of these natural wonders. At Luray, for example, discoverers Andrew Campbell and Benton Stebbins, even in their flickering candlelight, knew they had made a spectacular find when they descended for the first time, in 1878, into the vast dark chasm there. "The soaring cavern walls reflected every color of the rainbow. The light from their candles danced over the surface of crystal-clear pools. And every way they turned, there were formations more breathtaking than the last."

The same can be said of Weyer's Cave in north Augusta County; Endless Caverns near New Market; Skyline Caverns near Front Royal; and dozens of others throughout the commonwealth. These scenic wonders are today visited by millions annually. Yet in the early days of the frontier, they were often feared, and considered by some to be places of evil, and, in at least two instances, of hauntings.

Kercheval, in fact, reported on one of these in the 1830s. He told of visiting a place called Shaffer's Cave near Mt. Jackson in Shenandoah County southwest of Front Royal, close to present-day highways 11 and 81. While he said this site was "not very remarkable for its production of natural curiosities," he did uncover a foreboding legend there.

Here is what he wrote: "A large human skeleton was many years ago found in this cavern, the skull bone of which a neighboring man had the curiosity to take to his dwelling house. This aroused the ghost of the dead man, who, not being pleased with the removal of his head, very soon appeared to the depredator and harassed him until he became glad to return the skull to its former habitation. The ghost then became appeased and ceased his visits. It is said there are many persons to this day in the neighborhood, who most religiously believe that the ghost did really and truly compel the offender to return the skull."

Kercheval went on to add: "The author saw in the possession of Dr. Witherall, of Mt. Jackson, one of the arm bones of the skeleton, that part extending from the shoulder to the elbow, which was remarkable for its thickness, but was not of very uncommon length. At that time he had not been visited by the ghost to demand his arm; but perhaps he was not so tenacious of it as he was of his head."

But perhaps the best known, and possible the most frightening, of Virginia's cavern spirits, is the one which haunts a cave at Natural Bridge. Over the past two centuries there may have been more words of eloquence written about this splendid wonder, than about any other single entity in Virginia. Thomas Jefferson, who once owned this property, was in awe of it. Kercheval's description, 160 years ago, still holds true: "Descending into a deep glen, I had to dismount my horse and walk up the margin of a fine stream and beautiful clear water, until I approached within 70 or 80 yards of the arch, the view being obstructed by a point of rocks, until within that distance.

"Passing the rocks, the most grand, sublime, and I may add, awful sight that I had ever looked upon, burst suddenly in full view. It was a very clear day, the sun rather past meridian, and not a speck of cloud or anything to obstruct the sight. The author was so struck with the grandeur and majesty of the scene, as to become, for several minutes, terrified and nailed to the spot, and incapable

Natural Bridge

to move forward. After recovering in some degree from this, I may truly say, agonizing mental state of excitement, the author approached the arch with trembling and trepidation."

One might say that in the years since, many others have approached the neighboring Buck Hill Cavern with trembling and trepidation, too, but caused by a much different source; one not of this world. Within this magnificent area, which runs to a depth nearly 350 feet below the surface, visitors encounter one marvel after another: a flowstone cascade; a cathedral ceiling full of stone icicles; a colossal dome; a mirror lake; a "hanging garden of crowns;" and a waterfall room.

One may also see vast armies of bats clinging to ceiling crevices, and they tend to darken the atmosphere for an eerie spectral attraction, called by some the "unknown Eldritch horror." It is more commonly referred to as the Buck Hill Cavern Ghost. Writer

Constance Miller of Buena Vista, in correspondence with the author, says she has heard about this spirit since she was a little girl.

According to the legend, which is also told by tour guide Wanda Pickles and others at the site, Colonel Henry Parsons, the original owner of the caverns, hired a work crew in 1889 to build a 275 foot entrance way into the cave. Somewhere, deep in the recesses of the cavern, the workmen suddenly dropped their tools and equipment on the spot and ran as fast as they could back to the surface. Inside they had heard, they said, the low, wailing moan of a ghostly presence. No amount of encouragement of any kind could persuade them to reenter, and the project had to be abandoned.

Nearly 90 years later, Buck Hill was finally opened to the public, and the haunt, apparently, still is there! According to Constance Miller, a distant, but distinct moaning sound has been heard by visitors in 1978, 1980, 1985, and, most recently, in 1988. On this last occasion six people who had entered the cave followed the example of the workmen a century earlier; they fled.

No one knows who the ethereal being is, or why he, or she, is there, although those who have heard the chilling moans say it sounds like someone in terrible suffering.

CHAPTER 20

A Galaxy of
Gambling Ghosts

* * * * *

THE MAN IN GRAY AT WAVERLY
(Frederick County)

t last count there were no less than three historic homes known as Waverly in the
Virginia Landmarks Register. There is the Waverly in Leesburg,
Loudoun County, built about 1890, and described as "a symbol of
personal prosperity rarely expressed with such ostentation in the
Victorian architecture of Northern Virginia." There is Waverly Hill
in Staunton, a 1920s "elegant expression of the Georgian Revival
style." Then there is the Waverly in the Middleburg district of
Fauquier County, an ocher-colored mansion erected around an
18th century stone cottage.

A fourth Waverly is not in the Landmarks Register, although it
might well be a candidate for inclusion not only there, but in a
ghostly register as well. This house, built circa 1734, stands in
Clearbrook, Franklin County, about five miles from Winchester.
The first owner was Alexander Ross, a prominent Quaker
Scotsman, and it once was sold to a great-nephew of George
Washington.

As with most old mansions in this area, Waverly saw its share
of action during the Civil War — it is said that Winchester
"changed hands" something like 60 to 70 times during the conflict

— and the house still has some scars and specters to prove it. One of the family portraits that hung there during those times was punctured by a Yankee bullet, and the home was visited on occasion in post-war years by "the ghost of a man in gray," who some feel was a Confederate officer.

He was first reported by a woman named Lily Jolliffe, a neighbor, who told of manifestations while spending the night in the house. In the guest room over the parlor, she bolted her door and retired one evening. A little later she was awakened by footsteps coming down the hall. Believing it to be her hostess, she called out, "Wait, I'll let you in." But even before she could get out of bed, the door opened and a "man in gray" walked in and went over to the window and looked out. He then turned, came to the foot of the bed, glared at Miss Jolliffe "for some minutes," and stalked out of the room, bolting the door behind him. The lady was, to say the least, considerably upset by the experience.

The next day she told her father about the incident, and he told her one better. Some years earlier he used to play cards in the mansion with three other gentlemen. One night, as they played in the room over the parlor by candlelight, the door opened and the same mysterious man in gray entered. He apparently had a dislike for gambling, because he strode straight to the table and blew out all the candles. The four astonished card players scrambled for the exit in the darkness.

This particular spirit apparently had been seen by a number of people. One former resident, Mrs. Dabney Harrison, later told Miss Jolliffe that she had seen the man several times, always in the same room. She particularly remembered one occasion when her dog, "trembling all over," leaped in bed beside her. As she roused, there was the man standing at the foot of the bed.

Mrs. Harrison also recalled the time when the hall clock, which had been broken for several years, suddenly struck one night — 79 times! Shortly thereafter, her grandfather, who had been in fine health, died unexpectedly. He was 79-years-old!

Winchester Star staff writer Linda McCarty went back to Waverly recently to do a Halloween feature on the house and its hauntings. The current owners, Kenneth and Tricia Stiles, told her that they had had no direct encounters with visitors from another world, but that there had been a couple of curious "things" which happened shortly after they moved in about a dozen years ago. One woman at the house one day said she definitely heard footsteps upstairs, but a cautious search revealed nothing. A few weeks later a couple was painting the kitchen cabinets. They were using blue paint. The man bent down to apply more paint on his brush, and when he looked up *red paint* was dripping down from the blue cabinet door he was working on!

If the "gray man" had been in the Confederate Army, this might explain his displeasure at anything colored blue. The Stiles also said that they had an unusual experience with their hall clock. It had been given to them by a friend. "It worked fine until our friend died," Mrs. Stiles noted. "Then it just stopped and has never worked again."

Three months after her initial article ran, in October 1993, writer McCarty did a follow-up, offering a possibly plausible clue as to the identity of the man in gray, and why he was at Waverly. After extensive research, she discovered that a Colonel Charles Christopher Blacknall, from Granville County, North Carolina, was wounded during the battle of Third Winchester near Opequon Creek off Berryville Pike. Commander of the 23rd North Carolina regiment, Blacknall was shot in the right foot, the ball shattering several small bones.

After being treated in a hospital, it is believed that he was moved to Waverly to recuperate. There, his leg was amputated, and he seemed to be recovering, but he died a few days later of "intestinal and digestive problems." Mrs. Anna Washington, who had helped care for Blacknall at the house, wrote the colonel's wife and told her he had been buried at the Episcopal Cemetery in Winchester. She asked Mrs. Blacknall's permission to have the body moved to Stonewall Cemetery where many other Confederate soldiers were interred. The permission was granted.

"Is the 'man in gray' the young Colonel Charles Christopher Blacknall?" writer McCarty asked, completing her article. "Is he desperately searching for a way to get home, a way to see his wife and children again?" One might also ask that if it is the colonel's spirit, is that why he has been seen over the years walking across the room above the parlor in Waverly, staring at whoever is in the bed? Is that the room in which he died? And, finally, was he a strictly religious man who could not abide card playing?

If so, then the mystery would be solved!

* * * * *

THE HARD LUCK POKER PLAYER AT THE BUCKHORN INN
(Augusta County)

he Buckhorn Inn, about 12 miles west of Staunton on Highway 250 near Buffalo Gap in the George Washington National Forest, advertises genuine "Shenandoah Valley food." When asked what this includes, one of the inn's managers, Mary White, says, "Some of the best fried chicken around. We have a nice tenderloin with gravy, our cheese is baked right into the macaroni, and our sauerkraut is extra good. It's just good cooking the way grandma used to do. We cook a lot of our foods seasoned with ham." And for desert, she says try the peanut butter pie, the peanut butter fluff, and the "strawberry streusel," a three-tiered concoction that includes a layer of pretzels, a layer of cream cheese with whipped topping, and a layer of Jello with strawberries.

The inn today has four dining rooms, and six rooms upstairs for lodging. It also has a roaring past. It dates back to the second decade of the 19th century, and was, for years, a favorite stage-coach stop for travelers heading for the famous health spas of Warm and Hot Springs, a trip that reached peak proportions in the 1880s. It also served as a military hospital during the Civil War.

But the resident ghost at Buckhorn is not a Confederate or a Yankee soldier, as one might expect. He is rather, a late-19th century card player who either was: caught cheating or winning too much; or caught someone else cheating or winning too much, but was a slower shot. No one seems to recall. It is only known that he was killed over a poker game.

"Oh, he roams around the halls upstairs at night," Mary says. I've never seen him, but a number of our overnight guests have said they have heard and seen him." The hard luck gambler has appeared in apparitional form on occasion, dressed in the mountain garb of the 1890s era. He apparently is harmless, and even tends to lend a certain degree of old-time charm to the inn. It is speculated that he wanders about still searching for the card game that broke up abruptly so long ago.

* * * * *

THE GHOST STILL LOOKING FOR A GAME
(The Shenandoah Valley near Harrisonburg)

n the 1890s and after the turn of the century, the mountain community in Beldor Hollow, later called Sun Valley, was a favorite meeting place for weekend poker games. The spot was ideal — nestled in the quiet solitude of the mountains, far from the usual interruptions of more inhabited areas. According to a report some years ago in the Harrisonburg Daily News-Record, around 1912, a group of men, all on horseback, rode up to a cabin in the Sun Valley area for a friendly hand or two of cards.

Throughout the course of the game, the "atmosphere turned less than congenial." A dispute about the game broke out, and was settled with a gun. When the smoke cleared, a man named Gilmer was dead. Apparently, said the report, "that man's spirit just wasn't sure that his death meant the end of the game." Local legend has it that Sun Valley residents still can hear the sound of the dead man's horse clopping through Hawksbill Creek, a clear, small stream that runs down the hollow. The ghost is returning on his horse to the scene of the murder, people say.

An area historian named Robinson claims that once he heard, "just as plain as day," the sound of hooves amidst the gurgling water when he was at a house in Sun Valley. He knew of the legend, and convinced that someone was playing a practical joke, he and his companions raced outside to catch the culprit in the act. They found nothing — "no jokesters, no horses, nothing but the babbling creek!"

* * * * *

THE SWASHBUCKLERS AT CARTER'S GROVE
(Williamsburg)

(Author's note: I covered the ghosts of Carter's Grove, the magnificent colonial plantation house near Williamsburg in James City County, in Volume I of "The Ghosts of Virginia." The chapter was titled "The Puzzling Riddle of the Refusal Room," and it told of carnation petals being ripped to shreds and strewn in the house at night by spectral hands.

Carter's Grove

Since publication of that book, in 1993, I have come across another reference to spirits there. This was reported in the October 1928 issue of a long-extinct magazine of Virginia called "The Black Swan." Here is what was written by T. Beverly Campbell:)

t is said that three pirates are buried beneath its (Carter's Grove) cellar, and we are told that on several occasions these buccaneers have been seen seated in this cellar at a game of cards, but as yet none of those who have seen the apparitions have lingered to watch the game over the shoulders of the pirate ghosts."

* * * * *

THE APPARITIONAL CARD DEALER
(Big Stone Gap)

(Author's note: This account is taken from the archives of the Blue Ridge Institute of Ferrum College. It is part of the James Taylor Adams collection. Adams was a prolific researcher, interviewer and writer who chronicled life in Southwest Virginia from the 1930s through the 1950s. He and others scoured the hills and valleys of this area recording folklore that had been handed down, generation to generation, for more than 200 years.

The following is from an interview by James M. Hylton. It is part of the Adams collection, and is reprinted here courtesy of Clinch Valley College and the Blue Ridge Institute. Here is how Hylton prefaced it: "Related to this writer January 14, 1942, Wise, Virginia, by Logan (Loge) Tonker, aged about 40 years, who is a WPA worker at Big Stone Gap, and who delves into tales and herb medicine a good lot of his time. He was in Wise on business this date and upon request refreshed his memory to see if he could recall about a house that he told this writer about some time ago... He believes in witchcraft to some extent and in old signs and sayings... He says this experience happened to him in Big Stone Gap and in an old red brick building that stands on Shawnee Avenue in the western end of town. It was a good building in the old days and in the days when the county was very young and law and order first came to the Gap. It has fallen away somewhat and is showing its years. The red bricks are dropping from the top edges one by one and it has been vacant now for many years.

"The men of the lower ebb and flow of life used to play 'poker' there in the past years and about 40 years ago a man was killed in an upper room on the back side. It had been passed around from mouth to mouth that the house was 'hanted.' Of course, the people of the better class who were educated and more refined, would hear nothing of it, but among the ones of the poorer class who had their own superstitions, it was a general knowledge about the old 'Baker Building' being 'hanted.' Logan tells here the following story or experience he had himself there.")

I'd always heard that the Baker Building in Big Stone was hanted. As I'd lived there most of my life, I allowed I'd see for myself what it was all about. I'd heard that at 8:25 p.m. at night that iffen you'd go there upstairs, you'd see this feller come in through the wall and make a move as iffen to set down and make motions with his hands as if dealin' cards.

"I'd got purty full one night and some fellers wuz talkin' about it, and I decided to see for myself, so around to the buildin' I went. I set thar about a half hour when I heard the L & N coming down from Norton, and I knowed I was on time for it runs on time and is due here at 8:30, so I waited and looked to see what I could see.

"Well, it weren't long 'fore the first thing I knowed I was lookin' at a light like the shape of a man and it'd come right through the wall, too. It stood there while the train was passin' and then at once it got smaller like somebody settin' down and iffen I'd not had my guts a full of wine I'd never stayed thar like I did anyway. Well, it set down like I say and it looked like a man settin' thar dealin' cards over a table and I figured as I'd seen enuff 'bout then and skeedadled outta thar fast as I'd ever run before in my life, I know. Later, I told it round town and some others tried it and found out the same as I did. The house is still thar and you can try it for yourself sometime iffen you give yourself the hankerin' to do it, too. I've seen and heard lots a stuff, but that beats me I'm a tellin' you right now, yes siree."

(To this, interviewer-writer Hylton added: "I have investigated this and some say that it is true that you can see this sight when you wish at 8:25 p.m. each night. Others say that it was the train passing over a railed bridge in the distance and casting the flickering light on the wall, and that since the train has been discontinued, it can't be seen. But others say that you can see it for yourself now as you could for many years. At any rate, they never play poker there in the nighttime anyway.")

Intriguing Images at Stately Salubria

(Culpeper County)

(Author's note: There is a mystique about stately old Salubria which has intrigued me. Perhaps it is the fact that there are tantalizing clues about dark deeds at this Georgian mansion which seem to lie just beyond the researcher's attempts to unmask them. More of these have surfaced since I first wrote about the house in "The Ghosts of Fredericksburg and Nearby Environs" in 1991.

First, what do we know about Salubria? According to the Virginia Landmarks Register, it was built circa 1760 for the Reverend John Thompson. It features "outstanding interior panelling, and its otherwise plain facades are given an elegant rhythm by the use of segmental brick arches above all the openings."

The good Reverend Thompson was first married to Lady Spotswood, widow of Governor Alexander Spotswood. It is around her that some of the first reports of hauntings surface. There is, for example, a book called "Germanna," which contains a ghost story in which Lady Spotswood is "trapped in a secret room while hiding silver during the Revolutionary War." Unfortunately, the facts are that she died well before this time, and, in subsequent renovations of the house, no secret rooms or passages were found.

It is believed that Lady Spotswood is buried on the grounds, at Stevensburg, about seven miles from the town of Culpeper, although her final resting place cannot be found today. There is a legend about her son, Robert, who was killed in the French and Indian War. His body was never discovered, however, the Lady was sent one of his moccasins which was preserved as a family

Salubria

relic. Supposedly, as long as the moccasin was in the house, "fate
dealt kindly" with those still living at Salubria. After its mysterious
loss, at a date not recorded, none of the family held onto the
old mansion for any length of time. It also is said that at times,
occupants of the house have distinctly heard the tread of the
lone moccasin over the floor of the upper hall and in Lady
Spotswood's room.

The property was acquired by the Hansbrough family in 1792.
They changed the name of the house from "The Grange" to its
present name, meaning healthful. It was sometime after this that
the most interesting "suggestions of the supernatural" arose. The
following appeared in an article in a now-obscure magazine called
"The Black Swan," in October 1928: "Through inheritance, the
property came into the hands of three sisters named Hansborough
(sic)." Their reign must have been extraordinary to say the least.
The Black Swan article states: "One of them is reported to have
killed a slave and buried the corpse beneath the cellar. All three
committed suicide, two by hanging themselves, and the third one
by drowning herself in the well."

The article continues by saying that many years later a lady
who was stopping at this house was badly frightened when the
mirror before which she was arranging her hair preparatory to
retiring, "clouded over with a peculiar gray mist." Margaret
DuPont Lee, in her 1930 book, "Virginia Ghosts," elaborated on
this phenomenon. She said the lady was a Mrs. Grayson who was
quoted as saying at the time, "A white mist seemed to have
enveloped my form. I could not move nor utter a sound. As I
looked intently, the mist slowly took the form of a face peering

over my shoulder and reflected in the glass before me. I felt oppressed and unable to move." At this point, Mrs. Grayson screamed and fainted. An investigation yielded no mortal cause for the manifestation.

The magazine article also told of an occasion when "two children were nearly frightened out of their wits in this house by the appearance of the ghostly figure of a woman in white, with her hair hanging down." The image then "floated" down the hall and disappeared. A servant told the boys they had "seen the spirit!"

The intrigue lies amid the hidden identity of this ghostly woman. Was it Mrs. Spotswood, searching for the lost moccasin? Or was it one of the Hansborough sisters returning in remorse?)

The 'White Lady' of Avenel

(Bedford)

(Author's note: A couple of years back, when I was doing research for my book, "The Ghosts of Charlottesville and Lynchburg and Nearby Environs," I came across a yellowed newspaper clipping about a ghost in a house called Avenel. For one reason or another, it did not get included in that collection. Subsequently, I received an interesting letter from a lady named Betty Lambeth Gereau, a member of The Avenel Foundation's board of directors. She brought me up to date on this historic house and its spectral presences. The Foundation bought the house in 1985, and has been in the process of restoring it to its antebellum grandeur.

Mrs. Gereau also sent me a thick packet of information about Avenel. "The elegant home," she wrote, "conjures up visions of times that were more gracious than our own, and our imagination is kindled by recollections of life within its walls. Avenel is, in fact, far more than a house. It is also a legend and a landmark for those who live in the area, an integral part of their heritage."

She told me that the restored mansion "will meet Bedford's pressing need for an attractive, convenient, spacious place for people to gather for business or pleasure. It will be the site for meetings of business and professional groups and for civic clubs, as well as a gracious setting for wedding receptions, Christmas parties, luncheons and dinners by appointment, and many other types of social events." She added that, once renovated, Avenel will be available for overnight accommodations including breakfast.

She also knew how to pique my interest, for she said, "to this day we still have unexplained happenings!" With this, she included several newspaper and magazine clippings all describing a supernatural presence in the grand old house. I was hooked.)

It is interesting to note how many builders of Virginia's beautiful old manor homes erected in the late 18th and early 19th centuries seemed to have been influenced by the classic writings of Sir Walter Scott. One is reminded, for example, of a 1780 house in Rustburg named "Ivanhoe," which, coincidentally, is haunted by the ghost of a murdered peddler, and features a mysterious bloodstain which keeps disappearing and reappearing in the room where the peddler met his fate.

And so it is, that when William Burwell had his dream mansion built in Bedford in 1836, he called it Avenel, the name stemming from another of Scott's masterful novels. This one was "The Monastery," and, ironically, it included an apparition called "The White Lady of Avenel!" How vividly prophetic that title turned out to be, will soon be revealed!

Burwell, incidentally, was elected to the Virginia House of Delegates in 1838, and was instrumental in obtaining the charter for the first railroad in Piedmont Virginia. The railroad came to the town in 1856, and its tracks cut across the southern side of the Avenel plantation.

In the stylish pre-Civil War era, Avenel was one of the grandeur homes of central Virginia. The stately house has two-foot-thick walls, five bedrooms, a parlor, dining room and kitchen. There are no less than eight fireplaces, ornate ceilings, a wraparound porch, and a double staircase. A separate building houses the original kitchen. The interior has remained virtually unchanged over the past 150-plus years.

In its glorious heyday, Avenel was the very essence of Southern hospitality. It was the center of a vast plantation, spread out at the foot of the Peaks of Otter. In 1910, Mrs. Rosa Burwell Todd, one of Burwell's four daughters, gave an incisive glimpse into what life was like when she wrote a magazine article about the house. It was, she said, "an ideal home in the 1850s before the war clouds began to gather, and the servants were as proud of its fame for hospitality as the master and mistress. Kitchens were always far from the house in olden times for the servants were too abundant in those days for the distance between stove and table to be considered of importance. These dusky attendants were trained to bring in hot breads, biscuits and cakes in rapid succession, each seeming to be hotter and lighter than the one it succeeded...

"Friends were highly valued in those easy going times, and men retained their college contacts even to old age by keeping in close touch with each other. And how those old friends did enjoy discussing the many subjects of mutual interest, their life-long associations brought about them, as they sat under the big oaks on Avenel's broad lawn ... where so soon ladies of the neighborhood were to gather to make clothing for men at the front and provide their contribution to hospital supplies."

One of the frequent visitors to Avenel was Dr. George W. Bagby, author of "The Old Virginia Gentleman." He once wrote, "Avenel and its inmates constitute one of the deepest and most beautiful parts of my very life. They inspire the best writing I ever did." Such writings, in turn, caused another famous author of the time, Thomas Nelson Page, to comment that it was Bagby who "opened his eyes and whispered into his ear the charm that sang to his soul of the South."

Fortunately, the house was spared during the Civil War, although, as Letitia Burwell penned in her memoirs, "The Yankee soldiers pulled down all the Avenel fences to make their camp fires." It was shortly after the war that the mansion received perhaps its most distinguished and revered visitor — General Robert E. Lee. He and his daughter, Mildred, stopped over after a trip to the Peaks of Otter.

Letitia also told of his coming. "His circumstances and surroundings were now different; no longer the stars and epaulets adorned his manly form, but dressed in a simple suit of pure white linen, he looked a king and adversity had wrought no change. Trust in God kept him calm in victory or in defeat." Lee took tea at the house and spent the night. The next day, as he departed, Mrs. Todd wrote: "That afternoon, General Lee, with his daughter by his side, rode through the village of Liberty, now Bedford, on their return home, the citizens waiting eagerly to see him once more. As he rode down the street, with his hat in his hand that he might show his appreciation of their homage, every head was bared as they waved a farewell to their beloved general, and a mighty silence came over them as Traveler, bearing his honored rider, toiled slowly up the rugged hill leading from the narrow village street."

The visit inspired Elizabeth Baskerill Wall to write: "The old house, guarded by its mammoth magnolia, crepe myrtle and holly trees has become a landmark. And Lee is remembered within it as neighbor, kinsman, father and friend — himself the ideal Virginia Gentleman ..."

The first known appearance of the "supernatural presence" at Avenel surfaced in 1906. So pronounced was the impact of this and subsequent visitations, that the house quickly garnered a reputation as being haunted; a reputation so well circulated among the townspeople that few dared venture into the house, and many would walk across the street rather than pass close by.

The sighting is most appropriately told by Peggy Ballard Maupin, now in her 90s. She lived in the house for more than 80 years. Her father bought Avenel from the Burwell family in 1906, when she was a small child. "When we first saw 'her,'" Mrs. Maupin tells, "my mother and a whole crowd of us were at the end of the porch. It was about dusk when the 'White Lady' walked up the lane that passed in front of the house. My mother said 'Do you see what I see,' and just then the apparition disappeared in an old oak tree." Mrs. Maupin adds that she and several others saw the figure, but no one could explain it. The vision was described as being a very fashionably dressed woman, but in clothes of a much

Avenel

earlier era. She was carrying a white parasol. Later, the figure was seen again, this time walking with a gentleman "dressed also in clothes of another age."

Mrs. Maupin believes it may be the ghost of Fannie Steptoe Burwell, who lived in the house generations ago. Mrs. Maupin's husband, Harry, a respected town druggist, was firm in his disbelief, until an eerie personal encounter suddenly changed his mind. Mrs. Maupin says, "he was seated on his bed, ready to retire, when he looked through his open door. 'She' went slowly by, in the same white, full gown with her face in the shadows." The specter passed the bedroom and disappeared down a dark hallway. "It really scared him when he saw it," Mrs. Maupin said, recalling that he had goose pimples all over his arm "to substantiate his fear." Harry adamantly declared that "it definitely was not auto-suggestion or some other psychological phenomenon." He saw what he saw even if he couldn't explain it.

There have been numerous other inexplicable events in the house ever since. There is, for instance, a door in an upstairs bedroom which, say several overnight guests, mysteriously opens precisely at midnight. High above the back stairs landing is a wide double-sash window. Many say a face can be seen in this window, and even in pictures of the window. It is reported to be the face of a dark man, possibly a former slave or servant at the house. The 'face' peaks down at onlookers through the lower sash, sending a tingling chill through those who have viewed it.

Early in 1993, writer Chuck Kincaid was invited to Avenel to write about the resident ghost for Roanoker Magazine. He spent several hours in the house alone and was duely impressed. He described hearing an unusual and unexplained sound in the back of the empty home. He said it was not caused by any rational means, such as traffic, appliances, voices, or the wind. He said it was "more like a flutter. It's like a swishing sound. It's like a moth hung up in curtains." But he noted that there were no curtains, only bare windows. Tracking it closer, Kincaid reported it to be "a constant breathy murmur." He sensed it was coming from a back stairway. "We listened to the whispering, trying to locate it. It seems like a movement." That apparently was enough to convince him. He hastily moved out of the house and onto the porch. In his article, he concluded his conjecture about the cause of the sound. "But for all the world it sounded like the rustle of a hoop skirt."

"To this day we still have unexplained 'happenings' at Avenel," Betty Gereau wrote. She says that once she went into the house when no one else was there to pick up some brochures. "I heard this loud banging upstairs. I must admit I was shaken. I couldn't figure out what was causing it. I went upstairs to look and all I could see was a bunch of wasps flying around. I never did learn what was making the loud sounds.

She and others have noticed another ethereal occurrence. In an upstairs bedroom, called the Lee room, for this is where the general slept when he visited Avenel, the bedsheets and the pillow give the appearance that "someone or something" had laid down there after the bed had been made up. "There is a definite depression on the pillow and on the bedsheets," she says.

A few years ago, because much of the original furnishings had been lost, several portraits from another house were given to the Avenel Foundation for hanging in the house. Whoever the ghost is, she or he didn't care for these "intrusions." Several times the portraits were found moved about by unseen hands, sometimes they were taken off the walls and placed on the floor, and on one occasion, portraits were found turned around, facing the wall. Mrs. Gereau says "'she' was not happy with them." Later, when some original Avenel portraits were found and returned to the house, and the other ones taken down, the manifestations ceased.

This lends credence to the theory that the ghost is that of Fannie Steptoe Burwell, who lived in the house for so many years. She is described by all as being a benevolent haunt, merely making her presence known on occasions when she is not pleased with what is happening at Avenel.

This seems plausible as many ghosts in Virginia houses are said to do this. But one wonders. In Sir Walter Scott's novel, "The Monastery," the story is set in the borderlands that lie between Scotland and England. The time is during the 16th century. The Avenel here was an ancient Scottish castle, complete with moat, drawbridge and knights in armor. The gateway bore the armorial crests of the House of Avenel and included a figure "shrouded and muffed." The figure was generally thought to represent the mysterious being called "The White Lady of Avenel."

In the novel, the House of Avenel falls upon hard times and it became the duty of the White Lady — the "Maiden of the Mist" — to intercede on behalf of the dwindling heirs in an "altogether unnatural" way. This she did with some determination, for with the fall of the House of Avenel, she was destined for oblivion — a fate reserved for astral spirits of the day.

Scott wrote his novel in 1820. Avenel in Virginia was built in

1836. As one newspaper columnist observed long ago, it is therefore apparent that the White Lady "could extend her astral existence by updating her residence and moving into Avenel of Bedford. For it is most certain that her Scottish alliance could not outlast the star that ruled it. One can only assume that this is exactly what happened."

CHAPTER 23

Does A Ghost Guard The Beale Treasure?

(Montvale — Bedford County)

he ghost of Thomas Jefferson Beale — if there is one — must either be crying in complete, total, absolute frustration ... or laughing so hard his sides ache. Beale, you see, is the Virginia gentleman, or hooligan, and there are strong arguments for either choice, who is said to have buried a legendary horde of gold, silver and precious gems somewhere near the town of Bedford, west of Lynchburg. The cache allegedly included nearly 3,000 pounds of gold, more than 5,000 pounds of silver, and hundreds of thousands of dollars worth of jewels. According to the legend, Beale and his associates buried the treasure in iron pots in the ground, leaving behind a complex code, which, once broken would reveal the precise location of their loot.

But nearly 175 years later, a burning question remains unanswered: was any treasure buried at all, or did Beale pull off one of the greatest hoaxes in history? If he did, his spirit must be rolling in laughter at the thousands — thousands — of people who have searched in vain, some squandering their own life savings in the process, for the pots of gold. But if he really did hide a fortune, then he must weep ghostly tears because no one has been able to find even a single coin.

Whether, in fact, Beale buried anything at all has become almost anti-climatic because even if it was proven he didn't, undoubtedly there would be legions of amateur adventurers who would never believe it, and would keep on digging. Because over the years the Beale treasure has almost become bigger than life. It has been the subject of countless newspaper and magazine articles, books and television programs — to the point where it is beginning to rival some of the top unsolved mysteries of all times, such as the Lost Dutchman mine in Arizona, and the eternal search for the Abominable Snowman. It certainly must qualify as Virginia's most enduring and alluring mystery.

The enigmatic Thomas J. Beale is believed to have been born around 1792. Some who have written about him described him as "a gentleman well educated, evidently of good family, and with popular manners." Others have said he was a black sheep, "gun slinging genius" who was constantly bailed out of scrapes by his more respectable brothers. There is one account that, as a young man, Beale shot and killed a man in Fincastle, Virginia, which led, indirectly to his finding of a king's ransom out west. Beale claimed, however, that he and 30 individuals "of good character" were "seeking adventure" when they left on a two-year expedition hunting buffaloes and grizzlies. The year was 1817.

It still is a puzzle as to exactly where this curious troop of Virginians wound up in the west. Some have said New Mexico, some Arizona, and some "south-central Colorado." There is no consensus, but most researchers feel Beale and the others were somewhere in the vicinity north of Santa Fe when they discovered gold in a small ravine. They mined it for several months and then their pile grew so large they became apprehensive. So the men designated Beale to lead a small contingent back with the gold to bury it in Bedford County, in a remote area between the mountains. Their trust in Beale apparently was without question.

And so, in November 1819, Beale arrived back home with two wagon loads of gold and silver nuggets. In the Goose Creek area, Beale followed a narrow and seldom-used trail leading into a gap in the foothills of the Blue Ridge mountains, within sight of the Peaks of Otter. As snow fell, the party dug a large square pit six feet deep, lined it with flat stones, placed the gold and silver filled pots on the stones, and covered everything up with dirt, rocks and forest debris.

Beale then went back 2,000 miles to the mining site. Later, he repeated his long trek east with another load of the precious metals. This was buried at or near the original site in November 1821.

This part of his task completed, Beale, with the help of one or more of his partners, next devised an elaborate system of incredibly complex codes, which, when broken, would reveal where the treasure had been buried. They covered three sheets of paper with long series of numerals. Cipher number one tells how to find the hidden pots of gold, silver and jewels. Cipher number two describes the complete contents of the treasure vault, and the third one lists the names of the 30 men who were to divide the contents equally.

When this was done, the codes were carefully placed in a metal strongbox, fastened with a tough lock. The nine men who had buried the ore, agreed to leave the box with Robert Morris, innkeeper at the old Washington Hotel in Lynchburg — a man they all knew and trusted. They stayed at the hotel for a few days, then left again for the west to continue their mining.

Morris never was to see Beale or any of the other men again. The mystery was beginning. Two months after the adventurers had left Virginia, Morris did get a curious letter from Beale posted from St. Louis, then a small hunting and trading post on the western frontier. It said the papers in the strongbox would be meaningless without the proper decoding keys. These keys, Beale stated, were in a sealed envelope that had been given to a friend in St. Louis with instructions to mail it to Morris in June 1832 — ten years later — if by then the band of 30 men had not returned to claim the money.

Morris hid the box under some clutter in an old shed adjacent to the hotel. The ten years passed, and not only had no one from Beale's party come back, but there was no letter from St. Louis. Yet, incredibly, Morris had forgotten about the box. It was not until 1845 — 23 years later — that Morris stumbled upon the strongbox while searching for a harness in the shed. He had the lock broken and opened it. Inside were some old receipts, a couple of letters, and the three coded sheets of numbers. One of the letters, from Beale, told the details of their western expedition, how they found the gold, and how, and in general terms, where, they had buried it.

Morris tried to decipher the codes, but, as have thousands of others since, found them too difficult. Again, inexplicably, he set the box aside. Seventeen years later, a year before he died, Morris, by then reasonably sure that no one was going to return, handed the box and its contents over to James Ward, a trusted family friend. Driven more by curiosity than greed, for he was a man of "independent means," Ward worked day and night on the intriguing codes. Purely by accident he discovered that the second code was keyed to words in the U.S. Declaration of Independence. Laboriously, he deciphered it. It read: "I have deposited in the county of Bedford about four miles from Buford's Inn in an excavation or vault six feet below the surface of the ground the following articles belonging to the parties whose names are given in number three (the third coded sheet) herewith. The first deposit was ten hundred and 14 pounds of gold and thirty-eight hundred pounds of silver. This was deposited November 1819. The second deposit was made December 1821, and consisted of nineteen hundred and seven pounds of gold and twelve hundred and 88 pounds of silver. Also jewels obtained in St. Louis... The above is packed securely in iron pots with iron covers. The vault is lined with stones and the vessels lie on solid rock and are covered with other stones. Paper number one describes the exact location of the vault so no difficulty will be had in finding it."

Ward then worked continuously on the two remaining unbroken codes ... "till his determination and his family fortune ran out." Finally, in 1885, he gave up and published the "Beale Papers" which included copies of everything that had been found in the box, as well as the deciphered code number two and an account of his own efforts to break the other two. He also issued a warning, which has turned out to be excellent advice that has rarely, if ever, been heeded. He said, "devote only such time as can be spared to the task, and if you can spare no time, let the matter alone."

The Beale Papers spread across Virginia like wildfire, and from that time on, for well over 100 years, vast hordes of fortune seekers have descended on rural Bedford County to search for the lost gold and silver. Literal armies of cryptographers, computer programmers, historians, professional treasure hunters, and just plain common folks, from all over, have tried to decipher the codes, running the numbers through thousands of books, documents and other papers that were published before 1822. And thousands of tons of Bedford dirt have been dug and redug all across the county. Even with all the tools of modern technology — the most advanced computers, the most sophisticated metal detectors, and the powerful arms of backhoes and the blades of bulldozers — nothing, not even a minute nugget, has been found. Ironically, small fortunes have been lost in the insatiable search that has yet to be quenched.

Millions of words have been written about the Beale treasure, thousands of maps have been drawn up, and countless teams of experts, including one called the Beale Cypher Association, have been formed — but all efforts have been in vain. The rich cache, if it exists, remains as safe in the ground today as it did the day Beale and his team buried it.

There are many who believe the treasure is one of the most elaborate and cruel hoaxes ever devised. But for everyone who doubts its existence, there are ten who will not let go of the dream of a lifetime. The hunt goes on. Each spring and summer new and renewed hope blossoms and yet more people come to Bedford to try their hand as others work incessantly into the wee hours of the mornings at home trying to break the maddening codes.

Is the treasure real? Will the codes ever be denuded and the grand prize found? To long-time Bedford County residents, such questions seem almost academic today. Many of them are convinced the ghost of Thomas Jefferson Beale hangs close in the vacant valleys between the mountains somewhere out near the vicinity of Buford's Inn, either laughing or crying, as a haunting reminder to the foibles and frustrations of his fellow man in the eternal quest for fame and fortune.

*****

(Author's note: After this chapter on Beale was first published, in 1992, in "The Ghosts of Charlottesville and Lynchburg," I uncovered some "treasure" of my own; I came across material that did, possibly, link sightings of Beale's ghost to the Bedford area. In a newspaper interview nearly 20 years ago, Mrs. James Howell and her husband reported that they had sensed Beale's presence and seen his apparition in the Buford Tavern at Montvale, which they owned. It was once a convenient stopover for travelers to Big Lick and points west, and the Howells converted it into a residence upstairs and an antique shop downstairs. Beale is said to have stayed in a room on the second floor during his visits to the area.

The Howells moved in about 1967, and began feeling that "something" was in the house with them shortly after that. About three or four years later, Beale's apparition appeared. "It was dark," recalls Mrs. Howell. "We had gone to bed, but we weren't asleep yet. 'He' came down the steps and came to the foot of our bed. He stood there a few minutes, looking at us, and then went on out the other door."

Mrs. Howell says their dog, a black toy poodle, also knew then the spirit was near. "It's the funniest thing," she notes. "She never barks, never growls or anything, but every now and then, we'll be sitting here and she has this low growl down in her throat for the longest time. I know she senses 'he's' in here somewhere. 'He' always comes at night, and yes, it's quite often. It's hard to tell, but for a week at a time I can tell he's here and then it will go away and it'll be a while before 'he's back." The ghostly feeling, she adds, is strongest in the room Beale stayed in when he was in the area burying his treasure.

"We're not afraid of him," Mrs. Howell says. She believes it is Beale's spirit because of the apparel the apparition was wearing when she and her husband saw it. "He was wearing dark clothes and a wide brimmed hat!

"Wouldn't it be nice if he told us where the treasure is."

CHAPTER 2 4

The Persnickety Spirit of After Years

(Buena Vista)

tretching between towering mountains and the North River, in Rockbridge County adjacent to Lexington, north of Lynchburg, is the colorful city of Buena Vista. It was a thriving boom town in the 1880s and 1890s, being centered on the "great road west," at the intersection of railroads. A report written in 1889 states: "The landed estate of the Buena Vista Company has been made by the consolidation of the historic iron and agricultural lands of Samuel F. Jordan, known as the Buena Vista property, the Green Forest farm and the Hart's Bottom farm; all together making about 13,000 acres ... Most of the lands of Green Forest and Hart's Bottom, amounting to over 1,000 acres, have been laid off into streets and building lots."

Industry then included paper mills, iron ore, silver manganese, and coal mines. It was during this expansive period, when the mining prospects of the region were being widely promoted, that a number of large, imposing homes were built. One of the few still remaining is called "After Years," built for Colonel Charles Gordon, an enterprising industrialist, who owned the Buena Vista furnace. The house has three stories, 23 rooms, and sits imposingly at 2252 Maple Street. In recent years, however, its grandeur diminished after decades of deterioration.

The roof was falling in, plaster cascaded to the floors, and the once-elegant porch was crumbling. It was deserted and decrepit, and gained a sinister reputation as being haunted. "It was," says

After Years

present owner Pat Wohlrab, like the Addams family house." Pat
and her husband bought the property in 1988. "It was a mess, and
there were times when I thought I was just plain crazy buying it.
Yet, I had always admired After Years, and I had always wanted to
live there."

The psychic emanations began even before she moved in. One
day as she sat on the hall stairway thinking about how to refurbish
the house, Pat says she was overcome by a benevolent feeling. "I
don't know how to describe it. It's hard to put into words. As I sat
there, the house definitely seemed to warm up. I got the feeling
that there was a presence there and whoever or whatever it was, it
seemed pleased that someone at last was moving in and going to
take care of things."

The manifestations continued in swift fashion after she moved
in. "All sorts of strange things began to happen," she recalls. At
first, there were terrible, foul smells, evil smells. We never did find
the source, but after a while they disappeared. So did my hus-

band's aviator sunglasses. They just vanished. In fact, a lot of things seemed to disappear and then show up again, unexpectedly. This happened to our keys. It happened to my mother's sewing box one night. The next day it showed up in the hall with a bright fabric over it. Once, the shower curtain and a towel in the guest bedroom disappeared. Then they abruptly resurfaced in the bath tub!

"And there were footsteps. We heard them often, shuffling about upstairs when no one else was in the house," Pat continues. "There were other unexplained noises and incidents. For instance, the light on the back porch had not worked since we moved in. One evening as we were driving back from Lynchburg, we saw that this light was on. How did that happen? There were definite cold spots in the halls and rooms. There seemed to be an aura present. And once, my mother saw what she said was a 'fleeting shadow' as she left a room. Also, doors and windows would mysteriously open after I had locked them. Between all these events, and the past reputation of the house, we had a difficult time getting baby sitters. People actually walked across the street to avoid passing in front of the house."

One day Pat and her husband were sitting in the kitchen at a table, talking about what color to paint the house. "We said, let's paint it mauve, and just as we did, a pitcher of apple juice sitting on the table turned over on its own. We just looked at each other. Them, when we resumed the conversation, a ketchup bottle fell over and spilled. It was obvious to me, the ghost didn't like mauve!"

After extensive research into the history of After Years, Pat came to believe that the sometimes mischievous spirit which seemed to exist in the house might be that of "Uncle" Will Dickinson. "I learned that he lived here from the early 1900s to the 1920s, and he loved the place. I felt that he was still around, checking on us somehow to insure that we took good care of it. He had been unhappy about the house's deterioration."

In time, Pat became accustomed to Uncle Will. When the keys disappeared, she told him to return them and ultimately they showed up on a sideboard. "He definitely is a benevolent existence," Pat says. "Finally, I just had an old fashioned talk with him. I told him, you lived here once, and I live here now. We have to learn to co-exist. Now, we have to establish some ground rules. Don't frighten the children, and don't show up unexpectedly."

Pat says After Years has been relatively quiet ever since.

The Sinister 'Black' Sisters of Christiansburg

(Montgomery County)

(Author's note: For years, I had been hearing about them. It seemed like every time I sold books at a fair or craft show, or spoke to a group, someone would inevitably ask, "have you heard about the Black sisters of Christiansburg?" I hadn't, but each time they were mentioned, the intrigue intensified. No one knew much about them, only that they were very mysterious, they lived in Christiansburg sometime around the turn of the 20th century, they ran "some sort of school" and they either were evil themselves or somehow caused evil. Also, people in the town swore they still saw apparitions of the always dark-clad sisters roaming the halls of Christiansburg Middle School, which was erected on the site where an earlier building once stood.

I must confess, the Black sisters caused me quite a problem. The harder I looked for references about them, the less I found. Finally, I learned that they weren't really the "Black" sisters at all. They were the "black" sisters. They earned this sobriquet because they always were dressed in black, mourning-type clothes, usually with heavy dark veils. Once I stopped looking under "B" in dusty state and county history books and files, I started getting some-where. On a research trip to Roanoke, I found a copy of Lula Porterfield Givens book, "Christiansburg, Montgomery County, Virginia, in the Heart of the Alleghenies." In it, I delightedly found an entire chapter on the "black" sisters. Even better, I discovered that an entire book, "Three Sisters in Black," by Norman Zierold, had been published a quarter of a century ago. I tracked down a copy in the Salem Public Library.

What I read was at once absorbing, macabre, evil, mysterious and frightening. Though the events occurred nearly 100 years ago, in the early part of the 20th century, mystique still surrounds these eccentric and enigmatic sisters. Had I not known better, I would have guessed this had been a tale dreamed up by Edgar Allan Poe, rather than having been one that actually happened.)

O n Monday afternoon at 4:40 p.m., November 27, 1909, a woman, with a soft, cultivated and Southern-accented voice, called Sergeant Timothy Caniff at police headquarters in East Orange, New Jersey. She said there had been an "accident" at her residence at 89 North 14th Street, a young woman was dead, and could the sergeant send the coroner over to take care of things.

Dr. Herbert M. Simmons went to the house and was let in by a woman named Virginia Wardlaw. She was dressed from head to foot in black. In an upstairs bathroom, the only one in the entire house, Dr. Simmons found the nude body of a young woman in the small, half-filled bathtub. The emaciated looking figure was in a crouching position, legs doubled up at the knees, the head submerged in the cold water, directly under the faucet. To Simmons, the young woman must have once been very beautiful, but it appeared that she had virtually wasted away. She couldn't have weighed more than 80 pounds.

Pinned to a robe in the bathroom was a somber note. Dr. Simmons read: "Last year my little daughter died; other near and dear ones have gone before. I have been prostrated with illness for a long time. When you read this I will have committed suicide. Do not grieve over me. Rejoice with me that death brings a blessed relief from pain and suffering greater than I can bear." The note was signed "O. W. M. Snead." Simmons learned that this was Ocey Snead, the niece of Virginia Wardlaw.

Almost immediately, the doctor grew suspicious. First, although the death call had just come in during the last hour, Simmons knew from his examination that Ocey Snead had been dead for at least 24 hours! When he asked Miss Wardlaw about this, she said she hadn't seen her niece since the day before. Strange, the doctor thought, that she wouldn't check on her for a whole day. Even stranger that the woman didn't have to go to the lone bathroom in all that time. Also odd were the facts that: there was no heat in the house; there was no food in the kitchen; there was only a stick or two of furniture in the entire house, including just one cot; there were no towels in the bathroom; and there were no pens or writing implements. This led to some obvious questions. Why was there no heat, food or furniture? Who takes a bath without a towel? How did the suicide note get written? What was going on?

When the doctor suspected foul play, he called the police. And when they couldn't get any satisfactory answers from Virginia Wardlaw, they took her in for further questioning. Over the next several days evidence began mounting which pointed to possible murder instead of suicide. Neighbors reported that ever since the two women had moved into the house in East Orange it had been unusually dark and quiet, with one exception. The night before Ocey Snead's body had been found, the shadows of several persons were seen passing behind the pulled curtains.

Where had the two women come from? Detective work traced them back to a house in Brooklyn. There, it was reported, Ocey had lived with three older women who were always dressed in black. Subsequent investigation revealed that Ocey had moved here with a young man about a year and a half ago. Several months later, the women in black had joined them, and then the young man left. Several witnesses, including a doctor, said that Ocey seemed to be deathly afraid of the women, and it appeared that she was being slowly starved to death.

When it was learned that Ocey had several life insurance policies worth thousands of dollars, and the beneficiaries would be the three women in black, motive was established, and Virginia Wardlaw was charged with murder. The New York newspapers had a field day. Ocey, said one paper, "was held a prisoner by three slovenly creatures of middle age... The people, and their way of living, were a deep and sinister mystery to all who lived in the neighborhood. The place was shunned as if it sheltered a pestilence... Ghoulish greed for wealth possessed by the victim is, in the opinion of the police, at the bottom of the case."

As the investigation deepened, more macabre incidents came to light. Two lawyers said they were called to the Brooklyn house once to help Ocey draw up a new will. They were appalled at what they saw. They said the house was bare, without even a single chair on the first floor. In an upstairs bedroom, they said Ocey's "face was sallow and emaciated, giving almost the appearance of a corpse." The lawyers said the women dressed in black sat next to Ocey and that "they chanted at times, while making strange passes and motions toward the sick woman." Once, when the older women left the room for a minute, Ocey whispered to the lawyers, "please take me away from here. They are starving me to death and they will not give me any medicine."

As the testimony and other pieces of the intriguing puzzle began to fit into place, police arrested the two other women in black. They were Caroline Martin and Mary Snead, and they both were sisters of Virginia Wardlaw. Ocey was Caroline's daughter.

Further probing led to the finding that the three sisters were all members of a very prominent Georgia family. Caroline, the oldest was born in 1845; Mary in 1848, and Virginia in 1852. Their father was John Baptist Wardlaw, born in Georgia in 1816. He became one of the most prominent Methodist clergymen of his time. The three sisters were all given excellent educations, and all three became highly respected teachers. Caroline taught in private and public schools in New York, as did Mary. Virginia taught at the Price School in Nashville, Tennessee, and "established a glowing reputation for her progressive methods of instruction."

In 1892, Virginia was offered a job as president of Soule Female College in Murfreesboro, Tennessee. Soule had been founded in 1851 and was considered one of the finest educational institutions in the South. Five years later, Mary Snead, who had recently become a widow, joined her sister on the faculty at Soule. Both Virginia and Mary were well liked and respected, although they were considered somewhat eccentric because of their peculiar dress. As author Norman Zierold put it, "In the South, where strange legends abound and original behavior amuses and fascinates, the wearing of black added to the occultness of the pair ..."

For nine years, things went smoothly at the college. Then, in 1901, Caroline Martin, the oldest sister, arrived in Murfreesboro, and slowly, almost imperceptibly, conditions at the school began to deteriorate. Caroline became the dominant spirit of the institution. Although extremely entertaining and persuasive at times, she also ruled with "a rod of iron, harsh and abrupt." She seemed to have a Svengali-like hold over Virginia and Mary. This was not unnoticed by the townspeople.

Rumors about the sisters' weird behavior circulated everywhere. These were fueled in part by Caroline's maid, who said: "She was powerful queer about her clothes. She would wear a nightgown all day except when she went out, and then she would put on an old black skirt and waist without anything under them. Sometimes she would go without any stockings and sometimes with only one. She would go three or four weeks without change of clothing. She would stay in bed for weeks at a time, her hair down wild and loose. She didn't take care of her hair nor her body. I don't remember her ever using the bathtub. She wouldn't even let me change the bedclothes when she went away.

"Her room was the nastiest thing I ever saw. She never let me clean it in the two years I was there. All over the floor was food and coal and ashes. She would never let me take any food away from her room after I had brought it, but it would stay there until it rotted... She kept a big box of money in her room and would scatter the five and ten dollar bills about on the floor just for the pleasure of throwing the money. Mrs. Martin kept a double-barreled shotgun right at the head of her bed. One night I saw her sitting on the cot laughing, with the gun between her knees. She had just shot a hole in the ceiling."

College bills fell months behind in payment, and Soule College fell into a "precipitous decline." The three sisters were constantly seem roaming about the buildings, wandering mysteriously through classrooms and down hallways. Often students in the courtyard would see Caroline glaring down at them from a high window. One night a student awoke with a fright to see all three gathered around the stove in her room, "mumbling and chanting." No one was allowed into the house the sisters lived in. The blinds were always down. Only at night did the three sisters venture forth, trailing their long black capes, seemingly in perpetual mourning, "Whether for those already dead or those about to die, no one knew."

To townspeople, little Ocey seemed to be a prisoner in the house. Said one resident: "From the moment we learned that they had placed a policy for upwards of $15,000 on the young life of Ocey Martin we knew she was doomed." Many speculated that Ocey, who bore a striking resemblance to Virginia Wardlaw, was actually Virginia's daughter and that Caroline had taken her to "protect Virginia's maiden status."

As the sisters' sinister reputation grew, students began leaving Soule in droves, and finally the sisters were ousted from their positions. They disappeared in the middle of the night early in 1905, still owing rent on the house where they had lived.

It was at this point that the black sisters turned up in Virginia. Their great aunt, Oceana Seaborn Pollock, then 93-years-old, was owner and director of the well regarded Montgomery Female Academy in Christiansburg. She asked Virginia to take over leadership of the institution, which she did, thus beginning an even more incredible and monstrous chain of events. As had happened in Tennessee, soon after, the other two sisters arrived in town. Caroline Martin next travelled to Lynnville, Tennessee, and insisted that her nephew, John Snead, Mary's son, leave his position there to become a teacher in Christiansburg. John at first balked, but later, seemingly under Caroline's hypnotic-like power, gave in and left his wife.

Her health subsequently declined and she was placed in a sanitarium. This appeared to break John's spirit. On a train with Caroline near Roanoke, he fell off, nearly killing himself. While Caroline insisted it was an accident, the train's brakeman was certain it was a suicide attempt. Several weeks later John was found drowning in an open cistern. He was rescued at the last minute.

The 'Black' Sisters

Again, it was believed he was trying to take his own life. One week later, teachers rushed to John's room at the school at eight in the morning, and found him "thrashing about" on the floor, his garments consumed in flames. He had apparently soaked his clothes in kerosene. He died three hours later. It then was learned that John had been heavily insured, and that he had recently changed his beneficiary from his wife to the black sisters!

Next, Caroline went back to Tennessee and persuaded Mary's other son, Fletcher, to come to Christiansburg. When he did, a hastily arranged marriage took place — between Fletcher and Ocey - even through they were first cousins. Both Fletcher and Ocey also were heavily insured.

Meanwhile, the persistently strange habits of the three sisters began causing alarm all over Montgomery County. As author Zierold said, "the ever spookier happenings at Montgomery College caused increasing consternation. A dread and horror of the women in black developed..." To this, in the history of Montgomery County, Lula Givens added, "Sinister events had created fear among the residents of this old Southern town. People hesitated to answer a knock on their door. Too frequently, on one pretext or another, the sisters were there... veiled in black, somber and austere. One lady whose parents lived here at the time said people were afraid to go on the streets at night."

A local cab driver said the sisters often hired him at night to drive them to a cemetery. They always told him to wait, but one evening, curiosity got the better of him and he followed them through the tombstones. In the dim moonlight, "he saw them gather about a grave. They made gestures skyward and murmured garbled incantations which he could not understand. He later told that his whole body shook with fear, so strong was his feeling that evil was near!"

Mrs. Givens also reported that "legend says girls would awaken at night to find the black-robed sisters standing on each side of the bed... withdrawing without explanation of their appearance. Like experiences spread through the dormitories of the college." It was no wonder, Mrs. Givens added, that girls packed, got their luggage to the depot, and took the first train home. In this manner, the "fabric of the school swiftly disintegrated." Indeed, Zierold notes, "disorder went past endurance as gangs of older boys went on marauding expeditions (at the school), trying to see how much damage they could do to the premises." Again, bills went unpaid, and claims against the sisters mounted.

In the midst of such chaos, the sisters abruptly left Virginia, and the scene then shifted to New Jersey and New York, and the disappearance of Fletcher Snead and the mysterious death of Ocey Snead. Eventually, the three sisters were tried for their implications in the murder of Ocey. Fletcher was finally found. He was a cook in a remote Canadian lumber camp, and was found not to be connected in any way with Ocey's fate.

Mary Snead pleaded guilty to manslaughter and was released in the custody of her son, Albert, who took her to his ranch in Colorado. Caroline Martin, defiant to the end, was sent to the New Jersey state prison, where her "emotional behavior became so unstable" that she was transferred to the State Hospital for the Insane and died soon after. Virginia Wardlaw, the sad figure who seemed to be so dominated by her older sister, starved herself to death in jail by refusing to eat while awaiting trial. Her body was sent back to Christiansburg and she was buried in the Sunset Cemetery not far from the site of the Montgomery Female College. The main building there was torn down some years ago and a new one built. It is now the Christiansburg Middle School.

Thus apparently ended the incredible and dramatic saga of the infamous black sisters. But did it? There have been numerous reports over the past several years of sightings of wispy apparitions, fleetingly glimpsed, peering out of the windows at the middle school. What is singularly unusual about this is that, almost without exception, such ghostly apparitions always appear to be white or grayish-white. Witnesses in Christiansburg who have reported seeing the figures darting about in the school unanimously said they were dark — as if dressed in black!

CHAPTER 26

The Highwayman Who Saw The Light

(Franklin County)

ou likely won't find the name of Joseph Thompson Hare in any of Virginia's history books, or in any other respectable history book for that matter! In fact, he wasn't even a native. He was born in Chester County, Pennsylvania, in 1780. And in a way it's somewhat of a shame that there are so few references to Mr. Hare, because he undoubtedly was one of the most colorful, charismatic and swashbuckling rogues of the early part of the 19th century. His exploits, covering travels from New Orleans to Baton Rouge, Nashville, Knoxville, Washington, Philadelphia, New York and Canada, are truly legendary.

He was, above all else, a highwayman; a robber who laid in wait for unsuspecting travelers in the frontier wilderness. But he was also much more. He was as well known for his superior courage and generosity as he was for his daring and bold criminal escapades. He was, by some, likened to an American Robin Hood, although this is probably much too kind an accolade for him. During his relatively short lifetime he successfully fought off attacks by Indians, a host of most unsavory characters, scores of pursuing lawmen, and a giant panther (for which he gained much fame.)

He had a lifelong struggle, lost in the end, trying to convert his considerable talents to lawful practices. He is included in this collection of ghosts because it was in Virginia that he encountered an

155

eerie apparition, which, for a time at least, changed the direction of his life.

It is said that Joseph Hare came from a respected, well-to-do, comfortable family. The oldest of six children, he apparently was wayward and self-willed from a very early age, and when his mother died when he was only 16, he "stood the victim of a vitiated will that was destined to be the tyrant of his future life," and "he plunged more deeply into wild and vicious courses," according to one 19th century biographer.

It was then that he began a twisted career by stealing $500 from a neighboring farmer, a caper so easy and exhilarating to him that, he "plummeted openly into excesses of the most disreputable character." Soon after, he left home for good and set out for New Orleans. There, he became "initiated in the mysteries and low trickeries of gaming, and familiar with all the practices and arts of professional thieves." He associated himself with some "desperate fellows who were in the habit of knocking people down and robbing the streets."

After a while he tired of this, possibly influenced by the tightening security in the streets of New Orleans, and he struck out on the road. As his biographer wrote, "The amounts (of money) carried by travelling parties were very large, and a highwayman with a large imagination and a disposition as sanguine as that of Hare, might calculate, without any great extravagance, upon becoming rich in a single lucky chance."

It was during this early period that Hare began gaining a reputation for having compassion for his victims, a highly unusual trait for a man in his profession. When, for example, he robbed a man of $250, the victim protested that it was all the money he had in the world. Hare gave him back $40 and told him to "thank his lucky stars that he had not fallen into the hands of men who were entirely devoid of principle!"

Hare's mode of operation was simple. He usually worked with two or three confederates. They would lay in hiding at some remote but well travelled spot. Then, when an unsuspecting party would come along, he would bound out in the center of the road and demand them to "deliver or die." "I want your money," he would say, and "if you show the least disposition to resist (we) will blow you to hell in the twinkling of an eye." The threat was enough. Rarely, if ever, did he have to resort to violence.

Over the next few years, Hare and his merry band roamed the southern countryside waylaying whoever was unfortunate enough to cross their paths. He escaped death a number of times, once after barehandedly fighting off the attack of a large panther, and once by dodging a bullet fired by an assailant at point blank range. He also spent much of his time keeping one step ahead of persistent posses and pursuers, often holing out in desolate caves.

By the year 1807, it appeared that Hare had tired of this type of life. With a stake of $4,000, he said, "I thought that perhaps no better time would offer for me to carry out my old intentions to reform... In this indifferent and unceremonious manner, did I sever all the links of connection which had lasted for a period of years, and which was characterized by the most close and confidential intimacy. Such, and so brittle, are the friendships which are made in crime."

In Knoxville, Hare received a letter from a friend in Richmond. "It informed me that the writer had taken permanent residence in that city, and it invited me to come thither at once, promising that if I did, I should have a chance to make $15,000 or $20,000. Here," Hare said, "was a splendid temptation to fall against good resolutions. I confess I was unable to withstand it."

It was at his juncture, as Hare travelled from Knoxville to Richmond, that he came upon a singular adventure which included his shocking encounter with a vivid apparition. The following is an account in his own words.

"At Abingdon I fell in with a drover of Franklin County, who was on his way home from Kentucky, where he had been on a trading excursion, and on a pretty profitable one, too, as I thought from the display which he made of his money. The devilish infatuation of my previous course of life seized possession of me, and in despite of all my previous resolutions, and of the important prospects which I had at Richmond, I determined to rob him. With this view, I kept in his company, but though I felt a secret repugnance to the act, and experienced a gloom of mind that I ought to have taken as a forewarning of my fate, I could not shake off the fascination which had seized me, but still kept on, like an ox going to the slaughter, as the Scripture says, or 'a fool to the correction of the stocks.'

"The warning clung to me so well that I had even followed the drover to within 15 miles of the court house in Franklin County, before I could make up my mind to carry out the purpose, which I had performed with so much alacrity in many instances before, but stimulated by the blind confidence of a long career of wicked fortune, I suddenly resolved, and dashing up to his side, half mad with my own irresolution, I fiercely demanded of him his money or his life.

"He hesitated for a moment, and then paid me over, with trembling hands, the sum of $450, which he declared was all he had. Without pausing to test his declarations by a search, or even to disarm him, I seized the money with eager haste, and turning my horse, struck in my spurs, and galloped away as if flying from the most sharp and inveterate pursuit. I turned my head but once in my flight, and then beheld the drover gazing after me as if undecided whether to give chase or not.

"I plunged my spurs still deeper in my horse's side, and watched his strides with the intensest interest of apprehension. I cannot account for the extraordinary feelings which had seized possession of me, unless it was a warning from some mysterious and supernatural power, or a forerunner of what was about to happen. I felt like a man under the influence of some hideous nightmare, and every time I urged my beast to speed, it seemed to me as if a crowd of fiends were whistling in my course, and on the point of laying their avenging grasp upon my shoulder. I rode and rode, without one moment's disposition to hold up, and when the powers of my tired animal began to flag, I kept moving forward in my saddle, like a steersman in a boat, in the hope that that would aid my motion. While proceeding in this way, a thing occurred, from the recollection of which I shrink, even in this dreadful hour.

"The moon had risen during my flight, and about nine o'clock, which was the third hour of my race, she was an hour high, and, consequently, bright and full. I had been galloping through a long stretch of narrow road, the bordering trees of which shut out her beams, and left the surface of the path in gloom.

"Suddenly I merged into an open rise, and there, in her silvery light, stood, right across the road, a pure white horse — immovable as marble, and so white that it almost seemed to be radiating light. I was a little startled by the first glance at the apparition, but expecting it to give way, I pressed towards it. But it did not stir, but stood with its small graceful head stretched out, its tail slightly raised, as if in a listening attitude, and its ears cocked sharply forward and strained towards the moon, on which its gaze seemed to be unwaveringly fixed. When within almost six feet of it, my horse suddenly recoiled upon its haunches, and, opening his nostrils with affright, gave a short cry of terror, and attempted to turn around.

"I trembled in my saddle as if struck with a sudden ague, but not daring to return into the gloom behind, I closed my eyes, bent my head, and driving my sharp heels deep into my horse's side, pressed onward at the fearful object. My steed took but one plunge, and then landed on its fore-feet, firmly resolved not to budge another inch.

"I opened my eyes, and the apparition had disappeared. But an instant had elapsed and no trace of it was left. My most superstitious terrors were then confirmed, and I feared to go forward over the charmed space where the strange figure had stood. I recollected a roadside inn which I had passed a mile behind, and touching my rein, my horse turned swiftly round, and obeyed the summons with a fleeter heel than he had shown previous to his fatigue.

"I have been told that I was laboring under a state of mental hallucination that night; an illusion superinduced by a peculiar state of nervous agitation, and that these things were mere chimeras of a feverish brain; *but I know better*, for I subsequently experienced similar forewarning and forerunners of misfortune.

"The vision was the cause of my arrest, for during the night, a party of 15 men, consisting of the drover's friends, surrounded the house and bore me off to Franklin County prison."

To this striking account, his 19th century biographer added: "The specter was present to his sense, and having terrified him from a sure escape and delivered him up into the hands of his pursuers, may be recognized as the supernatural decider of his fate."

Hare was to say later: "I think this white horse was Christ, and that he came to warn me of my sins and to make me fear and repent."

His biographer then added: "In a state of mind superinduced to the heaviest gloom, by a profound belief that he was in the hands of a superior and controlling destiny, Hare suffered himself to be bound without remonstrance, and passively led off amid the taunts and angry epithets of those who had taken him captive. He sat slouchingly astride the dull beast which had been allowed to him for the journey between the inn and the county prison; his head drooping upon his breast, and his manner giving no evidence that he was conscious of anything which took place about him. He answered no interrogations, he did not even lift his head to show he had observed them, and even when, to test the extent of his doggedness, the regulators proposed to save further trouble by hanging him up to the next tree, he maintained the same moody silence as before."

They did not hang Hare, then, however. He was found guilty of highway robbery and sentenced to the state penitentiary for eight years. With good behavior, he was out in five years, and for a time at least seemed to have gone straight. "I felt very sad," he said, "at the isolated and degraded condition to which my offenses had brought me, and then, again, saw in its true light the folly of a career in crime. It had stamped the mark of shame indelibly upon my heart, if not upon my brow, and I felt that crushed, disgraced, and deserted as I was, I had not the manhood left to stand up and look the great, wide, cold, and unforgiving world, with which I had to struggle, in the face. For the first time in years I wept, and my tears were those of sorrow and repentance. I resolved to live honestly for the future."

But, alas, temptation overtook Hare again. This time he wended his way north, to Philadelphia, New York City, Albany, Boston, and eventually Canada. He stole $30,000 from a man along the way, was caught, and went back to prison for two years. Released again, he fell in with one of his younger brothers and another man, and they held up stage coaches carrying U.S. mail. Eventually, he was caught once more, and this time he was found guilty and sentenced to die.

On the morning of September 10, 1818, Joseph Thompson Hare and one of his bandit companions were hanged. As his biographer described the scene: "Both displayed the utmost fortitude, and with firm steps advanced towards the spot of execution... A brief but awful pause ensued, when the executioner, severing the cord with a single blow of his axe, launched the wretched men at the same moment into eternity."

CHAPTER 27

By The (Grave's) Early Light

(Franklin County)

H e was a brooding genius; an individualist with a perplexing, eccentric personality that virtually defied rational analysis. He has been described by biographers as having been, all at once: cynical, witty, ambitious, self-reliant, practical, unbearably acidic, unquestionably loyal, and aggressively bold. Robert E. Lee called him a determined, resourceful, and energetic leader. Indeed, an aura of legend surrounded his military career and he became a legitimate folk hero, revered by Virginians to this day.

In his great gray coat, wearing his "ancient" white slouch hat adorned with a black plume, and ever chewing a wad of tobacco, he struck an imposing figure. The sheer force of his powerful character, combined with his tenacious fighting ability, and his daring bravery, earned him the die-hard respect of his enemies, peers and subordinates alike. One example: at the second battle of Manassas, instead of withdrawing after his regiments depleted their ammunition, he inspired his soldiers to remain in position and *hurl stones* at the advancing Union troops!

This was Jubal Early, General, Confederate States of America. A champion of the Southern cause who went to his grave in 1894 wearing a gray suit and cuff links imprinted with Confederate flags, Early was a native of Franklin County. His father, Joab Early, owned a sizable, thriving plantation in the county's Red Valley section about 18 miles north of Rocky Mount, between Roanoke and Martinsville.

One might consider that Jubal Early had just cause to return to his native state in spirit form and continue to lead phantom charges. He did, after all, spend the last 30 years of his life seeking a justification for the Southern secession and an explanation for the ultimate defeat of the Confederate forces.

But it is not Jubal's ghostly form that has been sighted roaming across isolated, long-deserted cemeteries in the Burnt Chimney region of Franklin County. It is, rather, the specter of his brother, William Early, who continues a ghostly search for his life's savings; savings which disappeared from his grave in a bizarre manner 130 years ago!

William Early's nocturnal ventures manifest themselves as a strange light in the mountain foothills; a light that has been seen but never explained by hundreds of area witnesses over several generations. "Many people have seen it," says local historian Gertrude Mann, "but nobody knows what it is." It is said to be the gentle golden light of Early's lantern, as his spirit wanders restlessly from tombstone to tombstone, searching eternally for his lost money.

The legend has an intriguing background. William Early is believed to have died in the mid 1860s, and was buried "with his money beside him" Just why his wife and children allowed this has never been known. (Maybe he thought you really could take it with you!)

Nevertheless, in time his widow fell in love with the farm overseer, and they decided to get married. This appalled Mrs. Early's children, who felt their mother was lowering herself in society. So they decided to do something about it. As one newspaper reporter wrote, "they decided to stop the wedding with the help of an uninvited guest." It was deemed that drastic measures were necessary, and their actions were shocking to say the least.

William Early's sons went to their father's grave, dug up his coffin, and carried it back to the family farmhouse. There, they stood the glass-covered coffin at the base of the stairs, to greet their mother when she descended the steps in her wedding gown!

Alas, the macabre plot did not work. Mrs. Early defiantly strode past the corpse and walked into the parlor where her marriage with the overseer took place. Chagrined, the sons reburied the remains of their father in another grave site, the exact location of which is today unknown. Somehow and somewhere in the process, William Early's money was either lost or stolen.

Ever since then, Early's light has been sighted dancing across the remote grave sites in the Burnt Chimney section of Franklin County. Many have seen the light move about in the eerie darkness. Many have chased it, seeking a sane and sensible explanation for its appearances. No one has succeeded in doing this.

Some residents dismiss the light as being caused by swarms of fireflies. But there are no fireflies in the dead of winter! Some have said it is the light of hunters' lanterns. But no hunters have ever stepped forward to justify this possibility. It is, say oldtimers, the ghostly light of William Early, brother of General Jubal Early, who cannot rest in peace until he finds his money, lost more than a century and a quarter ago!

CHAPTER 28

The Remorseful Duellist and Others

(Christiansburg and Fredericksburg)

ertainly one of man's more curious and morbid rituals in recent centuries was the dubious art of duelling. It was largely a practice of macho gentlemen; the ultimate (and often fatal) method of settling an argument. Weapons generally involved swords or pistols, although sometimes other arms were included, such as rifles. Historians say the early colonists brought many fashions to Virginia in the 17th century, but duelling was not one of them. In fact, this quaint custom was virtually unknown in this country, with a few exceptions, until well after the Revolutionary War.

One of the exceptions came just a few years before the war, in 1766. It involved two fairly prominent Virginians of Hanover County: Colonel John Chiswell, and Robert Routledge, a Scotsman. The scene of this conflict was the old tavern at Hanover Courthouse, the choice of weapons was swords, but the reason for the fight has been lost in the sands of time.

Nevertheless, Colonel Chiswell, according to one contemporary account, slew Routledge and then "he wiped his bloody sword on a cloth, and sat down and drank a bowl of bumbo" (a very potent, grog-like drink.) Chiswell was brought up on charges, but he took matters into his own hands, for after considerable brooding over the tragedy, he killed himself.

It appears that most of the survivors of these barbarous acts grew ever more remorseful afterwards, wondering why they had let things go so far in the first place. But sometimes the participants got a second chance to let cooler heads prevail. Such was the case in the celebrated duel, in 1826, of two Virginia giants, Henry Clay and John Randolph. After Clay had determined Randolph had impugned his integrity, he threw down the gauntlet and Randolph obliged. Pistols were chosen. Unknown to Clay, Randolph told a friend, "I have determined to receive without returning Clay's fire; nothing shall induce me to harm a hair of his head. I will not make his wife a widow or his children orphans."

Thus, when the shots rang out, Randolph's bullet harmlessly struck a stump behind Clay, while Clay's shot narrowly missed its target. So they did it again. This time Randolph, declaring loudly, "I do not fire at you, Mr. Clay," shot in the air, while Clay's bullet pierced the skirt of his opponent's coat. Realizing what Randolph had done, Clay rushed forward and explained, "I trust in God, my dear Sir, you are untouched," to which Randolph, smiling, responded, "You owe me a coat, Mr. Clay. I am glad the debt is no greater."

But all too often, the outcome of such cruel encounters was tragic. And, at times, it resulted in ghostly manifestations. Such occurred, for example, in one of Virginia's most notable duels. The principals were Tom Lewis, a 22-year-old attorney, and John McHenry, 42. They had been the best of friends but had become involved in a bitter dispute over politics. The scene was a hillside near the Montgomery County Courthouse in Christiansburg, in the vicinity of, appropriately, Sunset Cemetery. It was the first known American duel using rifles as the weapons.

Thirty paces had been stepped off after last-minute appeals to stop the madness had proved futile. McHenry, a crack shot, fired a split second before Lewis, striking his victim in the heart. But as Lewis fell, his bullet punctured McHenry's liver. Lewis was dead when he hit the ground. When attendees told McHenry this, he said, "Poor Tom, poor Tom, he was the best friend I ever had!"

McHenry was taken into town and lived to see the Lewis funeral procession pass by. Looking out from his window, he uttered, "There goes the best friend I ever had." McHenry died the next evening, remorseful to the end. He was buried in the Craig Cemetery. His grave was visited and well maintained for some time afterwards, and people brought flowers.

But then strange things began to happen, especially at night. It is said that the sounds of moans and soft sobbings could be heard. It so frightened visitors that they stopped coming to McHenry's grave, and in time, the site was lost amid the towering dark firs. There are those who say, even to this day, it is the restless spirit of John McHenry, still guilt-ridden, seeking forgiveness for the fact that he needlessly shot and killed his best friend.

Perhaps McHenry's ghost could take some comfort in the fact that this tragic event did, in fact, help influence, in 1810, the passage of the Barbour Bill outlawing duelling in Virginia.

And, finally, there was the duel of two promising young men, William Thornton and Francis Fitzhugh Conway at Alum Spring Rock near the Courthouse in Fredericksburg in December 1803. Both courted the beautiful Nellie Madison, and this eventually led to "some unpleasantness." On the field of honor, both fired and both fell, mortally wounded.

The Virginia Express of Fredericksburg duly reported: "With infinite regret, we communicate to the public, an event the most distressing in nature, and fatal in its consequences of any within the compass of our recollection. On Monday last Mr. William Thornton and Mr. Francis Conway met, in consequence of a previous misunderstanding, in the neighborhood of this town, and sorry are we to announce that the event proved fatal to both parties. In the fatal bout they both departed this life.

"By their untimely fate two weeping Mothers are left to deplore the loss of two dutiful sons, their children two affectionate brothers, and society two most promising citizens. The surviving relations are in a situation easier to be imagined than described.

"We sincerely regret the frequency of a custom so prevalent in our county, and hope the melancholy catastrophe, here related, will prevent others from endangering their own lives, or embittering the days of their surviving relatives."

An eerie footnote to this misfortune was brought to light in a book, "The Old and the Quaint in Virginia," by Georgia Dickinson Wardlaw, published in 1939. In the book, the author states that neither of Francis Conway's parents had any knowledge of the impending conflict, "but on the morning of the fatal day, Mrs. Conway is said to have appeared very agitated as she took her place at the breakfast table. When asked by her husband why she seemed so distressed, she told him of a dream she had during the night, in which a man on a white horse had hastened to the house, bringing a message that their son had been killed. Mr. Conway refused to share his wife's feeling of alarm, and did all in his power to calm her. A short while later, as she stood by one of the front windows, she fell to the floor in a faint. Rushing to her side, her husband lifted her in his arms, and as he turned to walk away, looked out the window. There, riding at full speed was a man on a white horse, bringing the death-message foretold in the dream."

Apparitional Actors at the Barter Theatre

(Abingdon)

(Author's note: Ghosts of the theatre date back as long as plays and other forms of entertainment have been performed from a stage. There were spirits in the Greek amphitheatres, and specters were both in the scripts and behind the scenes in Shakespeare's time. Who were they, and why did they reappear in such public places? Frustrated actors and actresses? Bankrupt backers and producers? Put-upon stage hands? Unknowns still seeking stardom in the hereafter?

In my book, "The Ghosts of Tidewater," 1990, I wrote of a spectral lady given the name Lucinda. She has been seen occasionally flitting about the stage at William and Mary's Phi Beta Kappa Hall in Williamsburg over the past 30 years. A number of witnesses claimed to have seen her or felt her presence.

One example: In the late 1960s, three male students, two of whom claimed to have psychic sensitivities, turned out all of the lights in the hall one night after a play rehearsal, and sat in the darkness to see if the ghost lady would appear. They were seated on the edge of the stage in front of a lowered pit, when "something" flew out of the pit towards them, which they later described as a "rush of air, almost transparent, weird and cold." This convinced them and as they ran across the stage, they said "the mass" seemed to chase them. It brushed past one of the students' ear, and he said it smelled like the "odor of dark crypts." Lucinda's identity has never been determined, although the strange incidents in Phi Beta Kappa Hall have continued through the years.

I have heard, too, of a benevolent spirit named "Ruth" who allegedly roams the stage at the Fort Lee playhouse near Petersburg. One play director there reported seeing her image walk on stage while he was working there late at night. He believed her to be a "patron of the arts."

There are, assuredly, many other theatre haunts around the commonwealth. Probably the one, or ones, most famous, most written about, and most experienced by the largest number of people, frequent the historic Barter Theatre in Abingdon, in the deep corner of Southwest Virginia.

The theatre is just across Main Street from the Martha Washington Inn, which, incidentally, also is haunted (see "The Ghosts of Virginia, Volume I"). The building itself dates back to the 1830s, and originally was built as the Sinking Springs Presbyterian Church. Later it was run by the Sons of Temperance and was known as Temperance Hall.

There is a colorful description of the area in, "Virginia, A Guide to the Old Dominion," compiled by workers of the writer's program of the Work Projects Administration of Virginia in the depression era 50-plus years ago. "The Barter Colony occupies the three brick buildings formerly used by the Stonewall Jackson Institute, a Presbyterian girls' school founded in 1869 and closed in 1932. Around an inn, theatre, work-shop, and dormitory revolves the life of the Barter Theatre, established in 1933 by Robert and Helen Fritch Porterfield."

Robert Porterfield was born in 1905 near Austinville in Wythe County. He was destined for the stage. His father had wanted him to be a preacher, but as a young man, Robert answered his call by moving to New York City to attend the Academy of Dramatic Arts. He appeared in a number of "bit" roles on Broadway in the late 1920s and early 1930s. Whether or not Robert would have made it as a star will never be known, for when the Great Depression hit, the lights in hundreds of theatres across the county went dark, and thousands of performers were thrown out of work. Few people had money enough to attend shows.

But Robert was more than a budding actor. He had a flair for the overall business of show business, and he had an idea. Why not take a troop of actors to Southwest Virginia and establish a repertory theatre there? If they accepted produce, meats and other edibles as the price for tickets, at least they wouldn't starve. And so, in 1933, he brought a group of unemployed actors and actresses to Abingdon, bought the building across from the inn, and opened the Barter Theatre. "Edible commodities, from calves to huckle-berries, are accepted on payment for tickets," said one writer in the 1930s.

The first play, John Golden's "After Tomorrow," was held in the theatre on June 10, 1933, and the audience arrived "lugging country hams, baskets of eggs, homemade pickles and jams, a rooster, a squealing pig, and a devil's food cake. Porterfield once said "nine out of ten theatregoers paid their admissions in any-thing from beans to cottage cheese. We ate well, and the 'culture hungry' Virginians thrived on our entertainment." The late comedian Fred Allen once said the only way Porterfield could tell if he had had a successful season was to weigh his actors. In addition, the resourceful producer paid off the writers whose plays he staged with country hams. These were well received, it was noted, by all but George Bernard Shaw, who protested that he was a vegetarian. Porterfield shipped him a crate of Virginia-grown spinach.

The theatre's survival through the depression and success afterwards exceeded Robert's fondest dreams, especially in artistic terms. Over the next 40 years some of the biggest names of stage, screen and television, cut their thespian teeth on small town stages such as the one in Abingdon. Among those who trod the boards there were Gregory Peck, Hume Cronyn, Ernest Borgnine, Patricia Neal, Ned Beatty, and Claude Akins.

Robert Porterfield died in 1971, but he was so profoundly devoted to his beloved theatre, that, it is said by many, he has never left it. There are scores of actors, stage hands, viewers, and others who swear they have seen the amiable founder still roaming around backstage or in the aisles dressed in his omnipresent gray sweater. During plays, some performers have claimed to have spotted him in the audience. Actress Cleo Holladay told Mark Dawidziak, author of "The Barter Theatre Story," that she looked up from the stage one night and saw a man in the last row in a white dinner jacket. She was convinced it was Porterfield, and said "that was the same night the pipes rattled and we took it as a sign that Bob approved of the show."

Others have seen a mysterious figure flitting about inside the building in the late hours of the night when everyone has gone home. However, when the theatre is searched, no one is found. Once, a Barter employee was walking by when he saw a man in a gray sweater sitting on a stoop. He recognized the figure as that of Bob Porterfield, and, without thinking, he spoke to him. Then he suddenly realized Porterfield had been dead for several years. He looked back, and the apparition had disappeared.

There is said to be another roving specter in the Barter Theatre, and this one apparently is the antithesis of Porterfield's friendly spirit; it has been described as malevolent and vindictive. Folklorian author Charles Edwin Price, in his excellent book, "The Mystery of Ghostly Vera, and Other Haunting Tales of Southwest Virginia," published by the Overmountain Press in 1993, said, "its presence filled the living with "dread and deadly danger. And no one knows its identity."

According to one popular legend, in the theatre, the noted actor Ned Beatty — remember him from "Deliverance" and many other films — once was so frightened in his dressing room by this unnerving haunt, that he ran out of his dressing room and into the street to get away from it.

Equally chilling was the experience of Barter publicity director Lou Flanigan a few years ago, as recorded in Dawidziak's book. Flanigan said he "felt a presence," one that somehow seemed to be so evil, he felt he had to get out of the building at once. "I had this horrible feeling that something was going to get me," he recalled. He raced across the stage, went down the stairs past the dressing rooms and ran toward the stage door that leads to an alley. All the while he had an overpowering feeling of fear. "If I had turned around and seen it," he told Dawidziak, "it probably would have been fatal. It was like it was following me." To add to his terror, Flanigan couldn't get the stage door open. Frantically, he kicked at it, it opened, and he darted outside. "One second more and I'm sure 'it' would have grabbed me," he said.

C H A P T E R   3 0

The Last Ride of
'Old Dry Frye'
(Southwestern Virginia)

(Author's note: For five years, from 1937 until 1942, scores of writers working under the Virginia Writers' Project, part of the Federal government's depression era Work Projects Administration, combed the hills and valleys of the Old Dominion and interviewed thousands of residents. They covered a variety of subjects, but mostly just talked to plain people about their lives — their jobs, their families, their farms, their joys, sorrows and aspirations. The writers lucky enough to be assigned to the Southwestern end of the state also collected a rich assortment of Virginia folklore; oral histories of traditions and legends which had been handed down in the hills and mountainsides for generations.

Among this lode were veins of ghost tales. Some were believable and sworn to be the truth. Some stretch one's imagination to the limit. As the old saying goes, paraphrased, let the reader beware. Following are two of the more colorful stories showing that the mountain folks had a sense of humor, taken from the Writer's Project files, which are housed in Virginia State Library archives in Richmond. I spent hours there poring through the tens of thousands of manuscript pages, some typed, some handwritten. The first item is titled "Old Dry Frye," and was the result of an interview of a person unnamed by Richard Chase in the village of Proffit. The date was April 10, 1942. I have done slight editing only to improve the readability. I think such legends are priceless. Enjoy!)

ld Dry Frye was a preacher. Not much of a one. Preached for his health, I reckon, and what chicken he could get. Anyway, he'd been going down to where a man named Johnny Martin lived at. Johnny Martin had a pretty wife, fairly young, and Old Dry Frye, he would go there when Johnny wasn't at home. But one Saturday night he miscalculated; went down to Johnny Martin's house, and Johnny *was* at home!

"Johnny was pretty mean, and he didn't care about knockin' folks in the head. So when Old Dry Frye knocked on the door and poked his head in the house, Johnny Martin come down with a stick of stovewood — Whap! Hit him harder than he aimed to. Killed him!

"'Law me!' he says. 'Now what'll I dow?'

"So Johnny figured a while, then he took Old Dry Frye down the road a piece and stood him up at another man's door and went on back home and got in bed. And pretty soon, when that man had to go out after a turn of wood, he opened the door and in fell Old Dry Frye. That man's old lady like to have throwed a fit, it scared her so, but he wasn't scared much. He just studied a while. He knowed where Old Dry Frye had had a habit of going, so he took him right back and stood him up at Johnny Martin's door, and knocked, and pulled on back home.

"Johnny Martin was scared to get up and answer, but directly he put on his britches and finally he went on and opened the door, and when Old Dry Frye fell back in the house, Johnny Martin says, 'O law! He's come back to ghost me!'

"Well, the next morning was meeting day at the church and Old Dry Frye was due to preach that Sunday, so Johnny Martin decided what he would do. Way along late in the night he took Old Dry Frye up to the church house and throwed him down at the edge of the pool — big baptizing pool they had in that church, deep 'un too. And then he set a chair right close and gathered up Old Dry Frye and set him in it. Put his elbows on his knees and stuck his hands up under his chin, propped him up that-a-way. Then Johnny Martin, he went on home and slept sound.

"Next morning a boy come to the church house pretty early to make up the fires. He seen Old Dry Frye a settin' there and says, 'Howdy, Mr. Frye.' Old Dry Frye never spoke. The boy come a little closer and says, 'Howdy, Mr. Frye.' Old Dry Frye set right on. The boy come right up to the edge of the pool and says, 'I said howdy, Mr. Dry Frye.' Mr. Dry Frye never answered yet. That boy, now, he was a fiesty young 'un he didn't care how he spoke to nobody. He says, 'Look-a-here, Old Dry Frye, if you don't say howdy back to me, I'll knock your elbows out from under you!'

"Well, when the old man still wouldn't speak, that fiesty boy reached over and knocked him a lick and over in the pool Old Dry Frye went, sunk right on to the bottom and clean out of sight! That boy thought he'd drowned the old preacher sure, and he was scared to death. But he couldn't do nothin' about it right then 'cause it was getting close to church time, and a few folks had started gathering and he hadn't built his fires yet. So he went to making up fires and didn't let on like nothin' had happened.

"And the folks all gathered and waited for Old Dry Frye to come and preach, and he never came, and nobody knowed where he was at. That boy would let out a giggle where he was settin' on the back row and the other boys would ask him what he was laughin' at, and he's just get tickled again and not tell 'em nothin'. So finally they just sung a few hymns and took up a collection and got up to leave. Johnny Martin was there and he sung as loud as anybody else and that Sunday, instead of a five-cent piece like he always done, he put a half dollar in the plate. And after the meeting broke and everybody went on off, that boy, he locked up the church and went on home to dinner.

"Then, 'way along late that night, he went and unlocked the church and got the old preacher out and put him down in a sack, got his shoulder under it, and started slippin' off to hide him somewheres. The moon was shinin's pretty bright time he got off a ways, and he crossed over a fence directly and went up a hill through an old field, a-stumblin' along under that sack.

"Now there was two men comin' down on the far side of the field right then, had 'em a sack a piece on their backs. The boy never seen them, but they saw him, and time they did, they both dropped their sacks and run lickety-split back over the ridge of that hill. The boy kept on up the hill, come across them other sacks directly, and he throwed his sack down, went and looked in the other ones. It was two big dressed hogs them two fellers had stole. So that boy drug his sack over there and left it, picked up one of the hogs and took it on back home.

"So the two hog-stealin' men looked back over the ridge directly, seen the two sacks a-layin' there, and the one-sack boy gone, and they come on down, picked up the two sacks and went on home. They went to the smokehouse and hung their sacks up. It was dark, you know, and they couldn't see very well what they were doin'.

"Next morning' the old woman got up to cook their breakfast, went out to the smokehouse to cut some meat. She reached up with her knife — and there hung Old Dry Frye. She hollered and dropped her butcher knife, and got away from there in such a hurry that she tore down one whole side of the smokehouse, broke off half the back porch, and knocked the kitchen door clean off the hinges! She was sorty scared.

"She hollered and yelled, and told them men there was a dead preacher man hangin' in the smokehouse in place of a hog. The men came runnin' out in their shirt-tails and looked, seen Old Dry Frye hangin' up there by his heels, and one of 'em says, 'I *thought* my sack was awful light comin' in last night, and that hog's hide *did* feel sorty funny when I hung it up in the dark.

"Well, just a day or two 'fore that, they had rounded up some wild horses that run out in the mountains around that place, so they went and picked out the wildest one in the lot, put an old wore-out saddle and bridle on it, and stuck Old Dry Frye on. Tied his feet underneath, tied his hands to the front of the saddle and pulled the reins through. Then they slipped out and opened the gate and let the horse go. Down the road he flew, with the old preacher on his back a-bouncin' and tossin' every whichaway, and them men run out and went to shootin' and hollerin', 'Stop him younder! He's stole our horse! Somebody stop him!'

"Everybody come out in the road a-shoutin' and a-hollerin' and shootin' around, but the horse went so fast he was gone 'fore anybody could say scat. Took out up the mountain and right through the brush and in amongst the trees and up over the ridge and out of sight over on the Kentucky side.

"And as far as I know, Old Dry Frye and that horse are over there yet a-tearin' around through that wilderness.'

* * * * *

(Author's note: This second account is excerpted from the book, "The Mountains Redeemed," a sort of personal history of the mountains and valleys of Southwest Virginia. It was written by Sam M. Hurst, and published in 1929. It involves a young doctor, who in his zeal to learn more about human anatomy, robs a grave to have a corpse to practice on, only to be frightened out of his wits.)

he poor fellow died and was buried out in some lonely country spot. The young 'doc' knew of his death and the place of burial. In the early night-time he hired someone's horse and buggy and went out alone and resurrected the 'stiff' before his time. He sat him upright in the buggy, tying him to the back of the seat so he would maintain his rectitude and dignity — a seat of honor right by his side!

"The 'couple' drove along without a word until they come to a way-side saloon, when 'doc' feels that he needs some 'medicine' to tone up his nerves. He gets out and goes into the saloon and gets a 'dram,' and takes a pint along with him for good measure and emergency. While he is in the saloon, someone who is 'on to' the doctor's game, quickly cuts the straps, lays the awaiting 'friend' privately aside, and gets up in the seat himself, and sits there with all the dignity of his predecessor. The doctor comes out and gets in and taking the reins, quickly drives off.

"After going a short distance, he takes another drink, and in spirit of braggadocio, sticks the bottle up under his 'stiff's' nose and says, 'Have a snort, old pard!' The 'stiff' replies, 'I don't care a damn if I do!', whereupon the doctor immediately drops the driving reins, leaps unceremoniously from the buggy, and almost without awaiting to alight, picks up his feet and runs down the road as fast as a ghost-pursued man can make his pendulums vibrate! The 'ghost' drives on and never comes in sight of the fast-fleeing doctor! The doctor had to look elsewhere for bones! We are not sure but that he quit medicine and went into the ministry!"

CHAPTER 31

A Case of Tragic Clairvoyance
(Abingdon)

(Author's note: Clairvoyance has been defined as the power or faculty of discerning objects not present to the senses. It also is the ability to perceive matters beyond the range of ordinary perception. In Virginia lore, there are a number of instances in which clairvoyant persons have, in various forms, inexplicably envisioned tragic circumstances. One of the most noteworthy, and well documented, was covered in my book, "The Ghosts of Williamsburg and Nearby Environs," published in 1983.

It involved former President of the United States John Tyler and his second wife, Julia Gardiner Tyler, who then lived at historic Sherwood Forest, on Route 5, roughly halfway between Williamsburg and Richmond. Here is what I wrote: "In January 1862, Tyler (then a member of the Provisional Confederate Congress) rode to Richmond, 35 miles away, to attend a conference. Julia and their baby daughter, Pearl, were to join him a week later. Before that could happen, however, Julia had a nightmare in which she envisioned her husband dying in a large bed with a headboard of a 'great carved eagle with outstretched wings.' She was so upset at the vividness of her dream she went at once to Richmond by carriage. However, he was found perfectly healthy and scoffed at his wife's disturbing vision.

Two days later he suffered an attack at the Exchange Hotel and died in a bed that in detail matched precisely the one Julia had seen in her dream!"

I reported a second such incident in "The Ghosts of Tidewater," published in 1990. In what was called a "crisis apparition," a sea captain named David Duncan was anchored on his ship, "The Sea Witch," in the harbor of Genoa, Italy, on May 12, 1823. He was, interestingly, reading a volume by the 18th century poet Edward Young called "Night Thoughts on Life, Death and Immortality." The exact poem he was reading described Death as an 'insatiate archer."

Suddenly, he envisioned a fire at the foot of the main mast. He ran from his cabin and when he reached the deck the fire seemed to blossom. In the midst of the flames he clearly saw the wraith-like form of his wife frantically clutching their son and daughter. Her screams pierced the silence in the harbor. "David! David! Save us!" she cried. And then, in a flash, she was gone, as was the fire.

Although crazed with anxiety, it was not until sometime later, when his ship finally docked at Norfolk, his home, that Captain Duncan learned the awful horror of his illusion had been real. His wife and two young children had indeed perished in a fire in their apartment on May 12, 1823!

And so, he placed a horizontal, raised tombstone, inscribed with his wife's name and the date of death over the single grave site in St. Paul's church yard. To this, he had the stonemaker carve the two lines of verse he had been reading when his loved ones died: "Insatiate archer, could not one suffice? Thy shaft flew thrice and thrice my peace was slain."

These two incredible events thus serve as a backgrounding prelude to the following account which was described in a faded, yellowed, 1931 newspaper clipping I found in a dusty scrapbook in the backwall recesses of the Roanoke Public Library. Excerpts from that account, which need no enhancements, follow.)

O n the western edge of Abingdon two old brick homes, one on either side of the Lee highway, attract the attention of passers by. They are plainly types of the old time residence of the better class of well-to-do citizens, and each has in reality a history of its own worthy of preservation.

"Then to the north of the road is the Bradley home and for more than a hundred years the Bradley house has been there. First it was a log house built on lots sold to James Bradley in 1796 by David Craig, who came down from Pennsylvania...

"For many decades the Bradley house was a noted roadside tavern something over a mile from the town. The brick residence, its successor, was built on the same site.

"Connected with it is one of those very remarkable stories of incidents said to happen with certain psychic individuals which seem increditable (sic), yet are so well attested as to compel acceptance as rare and inexplicable phenomenon...

"Colonel Thomas L. Preston, an old school gentleman of the highest type whose word none would doubt for an instant, had the facts first hand. He records the story in his reminiscences and vouches for its truth. It lives among the traditions of Abingdon.

"Colonel Preston says that a young merchant from Mississippi a few weeks after his marriage to the daughter of a wealthy citizen of that state, had left his home and gone to Philadelphia for a new stock of goods. A little while before he was expected to return, the young bride became anxious and depressed. She was laughed at for pining for her husband. But her depression deepened and she insisted that he was seriously sick.

"One morning soon after breakfast, when the depression was worse than usual, she went to her chamber. Soon after entering it she was heard to fall. The family hastened to her and found that she had fainted.

"The first words she uttered on regaining consciousness were: 'My husband is dead and not a friend was with him. I saw him die.' Then covering her face with her hands she said in the deepest anguish: 'I see the room in which he died, and the house and everything about it. I see it all. The little chamber upstairs in a brick house close by the road, with a window looking over a porch, and in front a rocky hill with a double log barn upon it and nearby a creek, where there is a tilt hammer. Oh I see it all, and my dear husband dead and alone.'

"So inconsolable was the bride that her brother decided to look up the bridegroom, taking the road by which he was expected to return. When he arrived at Bradley's he was so impressed with the resemblance of the place to his sister's description of her vision that he dismounted, and on meeting Mr. Bradley, asked if there had been a sick man from Mississippi stopping with him. 'Yes,' Mr. Bradley replied. 'He came here sick and died in the room upstairs. I wrote to his family but have not received an answer. All his effects and money I have kept safely.'

"It was ascertained that the man died at the hour that his bride fainted at her home in Mississippi. From the window of the upper chamber the scene was identically the same as that described by the disconsolate bride. It is needless to add that she had never been in that part of Virginia."

C H A P T E R   3 2

The Corpse Who Demanded To Be Reburied

(Lee County)

(Author's note: I should know better by now, but it still never ceases to amaze me as to how strikingly similar some of Virginia's most unusual ghost stories seem to be. And I'm not just talking footsteps, or bangings, or moans, or cold spots or any other of the more common manifestations of spectral phenomena. I'm speaking of some rather complex cases in which the spirits — although they may be hundreds of miles and hundreds of years apart — seem to follow the same pattern, at times so closely that one might wonder if one ghost were not somehow the reincarnation of another!

If the reader has the first volume of this series on Virginia ghosts, it may then be remembered that a woman named Mary Bowman of Virginia Beach, herself metaphysical, had the eerie experience of hearing a voice from the beyond calling whenever she drove past a certain section of countryside. It was a girl's voice, clear and distinct, and it was calling for help. As Mary's vision grew in intensity, she saw flash images of a brick wall, a rambling farm house, and a young woman, perhaps only 18 or 19. As Mary phrased it, "I saw a picture of a girl. She had blonde hair. She was lying down, as if she were in a coffin. She appeared to be wearing colonial-era clothes, with billowing sleeves, and I got the feeling that she lived 200 years ago."

It eventually became an obsession with Mary to find out who this girl was, where she was, and what she wanted. Why was she crying for help? Eventually, Mary saw, in real life, the brick wall and rambling farm house she had seen so many times in her visions. She drove to the house, knocked on the door and a man answered. She told him of her obsessive dream. Rather than think her crazy, he took her to his garage and showed her a pile of human bones. He said they had been in an unmarked grave unearthed by bulldozers in the area.

Immediately, Mary knew why the woman had called out for help. She had wanted her remains properly buried. When this was done, the spirit was finally at rest, and Mary, too, felt a tremendous relief. The vision and the voice disappeared.

There is a rather close parallel to Mary's experience. It, also, was recorded in the first volume, and involved the apparition of a woman with a tortoise shell comb in the back of her hair. She was seen over a long period of time in a house in Richmond. No one knew who she was, or why she appeared. Generally, she would be seen walking down a hall and then she would vanish. Some years later, during renovations to the house, workmen found the skeletal remains of a small woman, with a tortoise shell comb in the back of her skull, in a shallow grave only a few feet from the front of the house. These remains were given a proper reburial, and the woman's ghost was never again seen in the house.

Both of these encounters serve at a prelude to yet a third instance where a voice (and in this case a sighting) from the past returned to let someone know they cannot be at permanent rest until their mortal remains, improperly disposed of, are recovered and reinterred. This third example was first uncovered in a depression-era writers' program by a researcher in 1942. The story itself dates back considerably earlier — no one knows just when it was supposed to have occurred — and was handed down in the mountains of Southwestern Virginia for generations. It most recently was republished in Virginia Cavalcade Magazine, put out quarterly by the Virginia State Library and Archives, in 1993.)

ee County is about as close as one can get to Tennessee and Kentucky and still be in Virginia. It lies at the very Southwestern "toe" of the Old Dominion. The Cumberland mountains run on the Kentucky line, Powell mountain is on a part of the Southeast border, and there are several other ridges in the county. In 1845, historian Henry Howe wrote: "Much of the land is of a very black, rich soil. The staples are beef, pork, and horses. The people of this county make their own sugar and molasses from the maple sugar tree, which grows in great abundance ... Jonesville, the county seat, lies 284 miles from Richmond and 65 miles from Knoxville, Tennessee. It stands on a beautiful eminence, in the midst of wild mountain scenery."

It was amidst this setting that WPA worker Richard Chase heard "The Ha'nted House Tale" of Lee County. Following is a paraphrased version of the legend Chase recorded from a mountaineer: One night in a driving, freezing rain storm, "somewhere over toward Blackwater," a preacher stopped at a house and asked if he could spend the night there, a common custom in those days, especially in mountainous regions of rural Virginia. The man said he didn't have any room in his house, but there was an old empty house in a field against the mountain, and the preacher could stay there if he wished. So the men had some supper together, than the man took the preacher over to the isolated house and helped him gather some wood to make a fire for the night.

The preacher, who later related his experience to the grandfather of the man Chase interviewed, built up a "good fire," sat down in a "rickety chair," and read in his Bible for two or three hours before falling off to sleep. He woke up some time later as the fire was about to go out. He struck a match to see what time it was. Almost midnight. He started to get up to put another log or two on the fire, but instead just sat there for a minute or two, listening to the still pounding rain on the roof.

Suddenly, he heard a terrifying noise. The preacher said it sounded "like a wheelbarrow load of rocks" falling against the roof of one side of the house. He went out to see what caused it, but "there wasn't a sound of anybody or anything except the rain fallin.'" So he went back in the house and put some wood on the fire. He then heard what he said sounded something "like a rooster startin' to crow right at the door but it cut off quick like somebody hit it with a rock and knocked the crow out of it."

This might have been enough to have driven even hard-bitten men back out into the rain to seek some other, less eerie shelter. But the preacher sat back down and started reading his Bible again. "All at once he heard somebody moan." He couldn't tell where this came from. He put down his book and stoked up the fire. Then, as it was described, he heard "the awfullest moanin' and groanin' ... all through the house. Sounded like a woman goin' through the rooms sobbin' like she was lost. Then it sounded like it was comin' from the cellar, just like somebody strugglin' and dyin.'"

The "woman," or whatever it was, then screamed "somethin'

awful three or four times and stopped all at once." The next sound was even more frightening. The preacher heard footsteps coming up toward a door at the back of the house! Shaken to the core by this time, he grabbed a stick and stood with his back to the fire. Ever so slowly, the door opened, and the apparition of what appeared to be a woman formed. He could only make out a "sort of dim shape." Scared speechless, the preacher grabbed his stick tightly. The figure seemed to be sobbing, then it disappeared and the door closed.

The preacher tried to resume his reading, but the groaning and sobbing continued. Then the door opened again and the vision reappeared. "In the name of the Father, The Son, and The Holy Ghost!" the preacher exclaimed, "what do you want?" The spirit "sobbed sort of quick, like it was catchin' its breath and come on up to him like it was half floatin' and half fallin' and grabbed him by his coat lapels!"

This close, he could see that it was the apparition of a young woman, probably in her early twenties. She had on a faded dress, and "her hair was hangin' all tangled up around her head. She smelled earthy, *she didn't have any eyes, just black holes where her eye sockets was, and she didn't have any nose to her face!*" At this point the preacher was having great difficulty breathing, and his fear was so paralyzing, he couldn't even raise his stick an inch.

"I want to be buried," the vision spoke. "You'll find my bones buried under the hearth-rock there. My sweetheart killed me for my money and if you do what I tell you, you can come back here tomorrow night and I'll tell you where it's hid." The preacher, frozen, listened intently as the voice continued. "You take all my bones but the end of my left hand, little finger, and give me a churchyard burial. Then you invite all the folks in this neighborhood to a supper and put my finger bone on a plate and pass it around and it'll stick to the hand of the one who murdered me."

With this, the apparition sobbed, sank down on the hearth and evaporated before the preacher's eyes. Sighing heavily, the preacher finally managed to move. He couldn't sleep and he couldn't read. He just sat there trying to make some rational sense out of what had happened. There were no strange noises or visions the rest of the night. The next morning he got up, went to the main house, and told the man there about his experience with the haunt. Together, they uncovered the bones, reburied them in a graveyard, and "that preacher gave her a good funeral."

That night a big supper was held with several men attending.

A plate with the fingerbone was passed around, and when it got to a certain man, it stuck to his hand. "He started hollerin' and tryin' to get it off but it stuck just like it had growed on him." He was, then, a pretty old man, and "nobody had ever suspected him of that killin.' " Although the time of the murder was not specified it is speculated that it must have occurred 40 or 50 years earlier. The man was so horrified by the bone sticking to his finger that he confessed to the crime and was subsequently hanged.

The preacher went back to the deserted house the next evening and the apparition reappeared and told him where to find the money. It was said that the house "wasn't haunted anymore after that. But the ha'nts handprints were seared on the stranger's coat lapels where she took hold of him." It was said, "it looked just like they were burnt in!"

C H A P T E R 3 3

The Baffling Mystery of The Bouncing Bed
(Lee County)

Deep in the mountains of Southwestern Virginia the folklorian legends of generations and centuries ago are so well entrenched that sometimes today it is difficult to separate fact from fiction. This is one of the few areas left in the United States where the true and time-honored art of story telling is still alive and well. Here, in the "toe" of Virginia there are all sorts of heroes and heroines, villains and scary things. There are witches and their evil spells; notorious outlaws who vanish in the foothills when tracked; moonshiners and their contraption-like stills hidden deep in the forests; elves, gnomes, fairies, and all sorts of charmed and enchanted animals.

In such a wonderland of all-but-forgotten lore, there also is a treasure trove of ghost stories and other acts and occurrences of eerie and inexplicable character. One such tale, still told with relish and delight, is that of "Bertha's Bouncing Bed." Actually, "tale" is somewhat of a misnomer here, because in this instance, the psychic phenomena, which occurred over a lengthy period of time, was, in fact, witnessed by hundreds of people from miles around, including a number of experts. There was some controversy over the authenticity of the episodes, but most people were convinced they were genuine.

One of the more definitive accounts of the activity was recorded in 1938 by I. M. Warren as part of the Virginia Writers' Project during the last years of the great depression. In his travels, writer Warren tracked down the origins of the bouncing bed. The site was on the north side of Powell's Mountain in Lee County, about eight miles from Jonesville, the county seat. There was situated a small three room log cabin owned and occupied by Robert Sybert and his wife, Rebecca Jane.

They had moved to this isolated, hilly and desolate section of Southwest Virginia in the 1880s from Missouri, bringing their household furniture with them, including the infamous bed. They had one married son, Robert, who lived near them. He had four children, one son and three daughters. The oldest daughter was named Bertha Marie. She was nine years old in 1938, and for some unexplained reason, lived most of the time with her grandparents. She was described as being small and slender, weighing only 41 pounds. She was said to have a bright mind, made excellent grades in school, and was "apparently a normal child."

As Warren reported; "The peculiar occurrence consisted of a quivering shaking movement of the bed in which the child slept, and so persistent became the sketchy tales of the quivering, quaking bed and the uncanny scratching noises, that citizens of substance, usually quick to dismiss weird accounts from the backwoods that smack of the supernatural, began to look into the matter.

The Syberts thus welcomed a delegation of witnesses to their humble home on December 18, 1938, and invited them to stay and "see for themselves." Mrs. Sybert, then 71, told those present that she had lived in the cabin since March 1888, and had given scant attention to unusual incidents that defy logic.

"Four weeks ago," she said, "Bertha began to hear unusual noises just as if someone were rasping a nail across the head of the old wooden bed in the corner. The noise continued for several nights, and all the time she blamed only a prankster 'who'd try to scare an old lady.' It continued night after night and the bed where the child slept began to quiver. This week," Mrs. Sybert continued, "it's been so bad that Bertha's bed bounces and shakes something awful. You can stand across the room and see it as plain as day."

The delegation was not disappointed that evening. "Sure enough," one witness exclaimed, "it began shortly after six o'clock p.m. The bed quivered and trembled, yet the house was steady." This led Reverend Victor Sword, a Baptist minister present, to comment: "I saw the trembling, but such things are just beyond my knowledge."

On another occasion, a town merchant named Raymond was

in the house, and he, too, was impressed. "The night I was there Bertha failed to go to bed at the usual hour and instead, sat upon a chair," Raymond said. "Shortly after six o'clock the chair began to tremble, and her feet weren't touching the floor! Don't ask me what causes it. It just can't be explained!"

Warren reported that the nocturnal quakings did not seem to be confined to the old wooden bed, but occurred in any bed the child slept in. At one point Grandmother Sybert thought that maybe if other members of the family came to the house the bouncing might stop. She invited her son, Robert, Bertha's father, and three other relatives. The experiment didn't work. "And it still goes on," Mrs. Sybert said. "It must be witchery, cause the old thing makes me sore through my back when I get in bed with Bertha. It upsets me too!"

The Syberts next tried music to see if it would soothe whatever it was that was causing the bouncing, but this didn't work either. Said Robert: "Music had no effect. It didn't make any difference whether sacred or rag-time music was played, Bertha bounced just the same. Last night we slipped away from the crowd (by now curious neighbors and townspeople had heard of the phenomena and came to the house in droves) and took her to Raymond Minor's home, about a mile away, hoping to get away from 'the development'. "Robert put his daughter to bed and Mr. Minor played sacred music. "Suddenly," Robert said, "Bertha and the bed began bouncing just like it did at home." Minor played rag-time music, and "Bertha bounced on." "We thought Bertha would be safe at my house," Minor commented later, "but it really happened."

Robert said, "two weeks ago they put a Bible under Bertha's head and the ghost failed to appear, otherwise she has bounced every night since November 16." On Monday evening, December 19, 1938, while a curious group was watching, the child suddenly cried out, "that thing is pulling my hair, grandma, and it hurts."

Over the next week, dozens of people came to the house as the strange events spread like wildfire through the mountain communities. Said Warren: "Doctors, lawyers, merchants and a minister, with others, have sought an answer or explanation to the bouncing bed riddle. A curious throng waded ankle deep through mud and driving rain and sleet on the night of December 23, to watch the capricious 'ghost.' 'Ghost' or 'witchery' is the family's answer to the strange quivering of Bertha's bed. Neighbors and visitors, after repeated visits to watch the child jostled about, haven't offered anything more tangible to hang an explanation on."

On Christmas Eve, radio station WOPI in Bristol stretched a wire from the nearest electrical source to the mountain cabin and placed a microphone under Bertha's bed, and sent the scratching noises out on the air. As Warren wrote, "this added new interest to the curious minded and on the next day, Sunday, Christmas Day, throngs of people, more than a thousand, visited Bertha's home.

During the week in December of the most intense activity, Dr. Axel Brett, professor of Philosophy, and Dr. George Haslerud, professor of Psychology, both from the University of Tennessee, came to the Sybert cabin to examine Bertha and the bed. They saw the bed "go through its gyrations and heard the scratching noises." All they said at the time was, "It's very peculiar."

However, after returning to the University, they issued a report "debunking" the phenomena. Their paper was carried in the December 28, 1938, edition of the Roanoke Times. They said: "We entered the investigation with an elaborate plan of controls for accomplices, slight of hand, and other possibilities. We were amazed at the simplicity of the entire performance and the obvious natural explanation."

And then the professors dropped a bombshell that reverberated throughout the mountains of Southwest Virginia: "We have no doubt that the child makes conscious, deliberate contractions of the buttocks which explains the peculiar swaying of the mattress. The movements can be duplicated easily. The squeakings and scratching are the result of the dilapidated condition of the spring and bedstead ... The darkness of the room helps to conceal much."

But instead of laying the issue to rest, the professors' report stirred up a fury of unprecented proportions. Warren noted that when the report reached the ears of the mountain people of Lee County, offering a physiological, rather than a psychological or psychic interpretation to the bouncing bed, "they rose to a rousing defense, challenging the scientific qualifications of the Ph.D's." The challengers included a former state senator, a physician, a hotel operator, Bertha's father and grandmother as well as many others "who were outspoken."

Bertha's father, Robert, was particularly irked. Warren, who interviewed him, said, "he cast a significant glance at a long rifle hanging on the wall of the mountain cabin, and looking across the room at a shotgun on another wall, he remarked: "They better not lie on us. I have something better than that to correct with!" Robert said their investigation was too brief. He said they only examined the bedsprings and stood around awhile and asked a few questions. Bertha's grandmother was equally adamant. "Them fellers are liars," she declared. "Tell them to come back and do it right. If I thought it fake, I wouldn't let anyone come in the house."

One credible witness to the bed bouncings was attorney and former state senator John C. Neal of Pennington Gap. He dismissed the conclusions of the professors by saying, "the examination was very lame indeed, an extreme surmise, indefinite and incomplete. The mystery is yet unsolved." To this, Dr. G. W. Young, area physician and surgeon, added: "the professors' investigation does not clear up the case."

To this day no one can convince the people of Lee County that the solution of the mysterious bouncing bed does not lie somewhere in the nether world of the supernatural. Perhaps the testimony of eye-witness Sam Elkins of Walling Creek sums up the general feeling best. He offered to bet money on the "haunt," saying, "I don't like for people who claim to be scientists to call our people liars!"

On Indian Incursions and Burial Ground

(Statewide)

(Author's note: The settlers of the mountains and valleys of the western part of the state had to be extremely tough, wily and resourceful just to survive the harsh conditions. Henry Howe, in his book, "Historical Collections of Virginia," written in 1845, said, "The inhabitants of the mountain counties are almost perfectly independent. Many a young man with but a few worldly goods, marries, and, with an axe on one shoulder and a rifle on the other, goes into the recesses of the mountains, where land can be had for almost nothing. In a few days he has a log-house and a small clearing. Visit him some fine day 30 years afterwards, and you will find he has eight or ten children — the usual number here — a hardy, healthy set; 40 or 50 acres cleared, mostly cultivated in corn ..."

The life of a Virginia pioneer was, to a large extent, a lonely one, fraught with daily perils. Disease often ran unchecked; wild panthers and bears roamed the woods freely, not to mention the rattlesnakes and moccasins underfoot. The work itself was back-breaking and only the strongest could manage it. Even the most basic supplies were miles away, as were the nearest neighbors. If all this were not enough to cope with, the greatest danger, certainly in the middle part of the 18th century, came from marauding Indians who savagely and indiscriminately attacked and killed the settlers at virtually every opportunity.

A vivid and frightening account of what this life was like was described in the book, "Virginia, A History of the People," by John Esten Cooke, published in 1893: "Of the strange and moving incidents which befell these old first settlers in the Valley, and on the far Virginia border, it is impossible to speak in this place. They were intruders and must fight; and in the histories of the frontier we have the picture of their daily lives. They fall by unseen bullets fired from the woods; the stockades shake under the blind rush of the dusky assailants; the flames of burning cabins light up the marches; wives and children are tomahawked or carried off to be tortured; — and this is what is going on, all along the Virginia border, in the midst of outcries and the crack of rifles, nearly to the end of the century … "

From such on-going warfare a number of heroic legends have emerged. I wrote of one, Mad Ann Bailey, in my first volume of "The Ghosts of Virginia." After her husband had been killed by Indians, "Twas at this juncture (she) donned semi-male attire … and took the gun, determined to protect herself and her little child and also avenge her husband's death … For the next 11 years she became a terror … She became a spy, messenger, and scout, killed more than one person's share of Indians (and) saved stockades."

Samuel Kercheval, who wrote the "History of the Valley," first published in 1833, spent a lifetime travelling about the commonwealth and interviewing hundreds of early settlers. In his book, he devoted several chapters to "Indian Incursions and Massacres." Following, are some excerpts from these writings, which include a couple of examples of the extraordinary courage and an incredible sense of survival possessed by the Virginia settlers. There are, also, a pair of psychic incidents, one of which proved to save an entire family's life from imminent hostile attack.)

Just before the massacre on Looney's Creek, (about 1758) seven Indians surrounded the cabin of Samuel Bingaman (in the western part of the state) … It was just before daybreak, that being the time when the Indians generally made their surprises. Mr. Bingaman's family consisted of himself and wife, his father and mother, and a hired man. The first four were asleep in the room below, and the hired man in the loft above.

"A shot was fired into the cabin, the ball passing through the fleshy part of the young Mrs. Bingaman's left breast. The family sprung to their feet, Bingaman seizing his rifle, and the Indians at the same moment rushing in at the door. Bingaman told his wife and father and mother to get out of the way, under the bed, and called to the man in the loft to come down, who, however, never moved.

"It was still dark, and the Indians were prevented from firing, by a fear of injuring one of their number. Bingaman, unrestrained by any fears of this kind, laid about him with desperation. At the first blow, his rifle broke at the breech, severing the stock to pieces; but with the barrel, he continued his blows until he had cleared the room.

"Daylight now appearing, he discovered that he had killed five, and that the remaining two were retreating across the field. He stepped out, and seizing a rifle which had been left by the party, fired at one of the fugitives, wounded, and tomahawked him. Tradition relates that the other fled to the Indian camp, and told his comrades that they had a fight with a man who was a devil — that he had killed six of them, and if they went again, would kill them all!"

Kercheval's second account of incredible heroism took place in 1782 at Fort Rice, which at that time was still part of Virginia. The fort was under siege, surrounded by Indians. "Abraham Rice ... mounted a very strong active mare and rode in all haste to another fort, about three-and-a-half miles distant from his own, for further news, if any could be had, concerning the presence of a body of Indians in the neighborhood. Just as he reached the place, he heard the report of the guns at his own fort. He instantly returned as fast as possible, until he arrived within sight of the fort.

"Finding that it still held out, he determined to reach it and assist in its defense, or perish in the attempt. In doing this, he had to cross the creek, the fort being some distance from it, on the opposite bank. He saw no Indians until his mare sprang down the bank of the creek, at which instant about 15 of them jumped up from among the weeds and bushes and discharged their guns at him. One bullet wounded him in the fleshy part of the right arm about the elbow.

"By this time several more of the Indians came up and shot at him. A second ball wounded him in the thigh a little above the knee, but without breaking the bone, and the ball passed transversely through the neck of the mare. She, however, sprang up the bank of the creek, fell to her knees, and stumbled along about a rod before she recovered. During this time several Indians came running up to tomahawk him. Yet he made his escape, after having about 30 shots fired at him from a very short distance!

"After riding about four miles, he reached Lamb's Fort, much exhausted from the loss of blood. After getting his wounds dressed and resting awhile, he set off late in the evening with 12 men, determined if possible to reach the fort under cover of the night. When they got within about 200 yards of it, they halted; the firing still continued. Ten of the men, thinking the enterprise too hazardous, refused to go any further, and retreated. Rice and two other men crept silently along toward the fort; but had not proceeded very far before they came close upon an Indian in his concealment. He gave the alarm yell which was instantly passed round the line with the utmost regularity. This occasioned the Indians to make their last effort to take the place and make their retreat under cover of the night. Rice and his two companions returned in safety to Lamb's Fort."

Consider also the miraculous escape of Mary Ingles, an incredible drama of extraordinary effort, endurance and survival. Along with several others, she was captured by marauding Shawnees in July 1755 near what is now the town of Radford. According to one persistent chapter in her legend, she gave birth to a child on the third night of her captivity, yet was able to mount a horse with her infant the next day, and continue the journey to their village.

Some time later, then in Ohio Territory, Mary and an older Dutch woman made an escape attempt with only the clothes on their backs, a blanket and a tomahawk each. It was to be a journey of extreme, almost unbearable hardships. Sleeping on the ground, in hollow logs, and, occasionally in a deserted cabin, they subsisted on black walnuts, wild grapes, papaws, roots, and, infrequently, on corn and turnips gleaned from abandoned farms.

When they reached the New River, the Dutch woman had become so crazed with hunger that she tried to kill Mary and eat her, but Mary wrenched herself free and hid. She found an old canoe, crossed the river and continued her flight. Forty two days later she staggered back into civilization, exhausted, her feet and legs painfully swollen.

The next spring Mary Ingles had a premonition that another Indian attack was imminent and she persuaded her husband to leave their cabin immediately. As they crossed the Blue Ridge Mountains headed toward the Peaks of Otter, the Indians massacred those in the settlement the Ingles has just left. Mary, it was said, bore a charmed life. One writer noted that "if adverse fate repeatedly marked her as a victim of firebrand, hatchet, or scalping knife, an interposing Providence just as often spared her." She died in 1815 at the age of 83.

The first of the two psychic incidents probably dates somewhere in the 1730s. It was related to Kercheval by Captain James Glenn, then 73 years old, and was confirmed by John Tomlinson, who was 92 at the time the book was published.

"There is also a tradition, and there are evident signs of the

fact, of another furious battle fought at what is called the Slim Bottom on Wappatomaka, (the ancient Indian name of the Great South Branch of the Potomac), about one-and-a-half miles from its mouth. At this place there are several large Indian graves, near what is called the Painted Rock. On this rock is exhibited the shape of a man with a large blotch, intended, probably, to represent a man bleeding to death.

"The stain, it appeared to the author, was made with human blood. The top of the rock projects over the painted part so as to protect it from the washings of the rains, and is on the east side of the rock. How long the stain of human blood would remain visible in a position like this, the author cannot pretend to express an opinion; but he well recollects the late General Isaac Zane informed me that the Indians beat out the brains of an infant (near his old iron works) against a rock, and the stain of the blood was plainly to be seen about 40 years afterward!"

The second, and more famous account of apparent psychic phenomena regarding Indian attacks, occurred on what is now county road 615 near Luray in Page County. The year was 1758. This episode was covered by Kercheval, and later by Depression-era writers in "Virginia, A Guide to the Old Dominion." At the time, John Brewbecker (now Brubaker) and his family resided on the west side of the South Fork of the Shenandoah River, on Massanutten Creek. Indian incursions in the area had been frequent, and the families lived in virtually constant fear.

One evening, Mrs. Brewbecker had a premonition of a pending attack. She told members of her family, and a neighbor, John Stone and his family, that she had a vision. As Kercheval recounted the occurrence: She could "see a party of them (Indians) on the side of the Massanutten Mountain, in the act of cooking their supper. She also declared that she saw their fire, and could count the number of Indians." The spot Mrs. Brewbecker pointed to was about two miles distant, and clearly out of the range of ordinary eyesight. No one else saw anything ... "And it was therefore thought that she must be mistaken. Persisting in her declarations, she begged her husband to remove her and her children to a place of safety; but she was laughed at, told that it was mere superstition, and that she was in no danger."

While the Stone family ridiculed Mrs. Brewbecker's premonition, she finally persuaded her husband to move their family to a safer place. The next morning, Indians raided and John Stone was immediately killed. Kercheval: "Stone's wife, with her infant child and a son about seven or eight years old, and George Grandstaff, a youth of 16, were taken off as prisoners. On the South Branch Mountain, the Indians murdered Mrs. Stone and her infant and took the boy and Grandstaff to their towns. Grandstaff was about three years a prisoner, and then got home. The little boy, Stone, grew up with the Indians, came home, and after obtaining possession of his father's property, sold it, got the money, returned to the Indians, and was never heard of by his friends afterward.

"The same Indians ... plundered old Brewbecker's house, piled up the chairs and spinning wheel, and set them on fire. A young woman who lived with Brewbecker had concealed herself in the garret; and after the Indians left the house, extinguished the fire and saved the house from burning."

It was later learned that the Indians, indeed, has encamped the previous night at precisely the spot on the mountain that Mrs. Brewbecker had envisioned; that it was exactly two miles off; and that the number of attacking Indians "tallied even in number with Mrs. Brewbecker's count!"

* * * * *

(Author's note: Two ghostly accounts involving Indian attacks are included here for organizational purposes. One occurred in Rockbridge County in 1742. The other took place in Loudoun County, although the exact date is unclear. Kercheval described it and attributed the date to 1736. J. V. Nichols, in his work, "Legends of Loudoun Valley," notes that the event may have happened as early as 1720.

PURSUED BY A HEADLESS PEDESTRIAN!

 tate historical marker A-43, located in Rockbridge County about a mile south of the town of Fairfield, is headlined, "McDowell's Grave." It states: "In this cemetery are the graves of Captain John McDowell and seven companions, who were killed by Indians near Balcony Falls, December 14, 1742. This fight began a war that lasted until 1744."

Occasional reports that this old graveyard is haunted have surfaced over the past 250 years. There is considerable speculation that it may be the spirit of McDowell himself still seeking redress from his cruel murder so long ago. Perhaps the most definitive recounting of a sighting of the apparition was made 35 years ago in a newspaper article that quoted John W. Smith of Lexington. Smith was described as "an earnest churchman and an honest man, not given to exaggeration."

According to Smith, when he was about 16-years-old, he was riding a horse from an evening party at the home of his kinsman, Billy Robertson, in Fairfield. He had borrowed the horse from his boss, who owned a sawmill at Timber Ridge where Smith was living and working.

Smith said at about midnight, as he was riding south on the highway at a point closest to the old McDowell Cemetery, in the drizzling rain, he "came upon a man walking in the rain." Smith said he addressed the figure, but received no answer. He looked closer, and felt a "terrifying pang of indescribable fear."

As Smith told it: "I saw he didn't have no head! Scared? It just about scared me to death! It would have scared anybody. No, I wasn't drinking. I didn't even know what it was to drink in those days. And it was light enough to see, if it was drizzling. He had on a long overcoat, and if that man had a head, I could not see it. He came out of that cemetery over there.

"I threwed the switch on the old horse and came away from there! The next day I told Mr. Ward about, and he said somebody had just been trying to scare me." Smith, however, remained convinced that what he saw was not of this world. If someone were trying to frighten him, why would they wait in the dark cemetery at night, in rain, at such a late hour? And how would they even know he would come past that way?

To this day, it is still believed by some of the area that Smith may have seen the restless spirit of Captain John McDowell seeking the scalp he lost to the Indians.

* * * * *

THE CLASH OF GHOSTLY TOMAHAWKS

 little east of Catoctin Mountain, within sight of Route 15 in Loudoun County, Northern Virginia, is a huge, curious, circular mound. It is now about 100 feet high, although the erosions of nature and the cultivation of man over two and a half centuries may have whittled it down considerably from a once even more imposing height.

It was here that in 1720, or 1736, or whatever year, a fierce and bloody battle took place between the Delaware and the Catawba tribes. The Delaware people, early in the 18th century, were located in what is now New Jersey, Delaware and eastern Pennsylvania. The Catawbas lived 500 miles away in western North Carolina and Northwestern South Carolina. Although such a great distance separated them, these two great tribes were at war.

One spring, a "large band of Delaware warriors," rode south and launched a series of surprise attacks on their enemies, destroyed most of their villages, killed many of the men, and took many of the women and children as prisoners, then headed back north. The scattered Catawbas quickly regrouped, formed their own war party, and rode after the Delawares.

They caught them at a site about four miles south of Leesburg, and there ensued the gory battle. There is confusion, here, too, among historians about what transpired. Kercheval, in 1835, wrote: "Every man of the Delaware party was put to death, with the exception of one who escaped after the battle was over, and every Catawba held up a scalp but one. This was a disgrace not to be borne; and he instantly gave chase to the fugitive, overtook him at the Susquehanna River, (a distance of 100 miles), killed and scalped him, and, returning, showed his scalp to several white people, and exulted in what he had done."

Loudoun County historian Nichols, however, says, "Though surprised, the Delawares fought desperately against their pursuing foes who, thirsting for revenge and intent on rescuing their women and children, battled with savage ferocity. Bows and arrows were cast aside and the struggle was hand to hand with tomahawk and hunting knife, wielded in unrelenting fury. Finally, the superior prowess of the Delawares prevailed and the Catawbas were forced to retreat without recovering their captive women and children from the enemy.

"But the Delawares had paid a fearful price for their victory. Many of their best and bravest warriors lay dead upon the scene of the contest. The distance was too great and the numbers of the remaining warriors too few to carry the bodies of their dead back to their own hunting grounds for burial as was their custom. So they assembled them near the center of the battleground on a level space not far east of the Catoctin Mountain and erected over their bodies a large mound. Then they conducted their tribal funeral rites, and departed with sad hearts and in silence for their homeland."

In his book, "Hauntings and Happenings of Loudoun," author Frank Raflo, citing Nichols, said, "for many years on each anniversary of this battle a band of Indians would silently emerge from the surrounding forest, conduct their funeral rites, leave some food and a few arrows on the mound, and then, as quietly as they came disappear into the shadows of the woodland. Each year the numbers taking part in these rites decreased until finally only one aged Indian came slowly out of the forest, made his weird incantations, left some food and arrows on the mound for use of the spirits of the fallen warriors in the 'happy hunting grounds' and then disappeared ... "

In time, white settlers moved west, and a family named Meade acquired the land on which the battle had been fought and the mound erected. Members of this family told of hearing each year, on the date of the anniversary of the fight, "the sounds of conflict around this mound." Their slaves were even more explicit. They said they saw the "shadowy forms of the tomahawks, observed the silent flight of the vanquished, and listened to the shouts of the victors!"

Watchdog of the Valley Frontier

(Botetourt County)

hey used to say, early in the century, that when the winds whipped up at old Greenfield mansion near Daleville in Botetourt County, a few miles north of Roanoke and west of Troutville, that the "God-awful" noises of heavy boot stomping and loud banging doors were made by the ghost of Colonel William Preston. The ghost appeared, it was said, to maintain a spectral watch over the spirits of marauding Indians who continued to threaten the peace of early valley settlers nearly two and a half centuries after the colonel had successfully fought them off in real life.

For above all else, William Preston was an Indian fighter. He was so dedicated to the protection of his fellow Virginians, in fact, that he once turned his own mansion into a fortress haven for men, women and children seeking shelter against enemy attacks. His fierce resolve and determination earned him the title, "the Watchdog of the Virginia Frontier."

Preston was born in Donegal, Ireland, in 1729, and was about eight years old when his father brought the Preston family to America. They settled in Augusta County. Preston's father died when he was 17, and he went to live with his uncle, Colonel James Patton. Patton was killed in a raid by Indians at Draper's Meadow near Blacksburg in 1755, and Preston was spared only because he had been sent to a neighboring farm to solicit help in harvesting. This event undoubtedly deeply saddened him, and helped foster a life-long pursuit of revenge.

As a young man, Preston became a surveyor in Botetourt County and worked in areas including the Catawba, Craigs and Purgatory Creeks. He later served with distinction in the Virginia House of Burgesses, and upon the formation of Botetourt County in 1770, he became one of the original justices, coroner, and colonel of militia, as well as the first surveyor there.

In the 1750s, there is some disagreement as to exactly when, Preston bought several hundred acres of land near the hamlet of Amsterdam, and built a house that came to be known as Greenfield. He built it on a hill because it provided a long-range panoramic view of the surrounding countryside. One wing featured tall columns and was originally erected as a combination log house and fort for defense against the Indians. At the rear of the house stood a log kitchen and smokehouse, with a well in the yard center, forming a square with the house that could be closed by a palisade in the event of an attack.

He apparently chose the site and design wisely, because in a letter he wrote in the mid-18th century, he describes the Indians as "being on the warpath," and added that within the walls of Greenfield were "80 men, 40 guns, and by the grace of God," he hoped to hold the fort.

Mrs. Preston seemed to be of a heroic nature, too. Once, when a 12-year-old boy came running from a neighboring farm, shouting that Indians had attacked his family, it was she who insisted that every man and boy at Greenfield rush to the defense of the family, while she alone maintained guard over the stockade. The rescuers rode in vain, however, as they found only scalped bodies of "every single person" at the farm. In a curious twist, the Prestons then chose to raise the sole survivor. Years later he saved Colonel Preston's life at the battle of Guilford Courthouse.

It was Preston who sent the first petition from a citizen of Botetourt County to the House of Burgesses. Unsurprisingly, it warned the colonial authorities of the imminent danger of an Indian attack. It is written that, as the first colonel of the militia in the County, Preston "was almost constantly engaged in either leading or preparing for expeditions against the Indians. During the Revolutionary War he was not only engaged in defending the outposts of Southwest Virginia against the Indians, but also in fighting the British Loyalists in their attempts to foment trouble."

Meanwhile, more and more additions were added to the house on top of the hill, and Greenfield began to assume a revered position as an historic landmark. George Washington came here during one of his last surveying trips to the frontier before the outbreak of the Revolutionary War.

Colonel Preston either knew, met or corresponded with most of the colonial leaders of the day. At one time there were more than 600 pounds of papers, documents and letters in the house; letters from such 18th century luminaries as Patrick Henry, Richard Henry Lee, Lord Botetourt, and Lord Dunmore. He also accumulated an impressive collection of Indian arrowheads, as well as guns, pistols and sabres. Fortunately, many of these invaluable papers have been preserved and are housed at the Wisconsin State Historical Society.

Having survived a lifetime of danger, dodging Indian bullets, arrowheads and tomahawks, the crusty warrior, the "lord lieutenant of the frontier," died, as he might have wished it, at a regimental muster held near his home, on June 18, 1783.

He left quite a legacy. Eight generations of the Preston family lived at Greenfield. The Colonel's son, John, gained fame himself serving as a general in the militia, as a legislator, and as treasurer of Virginia. Other descendents included General Francis Preston who fought in the Revolutionary War, and James Patton Preston, governor of Virginia in 1816. The estate included nearly 1,000 acres, vast apple orchards, a large herd of cattle, and thoroughbred horses.

Greenfield also housed a noisy ghost. So prevalent were the rumors that the mansion was haunted by the avenging specter of the colonel, ever vigilant in his guard against Indian attacks, that Preston descendents had a hard time hiring help to run the house and estate. Servants were wary of being in the mansion, especially after dark. For it was in the wee hours of the evening, particularly on windy nights, that the manifestations most often occurred. 'He' was said to then stomp about on the upstairs floors, opening and shutting doors with loud banging sounds. His grandchildren and great grandchildren would search the entire upstairs to find a plausible explanation for the sounds, never to succeed. It was, some said, Colonel Preston, making his presence known as if to warn all that they should never let down their guard.

Tragically, the old house burned to the ground in an early morning fire in 1959, and since then a state highway marker on Route 220 has been taken down. It is a shame, because it reminded present day Virginians of the life-long heroics of one of the commonwealth's most daring and dedicated defenders; a man who helped make Southwestern Virginia safe for settlement.

But, one may say, at least after the house was destroyed, the tireless spirit of William Preston could at last rest in peace.

CHAPTER 36

The Eerie Return of Chief Benge

(Flat Gap and Southwestern Virginia)

(Author's note: Among all the notorious Indian chiefs who ran rampant through the valleys and mountains of Virginia during the second half of the 18th century, torturing and killing hundreds of settlers, and burning their homes and fields, none was more feared than a Shawnee known as Chief Benge. For 10 long years in the 1780s and 1790s, he terrorized the furtherest regions of Southwest Virginia, launching raid after raid against the ill-equipped pioneers as they desperately tried to carve a new life out of the wilderness.

Benge actually was the son of a white woman who had been captured by the Shawnees, and an Indian brave. His mother escaped with him when he was nine years old, and returned to civilization. It has been written, however, that "Indian blood and nine impressionable years among his savage kin had bent the twig in a direction foreign to every Anglo-Saxon instinct," and at age 13, Benge returned to his fathers. He is said to have grown up to be "a marvelous specimen of physical manhood, renowned for his intelligence, strategy, strength, activity, endurance, and great speed in foot races."

Tradition says that Benge notched a tree on the High Knob Trail for each of his raids into the area. There allegedly were 13 notches on the tree. Following is the story of Benge's last raid, and after that, a report of the chief's ghost appearing to a man named Boyd Bolling, who told of his experience in 1942 to an interviewer for the Virginia Writers' Project. Benge's last raid is taken from accounts published in Summers' "History of Southwest Virginia," Sam N. Hurst's "The Mountains Redeemed," and other documents.)

O n the morning of April 6, 1794, brothers Peter and Henry Livingstone were working in the barn area of their family farm near Mendota, when Benge and a group of his marauders swooped down and attacked the farmhouse. The Indians set fire to the buildings, loaded their horses with plunder, took the brothers' wives and some slaves as prisoners, and rode off toward High Knob. By a miracle of fate, the Livingstone children were spared when they ran, unnoticed, to a neighbor's farm. By evening the Indians and their captives had crossed Clinch Mountain, and the next day they penetrated further into the woods. They camped at Stoney Creek, believing they had gone beyond the reach of any posses sent after them.

The next day the brothers were joined by a party of 13 men as they set off after Benge. Somehow, in their zealous pursuit, they got ahead of the Indians at Stone Gap, and realizing this, doubled back. They found two braves who had been sent out as advance guards and "dispatched" them, then headed for the main party. According to one report, they saw Benge in the distance, and observed him sticking his knife in the ground and "making magic" by circling the knife and muttering, "Ugh! Ugh! No white man near."

It soon became apparent that the magic didn't work. Vincent Hobbs and Van Bibber took careful aim with their rifles at Benge and an Indian next to him, fired simultaneously, and killed them instantly. In the ensuing battle, two more Indians were slain, five escaped, and the women and slaves were rescued.

It was written that much later, "An old, old lady, now dead, whose great-grandfather, James Huff, was in the Hobbs party, used to tell of how Henry Livingstone had sworn to drink the blood of Benge, and she would aver that after clasping his wife to his bosom, he ran with a tin cup to the rock where Benge's blood was flowing, and catching it full, quaffed it off thirstily."

It was further told that Benge's scalp was subsequently sent to the Governor at Richmond by Colonel Arthur Campbell, Indian agent, who also suggested that the state present Vincent Hobbs with a rifle, which it did — a silver-mounted rifle. Some say the skull of Benge reposed for years on an old chestnut snag where he was killed and that it eventually was sent to Richmond.

With his death at the rock by Benge's Creek just northeast of the town of Norton, the Indian raids ceased. Today, there is an historical state marker at the site. It reads, "The pass to the south was a secret route named Benge's Gap for an Indian half-breed who used it in making surprise attacks on settlers. The latter discovered the gap. When Benge was returning to it from his last raid, 1794, his party was attacked by settlers and exterminated."

In 1942, at Flat Gap, Virginia, Boyd Bolling told the following to a Virginia Projects writer: "I am sending you (an account of) the night I spent on the top of Stone Mountain on my trip. I dreamed of the forks of Honey River, or saw it in a vision ... It was my first day's hunt. I found myself alone on the top of Stone Mountain in sight of Norton. So I built my camp fire right where Benge and the big Indian were killed. So I cooked my quails (and ate) a hearty supper.

"Soon, the bright moon beams were streaming over the mountain tops, and the soft fall breeze was moaning so sweetly. I soon fell to sleep, not thinking there was anything to disturb me. All at once I heard a big rough voice say, 'White man sleep good.'

"So I jumped to my feet, grabbed my old long rifle. He says, 'Me no harm. I am from the spirit land.' I was about to shoot. He says, 'Put gun down.' I says, 'Who are you?'

" 'I am Benge, that noted murderer of the Indian gang. Hobbs killed me right here, caught a pint of my blood and drank it for capturing his wife ... I was raised an orphan ... Fell in among horse thieves. Had to take to the mountains. So I joined the Indians and led so many raids ... robbed, killed, scalped so many whites. So I was killed right here on top of Little Stone Mountain'."

At this point the narrator, Boyd Bolling, exclaimed, "I never slept no more that night!"

A Pair of Deathly Premonitions

(Carroll County)

here are, in the recorded annals of psychic phenomena, countless cases of what are commonly called premonitions of death. Many of these incidents involve dreams or nightmares, in which the dreamer envisions a close relative, often a mother, father, son, daughter, or brother or sister, husband or wife. The vision may be calling for help, or it just may appear, as if to say a final goodbye. In many more cases than can be dismissed by coincidence, the dreamer later learns that the person they visualized either died or suffered a terrible accident — at the precise time the dream occurred! Such phenomena have never been fully understood or explained.

What is much more rare in psychic realms is when someone has such a premonition, in dream form or otherwise, of their own death. Yet this apparently is exactly what happened to not one, but two persons involved in the same chilling event early this century at the Carroll County Courthouse in tiny Hillsville, near Galax, in the Southwestern part of the commonwealth.

For it was here, on March 14, 1912, that one of the most tragic episodes in the history of Virginia occurred. It has forever been known as the Hillsville shootout.

To understand exactly what happened and why, some background is necessary. This was hill country, and if the mountain folk who lived there could be summed up in one word, it would be "independent"; in two words, "fiercely independent." Through the latter part of the 18th century and through the 19th and well into the 20th, these pioneering people battled savage Indians, wild animals and the harsh environment of the land to build their log cabins and farm the rough hillsides to scratch out a living. They mostly kept to themselves and resented any intrusion on their privacy. They lived by their own code of ethics, which often included self-administered justice. In the backwoods regions this generally meant an eye for an eye.

Family and neighborhood feuds were not uncommon, and bullets were answered with bullets. As one writer noted, such feuds "have been marked by frequent assassinations and bloody battles. Women and children have been the victims as well as men, and not infrequently have whole families been wiped out before vengeance was satisfied. These have been carried on with utter contempt for the law. In fact, it would be counted a disgrace for any involved in them to appeal to the law. He would be branded a coward even by those upon whose side he had been fighting and would be cast out from among them."

One of the time-honored traditions of these people was the making of moonshine whiskey. It was, they felt, their inherent right to run stills, and when the Federal government decreed that taxes should be paid on such operations, the laws, and the taxes, were largely ignored. To dodge collectors, the moonshiners just moved deeper into the woods, and if law officers dared — and few did — come to track down the illicit producers of "white mule," they did so at the threat of facing an arsenal of double-barrelled shotguns and rifles manned by marksmen who could shoot the eye out of a squirrel at 100 paces. As has been written, "Time and time again the government has sent its officers at the peril of their lives into this wild and dangerous part of our country to suppress this species of crime, and many is the time they have never been heard of since."

This was the overall atmosphere that prevailed in Carroll County in 1912. One of the most feared clans in that day was made up of members of the Allen and Edwards families. Unlike the common stereotype of the backwoodsman, however, the Allens in particular were said to be respected businessmen and farmers and of average education. Still, the Allen men and their kinsmen, the Edwards, were described as possessing personalities "characteristic of many inhabitants of the Virginia highlands. They were rugged individualists — independent, proud, and generally hot-tempered."

The incident which directly led to the ensuing calamity is still somewhat clouded in confusion. There are at least three versions. One says that two of the young Edwards' boys had been arrested for moonshining and were being brought to jail in Hillsville. Another says simply that the two had been arrested on a "minor misdemeanor charge," while the third stated the Edwards boys had been captured for "disturbing a church meeting."

Whatever, they were manacled, on their horses, and being escorted in by either one or two deputies, again depending on varying accounts. Onto this scene came Floyd Allen, the 50ish uncle of the boys. In one version of what followed, he asked the deputies to unshackle the Edwards. The officers drew their guns. Floyd then went berserk, wrested the gun from one of them and smashed it on a rock. The officers fled. In another report, Floyd Allen met the deputies, and beat one of them senseless, leaving him for dead on the ground and scurrying off with the boys.

In either case, the result was a warrant for Floyd's arrest. He was indicted and released on bond. In the days leading to the trial, Floyd consistently vowed that he would never go to jail; that he would die before being confined. Those who knew him had no doubts of his sincerity. In the days before the trial, both judge Thornton L. Massie and commonwealth attorney William M. Foster received death-threatening letters from the Allen clan, saying revenge would be inflicted for any punishment rendered to Floyd.

The jury heard the evidence in the case for several days and then the verdict and sentence was to be handed down on the morning of March 14. The entire Allen clan, dressed in long coats, rode up to the courthouse that day and wedged their way into the packed courtroom. The night before Foster, expecting trouble, pleaded with judge Massie to deputize some men to protect the court. The judge refused. Nevertheless, Foster had court officials appear the next day carrying concealed weapons.

The jury filed in sometime after 8:30 a.m., and read a verdict of guilty as charged with the penalty set at one year in prison. The judge refused to continue Allen's bond and directed the sheriff to take charge of the prisoner. At that moment, all hell broke loose.

Floyd Allen arose from his seat, threw back his coat, revealing two revolvers, and proclaimed loudly, "Gentlemen, I ain't goin.'" Bedlam ensued. Sheriff Lewis F. Webb immediately rushed toward Allen, and at the same instant shots rang out from the courtroom. Judge Massie was hit five or six times and died immediately. The sheriff and Floyd fired away at each other in such close quarters, "that shots carried powder burns as well as bullets." The sheriff was killed and Floyd was hit by half a dozen or more shots.

The entire courtroom exploded in a furious eruption of shots that, one witness said, "sounded like the crackle of mountain laurel." Several members of the Allen-Edwards clan, with pistols and rifles, began firing, and their charges were answered from the guns of the court officers. The smoke from such a fusillade was so thick it was difficult to see anyone or anything. According to one contemporary written account of the scene, "A second after judge Massie had fallen over his desk, an outlaw blazed away with his Winchester, and commonwealth attorney William Foster threw up his hands and tottered backwards a corpse. Sheriff Louis Webb saw the shot and the man who fired it.

"Raising his revolver, he drew a bead on the outlaw, but before he could pull the trigger a shot from across the room struck him in the head, the revolver, still undischarged, flew out of his hand as he sank dying to the floor. The wounded also lay about the floor with the dead, and the place resembled a shambles ... Blood was everywhere ... While the shooting was in progress the spectators ... were making panic-stricken efforts to escape. A number of them had been hit by stray bullets and lay gasping on the floor. Those who escaped the leaden hail had scattered in all directions and were fleeing for their lives.

"Within less than a minute 75 shots were fired!"

In the pandemonium, the Allens and Edwards, including Floyd, who was riddled with bullet wounds, left the courtroom, mounted their horses, and fled. Dead were the judge, the commonwealth attorney, the sheriff, one member of the jury, and one witness. Several others were wounded.

Floyd was so badly hurt that he couldn't make it to the mountains, where the others headed for. He and his son, Victor, holed up in a local hotel. Such was the fear that the attack created in the town, no deputies tried to subdue them. They were arrested the next day after an army of law officials from all over Southwest Virginia arrived.

Over the next few weeks, a relentless succession of posses rounded up most of the clan. Only Sidna Allen, Floyd's brother, and Wesley Edwards, a nephew, eluded the manhunt by hiding in the mountains. They, too, were captured about six months later. A trial was held in Wytheville several weeks later, and Floyd and his son, Claude, were sentenced to death. A number of other members of the clan were sent to prison. On March 28, 1913, a little over a year later, Floyd and Claude were electrocuted in Richmond. Each man, it was said, walked "unflinchingly to the chair, calmly resigned to their fate."

Was Floyd Allen's fate preconceived? Did he envision how he was going to die even before the shootout? There is some suggestion that he did; that he had a premonition of his doom. He is said to have told this to his brothers as he awaited the results of his trial.

And what about the commonwealth attorney? Did William Foster foresee his future, too? Maggie Mae McManaway, then secretary to Foster was an eye-witness to the tragedy that auspicious day in 1912. In 1940, she was interviewed for a newspaper article on the shootout. The night before, she was with Foster when he had asked judge Massie to arm the courthouse with extra deputies.

"The next morning," she was quoted as saying, "Mr. Foster and I were in our office, and he appeared worried ... as he left to go to the courtroom he told me goodbye, and said I'd likely not see him anymore!"

Angelic Interventions

(Giles County and Powhatan County)

ince Babylonian, Persian, Egyptian and Greek times, angels have fascinated mankind. The word angel itself is a mutation of the Greek word "angelos," in turn a translation of the Persian word "angeros," or courier. And, of course, the great Greek God Hermes was the "Winged Messenger." Images of supernatural winged creatures have been found in ancient Mesopotamia and Sumeria. The popular image of angels as heavenly messengers is said to have originated in Persia's Zoroastrian faith and was then handed down to Judaism, Christianity and Islam. Halos and shining lights began to "accompany" angels by the fourth century after Christ.

It is commonly believed that angels may manifest themselves in many ways. Some experts contend that they make themselves most often known through "the inner voice," or in visions and dreams, or as bells and pillars of light. Yet it is also felt that angels have no standard form or appearance, but take whatever guise seems necessary to interact with humans in any given situation. They can thus appear as human beings of either sex, and as either adults or children, or as radiant beings.

Others suggest that angels are naturally occurring energies, and if they seem to humans to be visible at times and have form, it is because we are seeing them with the "inner eye," and projecting them into a visible form. Saint Thomas Aquinas, for example, whose views on angels continue to influence popular belief, said they are "intellect without substance; pure thought forms." However, he added, they can take on a physical body if they wish, and it makes their jobs easier.

Still, the entire subject of angels — their existence, their appearance, their mission — has been debated throughout history. In ancient times, angels were perceived to be evil, and caused great fear among an ill-educated and superstitious-conscious populace. Today, angels are overwhelmingly believed to be good and friendly; guardian angels, for instance, look after us.

One of the most celebrated cases of angelic intervention for the good occurred in the 16th century, and involved Benvenuto Cellini, the master Italian goldsmith, sculptor and author. In the year 1535, Cellini had been thrown into a dark dungeon. In despair, he attempted to hang himself, however, as he later wrote, a tremendous invisible force "knocked him back," and an angelic youth appeared to him in a vision and lectured him about the importance of living. Cellini later was released from prison and went on to become one of the most famous artists of the Renaissance.

Today, the most prevalent concept is that angels are our personal companions, guides and protectors. Many people believe they are with us constantly and only intervene openly when we are in trouble and need help.

Whether one personally believes in the existence of angels or not, there are a couple of intriguing instances in Virginia history involving angelic intervention. Although both were widely reported at the time of their happenings, they have been all but forgotten since. One included a host of angels and was witnessed literally by thousands of people. The other case pertained to a reference to an angelic visit that helped solve a brutal murder case.

* * * * *

AND THE ANGELS SANG

Nearly a century ago, probably early in the 1900s — the exact date has been lost — a band of angels apparently descended over the old Wabash Camp Ground near Staffordsville in Giles County in the extreme southwestern part of Virginia to join in hymnal singing at a great revival service. At the time this was a well-known camp ground which had been built along Wabash Creek on the site of the older Chinquapin Camp Ground which dated back to 1809. Revivals were very popular in the 19th and early 20th centuries, and the area included a huge shed for worship services, plus shelters for families, mostly consisting of log cabins. It was not uncommon for such services to draw several thousand people from the mountains, hills and hollows.

It was at such a service, possibly during the first decade of this century, that the angels allegedly appeared. Oldtimers in Giles County still tell of it. In a book, the Reverend W. S. Barbery quotes the Reverend W. E. Bailey who was pastor of a circuit that included the Wabash Camp Ground area and was present at the time of the occurrence.

"The circumstance took place on Monday, the closing night of the meeting … It was estimated that 5,000 persons were present. A number had been at the altar and professed conversion. Brother Frazier turned to me during the singing of a hymn and said, 'Ed, start that old hymn, 'Jesus, Lover of My soul'.'

"As we started the second stanza of this song, W. N. Wagner

called out above the sound of the voices of the congregation, 'Listen! Listen! The redeemed hosts of heaven are singing! I can hear the voice of my mother!' I then heard the chorus, softer than human voices, but clearly distinguishable through the remainder of the stanza. A thrill came over the audience and many pressed toward the front of the building."

Testimony of other witnesses quoted by Barbery in his book declared that the scene inside the shed, or tent, was "indescribable, the atmosphere charged with intense spiritual emotion, many faces gazing upward radiant with rapture and amazement as they heard what they believed to be responsive singing by unseen heavenly beings."

Three quarters of a century later, in a newspaper column, writer Goodridge Wilson added: "Some people now living believe angels sang above the shed on the Wabash Camp Ground in harmony with human voices inside during the closing hymn of a great revival service. Many people of a generation now departed firmly believe as long as they lived on earth that they heard heavenly voices from an invisible choir sing that night in response to soul stirring singing by the congregation."

* * * * *

AN ANGELIC SOLUTION TO MURDER

In an old book, "Legends of Virginia Courthouses," an unusual murder case is discussed. Again, the date is uncertain, although it probably occurred sometime during the 19th century. The site was an isolated farm house in Powhatan County which mysteriously burned to the ground one night. Foul play was suspected, and, sure enough, when investigators searched through the smoldering ruins, they found the charred body of Mrs. Skipwith, an aged woman who owned the house. She was lying across the corpse of a man who had served as her overseer and had cultivated her farm.

There were no apparent clues. A heavy rain had fallen before dawn, obliterating any tracks which might have been left. The motive for such a crime was fairly obvious, however, because it was known that the overseer had gone to Richmond the previous day, sold Mrs. Skipwith's tobacco crop, and had returned to the house carrying a sizeable sum in currency.

With little else to go on, Milton Bonifant, commonwealth's attorney for the county, did the only thing he could. He rounded up and jailed a number of suspects, all of who were known to have disliked the overseer. He also incarcerated three boys who were known to have been away from home late the previous night.

To help him, Bonifant called in celebrated Richmond criminal lawyer Louis Wendenburg. It was evident to these gentlemen that a brutal murder had been committed and the farmhouse had been burned to cover up evidence of the crime. But persistent interrogation of the suspects revealed nothing. Bonifant and Wendenburg were stumped.

As the two men talked, Bonifant said that one man Wendenburg had not seen was a big Negro named Jenkins. Incredibly, Bonifant said he had locked this man up "mainly for the reason that he *looks* as if he is capable of any crime, but so far as I know he is harmless." Then, Bonifant added something that immediately piqued Wendenburg's interest. "He hasn't a great deal of sense," the commonwealth's attorney said, "but the Negroes

around here stand somewhat in awe of him because he professes to be able to commune with the spirits."

Wendenburg immediately asked to interview the prisoner, and that evening he was taken to the cell. He carried a 38-calibre revolver in his overcoat pocket in case trouble developed. They chatted for perhaps a half hour or so, when the lawyer asked about the alleged supernatural powers the man possessed. "Jenkins," he said, "they tell me you are a mighty lucky man. They tell me you can talk to the angels."

"Yes, I can," the Negro replied. Wendenburg expressed wonder at the captive's ability to commune with another world, and said he himself was greatly interested in spiritualism, and could Jenkins bring down an angel in the cell now. "I'd like to see one," he said. Jenkins answered that if he brought one down only he and not the lawyer could see it. Wendenburg then asked Jenkins to produce an angel, and the prisoner responded that he would, saying, "you just keep still a minute." He then rolled his eyes and made "a few vague gestures" with his hands. To Wendenburg, the Negro seemed to go into a trance-like state. He was "apparently oblivious to everything around him. His figure became rigid, his eyes set."

Suddenly, Jenkins exclaimed, "there's she!" Wendenburg asked if the angel could see him, and the reply was yes. He then asked if the angel could tell if his wife was all right. She had been running a fever. Jenkins said the angel said his wife would be fully recovered in a day or two. For the next two hours or so, the lawyer kept asking innocuous questions of Jenkins and his angel. Finally, as midnight grew near, he asked if the angel knew how Mrs. Skipwith's house had caught fire.

Still in his stuporized state, his eyes glazed, Jenkins, without thinking, said that of course the angel knew. She knew everything! She says they set fire to it. "Ask the angel," Wendenburg continued, "if anyone saw them set Mrs. Skipwith's house afire." Responding impulsively, as if in a hypnotic state, Jenkins said, "She say there was three boys what was down the road a watching to see if anybody was coming, and they got tired and come up to the house and watched behind the trees."

Wendenburg couldn't believe his luck. He felt the Negro was unwittingly incriminating himself. "Ask the angel if she can remember what the men who set fire to the house looked like." Again, the response came gushing out, "Sure she recollect. She say there was five of them. She knows them. There was one stranger among them."

The lawyer immediately surmised that the stranger was Jenkins himself, so he pressed the point: "Get her to tell me what the stranger looked like." He had pushed too far, however. Jenkins finally realized what was happening. He jumped from his chair, "made all sorts of wild gesticulations and went, apparently, almost into a frenzy." "She done gone!" he shouted.

"Bring her back," Wendenburg demanded. "You mean to tell me that with all your supernatural powers and after you have been talking to her for three hours, she vanishes without a moment's notice?" "She done gone," Jenkins repeated. "She done gone for good. These here angels they don't never stay out after twelve o'clock."

Wendenburg then went back to commonwealth attorney Bonifant, who had fallen asleep, roused him, and told him he knew the solution to the murder. The next morning he brought in one of the three boys who had been jailed and told him that one of the murderers of Mrs. Skipwith and the overseer had confessed, and that if the boy would tell what he knew of the crime the court would try to lighten his sentence.

The youth broke down. He said he and the other two boys had been stationed at a bridge not far away from the house, and had been told by the five men to watch out for anyone coming. They had watched from behind some trees through the windows. They had seen Mrs. Skipwith felled with two powerful blows of an axe. Then, when the overseer returned to the house from Richmond, they had seen him killed at point blank range with a shotgun. The men had then piled brush around the house and set it afire. Later, the other two boys gave similar accounts.

As a result, the five men, including Jenkins, were convicted and sent to the electric chair, and the three boys were given sentences of five years each.

The concluding paragraph in the "Legends of Virginia Courthouses" account states: "So far as is known, this was the only case in Virginia criminal history in which an angel was invoked to fix the guilt in a brutal murder. And, it may be added, had it not been for the testimony of Jenkins' angel, the probabilities are that the mystery would never have been solved."

The Devil In The
Old Dominion
(Statewide)

o understand why there was so much wide-spread belief among 17th century Virginia settlers in the presence of the Devil in the colony, one must reach back to the Old World origins of our forefathers. Through medieval and renaissance Europe, it was commonly accepted as fact that all infidels and pagans were really direct worshippers of evil as opposed to good, and of Satan instead of God. Such sentiment ran particularly strong in England, where King James himself, in 1597, declared that the Devil was present wherever he found the greatest ignorance and barbarity, and that the abuses of witchcraft, "derived directly from Satan," were most common in the wild parts of the world.

Such beliefs were carried to America with the first colonists, and the power and fear that they exerted was perhaps best exemplified in New England with the famous Salem witch trials of the late 1600s, which resulted in multiple executions. In Virginia, as early as 1613, there are written references that the first plantations had been made "to resolve the works of the Divell," and that "Satan visibly and palpably raignes there, more than any other known place in the world." Thus, while Virginia was considered the golden land of opportunity, it also was thought to be a favorite dwelling place of evil, and therefore a battle ground for the "forces of Light and Darkness."

Throughout that first century in America, it is written time and

again by everyone from Captain John Smith on, that the Indians found in the colony were really devils incarnate. It is somewhat understandable that in such a pervasive atmosphere of ignorance and superstition, that Indians would engender such conceptions. For example, when Smith was first captured by Indians, he wrote that "round about him these fiends danced a pretty while, and then came in three as ugly as the rest, with red eyes, and white stroakes over their black faces."

Smith and others also wrote of "diabolic religious sacrificial ceremonies," and of "child sacrifices." Virginia Indians at the time worshipped a spirit called Okee, whom settlers described as a "Devil who sucks under the left breast in the best witchcraft tradition." In fact, it was widely suspected among the colonists that Indian priests were, in the words of one early letter writer, "no other but such as our English Witches are."

Of course, the many tomahawk-wielding incursions and full scale attacks of the Indians on the settlers, including the bloody massacre of 1622, did little to diminish the feelings that the savages were indeed spurred by Satanic spirits. But, in time, the "blame" for foul deeds, perhaps influenced by the witch trials in New England, began to shift from the Indians to women colonists.

The first such person to be accused and tried in Virginia was a woman known as Goodwife Joan Wright, or more commonly, "Goody" Wright. She had lived at Kecoughtan, but later moved across the James River to Surry County. It is on record that she was summoned to court in 1626. The charges, in today's light seem ridiculous, but at the time they were taken very seriously.

Goody Wright was, for instance, accused of casting a spell over a young couple and their newborn baby, which caused them severe illness for several weeks. Goody, it was said, was irate when she was dismissed as being the mid-wife for the baby's delivery because she was left handed. Next, a man named Daniel Watkins testified that when he told the suspected witch that Robert Thresher was going to give two hens to a woman, Goody told him he was wasting his time because "the maide he meane to send them to will be dead before the henns come to her."

And when the woman did die, it naturally added to Goody's sinister reputation. Subsequently, a woman named Rebecca Graye told the court that Goody had prophesied correctly that she, a Mr. Felgate, and Thomas Harris should soon "bury their spouses," and that another woman who complained of a "cross man to my husband" was assured that she should bury him shortly — all of which, it is recorded, "came to pass."

Still, despite the strong feelings that ran rampant in Surry County, there is no record of any conviction or punishment for the suspected bewitchings of Goody Wright. Thirty years later there is a documented account of a William Harding of Northumberland County, being accused of "witchcraft sorcery etc." He was tried, found guilty by a jury of 24 men, and sentenced to receive "ten stripes upon his bare back and forever to be banished this county."

It was also in the 1650s that the only known execution of an alleged witch occurred in Virginia, or rather more specifically somewhere at sea presumably near Virginia. Her name was Kath Grady, and she had been accused of causing either a storm at sea or a period of sickness aboard ship during its sailing from England to the colony. At that time, witches' malignancy at sea was a common superstition.

* * * * *

THE (NOT SO) WICKED WITCH OF PUNGO
(Princess Anne County)

We come now to the most famous witch case in Virginia's history; that of the legendary Grace Sherwood of Princess Anne County. This occurred in the era of mass hysteria following the Salem witch trials. No one knows how or why Grace was singled out as being a bearer of tragic events, but she was. She was a hard working woman, the wife of a carpenter, and the mother of three sons raised in Virginia Beach.

Perhaps she was a particularly ugly woman, or outspoken, or just plain unlikable, or all three.

Whatever, official court records indicate she was first brought up on the charge of being a witch on March 3, 1697. But when she and her husband counter-sued for defamation of character against her accusers, the affair was settled out of court.

Less than a year and a half later, Grace was back on trial again, and she fought back with a fierce determination. The record tells this story: "At a court held the 10th of September 1698, James Sherwood and Grace his wife suing John Gisbourne and Jane his wife in an action of slander, setting forth by his petition that the defendant had wronged, defamed and abused the said Grace in her good name and reputation saying that she is a witch and bewitched their cotton and prays judgment." The jury didn't take long to rule in Grace's favor.

The accusations, however, had a distinctly negative effect on her reputation, and soon after there was another suit and counter-suit with the charges bordering on the ridiculous. This time the accuser was an Elizabeth Barnes. She said Grace stole into her room in the dead of night, jumped over her bed and "rode and whipped" her to the point where she was so scared she couldn't make a sound. If Mrs. Barnes had any lingering doubts about dealing with a witch, they were dispelled with the way Grace exited the room. "She went out of the key hole or a crack in the door like a black cat!", Mrs. Barnes told the court. After four days of trial, this case, too, was dismissed.

Grace next appeared in the records in 1705 when she brought suit against one Elizabeth Hill for having "assaulted, bruised, maimed and barbarously" beaten her because she had allegedly put a hex on Mrs. Hill. Grace asked for an award of 50 pounds for the offense. Although the justices ruled in her favor, they granted her only 20 shillings.

Even this was too much for the Hills to take, so consequently they filed a formal charge of witchcraft against Grace. And here, the much harassed housewife, now a widow, made a tactical error. She failed to appear for the trial, and the sheriff was ordered to "attach her body" to answer the charges at the next session of court.

Further, it was decreed that she be searched by a jury of women for "any tell-tale marks on her body" which would indicate that she was indeed a witch. It should be explained that in those unenlightened days it was thought that the special mark of a witch

Grace Sherwood

was commonly a third pap or "teat" in an abnormal position on a woman's body. This was said to be withered and senseless except when sucked by the Devil. In 1705, the Rev. John Bell of Gladsmuir explained, "This mark is sometimes like a little Teate; sometimes like a bluish spot; and I myself have seen it on the body of a confessing Witch like a little power mark of a bleak color, somewhat hard, and withal insensible, so as it did not bleed when I pricked it."

Grace consented to the search. On March 7, 1706, a jury of 12 women, with the aforementioned Elizabeth Barnes as forewoman, reported to the justices that it had found "Two things like titts with Several other Spotts." This apparently threw the learned judges into utter confusion. Nothing like this had ever happened before. With the deftness of politicians, they referred the case to the Royal Governor and Council and the Attorney General of the Virginia Colony in Williamsburg. They threw it right back to Princess Anne County.

On May 2, Grace was ordered to be held in lieu of bond, and the sheriff was instructed to search her house "and all Suspicious places Carefully for all Images & Such like things as may any way

Strengthen the Suspicion." Next, she was ordered to be searched again for suspicious marks on her body, but this time a panel of jury women couldn't be assembled. Many by now didn't believe that she was guilty and refused to take part even under the threat of being held in contempt of court. Some were terrified.

As more or less a last resort, the court said that Grace "should be tried in ye water by Ducking." The quaint belief then was that if you tied up a suspected witch with a rope secured around her right thumb and left big toe and left thumb and right big toe and threw her into a body of water and she swam or floated, she was indeed a witch. If she sank, she was not, and if she was lucky she would be pulled from the water before drowning. Again, Grace consented to the test, probably because she was tired of the whole sordid episode.

The trial by water was delayed once because, of all things, it was too rainy on the day of the first attempt. Some said it was the Devil who caused this postponement. Finally, on July 10, 1706, at 10 a.m., Grace was trussed up in the appropriate manner and readied for her dunking in the Lynnhaven River. The event apparently was well attended by hundreds of the curious.

Somehow, Grace survived. She did not sink. Amid a loud chorus of cheers and jeers, she bobbed to the top of the water. In this most curious fashion she was thus adjudged as being a witch. Afterwards, five courageous and "antient weomen" searched her body again and declared on oath that she "is not like ym nor noe other woman yt they knew of having two things like titts on her

private parts of a Black Coller being Blacker yn ye Rest of her Body."

Armed with such irrefutable evidence, the justices ordered the sheriff to commit her to the Common Gaol of the County and "there to secure her by irons." How long she remained in jail has been lost in time, but apparently she was dismissed and sent home within a relatively short period to live out her life with what dignity she could muster. The court records show no further mention of Grace Sherwood until she made out her will in 1733. She died seven years later.

There have been many preposterous legends associated with Grace over the past 300 years, but none are really needed. The true story of her real-life ordeal is strange enough in itself. It is also the reason why Witch Duck Road in Virginia Beach is known today as Witch Duck Road.

A Boiling Cauldron of Witches

(Various Counties)

race Sherwood was, without question, the most famous witch in Virginia history. The fear of witchcraft ran rampant in the colony, especially in the Princess Anne County (Norfolk-Virginia Beach) area during the last decade of the 17th century and well into the early 18th century. This fear moved westward with the pioneering settlers and continued to figure prominently in the mountains and hollows for the next 200 years. In fact, there are still remote, isolated pockets, mostly in the southwestern area of the commonwealth, where a belief in witchcraft still persists!

Such beliefs in witchcraft and in a variety of superstitions, seem to stem from the fact that many of the pioneers lived miles from any other mortal beings, and had little or no contact with the outside world. Any schooling at all was a rare luxury for the children of such families. Consequently, in the midst of ignorance, legends were born. Unusual natural phenomena, for example, was viewed with dread. The sighting of a comet, or a solar or lunar eclipse signalled an omen of extreme ill fortune.

In his "History of the Valley," written in the 1830s, Samuel Kercheval wrote: "The belief in Witchcraft was prevalent among the early settlers of the western country (then Virginia). To the witch was ascribed the tremendous power of inflicting strange and incurable diseases, particularly on children, of destroying cattle ... and a great variety of other means of destruction, of inflicting spells and curses on guns and other things ... More ample powers of mischief than these cannot be imagined.

"Wizards (also popularly known as witch doctors) were men supposed to be possessed of the same mischievous powers as the witches; but it was seldom exercised for bad purposes. The power of the wizards was exercised almost exclusively for the purpose of counteracting the malevolent influence of the witches of the other sex. I have known several of these witchmasters, as they were called," Kercheval continues, "who made a public profession of curing these diseases inflicted by the influence of witches; and I have known respectable physicians, who had no greater portion of business in their line of their professions, then many of those witchmasters had in theirs.

"The means by which the witch was supposed to inflict diseases, curses and spells, I never could learn ... Diseases which neither could be accounted for nor cured, were usually ascribed to some supernatural agency of a malignant kind.

"For the cure of diseases inflicted by witchcraft, the picture of the supposed witch was drawn on a stump or piece of board, and shot at with a bullet containing silver. This bullet transferred a painful and sometimes a mortal spell on that part of the witch corresponding with the part of the portrait struck by the bullet. Another method of cure was that of getting some of the child's water, which was closely corked up in a vial and hung up in a chimney. This complicated the witch with a strangury, which lasted as long as the vial remained in the chimney. The witch had but one way of relieving herself from any spell inflicted on her in any way, which was that of borrowing something, no matter what, of the family to which the subject of the exercise of her witchcraft belonged.

"I have known several poor old women much surprised at being refused requests (to borrow something) which had usually been granted without hesitation, and almost heart broken when informed of the cause of the refusal.

"When cattle or dogs were supposed to be under the influence of witchcraft, they were burned in the forehead by a branding iron, or when dead, burned wholly to ashes. This inflicted a spell upon the witch which could only be removed by borrowing.

"Witches were often said to milk the cows of their neighbors. This they did by fixing a new pin in a new towel for each cow intended to be milked. This towel was hung over her own door, and by means of certain incantations, the milk was extracted from the fringes of the towel after the manner of milking a cow. This happened when cows were too poor to give much milk."

That such beliefs were held dear by mountain folk well into the current century was accentuated in the 1930s and 1940s when teams of interviewers combed the hills during the Depression-era Virginia Writers' Project to gather area folklore. The one thing that most impressed these writers was the genuine sincerity of the people recounting tales that had been passed down, generation to generation, for more than 200 years. They still believed these accounts to be true.

One of the hotbeds of such lore was "Witch Mountain" a few miles northwest of tiny Hillsville, the county seat of Carroll County, just off U.S. Route 221 near Galax. This mountain was said to be inhabited (it may still be!) by a sect who believed in witches and practiced witchcraft. The region's physical characteristics lend credibility to such assertions. The mountain has been described as "a high, rugged, dark mass; full of cliffs that cast weird shadows, and high reaching pines with witch-like arms reaching out into the misty haze. It is queer that the sun, apparently, was never seen to shine on the mountain. Always, no matter when you look, it is dark, gloomy and austere — an awe inspiring sight, shrouded with gloomy forebodings, just such a place as one would suspect to see or hear something mysterious."

Such was the fear of Witch Mountain that "those who utterly disavowed any knowledge of those living along the range, were always anxious to make their journey along the path leading along the base by the safe light of the sun. Those traveling at night would go many miles out of their way to avoid it, for many were the tales of dreadful mysterious happenings along its ridges."

One unidentified project writer who grew up in the shadow of the mountain wrote, "Even now, as I recall the desolation and gloom of that rugged mass of earth, I hear the doleful murmur of the pines as they whispered evil forebodings, I seem to feel the hair stand up along the base of my neck, as I did when a boy going to visit my grandparents, or on some errand for my mother ... I always ran the entire distance, my heart beating like a trip-hammer. I dreaded the trip from one visit to another."

Herewith, then, are some of the legends of the hills and hollows as told to the project writers and others.

AUNT NANCY'S LAMB: "One year Lacy, my husband, had an ewe die when foaling, leaving two lambs. One of these he gave to another ewe with only one lamb, but she refused to take the other one, so he brought it to me and I raised it by hand. One morning it was off its food and I was right upset. I put it outside, thinking there was something it could find for itself, but it just ran around and around, butting into things, the same as if it was blind. The poor little fellow seemed determined to die in spite of all the simples I could brew.

"That night I had him wrapped up, and lying on the hearth by the fire when old Jim Largin, the best witch doctor in the county, stopped by to borrow an axe. I got him to look at the lamb. He said it was bewitched and told me to have Lacy bring in a plow share and put it in the fire and before it was red hot, someone would come in, but to leave it in the fire until the person began to get sick, and when they did, my lamb would be all right; but that I must pull the plow share out and pour cold spring water on it to cool it off in a hurry, or the person would die.

"I was willing to do anything to save my lamb, so I got Lacy up out of bed, and made him get the plow share for me and I built a hot fire around it, lit my pipe, and set down to wait. Pretty soon, I heard rapping on the lean-to door. I opened, and let in a woman called Kate Upp, who lived about halfway up on the side of Witch Mountain. She said she wanted to borrow my wool cards (brush-like tools used to clean and straighten wool for weaving), but I knew better than to lend anything to a witch, for if you do you put yourself in their power, so I said my neighbor had my cards, combing wool for her quilts.

"She sat down, and pretty soon leaned over saying she was feeling faint like and asked for a drink, and for me to crack the door. About this time the lamb began to scramble about and got up and nosed me, like he always did when he was hungry, so I pulled the plow share out of the coals and poured on the cold spring water like I was told, and Kate left. I have always worried about that, for late the same month, some neighbors found her dead, just off the path leading up the mountain, and I wondered if I had left the plow share in the fire too long."

AUNT LUCY'S BEWITCHED COW: "Aunt Lucy lived in Montgomery County, not far from Christiansburg. Her descendents remember and tell her actual experiences with witches. She was an intelligent and highly respected old lady, living a simple life on her farm when she became greatly alarmed and distressed when her favorite cow was bewitched, and she sent for the witch

doctor, who, after examining the cow, said: 'surely your cow is bewitched.' She at once suspected either a man or his wife who lived in the neighborhood. This man and wife were considered very peculiar; they were poor, superstitious, ignorant people, whose habits and manners, also their mode of living, indicated that they had strange, uncanny beliefs.

"Aunt Lucy proceeded to try the old remedy so well known among the craft. She secured a silver dime and fashioned it into a bullet, with which she loaded her gun; then made two pictures, one of each of the suspected witches and fastened them to the side of her house, one over the other, and shot a hole through them, thus killing the witch. Her cow was immediately relieved of the 'spell' and her milk pure as before.

"This legend has been handed down to the third and fourth generation and related as an actual occurrence by those whose integrity and veracity cannot be questioned."

A similar tale involved an old man by the name of Tony Burris, a farmer who lived on the mountainside. "He observed that all his milch cows failed at one time to give any milk. He believed Polly Holders, a very poor, superstitious old woman, had bewitched his cows. He drew a picture of the old woman and shot it with a silver bullet. He hit the picture in the hip and, at the same time, old Polly Holder, the witch, was seized with a severe pain in her hip from which she could get no relief. Of course, the spell was broken and the cows gave milk as before. Polly was taken to the Grayson County Poor house where she died."

AUNT GRANNY'S PUNISHMENT: "In or about the year 1800, there lived a family on Bridle Creek in Grayson County. There lived with this family an old woman called 'Granny the witch.' Stephen Ward with his family moved into the county and settled on an adjoining farm. Soon, some trouble arose between the two families, and at the same time Mr. Ward's cow began to give bloody milk. Aunt Granny was accused of bewitching the cow. Mr. Ward learned in some way how to break the 'spell' and relieve the cow of the malady.

"One morning he milked the cow and put the milk in a vessel which he placed over a hot fire in his home. He then went out and got three peach tree switches, and as the milk boiled, he whipped all of it out of the vessel into the fire and it was consumed by the flames and hot embers, producing a peculiar kind of smoke.

"When the task was completed, a boy came running from the home where Granny lived and said: 'All of you come quick, Granny is very sick. She wants you to come over and see her.' Mrs. Ward replied: 'Damn her, let her die.' None of them would go to see her. Other people who did go said: 'Her eyes were about smoked out, and she had marks all over her face like she had been whipped.' The Wards were never bothered again with the cow giving bloody milk!"

GRANDMA'S BEWITCHED BETSY: "There lived on Back Creek, in Roanoke County, about five miles south of Roanoke, an old woman in an old house, built in the early 1800s, who was a firm believer in witches. The following was told by her grand-daughter as an actual occurrence.

"When I was a small girl I went to help grandma pick the seeds out of her cotton. Soon after supper I left grandma to wash the dishes and went into the room where the cotton was stored and lighted a candle. Soon, grandma came in and threw up her hands in holy horror, dashed across the room, and put out the candle. She excitedly exclaimed, 'Don't you know better than to light a candle so soon after dark. The witches will come snooping around.

"The next morning, grandma sent me to the barn to feed the horses. I noticed old Betsy, the gray mare, refused to eat. She stood motionless, with drooped head, seemingly exhausted. I rushed to the house and told grandma that something was the matter with Betsy. 'There now,' said grandma, 'I told you the witches would come last night.'

"Grandma got some asafoetida and tied it up in a little cloth bag and attached a long string to it and hung it around Betsy's neck. This broke the spell and drove the witch away. Soon, Betsy was all right again."

AN EYE FOR AN EYE? Somewhere near Bristol, a settler a long time ago had a flock of sheep. Suddenly, his sheep began to die, but no apparent cause could be found. Believing them to be bewitched, he hired a witch doctor who told him to go home and skin out the shoulder of a sheep and put it in an oven and bake it. While doing this, he was, by no means, to allow anyone to come in the house and borrow or steal anything from the house.

So the man followed the instructions, and began baking the sheep shoulder. Two hours after he started, a neighbor woman came to the house and asked to borrow some meal. She was refused. Then she asked for some water, and they told her they had brought no water up to the house that day. She left, but was soon seen approaching again, "walking faster than before." She seemed edgy and couldn't stand still. She then asked what they were baking, and she even tried to accidentally overturn the oven.

Finally, she left again, but within minutes was seen running back to the house. "For God's sake," she screamed, pointing to the oven, "get that off there! You are killing me. Look here!" She ripped off her blouse and exposed her own shoulder, "baked to the same crisp brown as the mutton shoulder!"

Quaint Customs and Strange Superstitions
(Statewide)

raditions die hard in the hills and hollows of backwoods Virginia, especially in the southwestern end of the state. One can still find there today isolated pockets deep in the mountains where the lifestyle leans more toward the 19th century than the 20th. Ancient superstitions doggedly flourish in these remote regions. Many of these deep-seated beliefs were brought over by the early settlers from the rural districts of mother countries ... England, Ireland, Scotland, Germany and others. Some legends were learned here from American Indians, and have been absorbed in the mountain culture.

Of course, the origins of superstitions date back to mankind's earliest days. They are the outgrowth of fear and ignorance, founded in primitive man's efforts to understand and explain the phenomena around him. These notions and beliefs were handed down through the ages as if they were contagious, and were prominently observed by such advanced civilizations as the Egyptians, Chaldeans, Grecians, Romans and others.

As the early Virginia settlers moved west into the hills and valleys, many, for generations, lived far removed from populated areas. Children, kept busy with farm work, had no time for school, and as the years passed, the superstitions and omens continued to hold considerable influence.

Newspaper columnist Lloyd Mathews once said, "In my years

of living among people of the hills, I have run across those whose very lives are guided and regulated by superstition day to day, year to year. There are certain things that may be done, and others that may not, lest bad luck follow. At the same time, there are many good omens, so the man who is careful to observe the signs, and abide by them, can just about control his destiny. There are enough mountain superstitions right here among us to write a book. Yet the majority of people, if asked if they were superstitious, would answer in the negative."

Funeral procedures stemming from superstition vary greatly — from laying offerings in the graves of loved ones to make their life easier in the next world — to driving stakes through the hearts of the departed to ensure they never come back. In the Eastern part of the world, cremation was thought to be an ideal "send off," in that it was believed the soul or spirit was helped on its way up to heaven by the flames, while the body was destroyed so that it could not haunt the earth. Burial, conversely, was designed to preserve the body, either because of the popular belief in the "Day of Judgment," or because the physical body was thought to be needed in the afterlife.

It has been, of course, fairly common practice to bury possessions with the dead. Ancient Egyptians interred riches, ornaments and household objects with bodies, expecting a "rich and luxurious" life after death. Vikings laid to rest their warriors with weapons at their sides, expecting a fight wherever they went. Such gifts had the purpose of pacifying the dead so they would not be tempted to return to their former residences as ghosts. In fact, the custom of placing wreaths of flowers atop and around coffins was originally meant not only to honor the dead with beauty, but also to act as a 'magic circle' to contain the departed soul and stop it from "wandering."

Furthering this theme, dead people in Scandinavia were buried with their shoes, so they could walk comfortably to the next world, and Zuni Indians placed bread with warriors who had passed on so they would not go hungry and come back looking for food. Twenty-five hundred years ago, wives, slaves and horses were buried alive when their kings died, to serve them in their next lives.

According to authorities, one of the purposes of placing tombstones over gravesites was to make sure the spirits were kept safely below ground.

Of all the curious European superstitions Virginia settlers

brought to the New World with them, perhaps the most bizarre came from England. There, up until the first quarter of the 19th century, those who committed suicide were banned from being buried in consecrated ground. They were, instead, interred at a crossroads and a stake was driven through the heart of the dead person. The tradition arose because at that time it was believed that people buried outside a churchyard would come back as malign ghosts to "torment the living," unless they were pinned to one spot by a stake. Also, if the spirit did somehow get free, it then would be "confused" by the choice of roads when it arose to the surface.

A great number of Virginia superstitions seem to center around death, dying and the sick, including how to treat the sick. In the fine book, "Romantic and Historic Virginia," author A. Hyatt Verrill, a half century ago, talked about some unusual practices regarding funerals. "The body, enclosed in a rough box of unplaned, whip-sawed or hewed boards, is carried to the grave and buried without services ... once the corpse is disposed of, the incident is ended ... and it is not unusual for a man to marry or 'take on' a new wife — often a sister of the departed spouse — as soon as her predecessor is under ground.

"Usually, too, a funeral is regarded as a sort of fiesta, to be celebrated by abstaining from all work ... and getting gloriously drunk on 'white mule.' ... The bodies are invariably interred with their feet toward the east, and always two shovels are crossed above the grave."

Author Verrill continues: "There are no monuments erected, but it is customary to place a good-sized boulder at the head of the grave with a smaller stone at the foot, and sometimes the name of the deceased will be roughly scratched upon the headstone when some member of the community is present who can form letters. But as the stones from the older graves are frequently removed and placed at the newer mounds, all traces of the identity of the dead are soon lost.

"To the hollow folk, this is desirable rather than otherwise, for they believe that to speak or even think of the dead will encourage ghosts or 'haunts;' and they shun the burial grounds on the stone-riddled hillsides and never go near except when it becomes necessary to inter another body."

In the upper echelons of Virginia society, funerals were looked upon, not only as solemn occasions, but also as opportunities for lavish feasts and parties. When someone died at a grand plantation, for instance, messengers were dispatched by horseback and by boat to notify friends and family, and they would assemble from miles around, some staying for days. Food and drink often cost far more than the coffin and other traditional expenses. There is on record the funeral feast of a Mrs. Frances Eppes, in 1678, which included a steer, three sheep, five gallons of wine, two gallons of brandy, 10 pounds of butter and eight pounds of sugar. They must have had a great time laying John McClanahan to rest in 1774, for among the provisions for mourners were three gallons of wine and 19 gallons of spirits.

Here are a few more superstitious beliefs, as collected from a number of sources:

* The dead are always to be buried "facing Jerusalem."

* The howling of the dog is considered a portent of death and calamity. (This dates to the time when men made deities of animals. As a deity, the dog was supposed to be able to foresee death and give a warning of it by howling and barking.) The presence of a strange black dog in a house also foretold death.

* To hear a ringing or "bell" in one's ears is a certain warning of impending doom. However, the ringing of bells or a death knell for the deceased is a very old custom which originated from a desire to frighten away the evil spirits that lurk about the dead body.

* If a sick person is changed from one room to another, it is a sign that he or she will soon die.

* Anyone who counts the carriages in a passing funeral will expire within a year.

* To accidentally burn sassafras wood in a fire means the death of some member of the household in the immediate future. The same fate awaits if three chairs are accidentally placed in a row.

* If there are cedar trees to be set out, let Mother Nature do it, because as surely as the tree that you set out gets large, someone very close is sure to die.

* Turn the mirror to the wall when someone lies dead in the house. Whoever looks into the mirror at such a time will also meet their Maker. (This superstition is practiced to "avoid seeing the evil spirits which cause death.")

* Other ominous omens include: a shooting star; a comet (foretold impending war or tragedy); an open umbrella held over the head while indoors; the cry of an owl or the screech of a raven; to hear a cock crow during the nighttime; or to have a wild bird fly into one's house.

* In some mountain areas, a black cat crossing in front of some-

one is not nearly as bad as having a gray cat do it.

* If one sees a new moon through the boughs of trees, clouds, or other obstructions, that person will have "a month of trouble."

If one travels the backroads even today in Rockingham County (Harrisonburg area), and in neighboring counties, he or she might still see some visible reminders of a bygone era, designed to ward off evil spirits. They are the hex signs on barns and other out buildings on the farms of descendents of Pennsylvania Dutch settlers in the Shenandoah Valley. The signs are in the form of circular symbols and birds. The tradition is that such signs, in generations now past, were used in the belief that they were helpful in keeping away witches and other bad spirits.

Many traditions center around New Year's day. First, one should eat black-eyed peas, and for best results, cook them with hog jowls. Never visit on this day, but if you must, be sure to exit by the same door you entered. And don't carry out ashes on New Year's. If you do, all of your coal and wood burned during the year will turn to ashes instead of heat.

Never tell of a bad dream before breakfast, for if you do, it will surely come true. Never give a friend a knife, lest you want to cut off your friendship. If you are suffering from a witch's spell, make a picture of the enemy and bury it under the 'drip' of the house.

And, of course, there are the customs involving cures. Some of these were handed down by ancestors; others probably came from Indians. Among the substances to be used in case of illness are: boneset, camomile, mandrake, ginseng, catnip, sassafras, wintergreen, mint, jimson weed, kidneywart, sarsaparilla, snakeroot and other medicinal plants. Also to be used are salves and linaments of birch and balm of Gilead, balsam, witch hazel, and bears' grease! The best remedy for snakebite? Raw moonshine. (It wasn't clear whether one injested it or had it poured on the wound.)

In the 1800s and early 1900s many mountain folks contracted tuberculosis. The best cure for this was said to be to swallow a live snail each night for a period of nine days! If the first nine fail to do the job, the dose may be repeated several times. The presence of snails in one's stomach, where they were supposed to remain alive for several days, was thought to be "objectionable to the devil or evil spirit responsible for the disease, while slime exuded by the snails was supposed to find its way to the patient's lungs and cure them."

There were, and in some instances probably still are, superstitious fears of ghostly or evil natural phenomena. Witches'

Mountain near Galax, for example has long been believed to be the lair of area witches who cast dark spells on anyone who crosses them. Tinker Mountain, just north of Roanoke, is better known as Dead Man's Mountain because its shape resembles a person lying in a grave. Still heard are claims that Oakton Mountain, "blooms" once every seven years, indicating a vast gold horde hidden there. Others are convinced the brilliant golden-yellow light that brings the crags into sharp relief and sends lambent flames upward to the peak of the mountain represent the manifestation of a "malignant devil" who dwells there.

Samuel Kercheval, author of the "History of the Valley," written in the 1830s, acknowledged that such superstitions represented "an endless variety of sources of hope and fear, with regard to the good and bad fortunes of life … " But, he added: "While dreams, the howling of the dog, and the croaking of the raven are prophetic of future events, we are not good Christians. While we are dismayed at the signs of heaven, we are for the time being pagans. Life has real evils enough to contend with, without imaginary ones."

Sound advice. But the traditions of the hill people in the backwoods of Virginia die hard. And, really, who's to say?

CHAPTER 42

Of Monsters, Mythical and Otherwise

(Southwest Virginia, Loudoun County, and Richmond)

(Author's note: In my previous volume on Virginia ghosts (1993), I discussed claimed sightings of a "Big-Foot-type" creature on Quantico and in Augusta County. I also included four incidents of spectral dogs in various parts of the state. And in my book, "The Ghosts of Charlottesville and Lynchburg and Nearby Environs," I reported on the appearance of an albino beast of unspecified nature which appeared in Orange County near the home of James Madison, fourth President of the United States. I had also heard mention of a legendary talking cat in Danville, although I was never able to track this down. The fact that animals play an important part in Virginia's ghost lore is further confirmed by the following episodes which have been uncovered in recent research.)

AN OBSCENE AND BLASPHEMOUS VISION

 uthor Frank Raflo, in his interesting short book on Loudoun County ghosts, published in 1978, relates a tale from a then-84-year-old man who told of a bizarre experience his two aunts had sometime during the first decade of the 20th century. The man was living with the aunts at Short Hill Mountain near Hillsboro. The two women went out one night to fetch some water from their pumps, when they heard "violent cursing" apparently aimed at them. The oaths seem to emanate from a grape vine that wound around the lattice over the front porch.

Shaken, one of the aunts called for help, and her husband ran out carrying a gun. As he did, the "thing" leaped out of the lattice work and ran to a fence in the yard. As it did, the two women and the man, astonished, all said they saw the same thing —"an animal about the size of a bobcat, perched on a fence, with *a man's head on it!*" The man fired at the creature, but it bounded off into the woods, and the man was too afraid to follow it in the darkness.

This report in itself, of course, might be challenged as imaginations run wild, were it not for a separate and confirming incident which occurred in an old house in Round Hill about three years later. The house, which has since been destroyed by fire, had been abandoned for some years and had garnered a reputation in the area as being haunted.

As author Raflo reported, a young man, dared by his peers, agreed to spend the night in the house. According to his account, everything was peaceful until about two a.m. It was then that he was startled "by the sounds of violent cursing." Suddenly, he said, an animal "about the size of a bobcat, but with the head of a man," appeared out of the darkened room and jumped on the table in front of him. The beast then said, "it looks like you and I are the only ones here tonight."

Terrified, the young man instinctively leaped out an open window and ran as hard as he could toward Hillsboro. Minutes later, winded and exhausted by the shock of what he had seen, he stopped to catch his breath. He looked up and stark fear overtook him again as he saw the horrendous beast perched on a fence in front of him. "We have had quite a chase, haven't we," the thing said. This time the man found enough composure to respond, "we sure did, but that isn't half the chase we are going to have!" With that he took off running again. He didn't stop again until he found himself in the Short Hill cemetery at Hillsboro, a distance estimated at several miles. There, in the stillness amid the tombstones, the man at last found himself alone. Whatever it was he had seen had disappeared.

Raflo points out that it would have been highly improbable that the young man had ever heard about the previous sighting at Round Hill.

* * * * *

ON THE TRACK OF THE WAMPUS CAT

ales of a giant cat which measures about four or five *feet* in length and walks on its hind legs have circulated in the mountains of southwestern Virginia and eastern Kentucky for well over a century. Scores of residents of this area have told of seeing such a creature — called a Wampus Cat — and the stories have been passed down generation to generation.

Folklorist Charles Edwin Price, in his 1993 book, "The Mystery of Ghostly Vera, and Other Haunting Tales of Southwest Virginia," tells of interviewing one man in Wise County whose father and grandfather both said they had run into such a cat. His father had been particularly lucid in his recollection. He had been out chopping wood one day when a huge cat-like animal appeared in a clearing in the adjacent woods. He described it as being fully four or five feet tall, and standing on two legs." It stared at him "eyes like fire." After a minute or two, it ambled off into the woods.

Price says such a cat has reportedly been sighted in places stretching from Chattanooga, Tennessee, to Roanoke, Virginia. Always, only one cat is seen, and Price believes it is the same one, and that it is, indeed, a ghost. He bases his assumption on an ancient Cherokee legend in which a young woman, to ward off a demon spirit, covered her face with a mask made from the preserved face of a wildcat. Such a sight, a woman wearing a wildcat's mask, Price surmises, might look very similar to the descriptions given of the Wampus Cat, thus it might be the woman's spirit which is occasionally seen.

Further emphasis is added to this ethereal theory by the fact that a man named Tim Smith, of Bristol, recently reported seeing such a vision on a street in downtown Abingdon. He said he saw two eyes peering at him through some iron steps and they looked not like human eyes, but more like those of a cat. When he shouted at whatever it was, he said he heard the distinct "hiss of a cat," and then both he and his wife saw "something" running away and disappearing into the darkness. They both agreed that it looked exactly like a huge cat running on its hind legs!

* * * * *

THE GREEN-EYED "MONSTER" OF RICHMOND

n July 1935, the Richmond Times Dispatch headlined a story that there was a haunted house "right in the middle of town." This helped stir a veritable sensation that lasted for several weeks, drew thousands of curious onlookers, including scores of experts on psychic phenomena, and spawned dozens of reported sightings and claims, some bordering on the outrageous.

It all began, simply enough, when a widow named Mrs. Georgia "Georjie" Douglas moved with her two daughters and two grandchildren into a rented house at 418 West Main Street. On their first night there they "retired early, only to be tormented for the rest of the night with a thumping under the floor." At first everyone assumed it to be a stray dog, and they ignored the racket which persisted for about three weeks.

It was then that Mrs. Douglas had a frightful experience that could not be ignored. One night at about midnight she heard a knock at the back door. She opened the door, but there was nothing there. There came a second knock. This time as she opened the door, as the Times Dispatch quoted her, "there stood a creature that looked like it was half dog and half sheep." Too horrified to move, Mrs. Douglas stood there for a few seconds, and the thing disappeared. She said it "had a face like a bulldog and a body of a sheepshound. It's ears, about a foot long, stood straight out, and it had two green eyes like a monster!"

The newspaper account created a storm of excitement. Neighbors and others came to the house and said they, too, heard the strange noises coming from beneath the kitchen floor. Soon after, more than 100 onlookers were present when the floor was torn up and four men crawled under the house to search for the source. They found "the tracks of a creature which apparently had four feet, each about the size of a human hand, with claws about 10 inches long."

At this point the entire city had become entranced with the phantom monster. Two nights later, more than 2,000 people came to the house in hopes of catching a glimpse of the green-eyed phenomenon. In such a carnival-like atmosphere, the absurd became the ordinary. People suggested it was: a giant coon; an opossum; a badger; an alligator; a crocodile; a beaver; an otter; an owl; a peacock; bear cubs; a polecat; an interbred dog and coon, opossum and cat, and a panther and beaver. Many others said it was "not of this world, but is a spirit in transit." A circus representative offered Mrs. Douglas $50 cash for it. A woman said it was a ghost. "That thing is a ghost trying to tell you where there's some money hidden," she wrote.

As the tension caused by the mystery beast mounted, fear literally overcame some Richmonders. One night a young woman visiting in the house fainted when a dog scurried by. On another evening more than a score of young boys crept up to the house, and when one announced "I hear it," they all ran away as fast as they could.

Such fears were fanned when two "ghost hunters" crawled under the house one night and found a woman's red hat and black pocketbook, and some suspicious bones. However, they proved to be the "relics of hams, chops, roasts and T-bone steaks." But then a story surfaced that the house had once been a gambling house and bar, and as the newspaper emphasized, "some remembered that a man had been killed in a card game and his body had never been found, and suggested that it was his ghost that was tormenting the neighborhood." To this report, Mrs. Douglas said that when she had moved in she had found a stain on the front-room floor that "no amount of strong lye soap had removed." People then told her that human blood could not be washed up.

Next came a report that an apartment house across the alley from the residence had once been a hideout for two "notorious criminals recently executed in Virginia's electric chair." Two local citizens then actually told the Times Dispatch that they had seen a ghost that had the body of one of the criminals and the face of the other.

"Ever since they heard about it," Mrs. Douglas said, "thousands of people have worried me with their suggestions. The crowd makes more noise than the thing that thumps!" So bothersome had the nightly crowds become, in fact, that some neighbors cascaded them with "tubs of water." It didn't deter the curious at all. It got so bad that realty agents, worrying about damage to their property, came out and nailed a cover over the monster's entryway beneath the back porch.

Traps were set, but these were eluded for several nights. Finally, one night three trappers successfully snared the evasive beast who turned out not be a representative from the other world after all.

The cause of weeks of excitement and fear all across the great city was …. . an opossum carrying a set of quintuplets in its pouch!

* * * * *

243

THE HAIR-RAISING 'THING' OF HIGHLAND COUNTY

f one can envision the map of Virginia as the silhouetted outline of a shoe then Highland County would be about the tip of the tongue. It is appropriately named, resting high in the Alleghany Mountains on the West Virginia border. It was here, many years ago, that the legend of a mysterious "thing" surfaced around Dixon's Hill, a windswept area near Corbett's Store at Mustoe; an otherworldly phenomenon that remains unsolved to this day.

One witness was a woman named Gladys Ryder Griffith who grew up on a farm in the region. From her early teens, she recalls family members talking about seeing and hearing "strange things." One manifestation was the sound of a crying baby when they went to fetch a bucket of water at a nearby spring. The crying would be heard until they would get down the hill some distance from the spring.

"I heard this several times myself, and it would make you shiver," Mrs. Griffith said. But this feeling paled in comparison to subsequent encounters with "the thing." She first heard about it from oldtimers in Highland County. They told of the night two balls of fire suddenly appeared out of nowhere and then disappeared. They told of hearing awful sounds, like a goose in distress. They told of several people coming across the hill one Sunday night. As they got up to a fence, "The thing" got into one young man's hair and frightened him so badly that he passed out and his friends had to carry him away. He never would go that way again.

Mrs. Griffith, then a spunky teenager, heard all these stories and "laughed at them." She felt secure with the knowledge that her father had once told her that if she ever encountered anything out of the ordinary to say, "In the name of the Father and the Son and the Holy Spirit, what do you want?"

And so, armed with this thought, she set out one Sunday evening with her boyfriend and a nine-year-old girl determined "to satisfy her curiosity." After attending church at Dry Branch, they walked toward the hill. "The moon was bright," she said, "and everyone could see quite clearly." When they got to the fence where "the thing" had scared the boy earlier, they stopped to rest. The three of them sat on the fence with Mrs. Griffith's arm linked through her boyfriend's arm.

It was then that they first heard the noise. She said it seemed to come up from a sinkhole below. "It kept coming up by the fence and getting closer." Her boyfriend said it was just a sheep under a tree. Suddenly, "something like a strong wind brushed her off the fence. She was so startled she forgot to say the words her father had taught her.

"The 'thing' climbed the fence and jumped down behind our backs," she said, but she saw nothing, even in the clear moonlight. Whatever "it" was, it followed the three of them down the path, "blowing down their necks." Mrs. Griffith said she was so scared and became so weak she could hardly walk.

Thereafter, whenever anyone talked about the Highland County "thing," Mrs. Griffith exclaimed, "I would know it was true. This is so true that I will make oath on a stack of Bibles!"

* * * * *

THE PHANTOM AT POLE CAT HOLLOW

(Author's note: The following account is taken from the James Taylor Adams collection housed in the archives of the Blue Ridge Institute of Ferrum College, and is reprinted courtesy of Clinch Valley College and the Blue Ridge Institute. Here, Adams interviewed Finley Adams on May 7, 1941.)

One time, oh it's been 40 years ago I guess, Buck Gibson lived down there on Smoot. Si Adams and Rob Holcombe got together and made up to go and get some liquor and go down to Buck's and get him drunk and have a big time. So they kotch their nags and pulled out right up the head of Smoot, going through by Sandlick Gap. Si told me about it. He said they was goin' ridin' along, the path just wide enough for one hoss. Rob was in front and they'd got right up there above Pole Cat Hollow when all at once Si seed Rob's hoss rare up on his hind feet and he heard Rob holler out sumpin.'

"He looked and jes ahead of 'em there, right in the middle of the path, was the awfulest lookin' thing he ever seed. It looked like a dog, but it was bigger than any cow he ever seed. Big as a hoss. It seemed to be settin' back on its hind parts in the road and its eyes was as big as plates and shone jes like fire.

"His hoss seed it, too, and began to rare and pitch. Rob's hoss wouldn't go another step. So there they was. They tried to go round it, but the hosses wouldn't go. The thing opened its mouth and Si said he could see down its throat and it looked like a roarin' furnace of fire. They decided it was the Devil and that it was there to turn 'em back from goin' after liquor. So they jes turned round and went back home and left it settin' there in the road."

Vampires In Virginia?

(Statewide)

he following item ran in the Alexandria Gazette 100 years ago: "The announcement on the streets this morning that grave robbers had visited this city last night and 'resurrected' several bodies from their resting places in the cemeteries, created a profound sensation, it being the first time that such a bold attempt at 'body snatching' was ever made in Alexandria. The bodies of two persons were taken from their graves, but before they could be 'spirited away,' the men who came for them were detected, when they fled, leaving the corpses lying on the cold earth beside the graves where they had been interred."

Such incidents were not unknown in Virginia in those days. There had been, for instance, a celebrated case reported in 1897 at the old city cemetery in Lynchburg were "rumors of sinister activities in the graveyard in the dead of night began to spread, causing terror among white and colored people whose relatives were buried there." An account at the time said, "newly buried bodies were disinterred by stealth, carried to the tool house, and prepared for shipment in barrels ... "

In the Lynchburg incident it was learned that the bodies were being sent to medical centers for use in experiments and teaching. This was also suspected of the Alexandria occurrence, with one intriguing exception. One of the bodies there was said to have been found with "two ridges around the wrist of each arm." This caused some morbid speculation that a vampire or its helpers had been at work!

Could this be?

What exactly is a vampire anyway? Isn't it a myth, a totally fictional character invented by the macabre imaginations of such brilliant writers of the dark as Bram Stoker, who authored the immortal work, "Dracula"?

Not necessarily so. A vampire, says Italian author Ornella Volta, who wrote a definitive book on the subject, is "a dead person who survives his (or her) own death by feeding on the blood of the living ... It also means anyone with a thirst for human blood ... and by a curious inversion of sense, is also applied to the living who disturb the peace of the grave as well as to the dead who arise to trouble the sleep of the living ..."

There seem to be some historical precedents supporting the fact that vampires indeed may have existed, especially in sections of eastern Europe in past centuries. According to Paul Barber, who wrote a book titled, "Vampires, Burial and Death," in the early 17th century, "a Serbian fell off a haywagon and into history as one of the most notable examples of documented 'vampirism.' The ex-soldier broke his neck and died from the fall, but soon after his burial he began to harass townspeople, even killing four of them. Suspecting evil, authorities exhumed his body and observed a lack of decay, fresh blood, and other 'evidence' that he was a vampire. At that point, the body was disposed of in a way supposed to eliminate further possibility of mischief, and the 'haunting' stopped. (His body was burned and his ashes scattered.) Similar tales have persisted for centuries all over the world, and the belief in vampires and others who rise from the grave is widespread."

In a book on "Strange Stories and Amazing Facts," editors of the Reader's Digest noted that "Travelers who visited remote parts of Transylvania in the 16th century returned with strange and horrifying tales of creatures that were neither living nor dead ... creatures that left their haunts at night and feasted on human blood." Such a species, it was noted, "is said to be recognizable by its gaunt appearance and pale complexion. It is said to have full, red lips and pointed canine teeth; gleaming eyes with a hypnotic gaze; long, sharp fingernails; eyebrows that meet; and hair on the palms of its hands. Its breath is said to be foul, and its diet of blood endows it with superhuman strength, despite its cadaverous, emaciated appearance."

And, in his book "World of Strange Phenomena," Charles Berlitz says that Bram Stoker's novel, "Dracula," was, in fact, based on "the blood-thirsty career of a real person." He was Wallachian Prince Vlad IV, also known as Vlad the Impaler, who ruled 15tl century Rumania with an "iron fist and sharpened stake." H earned his nickname because of his penchant for the wooden stake as a favorite tool of torture. Berlitz says thousands of Turkish soldiers and civilians, thrust on poles staked in the ground, died in agony at his hands.

"Vlad would dine among his writhing victims," Berlitz wrote, "supping and bathing in their life-fluid. So tightly did his terrible reputation grip the countryside that when he died in 1477, rumors surfaced that he rose from the dead in search of even more blood." The author concluded that such stories may have contributed to the popular notion that the only way in which to stop a vampire's deadly depredations was to plunge a wooden stake through its still-living corpse.

There is documentation, too, that not all vampires were men. Elizabeth Bathory, born in 1560, married Carpathian Count Ferencz Nadasdy at the age of 15. She was said to have been very beautiful. As she grew older, she desperately sought any means to maintain her beauty. This included the killing of servants and others so that Elizabeth might rejuvenate herself by bathing in their blood. Eventually, one victim escaped. Elizabeth's accomplices were executed and she was judged to be insane and walled up in her room for life.

The publication of Stoker's novel of "Dracula" caused a sensation of fear around the world; a fear that was further enflamed in Virginia with the breakout late in the 19th century of grave robbing. It was amidst such a swirling atmosphere of horror that a legend of a real-life vampire in the Old Dominion first surfaced. It occurred in the 1890s, during a boom period in and around Big Stone Gap in the extreme southwestern part of the state.

It began when a local farmer found two of his prize cows slaughtered in the field. This in itself was not particularly noteworthy, because wild animals such as bears and wolves roamed the woods freely in those days. What made this gruesomely unusual was the *way* the cows had been destroyed. Both beasts had been dismembered, leaving only the head and hindquarters of each remaining in the field. And, *both had been drained of blood!* Over a period of time other domestic animals were found butchered in the same manner.

Suspicion centered around a reclusive European known only by the name of Rupp. He had been among the thousands of outsiders and foreigners who descended on this rural area in the hopes of finding instant wealth in the mines there. Rupp lived in a crude log cabin deep in the woods far from any other human. He was rarely seen in town. The suspicion arose when two boys came upon his cabin, and, through a window, saw the hermit sitting before his fireplace eating a large piece of raw meat. The boys said it looked like the leg of a cow.

At this point, superstition and speculation ran wild, and the townspeople demanded that the sheriff arrest Rupp. But the law officer had no evidence. No one had seen him kill the cows, and, after all, there was no law against eating raw meat. Then, a few weeks later, the town drunk was missing. No one had seen him for days. Some time later, his body was found in the woods, completely drained of blood, and with an arm and a leg missing. The site was only a quarter of a mile from Rupp's cabin, yet still no action was taken.

But when a second murdered man, a traveling salesman, was found in the woods near Rupp's place — his body also missing limbs and drained of blood — a number of vigilantes decided to take matters into their own hands. Armed to the teeth, they marched at night to the cabin. The door was unlocked and when they went in they recoiled in horror. The smell was overpowering. Body parts were strewn all over the floor, a scene which sent several of the men outside, retching.

Rupp was nowhere around. The men then set fire to his cabin and it burned to the ground. A posse was formed the next morning and the surrounding woods were thoroughly searched, but nothing was found. Rupp was never seen again. But stories of his spectral return are still told in the Big Stone Gap area.

And, finally, there is a letter the author received from Jon Gary Boze of Richmond some years ago. Boze wrote that he had some supernatural experiences of his own. "My grandmother was a medium, and could tap a kitchen table up a flight of stairs by herself! I have seen many table tappings by my parents as a child, and I'll swear what I saw was real. In fact, the house my parents still live in was bought by them, brand new in 1963. It has had some strange occurrences. We've heard someone, or something ascending the steps, sometimes normally, sometimes very loudly. Once, in 1983, I personally heard this three times in one day. I'm not ashamed to tell you that this scared the hell out of me!"

Then Boze said that he had just read the author's book, "The Ghosts of Richmond," and was especially interested in the chapter on Hollywood Cemetery. "I've spent many a day wandering around (Hollywood)," he said. "I was surprised that there wasn't a passage on a man named W. W. Pool, who is buried there, and was

Gravesite of W. W. Pool

supposedly run out of England during the 1800s for allegedly being a vampire." Gary said he spent one entire day searching for Pool's grave and was about to give up when he finally found it on his way out. "It was on the side of a hill. He must have been a man of some means because he has an impressive tomb of white granite, with little statues of goats or lambs on it.

"I know this may sound crazy, but I have always heard that every Halloween night a group of Satanists gather around his tomb and chant incantations. I thought it was strange that only Pool's name and the year of his death are on the stone. There is no date of birth and no inscription. That was it. It seemed kind of cold."

Postscript: Gary Boze wrote the author again, before publication. "I went to Hollywood Cemetery today," he said, and found the tomb. All it says is 'W. W. Pool.' I checked at the cemetery office and they were nice enough to look up the information that they had on him. It seems he died at age 79 on February 26, 1922, and was buried February 28."

More Afraid of the Dead
Than the Living!

(Near Bristol)

(Author's note: The genuine fear that ghosts, or even the thought of ghosts, struck in the hearts of many people in the extreme southwestern corner of Virginia, apparently cannot be overestimated. This was especially true among the superstitious, many of whom actually feared the dead much more than the living. The following account exemplifies this in unusual clarity. It is taken from Sam N. Hurst's 1929 book, "The Mountains Redeemed." The author talks about the rarity of suicides in the late 19th century, and the fact that, in those days, suicide attempts were viewed contemptuously. Those unsuccessful in taking their own lives were treated like criminals; those who were successful, were buried unceremoniously and with disgust.)

e recall only one suicide in our early childhood, and that was after the Civil War," Hurst wrote. "There was a white family living on Allen Hursteen's farm upon the mountain side. He and his beloved spouse did not agree, but often quarreled. To add impressiveness to his arguments and cause, with a rope about 10 feet long, he proceeded to the garret, and, mounting a chair, he tied one end to the rafter and the other end about the neck of his wife's 'dear' husband, which her arms had entwined many-a-time, and, kicking not to go up but down, so down he goes with a thud, expecting no doubt his loving companion to cut him down before he lost too much of his breath, but she never came!

"So he went on his way to his eternal home without further argument or ceremony or the sweet privilege of 'making up,' Mr. Hursteen would not allow his body to be interred in the family graveyard where all the neighborhood buried, and as the next thing to the ancient custom of burying suicides in the public road, he was buried upon the top of the hill in the woods on the left side of the road leading to Max Creek.

"... We are sorry that such a horrible deed had been done in that peaceful and happy community; for Jesse Moore's suicide with a piece of the rope still dangling from the rafter in that old building, and his body lying all alone out there in the woods by the road side, filled the whole community with ghosts galore for many years, oftentimes in the form of little soft-footed, snow-white animals about the size of a cat, which would come running out of the woods in procession and jump upon the rump of passing horses, causing them to throw the riders sprawling upon the ground.

"We have seen half a dozen boys and girls riding double thrown down like scrambled eggs into a heap! We were able to capture one of those ghosts! Jesse could not frighten his wife while in life, but is able to terrorize everybody after his death. But that is the way of ghosts — there is no accounting for their peculiar performances. Many and many times, in passing that house with the piece of rope still hanging there, and in passing his grave with Jesse still sleeping there, (the author) would hold his breath until he had fully gotten by the place, and then he would run for dear life, expecting something to catch him in the back at every step! Ever since, he has been more afraid of men dead than living. You can somewhat figure on the actions of the living, but you can never tell what the dead will do!"

CHAPTER   4 5

A Treasure Trove of
Ghostly Tales
(Southwest Virginia)

(Author's note: As one effort to help get people back to work
during the depression, the government (WPA) commissioned a
project whereby writers were hired to fan out across the
Commonwealth of Virginia and interview people on a variety of
subjects. One part of this endeavor was to collect, and hopefully,
preserve the colorful folklore prevalent especially among the
mountain, valley and hill people of southwestern Virginia. This
included everything from home-grown medical cures to music.
Thousands of such interviews were recorded, mostly from 1937
through 1942.

Outstanding among this enormous mass of historical vignettes
is the collection of James Taylor Adams, a prolific writer from Big
Laurel, Virginia. Adams, in fact, had been collecting such data even
before the WPA work began, and he continued long after it
stopped. This collection alone, which includes other writers, numbers in the thousands of pages.

Buried in the files are more than 200 ghost stories! I was
graciously received by Roddy Moore and Vaughn Webb at the Blue
Ridge Institute of Ferrum College, and allowed access to these
priceless papers. They well would make a book in themselves. The
following selection from the Adams collection is hereby offered
courtesy of Clinch Valley College and the Blue Ridge Institute.

The interviews here were all done in the early 1940s by Adams
and by James M. Hylton of Wise, Virginia. They are presented vir-

tually verbatim, with the only additions of a comma here, a correctly spelled word there, for clarity. I am very proud to include these accounts, as they represent what I feel is the true essence of a good, old-fashioned ghost story; one which has been passed down family to family for up to 200 or more years. They also provide a rare glimpse into one part of Virginia's rich heritage and history. Enjoy.)

* * * * *

THE HEADLESS COMPANION

(WPA writer James M. Hylton prefaced the following account this way: "Told to me by Mr. Hector Lane, aged 45 years, and a son of Caleb Lane who is one of the early settlers of the Hurricane section and remembers the time when people put great stock in ghost tales concerning old houses and the sort. Caleb is the son of Jackson Lane who settled in this county from Scott County, Virginia. This tale has been handed down from him and he said it was a fact as he told it to them." The interview took place May 16, 1941.)

hey was a man by the name of Hawkins that had a pretty good old farm down on Steeles Fork and it was hanted and he wouldn't live there hisself, but hated to see the place go to the bad and he let it be knowed that he'd give it to anybody who would live there and fix the place up a little and keep it from fallin'd down in ruin. Well, they's lots of fellers that tried it but they's come from there tellin' the awfulest tales you ever heard.

"But one day Hawkins found a man who was a Bible read man and never feared any sech talk or doin's as they was tellin' about this place, and he being down and out, took the ole man Hawkins up on his proposition right away soon, and they made the deal that he'd go up thar and stay till the house was repaired up a little and that he'd give him a right out and out deed to the place as long as he lived. Well, this feller who was a Dixon and pretty smart, slipped out that night and took a friend 'long with him to the ole house and they made a big fire in the ole log fireplace and set down on a ole bench in front of the fire and took out a Bible and started readin' in it and talkin' about it as they read.

"Well, everything was all pretty warm and nice for a while, but soon after midnight they heard the awfulest noise you ever heered, nearly like somebody draggin' some chains down the ole log steps that led to the loft and it got closer and then they saw what it was. It was a man without his head and they was so scared they couldn't move and the man set right down on the ole bench by them and started nudgin' the one next to the end he was on and kept on till he nudged the one on the other end off into the floor.

"Well, the friend that hit the floor hit the door, too, and hit it fast and left there flying. Well, Dixon set there and he said to hisself, 'Just one here now,' but the man by his side without his head said that there was two and he was still with him. Well, Dixon let his feet and legs pay him tribute and out the door he sailed with the man right at his heels.

"Over the hollow and up a slope they went till Dixon got plumb outa breath and slowed down a little, but the man was right to his side and Dixon heered it say 'They's two of us yet brother,' and Dixon answered him and tole him they was two now but soon's he got his breath they would be only one. Well, that was the truth I guess, for he out run the hant I guess for he lived to tell it anyway. Hawkins later tore the ole house down and rented the place for pasture land, but later some of the folks said that the cows that ate the grass from the place acted kinda queer-like."

* * * * *

THE GHOSTS WHO EXTRACTED REVENGE

(Told to James Taylor Adams August 4, 1940, by Clinton Sexton, Jr., who learned it from his grandparents.)

ne time there was a man who lived at the forks of a creek. His wife had died and had two little girls. He married again and his second wife didn't like the children and wanted to get rid of them. So she killed them one day and took them up the left hand fork of the creek and buried them in a sinkhole and covered them up with some old logs.

"Then every night they would hear something just screaming and crying and coming right down the left fork of the branch. His wife told the man the children had gone over to their granny's to stay awhile. And when she heard the screaming and crying and scratching, she would pull the cover up over her head and scrooch down in the bed and say, "Oo-oo-oo! I'm afraid!

"The screaming and scratching and crying kept on every night, oh, for a week or more. All the neighbors come in to hear it and see if they could find out what it was. But they couldn't tell what it was, but they could all hear it, coming right down the left hand hollow just like it was right in the air and right in the house and all around the bed where the woman slept, but nobody couldn't see anything.

"At last, one night they decided they would keep it out. So all the men and the women in the neighborhood come to stay all night with them and they cut and carried in a whole heap of backsticks and foresticks, great old big logs, and they shut the door and barred it with the backsticks and other wood. Oh, they just had it nearly covered up with sticks of wood and when they heard it coming, crying and screaming down the left hand fork of the hollow, the men all got against the door, too. They said they knowed they would not let it in that night.

"On it come just screaming and crying, and it come right up to the door. Then it began to scratch at the door and screaming and crying. The woman, she scrooched down in the bed and started crying, too. In spite of all they could do, it tore the door down, but they couldn't see a sign of it and the next thing they knowed, the woman began screaming that it had her and there, right before their eyes, she was drug out of the bed and she was fighting and holding back, but right out across the floor she went just a screaming as loud as she could for them to take it off, but they couldn't see a sign of a thing.

"And then right out of the door she went, kicking and screaming and saying, 'It's got me! It's got me! I'm gone! And the last they heard of her, she was hollering for them to take it off as she went out of hearing up the left hand fork of the branch. They hunted everywhere, but they never found a sign of her."

* * * * *

THE STUTTERING SPIRIT

(Told to James Taylor Adams October 14, 1940, by Dicy Adams.)

ou wouldn't think a school teacher would believe in ghosts, but I am pretty sure my father, Shade Roberts, who was a teacher, did believe in ghosts and that dead people could come back and haunt the living.

"I've heard him tell about an old man who lived in the same neighborhood where he lived when he was a boy, growing up. This old man stuttered awful bad and when he tried to talk he made a funny noise. Pap said he got to mocking the old man and that one day the old fellow got mad and swore that he would get even with him if he had to come back after he was dead and haunt him. Pap said that that sort of bothered him and he thought a whole lot about it.

"After he was grown and the old man was still living, he forgot all about it. He went and joined the army and served all through the Mexican War. When he got his discharge, somewhere in Ohio, he struck out for home. In those days people had to walk wherever they went or ride horseback, and Pap didn't have any horse ... So he walked all the way home to the head of Guesses River in Wise County, Virginia.

"He said that he got in the neighborhood of home one night away along about midnight and being so tired and not wanting to go in and disturb the folks at that time o'night, he just crawled over in a field and laid down and tried to go to sleep. But he couldn't go to sleep because something wouldn't let him sleep. Something just kept making a noise right around him all night. He knew it reminded him of something, but it was a long time before it come to him what it was. It was plimeblank (exactly) like the old man a-stuttering. So he laid there till day light and the noise never let up. Right round and round where he laid.

"When day light started, it hushed and he got up and started on home. He stumbled over something and he seen it was a rough tombstone. He struck a match and looked at it and found that it was the grave of the old man that had said he'd come back and haunt him for laughing at his stuttering! He had died while he was away in the army and he'd not heard about it. Pap believed the longest day he lived that that old man had really come back from the dead to haunt him."

* * * * *

THE GALLOPING GHOST HORSE

(Told to James M. Hylton at Wise, Virginia, June 23, 1941, by Ray Horton, son of Eliza and Bruce Horton, who, said Hylton, "were reared in this part of the county and knew and believed many old folk tales and dreams they heard and experienced themselves during their life times. He (Ray Horton) recalls how they used to sit at night and tell him these old yarns until he would be afraid to go to bed by himself and would think about them for many days after as any other young man would have done.")

Back when I was younger and in my teens going to school I had to walk a lot of the time to school and was along the road by myself. I've set and listened to Mother and Papa at night tell tales you could hardly believe, but I know they were honest about it or they wouldn't let me get hold of any of them myself to tell other people. Back then though, it seems people believed in hant tales and things of that sort more than they do now.

"One time stands out more vivid than all the rest to me as it was printed on my mind forever, I guess. He (Papa) said one night he's coming home from work down on Dotson Creek, where he was working for Mr. Henry Stanley at the sawmill, and on a narrow rocky road and dark as pitch. He heard a horse coming at a fast run somewhere down the road behind him and got over to the side to let whoever it was by. Well, no horse or nobody ever did come in sight but he could hear it plain and stood where he was for a long time, and then it died down slowly.

"He knew they wasn't another road in many miles of that place and nothing but thick woods and he was always prowlin's in the woods himself when young, and knowed they wasn't any lanes or paths that a man could run a horse on in the day time, much less at night. He never thought much more about it he says until the next day when they was all at the mill workin' and news come that a Blevins woman and her seven-year-old girl had been killed. They had been to the store and grist mill to get meal and groceries, and a snake had scared the horse and it had run away and turned the wagon over in which they were riding.

"They lived about four miles from us and away off from the road he traveled that night. But Papa had told his experience the next day at the mill about the horse he heard running, but the other fellers all laughed at him then. It was a funny thing that the woman's husband was one of the men to told it to. He was at the mill when we heard the news he said and it liked to killed him on the spot when he heard it. The woman and girl was throwed from the wagon and their heads hit some rocks and they was both killed right there on the spot."

* * * * *

CHASED BY A DEAD HORSE

(Told to James Taylor Adams by Mary Carter, October 9, 1940.)

've heard a lot of strange things in my life and seed 'em, too. A lot of things I didn't know what was. Maybe it was sumpin' and maybe not. But the quarest thing I ever know'd a happin' like that didn't happen to me, but to brother Frank Adams. Best I can remember it was thisy way.

"Frank always wanted to be sort of biggity and fiesty ... always a doin' something different than other folks. Frank was quare. Pa had an old bay horse and the old horse got down with the bot or sompin'. They worked with him. Give him everything they could think of, and Pa is a good doctor thaty way, too. But he got worse and worse. At last he got plum on the lift. And Pa always said when a horse got on the lift you'd just as well to knock him in the head. You could swing a cow and get up and again, he said, but you couldn't a horse.

"So Pa told us children that the old bay horse sure going to die. Frank was a great big young man then and the old horse was down about a mile down the creek from where we lived. So one evening Frank, he slipped off down that way and when he come back he looked sort of sheepish and guilty of sumpin.' Pa asked him what was the matter and what he'd been doing. But Frank wouldn't tell. Pa went down to see how the old horse was getting along and come back and told us he was dead. Frank had killed him. Had knocked him in the head with a poleaxe. Frank owned up and said he was jes gettin' the old critter out'n his misery.

"That was in the spring of the year and it went on till fall. One night we was all settin' round the fire when in jumped Frank. And I honestly believe he was the worst scared feller I ever seed! He said that he was comin' long up the branch and jes after he passed where the old horse's bones was, he heard something like a horse comin' behind him. He looked back and seed the old bay horse jes as plain as he ever seed him in his life, a runnin' after him. Ever' now and then he would let out a snort. Frank said he started to run and the faster he run the faster the horse run. He liked to run hisself to death before he got home.

"He had nearly a mile to come. Jes before he got to the house there was a big flat rock in the road and he said that he looked back and the fire was jes a-flying out's that rock when the horse's feet struck it. And jes as he got to the fence in front of the house the horse turned and went back down the road with his tail over his back, jes a rarin' and a-pitchin' and snortin'.

"We couldn't never get Frank to pass that place again after dark. He'd stay all night over at Grandpap's or Aunt Peggy's before he'd come home after duskdark. 'Course I never seed this myself, but I know the way Frank acted he shore seed something. 'Course I can't say what it was. But he'd killed the old horse you know."

* * * * *

THE HAUNTED SPINNING WHEEL

(Told to James M. Hylton, September 30, 1941, by Dan Fraley of Wise, Virginia. The account had been related to Fraley by his uncle, George Beverly, then deceased.)

 used to go around and visit with first one of my children and then to the others, one at a time and stay a good spell before I went on to one of the other places. I recollect that Maude, my oldest daughter that lived out in a far end of Wise here, had a spinnin' wheel they'd bought from an old man whose wife had died up in the Hurricane (section), and then he'd sold most of the stuff out (that) he didn't need, but just enough to furnish a couple of rooms for hisself.

"One night when I was at her house and sleepin' in the room I always slept in when there, it was the room by the grate, and I'd seen it (the spinning wheel) before and never paid much attention to it only that it had been polished and cleaned. Anyway, it is a long time now as that was in 1912 sometime in the late fall and the nights were getting cool. Along 'bout 12:00 I was woke up by something I didn't know just what. Anyway, I knowed I'd been woke up and lay there wondering if some prowler had been 'round the house or what, or maybe some dog or cow had made a noise somewhere near.

"The way I was layin' my eyes were on that old spinnin' wheel and naturally I got to thinkin' 'bout it. Well, sir, as I laid there a lookin' at it I thought I saw the wheel give a turn around right fast and I thought I heard a little noise. Then I thought I was about half asleep and at first never paid no attention to it but tried to think why I'd been woke up. Try as hard as I could, I couldn't though and kept lookin' back towards that old spinnin' wheel and blamed my soul if it didn't turn clear 'round, the next time I looked at it. If I'd been drinkin' I'd swear it was the jimmies, but I hadn't been drinkin' and knowed it was really turnin' 'round, or that is I saw the wheel turn 'round right fast-like.

"Well, I ain't no coward myself and I just decided to stay awake and watch it and see if I could find out more about it. Well, every time I'd turn my head and look back, it'd turn around at least one time and sometimes more. Then the cold sweat stood out on my head and I had a feelin' that everything wasn't alright around me. I got up and I called Maude and told her and she said that I'd have to put up with it and I wouldn't notice it anymore. But I couldn't sleep that night no more.

"In the morning at the breakfast table she told me that the man's wife that sold it to her had worked herself to death nearly spinnin' for things they needed at home and it had caused her to lose her eyesight and later she died broken in spirit and health. She said the old spinnin' wheel just couldn't keep still she guessed as she'd heard some folks tell her that was the reason the old man sold it for nearly nothing.

"Well, it was enough for me and I never stayed in that room anymore although I went back lots I stayed shy of that old time spinnin' wheel. Even if it didn't disturb them it did me — I can't stand to get the jimmies over a little thing like that but it got my goat right then and there and I ain't aimin' to deny it either. I could almost see the old woman spinnin' at the wheel after I'd heard about it and if I'd slept in a room in where it was after that I didn't know but what she'd come around herself. So I steered shy of it." To this, Dan Fraley added: "They say the tale's the truth though, sure."

* * * * *

THE HAUNTED HEWED LOG HOUSE

(Told to James Taylor Adams, August 7, 1940, by Mrs. Celia Ann Banks.)

everal years before our marriage my husband's brother, Jim Banks, had been killed in an election day fight by one of the Hoggs, and from then on his house was said to be haunted. Sol (her husband) told me about, but he had never heard the haunt himself. One day we decided to go and visit his sister-in-law who lived about five miles from us on a creek. We went and that night we set up late and talked and the widow Banks told us of the many things she had heard and seen since Jim was killed. She said that the noise always started just as the clock struck twelve and if we would stay awake we would hear it.

"We all slept in the same room. After we laid down we kept talking for some time and I guess it was ten o'clock before we quit talking. I heard the clock strike eleven, half-past and scratch for twelve (here interviewer Adams notes that old makes of clocks were built so as to make a scratching sound five minutes before striking the hour.) My sister-in-law called Sol and asked him if he was asleep. He said no and she said it was about time now.

"Then, just as the clock struck twelve, something like a rooster flew up on the porch and started crowing, and then (it was) like somebody struck it with a board and knocked the crow out of it. And from then on for the next hour I never heard such things before or since in my life. Out in the granary we could hear something just like somebody measuring up wheat and corn; turning over tubs and barrels and rattling chains. Then there was moaning and groaning and like someone sobbing all around the house.

"None of us slept any that night. She told us that one time she got up and went into the granary to see if she could see anything and as she opened the door something like a big black dog with eyes as big as a saucer and as red as fire run out by her. Another time she sent the children to hunt the cows back on the graveyard hill and something like a barrel rolled after them and right on up to the house.

"We never went back anymore. Not long after that she married again and the haunt got so bad that her and her second husband pulled up and moved off and I don't think anybody ever lived there after that. And it was a good hewed log house, too."

* * * * *

THE CASE OF THE CIRCLE SAW

(Told to James Hylton, September 26, 1941, at Big Stone Gap by Logan Tonker.)

y Dad's Pap was Sam Tonker who always worked at the sawmill over in Scott next to Gate City, and was a mighty good man, too, from what everybody tells me. Anyway, I'd never thought much about how he got killed till I went over there the other Sunday to gather some fruits and got to talkin' to some of the older folks that knowed Grandpap Tonker and how he'd got killed there at the sawmill long time ago. It's been 30 or 40 years now I guess, and most of them had forgotten 'bout it, too.

"My Dad told me how his Pap got killed when he fell over the circle saw at the mill just before the whistle blowed for dinner. He lent over the saw for something and lost his balance, and fell on top of it when it's running wide open at full steam and it cut him in two. It made an awful funny sound you know as it went sawin' in his body and everybody around the mill knowed something like that'd took place 'fore they knowed who it was even.

"Well, them folks was sorta funny 'bout them things and took the saw off and rolled it into the meadow near there and left it and put on a new saw. Well, some time later a dog was a runnin' a cow through there and it cut a foot off on that saw blade as it was sharp and in good shape when they'd took it off, you see. Well, some of the Blackwell boys that lived there took it and leaned it against a shed away from their house and put it so's nothing could get hurt on it anymore I guess and left it there.

"Well, it wasn't long fore I know they told me 'bout it and Dad did, too, 'fore he died that at night the men and women folks got to hearing moaning or a dull like sound at night of some kind, and for a long time couldn't figure out what it was making the noise. They'd look in the barn, out in the field, in the yard, in the shed and under the ole barn, but for a long time never found out what it was and they got to then thinkin' there's something funny 'bout their ears or their heads, but they all knowed they couldn't all be wrong 'bout it.

"Then one night one of the older boys had been in town late and was coming in when he herd it and kept getting closer and closer to the sound so's he could find out what it was making the noise everybody else was trying to figure out. He kept coming closer and closer to the shed and then he saw what it was, and it made his blood run cold as he thought 'bout Grandpappy Tonker getting cut into at a accident at the mill, and it come into his mind where the saw played a part in it, too.

"The noise was coming outta that ole saw leanin' against a side in the shed. Well, he run to the house and got the rest of the men folks 'bout the place and they all went back and they all saw and they all heard, too. Well, they took the saw down to the river that very night and tossed it into the water and as it went down, round and round, it made a funny noise. Later, on a cold clear night, they say you could hear that same dull noise like it made when he fell over the saw and was cut into. Now at the spot where they throwed it you can hear the same. Some people might not think much about this but it's shore true."

* * * * *

THE GHOST THAT SCRATCHES IN THE ASHES

(The following was told to James Taylor Adams on November 14, 1940, by Eva Fair Pegwam "who learned it from her great-uncle, Samuel Simpson Adams, who had it from his mother, Celia Church Adams, 75 years ago." The interviewer says the incident "may be based on the Hamlin family tragedy near the present village of Hamlin in Russell County. Mrs. Hamlin and her children were killed by Indians there.")

Long, long time ago there was a man and his wife and three children living away back in the woods; far off from anybody else ... One day the man put a turn on his horse and started off to the mill. It was a long ways to the mill and he would be gone all day. He hadn't been gone but a little while till his wife heard somebody a-coming riding up the rocky road. She looked out and saw two Indians coming riding on their ponys. She told the children to crawl in the closet and no matter what happened to stay there and not cry.

"The woman didn't have a thing to fight with. They had but one gun and her husband had took it with him, and the axe was sticking in the chopblock out in the yard. So she got down on her knees and began to pray. The Indians come on up and got down and knocked on the door. She wouldn't open it. Then the chief broke it down. They come in and found her kneeling there on the hearth a praying. They took her up and tied her hands and feet and carried her down to the edge of a high cliff and danced around her and then threw her over the bluff into the river. Then they went back and got everything out of the house they wanted and burnt the house down on the three little children.

"That night when the man came back from the mill he found his house in ashes. He soon found the burnt bones of his three little children and their hearts. You know they say a person's heart won't burn. He hunted and hunted for his wife's heart, but, of course, he couldn't find it. So he went crazy and run off in the woods and jumped over a cliff and killed himself. A few days later somebody found his wife's body in the river.

"And now they say that ever since then, the ashes of that cabin stays right there and nothing will grow in them, and that many a person pausing there of a night have seen an old man with a long gray beard and a stick in his hand hunkered down there stirring in the ashes hunting for his wife's heart."

CHAPTER 46

Death Devil and Howling Dogs

(Author's note: Among the priceless Adams collection are a number of accounts of spectral dogs, and still-living dogs which many mountain folks believed sometimes signalled imminent death among families which saw and heard them. Following is a sampling.)

THE DOG THAT FOLLOWED ITS MASTER TO ETERNITY

(Noah Stidham of Norton, Virginia, interviewed by James Taylor Adams February 27, 1942.)

Way back about 50 years ago a man named Hubbard come into this country from North Carolina. He worked around on Cane Patch and took sick with fever and died there. I was a young man then and with some others, I went to set up with the corpse. They had him layin' out on some boards laid on two chairs, as was the custom in them days. It must have been about midnight when we heard something scratchin' at the door. We didn't pay much attention to it and then the door flew open and in run a little black dog. It run right round and round like it was huntin' for something and then rared up on the boards and scratched the cloth off the dead man's face.

"Everybody was so took that none of us thought to stop the

dog till we seed him pulling the cloth off of Hubbard's face. Then somebody jumped up and run him out and shut the door and latched it. Had an old fashioned turn latch on it. We set there talkin' about it, and thought it was a dog that had just wandered in. Then all at once it started scratchin' at the door again and I wish I might never die if the latch didn't fly around just like somebody had turned it and the door flew open and in come the dog and it sprang right at the corpse and on top of his breast, and before we would stop it, it started licking his face. I jumped up and run him out and shut the door and set a chair against it. And for the next hour nobody spoke. You could have heard a pin drapped, it was so still. I'll never believe that was any natural dog, for nobody in the neighborhood had sich a dog."

* * * * *

THE DOG THAT HERALDED DEATH

(Mrs. Dicy Adams, interviewed by James Taylor Adams, location unspecified, but in the Wise, Virginia, area, March 17, 1941.)

One time long ago there was a neighborhood away back in the mountains that was visited by a big dog which seemed to be the courier of death into the community. One day this dog showed up at a house and undertook to take up, but seeming to be vicious, the folks wouldn't let it stay. But he stayed in spite of them. Nearly everyday they would see him sneaking around in the bushes and at night they would hear him howling around the house. Then one day one of the children of the family took sick. Nobody knew what was wrong with the child. Just sick, and it got worse and worse, the more sick the child grew, the more the strange dog would howl. Then one night the child was mighty bad off and the dog would come to the door and scratch on the shutter. They would run him away, but he would come right back. Then the child died about midnight as the dog was howling outside, and the very minute the child breathed its last the dog stopped howling and was not seen around that house again.

"Time went on and the dog showed up at another house in the neighborhood and tried to take up. These folks had heard of its strange behavior at the other place and the death of the child and they decided to humor it, thinking by so doing, they might ward off its evil influence. But not so. The dog was petted and allowed the range of the premises, but he would howl through the night and slink about in the woods in the day time. It wasn't long till the man of the house was coming home from his work one night when he saw the dog coming towards him from a patch of bushes. The man told later that as the dog neared him that he seemed to become weak and sick, and it was with much difficulty that he reached home, the dog following after him, howling. So he took to his bed and everything known by friends and doctors was done for him, but he died one night as the big dog sat on his haunches in the yard and howled. Immediately after the man died the dog disappeared from that farm.

"A few days later he showed up at another clearing. By this time the beast was held in deadly fear. The man at this house loaded his gun and took a shot at him. Even at a distance of only a few yards the shot seemed to have no effect on him. So it went, until one day this man's little boy was sent to the field to drive home the cows. Soon after the boy passed out of sight they heard the dog howling in the direction in which he had gone. The parents became uneasy and went to look for the child. They didn't find him. He was never seen again. And the dog was not seen again."

* * * * *

THE DEVIL DOG

(James Taylor Adams once said: "I have heard my parents, grand-parents and other older people tell of the Devil visiting people in the form of a dog. These visits were usually paid to dying men who had lived a notorious, wicked life. I cannot recall these stories at this time, but one told me March 10, 1941, by Mrs. Mary Carter of Glamorgan, brings these tales to mind.")

ne time there was an old man. He was a rich old man and owned a passel of slaves. He was awful wicked. They said he's been married four or five times and all his wives took sudden sick and died or was found dead. All of his wives had a lot of money and when they died he got it. Well, I've heard Pa say that when this old man's slaves died he wouldn't let nobody come and help bury 'em. It was thought he killed his slaves.

"Well, when he come to die, a passel of neighbors had gathered in to set up with him. It was about midnight and he was awful low. Expecting him to die any minute. All at once they heard a noise at the door. Somebody opened the door and there stood a big black dog. It had eyes as big as saucers and they looked like balls of fire. The dog jes walked right in and reared upon the foot of the bed and looked at the old man. He screamed and tried to get out of bed. He said it was the Devil come after him. He jes fell back and was dead in a minute. The dog then jes turned and walked out and nobody ever seed it again."

* * * * *

THE DOG WHO BROKE A MAN'S TOE

(Finley Adams, interviewed by James Taylor Adams May 7, 1941.)

alking' 'bout ghost dogs, I guess you've heard about the dog ol' Si Collins seed. One night Si was out in the yard between the house and kitchen and he noticed the kitchen door was a-standing open and he looked in and seed a big black, shaggy-haired dog standin' in there by the table. Strange dog to him. He scolded him, but he never let on. Never moved. He scolded him several times, but he didn't pay no attention. He ventured in. He spoke to the dog and tried to march him out, but he wouldn't move.

"Si got mad. He drawed back and kicked at him. His foot went right on through (the dog) and struck the table leg and broke his big toe. I seed it. He couldn't wear a shoe for a month or two and hobbled around on a cane with his big toe all swelled up and turned blue. But after he broke his toe he run out of the kitchen and hollored for Aunt Paggy to fetch a light. She brought a light and they searched all over the place and couldn't find hair nor hide of any dog. He believed as long as he lived that it was the Devil he seed like a dog."

A Host of Haunting Humor

(Author's note: It is clearly evident from the interviews of James Taylor Adams and others, that the people of the valley and hills of Southwest Virginia, although largely superstitious and wary of ghosts, never lost their senses of humor, and loved to tell a "good one" on one another. Following is a selection of the strangest — and funniest — accounts which have been passed down through the generations.)

BIG 'FRAID' AND LITTLE 'FRAID'

(From an interview by James Taylor Adams with Mrs. Dicy Adams of Big Laurel, Virginia, date unspecified, but about 1940. It was passed down from her grandparents. Her great-grandparents came to this section about 1810.)

One time there was a man. And he had a little boy. And he'd send the little boy after the cows of an evening. And he would stay and stay and stay and stay. Wouldn't get the cows home till way after dark. The man would whoop the boy. But that didn't do any good. He would stay out just the same.

"One day he told the little boy that something would catch him some night if he didn't quit staying out that a-way. He asked him if he was afraid. The boy laughed and said he'd never seed a 'fraid." That give the old man the idea of how he would scare him. So he told him there was 'fraids,' and he bet him that he'd keep on laying out till one would get him some night.

"So the next evening they sent the little boy after the cows. Had to go a long ways, maybe a mile or mile and a half. After he had been gone a long time and it was getting duskdark the man told his wife he was going to cure the little boy of staying out that a-way, and he pulled a bed sheet off the bed and took off up the road.

"They had a monkey and it had been learned to do everything it seed anybody else do, so it pulled a white table cloth off of the table and took right after him. He never looked back and didn't see the monkey a following him. So he went on till he come to a briar patch and he wrapped the sheet around him and hid in the briar patch. The monkey, it wrapped the table cloth around it and slipped right in behind him. He never noticed the monkey. It wasn't long till he heard the cows' bells a coming and the boy whistlin' along behind them. He let cows get by and just as the boy was right fernence where he set, he raised up and stepped out.

"'Hoomph!' the boy said, 'a fraid.' About this time the monkey stepped out too. The boy laughed. 'Another fraid,' he said. 'Two fraids. A big fraid and a little fraid.'

"The old man looked around and seed the monkey standing there wrapped up in the table cloth and thought it was a ghost, and he took right down the road just as hard as he could go. And the monkey took right after him, right at his heels every jump. The man looked back and seed it was a coming and he run faster than ever, while the little boy clapped his hands and hollered just hard as he could: 'Run, big fraid, little fraid'll catch you.'

"And the man never tried to scare the boy with hants anymore."

* * * * *

A VOICE FROM THE GRAVE

(Marvin D. Julian, of East Stone Gap, Virginia, interviewed by James Taylor Adams, October 27, 1941.

ere is a right funny thing that happened right up here in East Stone Gap cemetery. It's been three or four winters ago that Lee Qualls died up in the valley and they buried him here. About the time they got him put

272

away they come up an awful snow storm, so they just left the tent over his grave. One of his cousins from Scott County was going home the next morning and went by the cemetery to visit Lee's grave. It was before day when he got there, and another snow storm broke and he went in the tent and set down.

"Worley Stidham, a young man up the valley was on his way to work at the saw mill and he cut through the cemetery. He saw the tent there and sort of scrooched up against one side to shelter out of the snow storm. He was too timid to go in. The feller, Qualls, in the tent, heard him run up to the tent and could see him pressed against the outside of the canvass. He talked, course, and he said, 'Bad weather out there?'

"The Stidham boy thought it was the dead man talking to him, and he liked to run hisself to death getting away from there, and swore that Lee Qualls (the dead man) spoke to him and asked him if it wasn't bad weather."

* * * * *

THE MAN THEY KILLED TWICE!

(Told by Clinton Sexton, Jr., 13-year-old, passed down by his great-grandmother, to James Taylor Adams at Big Laurel, Virginia, July 20, 1940.)

nce there was a man traveling through the country and night overtook him and he began inquiring about a place to stay all night. At one big house the man told him he could stay. So he put up his mule that he was riding and went in. There was a whole lot of people there and he noticed they acted queer. One would nudge another and they would go out and be gone a long time and other people kept coming in. And they would get back in corners and whisper together.

The old man come over and told him his bed was ready any time he wanted to go to bed. He said he was tired and believed he would go to bed, and a boy took him upstairs and showed him his bed in a little room. As soon as the boy had left the room, he heard the lock click on the door and found the door was locked. He looked around and there was not a window in the room anywhere. He felt around till he found a little table and it had a candle on it.

He lit the candle and started looking around. He noticed the quilts was pulled plum down to the floor all around the bed. He wondered why that was and he stooped down and looked under the bed and there lay a dead man under there. He knew then that this was a robber's house and that they killed everybody that stayed there. He didn't know what in the world to do.

"At last he made up his mind. He pulled the dead man out from under the bed and seen that his head was mashed all to pieces, and then he noticed something setting at the head of the bed and it was a big maul. He put the man in the bed and put the cover over him just like he was laying there asleep and then he stood right close up to the door.

"It wasn't long till he heard them a coming. He stood just as still as he could. They stopped at the door and he heard them arguing. One said, 'Now you know it's your time.' The other said 'No, you know I killed the last one.' Then they agreed for one to kill him and they unlocked the door and slipped in. Just as they cleared the door he slipped out. But he waited on the outside to see what they done. He heard them pick up the maul and then 'thump.' And one of them said, 'that was easy. He never moved after I struck him.'

"He didn't wait to hear no more, but slipped down stairs and crawled through a window and run out to the stable and throwed a saddle on his mule and hit out. He hadn't gone far till he met a man going after a doctor. He told him what he had heard and seen back there, and the fellow told him people had been suspicious of them folks a long time and that lots of travelers had put up there and never been heard of again. He told him to go on down to his house and stay with his wife and sick baby till he went and got the doctor and he would bring the officers with him. He did, and they found a whole pile of bones down under the floor where they had buried the people they had robbed and killed."

* * * * *

THE TALKING MULE OF THE MINES

(James Taylor Adams said the following had been told up and down the Clinch Valley and Elkhorn for years. He heard it as early as 1916. This interview with Leonard E. Carter of Glamorgan, who heard it 30 years earlier from a coal miner, took place February 12, 1941.)

I heard a feller at Glamorgan tell a tale one time about a hainted coal mine. He said it was at Pocahontas. One day, he said, two Negroes was loading coal when all at once a bony ol' mule trotted into their place. They thought it was a tram mule got loose from the driver, but they noticed it didn't have any gear on. That was strange but they didn't pay it any mind as all coal was hauled with mules then and the mines was full of them. You see, the coal is six or seven feet high at Pocahontas and they used big mules, not the little Santa Fe sort like they used to use 'round here.

"Well sir, this feller he said the Negroes jes worked on until the mule, it up and spoke and says to them: 'You git yore tools together and get outen here.' And the Negroes didn't wait to argue with it. They got! They told everybody what they'd seed and heard, but people jes laughed at them. Nobody believed them. A mule couldn't talk. But the next day the mule walked into a room in the mines where two Hungarians was loading coal, and speaking in the Hungarian language, told them to git their tools and git out. And they got, too. They told what they seed and heard. Then people begin to take notice. Funny, they thought a talking mule would run two crews out of the mines.

"A lot of fellers boasted that they jes wished it would come in their place. Well sir, nearly every time somebody got to boasting, it did visit them the next day. And the feller said the louder they boasted the faster they run. So it wasn't long till a lot of men was laying off, and the section in which most of the Negroes worked was closed down. They jes wouldn't go in the mines. Some of the miners would see a big rat run in their place and they'd walk right out and say they seed the talking mule.

"Things come to such a pass that one of the company men set himself up as a sort of detective to learn about the mule. He first went in the mine and all over it, but he coulnd't find a hair nor hide of it. Then he went to the office and looked over the books. At last, he found that two German (Austrian) coal loaders had been discharged about two months before and had soon left the boardin' house where they'd been boardin'. Then the feller set out again. A few days later he found the fired miners living in the old abandoned mine. They confessed that on the day they was fired that a mule had died and that give them an idea to put the company out of business. They skinned the mule and dried its hide and used it to scare the miners with."

A GHOSTLY RIDE AT NIGHT

(Robert Hammond, Tacoma, Virginia, interviewed by James Taylor Adams October 2, 1941, from an account Hammond heard from his father in 1891.)

've heard my father, Henderson Hammond, tell about an ol' haunted house in Scott County. Nobody could live thar or even stay all night. They was a sort of a brave feller in the neighborhood named Hammond, some of our kinfolks. Well sir, him and some other young men got together one day and agreed to go and stay in the haunted house that night.

"They met up and went long after dark awhile. Had to cross a high fence jes before they got thar. They all clumb upon the fence and was setting thar. All at once Hammond jumped off and the next thing they knowed they seed sumpin' jump up and him a straddle of its back and, kerstreak, it went away off across a field. They jumped off the other side of the fence and liked to killed theirselves a runnin' till they got home.

"Next morning they went over the Hammond's place to see if they could hear anything about him. He was there and told them he jumped off the fence right smack a-straddle of a cow's back and that he thought it was the haint a running off with him till he happened to notice its horns, then he knowed it was a cow."

*****

THE SPECTER AT THE SEVEN GRAVES

(Martin D. Julian told the following to James Taylor Adams at East Stone Gap, October 27, 1941.)

hen I was a boy like, we lived near a place where seven soldiers were buried. The graves were on a knoll and the road passed right by them and then crossed a shallow creek. The Baptist church was up just above the graves and the Methodist church just below. One night they were holding a meeting up at the Baptist church and two of our neighbor boys, Arthur Gray and Robert Carmichial, had went. They admitted afterwards that they were drinking a little.

"They left the meeting and walked off down the road. Came to the seven graves, as the place was called, and one of them bantered the other to climb upon a bank under some trees just across the creek from the graves and watch for the haint that was said to be seen there. They agreed, and clumb up on the bank and laid down. From where they were, they could see directly across the creek to the graves and the road coming over the rise by the graves. Now we lived just below the hill from the graves.

"Meeting broke up and everybody went home. It must have been about midnight when the boys thought they heard something over near the graves and looked, and there came a woman, or something, as they said, just like she was raising right up out the graves. She, or whatever it was, was dressed in white from head to foot, and seemed to be just floating along. They watched it and it come right on the edge of the creek and was heading straight for where they were. One of them jumped up and started to run up the road, and the other right after him. Just as they got started running, they heard a woman scream behind them, and they run that much the faster. It was a good two miles to where they lived, but they didn't stop till they got there. They were so exhausted that they both took down with fever and came very near dying.

"The strange part of it was that my sister, Hattie Julian, who was about 21 at the time, had a habit of walking in her sleep, and that night she had got out of bed, dreaming, she said, that she was going to meeting at the Baptist church, and walked up the road with nothing on but her night clothes. When she stepped into the water at the creek, it waked her, and she let out a scream. And that was the ghost the boys got so scared at."

The Phantom Pianist at Prestwould

(Clarksville, Mecklenburg County)

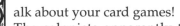

alk about your card games!

The colonists apparently took their gambling seriously. In the 1700s, the wily William Byrd II, the master of Westover Plantation in Charles City County halfway between Williamsburg and Richmond, was in the southernmost part of Virginia helping lay the state line along the North Carolina border. While in the area, he learned of the rich, fertile land along the rivers and lakes, and applied and received grants for more than 100,000 acres in the Dan River region.

He then built a plush hunting lodge there called Blue Castle to entertain friends. When the gentlemen were not out chasing fox, deer, bear, pheasants and other game and fowl, he made special accommodations for them inside. In the river entrance hall, for example, he had installed a huge cabinet large enough to hold both a barrel of whiskey and a barrel of brandy. Thus they could be seated at a table and gamble to their heart's content without ever having to send to the wine cellar or even step into the dining room for refreshments. It was said that here, on an octagonal Jacobean card table, "the gentlemen would play indefinitely."

When Byrd died, the estate passed on to his son, William Byrd III. He apparently possessed neither the business or the gambling skills of his illustrious father. It is written that to him arrived one fine day a caller, Sir William Skipwith, grandson of Sir Gray Skipwith. He came by the river "in a boat well manned by slaves and well supplied with wines of excellent vintage." It was an unlucky day for William Byrd III when he invited the stranger to come ashore and extended to him hospitality which included, since it was raining which discouraged hunting, a few games of cards. The game went on uninterrupted for three days. When Byrd ran out of cash, he put up Blue Stone Castle and the thousands of acres of the estate. He lost everything.

Skipwith's son, Sir Peyton Skipwith, then the only baronet born in America, inherited the property and in 1795 he had built a magnificent manor home on a superb site high above the Roanoke River at the junction of the Staunton and the Dan near Clarksville, about halfway between South Hill and South Boston. He called it Prestwould, after the ancestral Skipwith home in England. The house, says the Virginia Landmarks Register, is "an imposing expression of the elegant life style maintained by Virginia's gentry in the remote countryside." In her book, "Houses Virginians Have Loved," author Agnes Rothery said you approach Prestwould by a long unpaved drive. "The age of the plantation is immediately apparent by the immense oaks and cedars, the great magnolias with polished leaves, the massed clumps of ancient box, groves of smooth-barked crepe myrtle, tall hollies, and rare ivies."

The main house is surrounded by smokehouses, an ice house, corn house, wash house, slave quarters, hen houses, barns, tenant cottages, loom house and a plantation store. Today, the house retains an exceptional degree of its original interior and exterior detail, including three Federal era porches and distinctly regional Georgian woodwork.

One of the outstanding features of Prestwould is its exquisite French scenic wallpaper, by Zuber, dating back to about 1800. In the river entrance hall, for example, one wall is covered by a blue sky arching above a castle and trees faded green and brown "under which ride ladies and gentlemen." In the south parlor living room there are "ladies in directoire gowns and bonnets delicately stepping across rustic bridges, and gentlemen with swelling hips seated on garden benches, with classic pavilions crowning hills in the background and arches of broken stone framing fanciful seas."

Prestwould is perhaps best summed up by one writer who said, "It is a truly excellent example of good design, good taste and good workmanship ... From gaming pavilion to burial ground, it is a testament to the family whose ancestor won the plantation with a turn of the wrist, whose son built the house, and whose descen-

Prestwould

dents enjoyed its spacious amenities for so many years."
(Prestwould is open to the public from May through September. It
is operated by the Prestwould foundation, a non-profit organization for the preservation of the house and grounds as an historic
landmark.)

Some years ago Mary Skipwith Brown, then 90-years-old, the
great-great-great granddaughter of Lady Jean Skipwith, wife of Sir
Peyton, gave some insight into the character of her charismatic
ancestor in a newspaper interview. Lady Jean, she said, was a
highly independent woman. She systematically bought books "of
highly intellectual content" until, at her death, she held 850 volumes (which are on display at the house). When she married her
dead sister's husband, it was "so forbidden by the church in
Virginia that the couple had to find a church in North Carolina to
marry them."

Lady Jean, Mrs. Brown said, was an "icon for serious gardeners." In fact, her garden journal — she kept meticulous records on just about everything — was used by Colonial Williamsburg in laying out its gardens. The extensive Prestwould gardens were laid out in the Renaissance style by a local surveyor, Samuel Dedman. Lady Jean paid him 20 dollars. The gardens were restored in 1980 by the Garden Club of Virginia.

Mrs. Brown, who lived at the mansion until she was 12, remembered that the family had a cook, nurse, and a cleaning woman, "with many, many people living on the place." She recalled that each year a man came to grind cane and make sorghum. People lined up for it with buckets. The "big excitement," she recalled, was hog killing time, "when we'd all eat so much we'd get sick. My favorite was the tail cooked over the charcoal."

She said that in 1912, heavy rains washed out Indian graves on the property and "a major diversion" was collecting mountains of arrowheads and other artifacts which they traded off for books and candy. (A large collection of these artifacts nevertheless remains on display at Prestwould.) Mrs. Brown's favorite memory was that of Christmas time. "I remember Mama and Marshie in the kitchen in the basement cooking, cooking, cooking. Papa went hunting and came back with turkeys, geese and ducks. We children gathered chestnuts and picked out the meat for the dressing. I can still feel the sticky burr. The Christmas tree was a full cedar with little candles clipped to the boughs."

Lady Jean presided at Prestwould for 21 years with "a heavy dose of Scottish thrift. According to Sterling P. Anderson, Jr., a Skipwith descendent who studied her voluminous papers, "her parsimonious nature was largely known." For example, he cited the fact that she "mended and remended flour sacks until they barely held together." She was also said to keep a spy glass trained on the ferry (owned by the family) to make sure the operators "made a proper accounting of the day's receipts."

Lady Jean's last request was: "My desire (is) that my corpse may be interred in the same private manner in which I have lived, the funeral service of the Church of England may be read at the interment, but no sermon and no assemblage of people."

During the interview, the writer noted, as they discussed Lady Jean's "absorption in her music," that behind Mrs. Brown was an old piece of sheet music entitled "You Can't Stop Her." It seemed, the writer said, "close to psychic."

There are a number of reasons why the mansion should be haunted. Among the candidate ghosts are:

** William Byrd III, who squandered away the huge estate in the marathon card game.

** Sir Peyton Skipwith, who was, said Virginia Cavalcade Magazine, "to have many sorrows," and also because of his anomalous position as a baronet in the rebellious colony. Sir Peyton, in fact, was accused of treason during the Revolutionary War, but the case was dismissed in court.

** Lady Ann Skipwith, Peyton's first wife. She was the person described in "The Ghosts of Virginia, Volume I," who now haunts the Wythe House in Williamsburg. She was insanely jealous of her husband, and believed he had amorous intentions toward her sister, Jean. Possibly her feelings were somewhat justified in that Peyton married Jean after Ann's death following childbirth.

However, despite these reasonable causes for haunting, the manifestations which have been experienced at Prestwould don't seem to be linked to Byrd, Peyton, or Ann. Rosa Thames, a volunteer worker at Preswould, tells of the time a year or two ago, when an electrician came to the house to install a burglar system. He said that every time he went into the attic to work, he would hear doors slamming when no one else was around. He searched for the source but never found anything. He never could explain it, although some in the house said that either Sir Peyton or Lady Jean might have been making their presences known to anyone who was "making changes" in their house. This is a common cause for ghosts to assert themselves.

A case could be made that Lady Jean Skipwith is the spirit who came back to Prestwould. A delightful, 72-year-young lady named Ruth Skipwith Smith, who resides in Clarksville, sheds some light on the subject. Mrs. Smith is a direct descendent of Lady Jean, and lived at the house until she was three years old.

"Poppa sold it to a Mr. and Mrs. Goddard from New York," Mrs. Smith says. "I think Mrs. Goddard stayed there only one night, and then she went back to New York. She said her husband wasn't going to keep her in the sticks. I can't say whether or not she encountered any ghosts there, but maybe she did."

Mrs. Smith says that the house then was purchased by Dr. and Mrs. Price. Barbara Price also was a descendent of the Skipwiths. From the time she moved in, she heard piano and harpsichord music late at night, coming from downstairs. Lady Jean Skipwith was a noted player of both these instruments. Mrs. Price never could find any mortal source for the strains, and assumed it was the ghost of Lady Jean. Dr. Price, however, was a skeptic.

One night after they had retired, Dr. Price heard the piano music downstairs according to Mrs. Smith. He told his wife she must have left the radio on downstairs, but she said she hadn't. So he got up to check. When he went downstairs he found that the radio was off, but he could find no explanation for the music. "That actually happened," Mrs. Smith says, "and Barbara often said she would believe till the day she died, that it was Lady Jean."

The Recurring Wreck of Old 97

(Danville)

etween Pickett and Farrar Streets in Danville is a state historical marker which reads: "Here, on September 27, 1903, occurred the railroad wreck that inspired the popular ballad, 'The Wreck of the Old 97.' The southbound mail express train on the Southern Railroad left the tracks on a trestle and plunged into the ravine below. Nine persons were killed and seven injured, one of the worst train wrecks in Virginia history."

Motorists entering town on U.S. Route 58 now pass over the site generally unaware of the dark tragedy which shook the commonwealth nearly a century ago.

Curiously, there were at least four separate omens of pending ill fate regarding the final, fatal run of Old 97. The first was its late departure from the depot in Washington, D.C. North-bound mail trains were running behind schedule, and this delayed 97 for an hour; a fact that caused considerable concern, for this crack express train had a prideful reputation of being on time as it raced south through Lynchburg and Danville, and across the Carolinas to Atlanta.

The second omen centered around the engine itself, locomotive number 1102. A year earlier, her wooden cab had exploded into flames, causing a wild, out-of-control ride until the engineer and fireman were finally able to reenter after the fire had consumed the wooden portion of the cab.

Third, there was considerable grumbling among the crew

members on the fateful morning over part of the train's cargo: a large shipment of live canaries. This did not bode well at all for the superstitious-minded.

And lastly, there was the inexplicable incident which happened when 97 stopped at tiny Monroe, just north of Lynchburg, to change crews. The regular relief crew, for some still-unexplained reason, was, at the last minute, transferred to another train. That was a particularly scary omen to railroad old timers who believed a "strange hand on the throttle" was a portent of lurking danger.

That hand belonged to Joseph B. (Steve) Broady. Despite the best efforts of the regular crew, no time had been made up between Washington and Monroe, so it fell to Broady and his team to slice as much time as they could on the next leg of the run, from Monroe to Spencer, North Carolina. The train, which included the locomotive, two mail cars and two baggage cars, normally stopped in Lynchburg for several minutes, but on this day old 97 stopped and started up again so fast that 17-year-old Wentworth Armistead, who had been sent aboard at Lynchburg to check the locks on safes, didn't have time to get off.

It was now just past 1 p.m. The train was due in Danville at 1:40, and there were 64 miles to cover. Broady ran the throttle wide open, slowing only slightly for treacherous curves as the cars threaded through the hills and valleys of southern Virginia. Old 97 was hurtling so fast passengers complained they had difficulty in seeing the countryside.

The train whizzed past junctions at Altavista, Gretna and Chatham at record speeds, but at a terrible price. Engineer Broady was, in railroad parlance, "eating steam." On straight stretches, he ran full out, shoving his throttle and pulling the brake valve on curves only enough to permit safe passage. Railroaders called this throttle-brake, throttle-brake procedure "whittling," and while it speeds the pace of the train, it has a frightening down side — it consumes steam and air pressure faster than the compressors can produce it. Apparently, while Broady concentrated his attention on the unfamiliar (to him) terrain ahead, he either forgot or ignored the gauge that regulated his braking pressure. He seemed a man hell-bent on making up time at all costs.

And, in fact, Old 97 had made up about half an hour on the whistling run from Lynchburg, as it entered the most dangerous portion of its doomed journey, a three mile, curving down grade that led to the trestle crossing the Dan River on the outskirts of Danville. At the bottom of this long descent was the most dangerous curve of all, which veered sharply to the east. Below the trestle at this point was a 75-foot drop into a deep chasm over Still House Creek. On each side of the rails north of the curve were ominous warning signs: "Sharp Curve. Speed Limit 15 Miles Per Hour."

Broady apparently approached this treacherous stretch at full speed. Eyewitnesses say that Old 97 was going "faster than anything they had ever seen" as it hit the three-mile down grade. Only when he saw the warning signs did Broady shove in his throttle and pull back on the brake lever. To his horror, nothing happened. The air pressure was gone. Frantically, Broady began dumping sand on the tracks and tried to reverse the pistons.

It was too late. As one writer described the scene in a magazine article nearly 40 years ago, "The engine struck the first rails of the curve, wavered and swayed for a moment ... then continued straight ahead. With a sickening lurch, the stampeding locomotive left the track and bounded onto the trestle, bounding and skipping along the crossties while wood splinters flew in every direction. The mail car behind the tender left the rails, then the second car, the third and the fourth.

"The runaway express rolled to the right, leaped above the yawning chasm, and fell toward the bottom. With a thud and roar never before heard in Danville, the engine's left side struck the creek bed; she half-buried herself in the mud, the drive-wheels continuing to turn slowly. As steam spewed in every direction, the

Engineer Steve Broady and Old 97

four cars tumbled and shattered almost on top of the overturned locomotive, seemingly exacting revenge for their fate. The last car struck the pile of debris; its wheel bounded off; and it came to rest with one end pointing to the sky, as if gasping for air.

"For a long moment the awful silence of death hovered over the scene." It was soon broken by "the frantic shouts of rescuers, and the shrill songs of hundreds of freed canaries flying wildly overhead."

Broady and his two firemen were found near the locomotive cab. They had been "scalded almost beyond recognition." Broady's watch was found. It had stopped precisely at 2:18 p.m. Dead, too, was young Wentworth Armistead, who had not had time to get off the train in Lynchburg, and five others, including a new bridegroom. Rescuers dug through the 350 tons of wreckage for a day and a half. Although train 97 was cancelled, the engine was raised from the ruins, repaired, and placed on service for the daily Richmond to Danville run until 1935 when it was scrapped. The tracks were rerouted, and part of the ravine was filled in to support the present-day highway.

Certainly, any of the crewmen or passengers who died as a result of that fateful ride in 1903, one might say, would have just cause to return to the scene. Young Armistead surely would, or a remorseful Steve Broady.

Perhaps they do!

It has been told by Danvillians for nearly a century now that if one stands still on an autumn afternoon at a little past two, at the foot of that three mile down grade and listens closely, "Old 97, with Steve Broady at the throttle, echoes yet through the Valley of the Dan!"

*****

A coincidental footnote to this chapter was added 63 years later when the following dispatch was filed on September 28, 1963, by United Press International: "Yesterday, at about 1:30 p.m., Robert Burns George, 78, of Gretna Virginia, was killed by Train Number 21 as it passed through town. Number 21 replaced famed Mail Train 97 on its run from Washington, DC to Atlanta, Georgia. George, who was walking along the track, stumbled in front of the engine. He died on the anniversary of the wreck at about the time 97 would have passed Gretna, had it still been running. Moreover, he was killed in the hometown of the man who claimed to have written the great song ... and he was a nephew of that man, David Graves George!"

CHAPTER 50

Lightning *Does* Strike Twice!

TH~ FACE FROZEN IN THE WINDOW PANE
(Near Martinsville)

(Author's note: For years, I had heard about the image of a man's face which mysteriously appeared in the Hairston house at Beaver Creek farm in Henry County. Louise Miller of Huddleston, Virginia, then 74, told me about it, saying as a child she played in the yard there and had seen the impression a number of times, although she didn't know the details.

A friend, Vicki Lester of Richmond, who grew up in Martinsville, said she, too, had visited the farmhouse in her youth, and remembered it as being "spooky as hell." Initial research into such an intriguing phenomenon turned up nothing. Then, some months later, I got a letter from Carl de Hart of the Blue Ridge Regional Library in Martinsville. He had found a yellowed old newspaper clipping dating back nearly half a century. Following are excerpts from that article.)

he Hairston owners of Beaver Creek farm have a lengthy history in Henry County. Robert Hairston was high sheriff of the county in about 1780 ... His son, George Hairston, came to settle in Henry County in 1770, and bought Beaver Creek farm ... The original home on the estate was brick, but it burned sometime in the early 1800s. The present frame building ... was built in about 1837.

George was described as being a "brawny picturesque man, more than six feet tall and the father of 18 children; wore buckled knee breeches and a great beard, braided and thrust inside his shirt." He was "a robust figure in the history of the early frontier. He was born in Albemarle County in 1740, ran away to fight Indians at 17, became an Indian agent, land agent, and officer of militia, fighting Indians all up and down the frontier ... He reputedly bought his 30,000-acre tract in 1770 for 10 cents an acre.

"Marshall Hairston, who lived at Beaver Creek farm from his birth in 1802 until his death in 1868, was standing in front of a third-story window at the rear of the home on a summer day a few years before the Civil War began. He was watching slaves at work in the fields back of the home while an electrical storm came up. Suddenly, a bolt of lightning struck near the house which stunned Marshall for a few seconds.

"Sometime after this, persons outside the home looked up and there, on the window near where the man had been standing when the lightning struck, was a profile of a man. The man in the window portrait had overhanging eyebrows, a sharp nose, and sideburns. *So did Marshall Hairston!* ... The late T. E. Gravely, who remembered having seen Marshall Hairston, told the present owners of the home the picture on the glass was a good resemblance of the elder Hairston.

"Today, (1948), the window ... is partly obscured from view by trees. Ole 'Uncle Matt,' colored caretaker who has grown accustomed to seeing the window painting, says it used to be plainer from a point on the back lawn directly in front of the window. Now, however, this point is obscured by tree leaves, and visitors must stand to one side in trying to spot the likeness.

"From inside the home the window pane shows nothing that resembles a head. It is, however, discolored by a reddish tint, apparently in the glass. Whatever it is, it will probably last. According to 'Uncle Matt,' that one window doesn't get washed. The last one to try it, a relative of Matt's, reported his hand 'stuck to the glass'!"

* * * * *

THE END OF A 'HARD' MAN
(Fort Belvoir Vicinity)

t is believed that two of Virginia's most famous "Georges" — Washington and Mason — may have had a hand in the design of historic Pohick Church in the northern part of the commonwealth, near Fort Belvoir. They both served on the vestry at the time of its construction, 1769-1774. Much of the building's interior was desecrated by Union troops during the Civil War when it was used as a stable. Among the notables buried in the Pohick Cemetery is a Richard Chicester, who lived in the 18th century. The Chicesters were among the more prominent colonial families.

While Richard was a respected member of the community, first in Lancaster County in the Northern Neck, and later in Fairfax County, he had a sinister reputation among his slaves and servants. He was said to be a cruel master. They were so fearful of him, in fact, that, among themselves, they called him "Hard" Chicester.

The following anecdote was told the author at a Richmond craft show in 1993. It has not been authenticated, but, nevertheless is colorful enough to pass along with that in mind. The house servants said when Chicester died, "a red rabbit ran out from under his bed." The author has not been able to determine if this was an omen of evil or not.

It was further related that sometime after his burial in the graveyard at Pohick Church, a bolt of lightning struck his tombstone and ripped off the first three letters — R I C — of his first name ... leaving, for all to see, "Hard Chicester."

CHAPTER 51

More Samplings of Spectral Vignettes

* * * * *

A CATTY TALE
(Port Republic)

There exists a legend that a woman was murdered in the late 1800s at the Yellow House Inn in Port Republic, a few miles west of Weyer's Cave about midway between Harrisonburg and Waynesboro. It was said that her beheaded spirit would appear on the Inn's front porch and rock in a chair. It was further said that she especially liked to appear in this apparitional form on Halloween.

Sometime prior to 1914, because that is when the Yellow House Inn burned to the ground, three brave young men decided they were going to "face down" the ghost one Halloween. So when it became dark they sauntered up to the porch, sat down in rocking chairs, and waited. When nothing happened for several hours, they nodded off to sleep at about 1 a.m. A neighborhood tom cat jumped into another rocking chair to join them.

Later, one of the men's loud snoring apparently spooked the cat and it leaped out of the chair, pushing off its hind legs. The men then awoke, saw the empty chair rocking back and forth, and ran from the Inn as fast as their legs would carry them!

* * * * *

BEWARE OF THE RAGMAN
(Botetourt County)

century or so ago, seedy-looking, gypsy-like old men would push carts from town to town, door to door, collecting rags, which at the time, were used to make paper. Largely because of their nomadic rovings and unshaven, unkempt appearance, these "ragmen" gained a sinister reputation, and parents, wanting to instill fear in misbehaving children would tell them if they didn't straighten up, the ragman would get them.

According to one account in a 19th century Botetourt County newspaper, a young girl named Priscilla, in Fincastle, north of Roanoke, had accidentally spilled her father's supper and let her dog eat it. Priscilla's mother was upset. She told her daughter that she was going out shopping, and that if Priscilla didn't behave, she would give her to the ragman.

To add to this atmosphere of fear, it was Halloween, "when the moon shone orange from behind the clouds and the wind howled and made the leaves dance at night." Priscilla was sent to her room and told to go to bed. She nodded off to sleep. Sometime later, she was awakened by a loud rapping at the door. She presumed it was her mother, but when she answered, she was horrified to see a filthy old man standing there, "with his clothes barely stitched on and a snaggletooth gleaming from his mouth. She stared into the eye that wasn't covered with a patch and let out a little cry as it winked at her."

According to the newspaper article, Priscilla died of fright, "certain that her mother had sent the ragman after her."

* * * * *

THE RESTLESS TODDLER
(Roanoke)

or a long time, neighbors Pernela Turner and Vicki Fox were afraid to talk about it, especially to each other, for fear of being thought crazy. Pernela had been hearing "rattling" sounds and loud bangs emanating from the kitchen, but she never could pin down the source. Her sister, Linda Hobson, who also lived in the house, reported hearing "a spirit" calling her name. Meanwhile, next door, Vicki and others of her family were experiencing similar manifestations, including unexplained visions. She even had her pastor come to her house and rub the sign of the cross into her walls with anointing oil.

And then one day a possible cause for the phenomena was uncovered, literally. Moochie, Pernela's dog, dug up a 100-year-old tombstone in the backyard right along the fence line that separates her house with Vicki's. It was a tiny tombstone, and read, cryptically, "Ironton 1780-1." Archaeologist Mike Barber was called in and he said the information indicated the stone marked the grave of a one-year-old child, and probably was part of a small family cemetery. He didn't know what "Ironton" meant. Additional research seemed to show the child could have been kin to a Lord Ironton of England who settled in Alleghany County more than 200 years ago.

Historian Clare White, associated with the Roanoke Valley History Museum, suggested that since the grave was found only a short distance from the Wilderness Road — a trail many settlers followed into Kentucky — that the child possibly died as its parents forged west.

Both Pernela and Vicki, who compared notes once the grave was discovered, believe they have found the answers to all the strange things that happened in their houses. Since the site was recovered and Moochie was kept away from it, the odd occurrences ceased.

* * * * *

A SPECTRAL WARNING, UNHEEDED
(Franklin County)

 here is, somewhere in a deep ravine off state road 658 in Franklin County, a haunted hollow, where the axe-carrying specter of a man believed to have been Jesse Chandler still roams. Also in this vicinity was an old graveyard, deep in the woods off a road that once went by the John Reynolds Zeigler farm and across Pigg River. No traces of the grave sites remain.

Chandler died "a troubled soul," according to old timers who heard it from their people. It is said that one day he went into the hollow to cut down a large oak tree for firewood. Six times, "someone" called him back before he cut the tree. He kept going back to his work, and on the seventh time, the tree fell on him and killed him. He has been seen wandering about with his axe over his shoulder ever since.

* * * * *

FLOWERS FROM ANOTHER WORLD
(Bland County)

One of the last blatant Indian massacres in southwestern Virginia occurred in 1779 in Bland County, close to what is now the West Virginia line near Bluefield. In July of that year, it was reported that Elinipsico, son of the notorious Shawnee Chief Cornstalk, was on the warpath in the area with about 40 or 60 braves. Warnings had been dispatched to take extreme caution.

Pioneers, however, being fiercely independent, often did not heed such warnings, feeling they could take care of themselves. One such person was Jared Sluss, a tough, no-nonsense farmer. One day that summer, he and his 12-year-old eldest son, James, went out to work a field, over a hill and out of sight of his house. Mrs. Christina Sluss was at the house, and three of her children were playing in the yard, while a six-month-old baby had been tucked away in bed for a nap.

In a flash, a band of Indians attacked. Two of the children were killed, although a third, Marion, seven, escaped and ran to his father, who told him to run to the fort for help, which he did. But when others arrived, they found Jared and James Sluss dead, and Christina dying. She told of a fierce struggle they had put up before succumbing. The baby, Mary, had not been discovered and lived to be 104-years-old.

As settlers gathered to bury the family, it was said they could hear the taunting war whoops, howls and jeers of the Indians, who appeared on a ridge overlooking the cemetery in full view. The tragedy occurred on a farm called the "Old Crabtree Place," near Ceres.

In a history of Bland County, it is written that the site is "marked and identified each spring by a field of pure, white-scented daffodils, which were planted by the tender and loving hands of Mrs. Christina Sluss. Although the field where the daffodils grow *has been cultivated many, many times*, the appearance of the daffodils each spring represents a living memorial to a noble pioneer family whose struggles, death and noble deeds made our rich heritage possible."

* * * * *

THE LIGHT IN THE HILLTOP TABERNACLE
(Wythe County)

For years there has been a community argument going on in Austinville about the light that glows in the window of the 160-year-old Olive Branch Methodist Church; a night light that shines when all lights have been extinguished in the church. Skeptics say there is nothing supernatural about the light; that it is caused either by the reflections of car lights as they come around the curve leading up to the hill where the church stands, or that it is a reflection of high voltage wires which tend to "glow" when it is very dark. Still others say it is an "effect" of the furnace.

But many townspeople dismiss such assertions, saying the light is caused by psychic phenomena that cannot be explained by rational means. There is an old cemetery next to the church, and some believe one of the graves is "open ended" — that is to say the "restless inhabitant" there has access to two worlds, and comes back and forth at will.

The ghostly adherents point out that the car lights come from the north side of the building, but the mysterious window light appears only on the southern face. The same with the high wires. As to the furnace, it is in the basement, while the light appears on the first floor.

What is not disputed is the fact that the strange light has been seen by almost everyone. It has appeared for years. One person who is convinced that the light has spectral origins is Kenneth Dean, who in 1977, lived just down the road from the church. At that time he told a newspaper reporter that he not only saw the light, but one night "when I came by I saw this *white* thing floating across the road. Ask my mother, she saw the same thing."

Whatever the cause, it was agreed, long ago, that the light in the Olive Branch Church was enough to make members of the congregation there nervous.

*****

A VISION OF ONE'S OWN DEATH?
(Clarksville)

There are on record a large number of cases of deathly premonitions and crisis apparitions where people have seen vivid apparitions, or otherwise saw or felt the presence of a family member or loved one at the moment of their death, even though the person who died may be hundreds or even thousands of miles away. Mothers, for example, may see the vision of their sons at the precise moment they are killed in war, or die in a tragic accident, only to learn later that their vision was incredibly accurate.

But what of the victims of such tragedies? Can they, on the threshold of death, foresee it? Of course, much has been written in recent years about people who have been declared clinically dead and then been revived. Almost unanimously, those who have survived this have told about out-of-body experiences; of seeing a tunnel of light; and often, of seeing relatives and friends who had previously "passed into the beyond."

Does a person, in his or her last seconds, catch a glimpse of something no one else can see? Such may have been the case when 38-year-old Benjamin Douglas Goode died on May 18, 1928. His sister, Rose Chambers Goode McCullough, wrote a family history book in 1957 for her son, Edward Goode McCullough, titled "Yesterday, When It Is Past." In it, she described the scene when Douglas died.

"He was lying quietly, that last afternoon, with his eyes closed, perhaps asleep, or nearly so. His father, who had come over on his regular daily visit, sat near him, but so little was the end expected at that particular time that his wife had left the room and gone downstairs on some errand connected with the children.

"Suddenly and strongly, he sat up in bed, turning a radiant face toward something — someone — only he could see.

"'Why, I didn't know you were here!' he exclaimed joyfully—and was gone."

*****

A DEVILISH SEDUCTION
(Dinwiddie County)

t was probably the most notorious murder case ever reported in Dinwiddie County. On February 2, 1846, Frances Adolphus Muir went to the plantation, known as Grampion Hills, of William Dandridge Epes to collect a long-overdue debt. Five years earlier he had sold Epes 930 acres in the Darvills district of the county, but Epes had defaulted in his payment. The two men had lunch together, and then rode off in the afternoon to hunt for deer. Muir was never seen alive again.

His body was discovered on Epes' plantation several months later, was exhumed from its shallow grave, and it was found that he had been shot twice. A warrant for Epes arrest was issued, and he was captured two years later on the Brazos River in Texas, and brought back to Virginia for trial. A jury convicted him of first degree murder and he was sentenced to hang. Shortly before his death, Epes confessed. He said he had shot Muir in the back while hunting, and that, as Muir lay dying, he told Epes he "hoped to see him in heaven." Epes was hanged on December 22, 1848.

In a book on the history of Dinwiddie County, it is recorded: "The case, while of particular local interest, is classic, in that the evils of murder, deceit, robbery, forgery and falsehood finally were vindicated by the conviction and hanging of William Dandridge Epes.

"The Dinwiddie Court properly concluded that William Dandridge Epes was *instigated and seduced by the devil!*"

The Powhatan Poltergeist

(Powhatan County)

 he argument rages on.
When objects move inexplicably, is such phenomena caused by a poltergeist-type spirit, or is it triggered by a living person through a mechanism known as Recurrent Spontaneous Psycho-kinesis, or RSPK? The German word poltergeist (from poltern — to knock) means "a noisy, usually mischievous ghost held to be responsible for unexplained noise," such as rappings. Poltergeists also long have been credited with the supernatural ability to move objects and to throw things around on occasion. Some believe this is an angry type of ghost, or at the very least one who demands attention.

RSPK proponents, on the other hand, believe that such things as flying objects and unexplained loud noises, are, in reality, caused by human beings rather than ghosts, generally adolescent youth. The focus of investigations into such "disturbances" is on an individual or individuals at the center of the action. Some scientists believe that RSPK activity is triggered by tension of certain neurological features.

They believe that ideal RSPK "agents," especially children from about the ages of 8 or 9 until or through early teenage, fit into a set pattern. They usually have a low ability at verbal expression, are poor students in school, and are often disruptive in class. These characteristics are usually coupled with built-up hostility that is being repressed from consciousness. Such persons have a deep feeling of hostility and frustration, and have great difficulty expressing such feelings. Thus the feelings are somehow manifested in the movement of objects, light and heavy, small and large.

Just how they do this, how they possess such ability, remains a dark mystery.

Whether one believes in ghosty-type poltergeists, or real live ones, or is still unsure just what to believe, the following account of a much-studied case may shed some light on the matter.

This particular case occurred 20 years ago and received considerable attention at the time, including a lead article in 1974 in the Journal of the American Society for Psychical Research, by John Palmer, then with the University of Virginia's Department of Psychiatry, Division of Parapsychology at Charlottesville. It was remarkable for the intensity of the phenomena over a relatively short period of time.

The incidents began in December 1971 at a rural, virtually isolated spot in Powhatan County. The hurricane swirl of activity centered around a slight, shy, 10-year-old Black male, known as "J. E." He lived in a small, one-room frame house with elderly foster parents, then both in their mid-seventies.

J. E. was a likeable child. But he was also deeply troubled and it was suggested that he harbored a repressed hostility toward his foster parents. He had been abandoned by his natural parents at the age of four. He therefore felt some rejection, and had little self esteem. He also had a low IQ, a learning disorder, and was a poor student. He reportedly was disruptive in class and frequently disobeyed his teachers. To compensate for a likely inferiority complex, J. E.'s offensive behavior made him a problem both for his teachers and his foster parents.

It was against this background that the poltergeist activity began. For the first couple of weeks the manifestations consisted principally of "stomping noises" off and on in the area of the basement furnace. However, neither J. E. or his foster parents ever found any rational cause for such sounds.

The serious actions began in the kitchen in the afternoon of December 30, 1971. Thus commenced nearly two weeks of continuous whirlwind poltergeist activity that mystified and frightened J. E.'s relatives and friends and challenged experts of psychic phenomena who came to the area to study the disturbances.

On that fateful afternoon J. E. and his foster mother and father returned home from a trip to the grocery store. As they passed into the house from the kitchen, a boxed layer cake was laid on the kitchen table, a few inches from the edge. As the mother passed by the table, following her husband and J. E., the cake started to slide off the table! She pushed it back. Then, as she entered the living room, the cake started sliding again, and this time fell onto the floor.

Immediately after this, J. E. passed by the stove at the back of the kitchen. As he did, a frying pan that had been on top of the stove crashed down. Then, on three separate occasions, the kitchen table "rose on its hind legs!" Each time, the boy pushed it back down. Both his foster mother and father saw the levitations, but could offer no explanation for them.

The poltergeist apparently then took the weekend off, for nothing else happened until Monday, January 3, 1972. Then:

* As J. E. walked by, a metal dish pan containing several dishes *rose* from the sink "on its own" and fell to the floor, smashing the dishes. This was witnessed not only by the parents, but also by a neighbor woman.

* A pan of sweet potatoes sitting on a kitchen countertop, fell to the floor without anyone touching it. It was placed back on the counter, and slid off onto the floor again.

* That afternoon, as J. E. and his foster father were walking from the barn to the house, a light wooden stick, about three feet long, which had been standing against a fence post, mystically *sailed* through the air right in front of them!

* Then, in succession: a heavy metal stove, which had been standing upright beside the barn, turned over; a large metal wheelbarrow which had been lying upside down, turned over to its upright position as J. E. walked by; and a heavy wooden feeding trough turned over 180 degrees as the boy passed it.

* As J. E. continued walking: three standing fenceposts fell backwards; a six-pound brick flew off a concrete wall and smacked the ground; and a garbage can fell over, untouched.

* Later that afternoon, several adults and J. E. were standing in the backyard talking when a heavy metal lawn chair levitated a foot off the ground.

Next, an incredible series of inexplicable events occurred over a 20 minute period as J. E. visited his grandmother that afternoon at her house nearby. Stomping noises could be heard but not pinpointed. A glass flower vase on the dining room table tipped over, although no one was near the table.

Two dinette chairs sitting side by side at the front of the dining room table started rocking sideways on their own, and then fell to the floor. J. E. picked them up, and they fell over again. In the living room, two small pillows on the sofa *flew* across the room in front of several witnesses. Then an afghan shawl draped over the sofa flew over J. E.'s head and landed on the head of his grandmother, seated about six feet away! After this, two sofa cushions flew off the couch and landed about eight feet away.

With J. E. seated on the floor, the heavy sofa moved out toward him, covering about a foot in "two successive jumps!" As the astonished witnesses, including the grandmother and some neighbors, looked on, a cardboard carton containing over three pounds of food *flew* off the table in the corner of the living room, travelled about 12 feet, and landed in front of J. E. Right after this, three chairs, two of them large, padded chairs, fell over, tipped by unseen hands!

The grandmother and the guests were by now deeply frightened, and J. E. was ordered to leave the house. As he walked through the dining room into the kitchen, the padded metal stool he had been sitting on earlier fell on its side and *slid* about seven feet across the kitchen entranceway to the opposite wall! As he passed through the kitchen, a wooden table set against the inner wall turned outward about 45 degrees, "as if following him out." And as he left the house, a staccato series of "loud, firecracker-like noises" was heard in the direction of his house, where he was headed!

With little wonder, Palmer, in his Journal article, said, "this is clearly the most impressive set of incidents in the whole case." But the day wasn't over yet! Late on the afternoon of January 3, J. E. and his parents made a trip to a doctor's office. As they prepared to leave in a pickup truck, odd things began to happen. The truck apparently started up by itself. Then the car lights began blinking on and off, the side-view mirror turned itself around, and the accelerator pedal *flew* out the window! On the way to town a door flew open, and in the doctor's office, as J. E. sat quietly, a door slammed shut by itself, a wooden chair fell over, and a medicine cabinet door popped open of its own accord.

The next morning, as J. E., his foster father and a neighbor rode to the post office in the pickup truck, the bizarre events continued. The door handle on the passenger side jumped up, unlocking the door. As J. E. sat in the car while his father went into the post office, the ignition key *turned itself on*! The glove compartment in the truck then sprang open and the papers inside *flew* out of the cab. At about the same time, a comb on the dashboard began to float around the cab, much like objects float in a spacecraft in orbit. As J. E. gathered the papers and put them back, the neighbor, understandably spooked, hurriedly got out of the truck. The glove compartment then opened again, and a box of Kleenex and some papers began flying around the cab. This sequence occurred three times!

That afternoon J. E.'s real mother visited and she took her son to church. There, she saw: several long wooden benches fall over one by one; the bench on which J. E. was sitting, rock back and forth; and a wooden table fall into the aisle.

Although the intensity of the poltergeist-type manifestations reached its peak over this two-day period, the events continued for several more days. On the morning of January 5, for instance, the dresser in J. E.'s bedroom was observed *shaking*. Then the boy's foster mother heard a loud noise and rushed into the bedroom to find J. E. lying unconscious on the floor behind the dresser. He said he had been sitting at the front of his bed when the dresser began moving toward him, "forcing him to crumple behind the bed." As he did, a clay figurine fell off the back of the dresser onto his head and knocked him out!

Two days later, a roll of toilet paper *flew* a distance of about 15 feet from the bathroom past J. E.'s foster father who was standing in a hallway. Right after that an aerosol spray can also flew past him. Author Palmer was invited in to investigate the case during the first week of January, and although he did not witness any significant phenomena personally, other than a chair which fell over in his presence, he clearly was impressed with what his investigation uncovered.

In all, he recorded 47 separate incidents of poltergeist activity over about a two week period. Curiously, he noted that in every instance, J. E. had been at or near the center of activity, often within a few feet of the objects which moved. Thus, he determined that the boy was "clearly the cause of the disturbances." He reasoned that J. E. might have chosen RSPK as a "defense mechanism," and that in this case psycho-kinesis might have served as a release mechanism for hostile impulses "which a person cannot express in other ways." In his conclusion, Palmer said "I am not prepared to say that paranormal phenomena have been conclusively demonstrated in this case. ... The information presented hopefully is sufficient to allow the reader to judge for himself what subjective probability to attach to the genuineness of the phenomena. My own impression is that most of the phenomena were genuine ... "

Palmer went on to note that the strengths of the case included the large number of witnesses who claimed to have observed the events, and the fact that many of the phenomena were "of the type that could not easily be produced by trickery without being detected." This, he said, was particularly true of instances where large objects were seen to move. "Given the large number of incidents, many of which could not easily be produced by trickery, this fact is impressive," he concluded.

Nevertheless, there is still room to wonder if this was a dramatic demonstration of RSPK by an energetic, active, emotionally-charged 10-year-old boy who allegedly had deeply repressed hostile feelings toward his elderly foster parents, or was it poltergeist activity.

Palmer brings up a telling point for his conclusions by noting that on January 10th, 1972, J. E. left the house of his foster parents and rejoined his mother, and that no psychic phenomena occurred after that.

Yet J. E.'s foster mother never was convinced that it was nothing other than an evil spirit at work. She believed that the boy "had the devil in him," a remark that Palmer interpreted as meaning that she felt he was possessed by demons.

And, finally, there is this curious footnote. Palmer went back to the scene in rural Powhatan County a year and a half later as a follow-up to his studies. J. E.'s foster mother and his great aunt had both died during this period and his foster father had remarried. The foster father told Palmer that he interpreted the reign of moving objects as having been "portents from God of the impending deaths of these two people!"

The Pearisburg Poltergeist

(Pearisburg)

strikingly similar week-long series of incidents of heavy-handed poltergeist activity occurred nearly six years later at a mountain farmhouse near the small town of Pearisburg in Giles County on the West Virginia border. The bizarre events which took place here between December 19 and December 24, 1977, remain a dark mystery to this day and townspeople still talk of the "supernatural happenings."

This time they revolved around a nine-year-old boy whose identity was kept secret. He was a foster child, living with a 65-year-old woman named Beulah Wilson, and was described as being "as fine a kid as you could find, very polite and mannerly." And although many felt that it was he who caused the mystifying occurrence, neither he or anyone else seemed to know why the things happened as they did.

It began simply enough at about 9:30 on the evening of the 19th when apples and oranges started falling from a table for no apparent reason. At first, Mrs. Wilson thought her cat might have been responsible, but the cat was nowhere near the table. Then a cake pan and some silverware fell to the floor. She placed them back on a cabinet, and the cake pan fell again. When dishes started shattering and large pieces of furniture toppled over, Mrs. Wilson became frightened, and called a neighbor, and then she called a police dispatcher. Both later said they heard objects crashing in the background. Mrs. Wilson asked her neighbor if he felt an earthquake taking place. She then said something was tearing her house to pieces.

The neighbor, Martin Caldwell, went to the house and said, "I saw this old sewing machine rise about three inches off the floor and fall over. Everything in the kitchen was turned over except the Frigidaire, stove and washing machine. Caldwell was so shaken he moved out of his house for the next two nights! The first investigator to arrive on the scene was deputy sheriff Jimmy Niece. He said as he drove up he saw "a carton of soda bottles on the back porch fall to the ground." He said the bottles were in a rack and would have had to have been lifted out of the rack in order to fall to the ground. He didn't see anyone touch the bottles. Other deputies added that large cabinets and pieces of furniture were toppled or moved toward the center of three rooms in the house. None of them believed that the boy, or Mrs. Wilson for that matter, had the strength to move such pieces. One said, "It's unbelievable. I went up there checked for strings, trick mirrors, went under the house, checked the foundation and still couldn't find anything wrong."

The next evening Donald Wilson, Beulah's son, his brother and the boy, were in the house straightening things up, when the activity started again. A cabinet that had fallen over the night before, but had since been placed upright, toppled over again. Wilson said he could see the boy and that he did not knock over the cabinet. He said the three of them quickly left the house.

Beulah and the boy moved in with Donald and his family, partly to escape the strange happenings, and partly to elude the army of curious onlookers and television crews which had descended on the tiny community in efforts to see the evil spirits at work. The sheriff eventually had to seal off Mrs. Wilson's house.

Three nights later, on December 23, the events continued — this time at Donald's house. "The boy said he went to shut the TV off and the table moved. Then an 18-inch trophy in the room fell to the floor." The boy hadn't touched anything. "I called the local church people in and we prayed," Donald said.

On Christmas Eve the boy went upstairs and "things began falling again." "Books (from an upstairs bookcase in the hallway) were coming down the stairs like someone was throwing them," Donald said, although he could see the boy wasn't throwing them. "I shouted 'in the name of Jesus, stop it!' and took the boy outside the house." Only then did the disturbances stop.

At this point, Donald Wilson said he had had enough. Although he didn't understand what was going on, he felt the events were somehow tied to the boy, and he was afraid for the safety of his family. Wilson's 12-year-old daughter was in hysterics. He called county authorities and asked them to take the boy back. He was later placed with another family, and no further activity was reported.

University of Virginia parapsychologist Dr. J. G. Pratt came to the Pearisburg area and investigated the case. He suggested that the cause might be routed in "a peculiar manifestation of psychic energy ... along the lines of a poltergeist. There is a release of psychic energy. It starts suddenly for no real reason and seems to stop just as suddenly." Pratt added that he had "never encountered a case in which so much happened in such a short period of time."

Perhaps Martin Caldwell, the neighbor, summed it up best when he said, "I've gone over the thing time and again in my mind and I just don't have any explanation for it. All we can do is accept that it all happened and hope that time will end it."

The Gentle Spirit of Burnt Quarter

(Dinwiddie County)

urnt Quarter, a large, rambling frame house in Dinwiddie County, southwest of Petersburg, was built around 1750, and is one of the oldest continuously operated farms in the region. The main part of the 15-room mansion, a two-story building, is flanked on each side by one-and-a-half story wings, each having a gabled roof.

In addition to having its resident ghost, Burnt Quarter has survived the ravages of two great wars — The Revolutionary and the Civil War. In fact, the house got its name from an incident that occurred during America's fight for independence. Banastre Tarleton, the notorious British Colonel who nearly captured Thomas Jefferson in Charlottesville (see "The Ghosts of Virginia, Volume I, 1993), passed through Dinwiddie County enroute to Yorktown. He had the granary, and all the slave quarters and outbuildings on the plantation burned to the ground, but for some reason, inexplicable to this day, the main house was spared. From that time on, the estate has been known as Burnt Quarter.

For the next 80 or so years, the plantation experienced peace and prosperity, and was one of the ante-bellum social centers of the area. A young mistress of the household who got married there in 1854 is said to have descended the stairway in a dress that cost $1,000 with a $500 veil!

Such opulence ended abruptly during the War Between the States. It was largely on plantation grounds that one of the last and bloodiest battles of the war was fought, the Battle of Five Forks on April 1, 1865, just nine days before General Robert E. Lee surrendered at Appomattox. Lee and his soldiers had been entrenched in a last-ditch effort to protect Petersburg at all costs, since its fall would open the Union army's path to Richmond and the collapse of the Confederacy.

Realizing this, Federal General Ulysses S. Grant felt if Lee's railroad supply line could be severed at a place near Dinwiddie called Five Forks, where five roads converged, the end of the war would be near; Lee then would have to give up his defense of Petersburg. Historian Bruce Catton called Five Forks "a lonely country crossroads," and much of the battleground was on Burnt Quarter property.

The two forces squared off on April Fool's Day: the overall Union army commanded by Philip Sheridan; the Confederates by Generals George Pickett and Fitzhugh Lee. Although eventually heavily outnumbered, the Southerners fought fiercely and the battle lines waged back and forth across Burnt Quarter's fields.

At one point Pickett told Fitzhugh Lee to warn the Gilliam family, which then owned the plantation, to vacate the house, as it was directly in the line of fire. With the 'Confederates in the peach orchard at the rear, and the Union forces in the front, Burnt Quarter was used for protection by both forces. Mrs. Gilliam, the owner's grandmother, sent her daughters to the homes of relatives for safety, but she herself refused to leave, as she was "caring for" a sick servant.

The fighting raged on for several hours that day, so fierce at times, say historians, that "the front lawn was covered with wounded and dying soldiers." During this period the house was used as a headquarters for Union General Wesley Merritt, and later Burnt Quarter was converted into a hospital. While the mansion was occupied, soldiers slashed the family portraits adorning the walls. One of these portraits was of Mrs. Gilliam's late husband, who had served in Congress. Bullets tore into the walls, and one cannon ball nearly demolished the great chimney at the end of the drawing room.

Exhausted by "the harrowing experiences of the day," Mrs. Gilliam retired early as the night shadows were falling. The story has been handed down in the family that a musket ball passed through the wall of her bedroom, through the pillow on which her head lay, and then out the opposite wall, "without the slightest injury to herself."

On the lawns surrounding the house, however, lay the dead and dying bodies of dozens of soldiers and horses. There is a grave marker today in front of Burnt Quarter that says: "Buried in this yard six unknown Confederate soldiers killed in Battle of Five Forks April 1, 1865."

Outnumbered by 26,000 to 7,000, the Southerners under Pickett were finally beaten back and the railroad lines Grant had sought to hold were secured. It signalled the end for Lee's Army of Northern Virginia, and a few days later the surrender at Appomattox occurred.

A few years later, several Union officers returned to the house to conduct an inquiry into the battle. As they noticed the damage to the portraits, one of the officers, General Winfield Scott Hancock, offered to pay for their restoration. Mrs. Gilliam steadfastly refused. The family had patched them up, although the slash marks still showed. Today, a visitor to Burnt Quarter can still see the pock marks of bullet holes throughout the building. There is also a sizeable collection of minie balls.

One would suspect, with so much bloodshed and suffering, that any ghosts at Burnt Quarter would surely be those of the heroic young men, from both the North and the South, who died there so close to the end of hostilities; so close to going home at last. But such is not the case.

The sole reported spirit there, instead, is believed to be an amiable one who "never harms anybody, though her ghostly presence may be felt." It is "Nissy" Coleman, a descendent of the original owner of the house. She is said to visit — "so gentle a spirit should not be said to haunt" — her bedroom in the second floor east wing. The tradition is that "the rustle of her skirt" is heard on still nights as she ascends the stairway, enters the room, and "hovers about the bed." So strong was this presence, that even through she was known to be gentle and not to bring harm in any way, servants refused to remain in the house after dark.

Ghosts Unwelcome at Trapezium House

(Petersburg)

(Author's note: As I have often written in my books and said in my talks, based on the experiences of people I have interviewed over the years, most ghosts are either benign or friendly. Only in very rare occurrences are they harmful. And most humans who have lived with spirits have learned to peacefully co-exist with them. Some even enjoy the company of ghosts; most others tolerate them. Generally, fear of otherworldly presences is overcome in time, but not always. A relatively few seem never to be able to get over such fear, which in certain cases may border on paranoia. To these persons, ghosts represent evil or demonic activity, and they will go to the greatest, and sometimes most bizarre extremes to avoid any contact whatsoever. Their fear is genuine, and it borders on sheer terror.

Such was the case with a most unusual and eccentric gentleman who lived in Petersburg during the 19th century, and who literally spared no expense in his life-long efforts to thwart off what he perceived to be evil presences. But first, as a preamble, it is interesting to note another instance of such "de-ghosting" efforts. It involves perhaps the most famous "haunted" house in America — the legendary Winchester mystery mansion in San Jose, California. It also has probably been the subject of more articles and books than any other house in the U.S. involving psychic phenomena. Here are the basic details:

In the middle of the 19th century, a man named Oliver

Winchester, living in New England, invented a revolutionary mechanism for guns. This led to the development of the Winchester Rifle, and the founding of the Winchester Repeating Arms Company, which made Oliver an instant multi-millionaire.

It did not, however, bring happiness to his family. Instead it fostered eternal fear and grief. First, the young daughter of Oliver and Sarah Winchester died in infancy. A few years later Oliver died of tuberculosis, plunging Sarah into years of reclusive mourning. She was heart broken, distraught beyond help, and her health deteriorated.

Finally, in desperation, she went to Boston to see a noted psychic. She was told her husband and daughter had died prematurely because there was a dread curse on her family. The curse was caused by the Winchester rifle, which the psychic called a "blasphemous instrument of death." It had resulted in the slaughter of thousands of American Indians and others. "The spirits of the dead will drive you to your death, too," the psychic told Sarah.

Shaken to her core, Sarah asked the psychic what she could do. Start a new life, she was told. Go far away and build a new house, not only for yourself, but for the spirits of all those killed by rifle. As long as you keep building this house you will stay alive, the psychic said. Sarah deeply believed this.

She then, in 1884, moved across the country to San Jose and bought an eight-room farmhouse on 162 acres of land. She immediately hired a corps of 22 carpenters and told them to start adding rooms to her house. Thus began around-the-clock construction activity, seven days a week, including Christmas day, for the next 38 years!

One of the first additions to the house was a seance room. It was dark, had no windows, and was festooned with 13 ceremonial robes hanging on hooks on the walls. Only Sarah entered this room, always at midnight. Here, it was alleged, she communicated with the spirits, and solicited their ideas on what to build next. She wrote such ideas down and gave the orders to her carpenters the next day.

One of the house's oddest additions was an unscalable bell tower. A toller's rope hung down through the inside of a tower shaft to a secret room in the cellar, accessible through an underground labyrinth known only to a Japanese servant and his apprentice. Sarah had them toll the bell precisely at midnight, and at one and two a.m. It is said she did this to summon the spirits for her nocturnal seances. She felt these hours were critical to her visitors from "another dimension."

As the years passed, her house continued to grow in an eerie, haphazard fashion. There seemed to be no design or plan in mind, as the eccentric millionairess believed such a maze of confusion would discourage vengeful spirits. For example, stairways led to blank ceilings, hallways led no place, cabinets opened to solid walls, windows opened to blank walls. There were 47 fireplaces!

Sarah was intrigued by the number 13, which in her studies of ghost lore, she had learned was, in olden times, considered unlucky only for evil spirits. Consequently, nearly all windows had 13 panes of glass, many rooms had 13 windows, 13 palms lined the drive, the greenhouse had 13 cupolas, walls had 13 panels, staircases had 13 steps, and there were 13 bathrooms in the house.

Meanwhile, as more and more rooms were added, Sarah's incessant fear of being trapped by avenging specters seemed to increase. Her behavior reflected this. To get to her seance room, for instance, she would wander through an "interminable intricacy of rooms and passageways," push a concealed button, slip through a panel, pass through a window into another room and down a flight of stairs, then up another flight. She thought this would make it difficult for "anything" to follow her.

Her favorite place was the "Daisy Room," so called for the daisies in stained glass windows there. She was in this room on April 18, 1906, when the entire house shook to its foundations, plaster cracked on the walls and the building began to crumble. It was now seven stories tall, and the top three floors collapsed and fell into the garden. Sarah, pinned under the debris, fainted. This was the fateful day of the great San Francisco earthquake.

Although servants were able to free the terrified mistress of Winchester House, they were never able to convince her she had been the victim of a natural disaster. She felt it was the spirits coming to get her. She instantly hired more teams of carpenters to accelerate the construction! She also had the Daisy Room sealed off. No one entered it again during her lifetime.

Sarah liked to sip expensive, imported wines and liqueurs when she dined in solitary splendor. One day she went into the wine cellar, and came out screaming. She had seen the implant of a black hand on the cellar wall. Servants told her it merely was the mark left by a workman, but she would have none of it. It was, she said, a clear warning from demons of the evils of alcohol. She immediately had the wine cellar bricked off! It was so hidden in the maze of construction that it has never been found!

Sarah Winchester died in the house on September 4, 1922,

shortly after finishing a session in the seance room. At that time no one really knew how many rooms the house contained. Some rooms were so hidden by other rooms that they were lost forever. There was a key to each room, and the keys filled three large buckets! So confusing was the construction that every time a room count was taken, a different number was reached. Even today, house custodians are not sure how many rooms there are. Estimates range from 148 to 160 or more!

The house had gained such a sinister reputation over the years that after Sarah died, such famous personalities as Harry Houdini and Robert Ripley (of Ripley's "Believe It or Not") came to see it. In time it was made a national historic landmark. Many psychics also have come to the Winchester Mystery House. Most have said they felt definite "presences" there. It was as if, some noted, someone or something was watching them. "We are not alone here," one commented. Many psychics described a concentration of psychic energy in the house. Some who slept overnight there heard the grand piano being played by unseen hands. Sarah often played the piano in the late hours of the night.

So, it seems, the spirits of the dead still roam the countless meandering rooms and staircases of Winchester House. One wonders if Sarah is now among them.

But, as I have said, this is all prelude to the following similar — and equally strange — account of a Virginia house, also designed to discourage representatives of the spirit world.)

* * * * *

It is called the Trapezium House, and it is located at 244 North Market Street in Petersburg, Virginia. It has been an intriguing curiosity for nearly two centuries.

It was built sometime around 1815 or 1817, the exact date is unsure, by a man named Charles O'Hara, who assuredly ranks among the most eccentric and most mysterious personalities who ever resided in the Old Dominion. Little is known of this odd and charismatic gentleman, even though he lived in the middle of Petersburg for more than half a century. He spawned more gossip and inspired more legends that perhaps any other person in the colorful "Cockade City."

It is known that he left his native Ireland when he was

19-years-old. Some have said that he had gotten involved in some of the contemporary "political brawls" in Ireland and found it "expedient" to leave the country. One account has O'Hara landing in New York City and becoming a bookkeeper for a large firm. Another, has him emigrating to the West Indies where he accumulated a fortune. What is not known is why he came to Petersburg sometime in the first decade of the 19th century. He apparently came as a young man of some means, however, because he bought choice property and commissioned the building of his house.

Workmen no doubt thought O'Hara a bit touched in the head when he laid down his specifications for the structure; there were to be no right angles in the house whatsoever! Apparently, from what can be pieced together, O'Hara brought some (how many is not specified) West Indian servants to the town with him. One was a mysterious woman named Jinsie Snow. It is believed that she convinced her master that if there were no right angles in the house, this would ward off any lurking evil spirits. Apparently, the thought was such spirits could only hide in square corners!

Consequently, the house was constructed in the shape of a trapezium — a four-sided figure with no two lines parallel. There are no right angles in the house; even the stairsteps to the upper floors are set at odd angles with the wall. There is only one room on the first floor, and the other two floors have two large rooms each. Mantels, floors, and other architectural elements converge on an imaginary vanishing point, so the interior of the house appears to be elongated. This illusion may be caused by the irregular shape of the house, but it is more likely that the effect was deliberately planned. On the first floor, everything in the single room is off center, including the fireplace, windows and staircase. There is only one door, the front door. As one observer put it, "the house seems to expand as you go upward." Oddly, the cellar, where the cooking was done, can be reached only by a trap door under the stairwell. Also, the cellar ceiling is only four feet high. This led a visitor to speculate that O'Hara's servants must have been gnomes. One writer has noted that the house had "great architectural interest as probably the only one of its kind in the United States, if not the world."

But if the house seems unusual, to say the least, consider O'Hara himself. First, it is a puzzlement to this day why he chose to settle in Petersburg. As one historian said, he knew no one there, seemed to like no one, and allegedly "snarled at women and children" as they passed his place.

Trapezium House

As the years passed, O'Hara's reputation for the outrageous grew to legendary proportions. For example, on important British and Irish holidays, he would dress up in a full British uniform and sit on his front porch. Although there is no indication that he ever served in the military, he came in time to be known as "the General."

In a 1940 Richmond newspaper article he was described as having been "about as friendly as a black widow spider, and from all accounts not much prettier." In another account, recorded in a Virginia Cavalcade article 30 years ago, "O'Hara was one of the greatest oddities in Petersburg. There was nothing particularly attractive about him, but he had such an odd disposition and such peculiar ways as to bring upon him the notice of all who saw him. He is said to have occupied only the first floor of the house, which he never swept or scoured. The accumulation of dirt and rubbish gave the house the popular name of 'Rat Castle.' He is also supposed to have kept exotic pets, such as parrots, rats, and monkeys which added to the colorful aspect of his dwelling."

O'Hara never married, although there was some speculation that the enigmatic Jinsie Snow was his wife. This was never substantiated. He had no known relatives, and as he lay dying, conscious to the last, he said nothing about how his estate should be settled. It was left to the state. Several people in Petersburg took up a collection — he apparently had made *some* friends — to mark his grave. The stone bears a harp, symbolic of Ireland, and is in Blandford Cemetery on Cockade Avenue.

Today, Trapezium House is owned by the Association for the Preservation of Petersburg Antiquities, a group of local people dedicated to preserving historic buildings in Petersburg. The association was formed to save this interesting landmark when it was threatened some years ago with demolition.

It is now nearly 150 years since the death of Charles O'Hara, and the mystery continues to surround the man and his unique house. The questions remain Why did he come to Petersburg? Why did he build such an odd house? Was he indeed afraid of evil spirits? What caused this fear? And did Trapezium House, with its unusual configuration alleviate his fears?

Or, is it possible that he had his coffin, too, designed to have no right angles?

CHAPTER 56

The Troubled Haunt of East Clay Street

(Richmond)

cross the street from the historic Valentine Museum stands, at 1008 East Clay, the William A. Grant house. It is, says the Virginia Landmarks Register, "an early example of the Italianate style in Richmond. The style's massive scale and square proportions were inspired by the palaces of Florence." The mansion was built either in 1853 (the Register), or, according to Grant's great nephew, Robert Grant Willis, in 1857.

Willis has written that on completion it "dazzled all who gazed upon it and upon the marble steps ... that led to the balustrade-crowded portico protecting the massive double-doored entrance." Willis said his great uncle was reputed to have been the richest man in the city before the Civil War and had a "penchant" for the latest brass chandeliers illuminated by gaslight, imported Carrara mantels, and large mahogany pieces. At the time, it was considered "the finest house in town, valued for taxes at $20,000, and meticulously cared for by 12 servitors — a butler, coachman, footman, nursemaid, lady's maid, three parlor maids, seamstress, cook, scullery maid, and gardener."

Visitors to this showplace included Jefferson and Varina Davis, Robert E. Lee, John Tyler and Edwin Booth, among others, and the house today is included in the National Register of Historic Places. Grant, who owned a "thriving tobacco business" housed in his factory at the northeast corner of 19th and Franklin Streets, had a son, James, and a daughter, Mary.

To appreciate what follows, one must regress 130 years ago to the time of the Southern defeat in the Civil War, and the bitter resentment Richmonders held for the Yankees. As Willis has written, "It was the time in the procumbent defeated Confederacy when tempers and sentiments ran high, especially with their father (William Grant), who not only sustained staggering reverses during the conflict, but had been humiliatingly ordered by the Yankee conquerors to board and house three Union officers in his home for the duration of the Reconstruction."

It was amidst such an acrimonious atmosphere, that Mary, then a pretty girl of 19, committed "the unpardonable transgression of eloping with a Northerner." Willis says, "it is not certain whether Mary Grant's suitor was identifiable as being one of the Federal officers, but it can be assumed so, since all unmarried women of her social standing in that period were scrupulously chaperoned, even at church, and would never have been casually exposed to the amorous attention of just any man without proper introduction. Nonetheless, secretive as her affair might have been, love found its unbridled way, and the elopement took place."

And from this, a tragic event followed. "I had heard of the scandal in hushed tones all my life," Willis states, "and as recently as a week ago (1987) from my 94-year-old mother who, in a moment of lucidity, quietly cautioned, 'We are not supposed to remember that,' when questioned about the famous murder in our family."

To add insult to injury, H. Rives Pollard, the controversial editor of "Southern Opinion," had "published questionable references about the elopement. Pollard, Willis described in an article in the Richmond Quarterly, "was an arrogant sort, possessing many enemies; furthermore it was well known that he had often been involved in countless disputes, political and otherwise, and only two years earlier was engaged in a furious shoot-out with a rival publisher in the rotunda of the State Capitol. Fortuitously, Pollard missed his aim; the bullet which was intended for his adversary shattered instead the tassel on the cane of Houdon's priceless statue of Washington."

James Grant, on the other hand, was said by Willis to be, "by all accounts the fiery, poetic, aesthete of the family, adhering rigidly to the tenets of Victorian chivalry." This intense young man had served as chief courier for Confederate General J. E. B. Stuart during the Peninsula campaign in Virginia in 1862.

James considered what Pollard had published about his sister

1008 East Clay Street

an unpardonable insult to his family. How long he brooded about it is not known. However, one "bleak November morning" in 1868, as Pollard stepped from his carriage to enter his office, the 23-year-old James Grant shot and killed him. News of the murder spread wildly, and when James was arrested and brought to trial, as Willis says, "emotions were so aroused in his favor, an impartial jury had to be summoned from Norfolk."

It has not been explained why, but, ultimately, James was cleared of the charges brought against him, and returned to his father's home on East Clay Street where he "remained cloistered behind shuttered windows." Willis reported, "His whereabouts thereafter are murky, and any knowledge that came down through the years was so veiled in secrecy, particularly among relatives, that very little is known of him or his sister. What remorseful suffering he endured he kept to himself. He died a young man, in his thirties, and was buried in Hollywood Cemetery.

A month later, William Grant mortgaged the house and it was sold in 1871. Most of the subsequent owners, Willis says, were ill-fated in one way or another until the property was bought in 1892 by the Sheltering Arms Hospital, which remained in the building for 73 years. The house is presently owned by the Medical

College of Virginia and used for offices. Although the exterior is little changed from its 1857 appearance, the interior is "scarcely recognizable."

Gone are the "splendiferous gasoliers" ... the huge paneled doors that separated the great rooms from one another ... even the grand staircase. But apparently *not gone* is young James Grant, or rather his sad spirit.

Willis says, "During the late 1920s and early '30s, when as a small boy I would accompany my father on his rounds to attend patients in Sheltering Arms, I recall hearing stories from the staff about a strange moaning sound heard nocturnally throughout the upper floor. Surely, the sound of death was no stranger to the walls of this or any hospital, but the source of the mysterious moans could never be accounted for. It was almost a foregone conclusion that none of the doctors or nurses present at that time knew of the building's history or remotely associated it with an assassin sixty years before.

"Reflecting today on that unhappy melodrama, I cannot but wonder if those inscrutable and eerie vibrations could possibly have been Cousin Jimmy's spirit restlessly roaming in search of lasting redemption.

"England is filled with such gothic tales, and Virginia is not entirely without its ghosts — a thought that gives one pause, as some day, in the overall plan, it is destined that I shall be buried next to James Grant in the family plot!"

CHAPTER 57

The Ghosts Who Love To Read

(Richmond)

f one lingers till closing hours at the stately Richmond Public Library, at the corner of First and Franklin Streets, it is entirely possible that he or she may well hear the riffling of the pages of a book, or the soft shuffle of footsteps in the darkened recesses of the stacks when no one is there ... or at least when no mortal being can be seen. For it is also entirely possible that such muted sounds are being produced by either one, or perhaps two gentle ghosts who, above all else, had a life-long (and now apparently an eternally-long) passion to read.

A number of patrons over the years have reported hearing such sounds in the shadowy corridors and corners of the Richmond building. And before that, 65 or more years ago, when the previous location of the library was a few blocks away on Franklin Street, such supernatural sounds were even more prevalent. That was when the library was housed in the former home of Major Lewis Ginter, one of the city's most important citizens of that era. (His house today serves as the Administration Building for Virginia Commonwealth University, and Ginter Park is named after him.)

And therein lies a story; a poignant story of love and deep abiding friendship which seemingly has endured past the realm of the living into the beyond!

Lewis Ginter came to Richmond from New York City and, in the post Civil War years, he made a fortune, mostly in tobacco. He was, says Richmond history buff Robert Grant Willis, "very cultured and widely travelled. He never married, but he loved to host parties in grand salons. He loved music, and one of his dreams was to build a grand hotel in Richmond, you know, after the Civil War we virtually had no hotels in the city. Everything was in ruins," Willis continued. "Major Ginter built the Jefferson Hotel on Franklin Street. When it opened in the 1890s, it, of course, was the most elegant hotel of its time, and today stands as a hallmark of a past era of grandeur."

Ginter was of German extraction, and before he came to Richmond he had started out in New York. There, he had a close lifelong friendship with another man, also with German ancestors. This bond between the two was recorded in a 1929 article in an old magazine on Virginia called "The Black Swan." Writer Vera Palmer said Ginter and his unnamed friend had little in common. Ginter was described as a "wide-awake, alert man of the world; the other a bookworm. They were young and full of the zest of life … each to be confronted with a strange tongue and an unfamiliar environment. And, in the process of gaining a foothold, they lost sight of one another for many years."

Ginter moved to Richmond while his friend remained in New York. They corresponded for a time, but then the letters grew less frequent and eventually stopped altogether. Over time, Ginter amassed a fortune and gained a reputation as both an astute businessman and a revered philanthropist. Some years later — the date is not specified — the Major travelled to New York on business, and incredibly, met the friend of his youth on the street. He was shocked. His friend "was obviously in dire poverty," his clothes frayed and threadbare. He admitted that from a material standpoint he was a total failure. He worked at a variety of odd jobs, "some of a menial nature," just to make ends meet. But he had read of Ginter's success in Richmond and he was proud his friend had done so well.

Ginter finally persuaded his friend to take him to the place where he lived, a tiny back room on the fourth floor of "an inconspicuous Brooklyn boarding house." The major was shocked again. The room was "absolutely bare of comfort." There was only a cot, a little stove, a cheap suitcase containing a few personal belongings … and books. Books were everywhere! Shelves "groaned" under their weight.

It was then that Ginter's friend explained what he had done with his life. The books, he said, *were* his life. He had spent every penny he made over and above that spent for the barest necessities — on books. He devoured them. Through them, he had "traveled the seven seas and scaled mountainous heights, physically and spiritually; their printed words gave back to him the riches of poets and philosophers, and the deeds of kings, queens and knights as they transpired within castles old." He had literally lived in the characters who he met in his beloved books. As author Palmer told it, "One day, in imagination, he was a millionaire or a noble lord, the next he might find himself a gay adventurer — even a buccaneer, while he would clothe himself in the vesture of sorrow, injustice and misery." Life, thus, was never monotonous, "even if he was sometimes hungry and often cold."

At first, Major Ginter could not comprehend the lifestyle of such a dreamer. He was "depressed and heartsore" when he left his friend, and he decided to do something about it in the only way he knew. He sent money to his friend. Then, on his next trip to New York, he looked in on him. He became indignant that his friend had not used the money to physically comfort himself, and chided him about it. His friend then promised that he would use the money to upgrade his impoverished condition. This time Ginter left him satisfied that he had succeeded in his quest.

Seven years later, the friend was dying and he sent for Major Ginter. He told him that he was sorry he had nothing to give him in return for his years of generosity. But the major told him he did have something. "If you really want to do something for me," Ginter said, "leave me your library, and it shall be cherished for the remainder of my life. I will value it not only because it was yours, but I mean to gain from its volumes something of that inner richness and satisfaction that has come to you." It was done. When the friend died, his books were shipped to Richmond. Ginter studied them for the rest of his life, and, in so doing, came to know what they had meant to his friend. And when the major himself died some years later, the books were donated to the library, where future generations could also benefit from them.

It is said that the friend never left his books; that he followed them south, and that his spirit could be heard and sometimes felt in the late hours after the Richmond Library was moved to Ginter's house, and even later, when it was moved to its present location. There have even been some reports that on occasions the sounds seem to be made by more than one entity.

Perhaps the two old friends now share the joy and fulfillment each individually found in the volumes when they were still alive.

CHAPTER 5 8

Legends of Unrequited Love

LOVER'S LONELY VIGIL AT CHATHAM
(Fredericksburg)

O f all the places in America where George Washington allegedly slept, dined, and was entertained, none apparently surpassed the hospitality of a magnificent Georgian mansion sitting high on a bluff just across the Rappahannock River from Fredericksburg. It is called Chatham — named by its builder, William Fitzhugh, for a friend and former classmate of his at Eton and Oxford — William Pitt, Earl of Chatham.

Washington was a frequent visitor here following the Revolutionary War — so much so, in fact, that he once wrote Fitzhugh, saying: "I have put my legs oftener under your mahogany at Chatham than anywhere else in the world, and have enjoyed your good dinners, good wine, and good company more than any other." Many other notables also visited Chatham during these years, including the Marquis de Lafayette, and an assortment of Randolphs, Lees and additional friends and relatives. The mansion became sort of a "free tavern" for the sophisticated gentry traveling north or south.

There was an early sadness associated with the great house, too. There is a sampler adorning the wall of an empty room there today. It was started by Patsy, the third daughter of the Fitzhugh family, as a memorial to her two older sisters who died at a very early age. In embroidery, it says:

"Here Innocence and Beauty lie, whose Breath
Was snatch'd by early, not untimely Death
Hence ... "

At this point, Patsy, aged seven, died. The sampler was then completed by another sister, Molly:

" ... did they go, just as they did begin
Sorrow to know, before they knew to Sin.
Death that does Sin and Sorrow thus prevent,
Is the next Blessing to a Life well Spent."

Because of the steady stream of "tourists," and possibly because of the sad memories of the lost children, Fitzhugh, ailing in health and plagued with debt, called himself a slave in his own house, and, reluctantly, decided to sell Chatham, his dream home, which he had built in 1768-1771. So, in 1797, he advertised, calling it "a brick house delightfully situated and containing nine commodious rooms, exclusive of a spacious hall or entry, two pairs of stairs, convenient passages, and good dry cellars." The grounds, he added, comprised pleasure and kitchen gardens, interspersed with scarce trees, choice flowers and flowering shrubs, fruit trees and berries. Adjacent were orchards of peaches, apples and pears. Features of the grounds were turfed slopes "created by great labor and expense."

And there was more. Detached from the mansion itself were various offices, kitchen and larder, housekeeper's rooms and laundry, storehouse and smokehouse, a dairy and springhouse, coach houses for four coaches, stables for 30 horses, a cow house with stalls for 36 head of cattle, a large farmyard with barns and granary, a variety of sheds, an overseer's house, a blacksmith shop, and quarters for more than 50 slaves!

It was, in short, a splendid estate of which a National Park Service brochure (The Park Service manages Chatham today) once said: "(with) its various outbuildings and dependencies, and the historic ground which surrounds it ... Chatham represents a small preserve in which the entire scope of Virginia heritage can be understood and appreciated."

Following a succession of owners, the mansion came into historic renown again during the Civil War when it was then the property of Major J. Horace Lacy, C.S.A. It served for a time as headquarters for Union generals Irwin McDowell, Ambrose

Burnside, Rufus King, Edwin Sumner and John Gibbon. It also suffered "wanton vandalism" according to the National Park Service. Yankee soldiers "removed original panelling to burn for firewood, pencilled graffiti on exposed plaster, rode horses through the mansion, and generally left Chatham a victim of the Civil War, as were countless other homes in the vanquished South."

One gentleman who had the opportunity to further inflict damage upon the mansion, but chose not to, was the redoubtable leader of the Confederate Army, Robert E. Lee. During the fighting at Fredericksburg, when General Ambrose Burnside was using Chatham as his headquarters, Major Lacy, owner of the house, rode up to Lee and said, "General, there are a group of Yankee officers on my porch. I do not want my house spared. I ask permission to give orders to shell it." Lee is said to have smiled, and replied, "Major, I do not want to shell your fine old house. Besides, it has tender memories for me. I courted my bride under its trees."

Abraham Lincoln visited Chatham at least twice during the early years of the war and may well have been treated to "a gourmet lunch," as General McDowell had two French chefs on the premises. More importantly, as "men, horses and guns swarmed over the Lacy plateau," the house became a field hospital for wounded Union troops after the battle of Fredericksburg. The famous nurse and later founder of the American Red Cross, Clara Barton, courageously tended to the sick and the lame here, as did the great American poet, Walt Whitman, who came to check on his wounded younger brother.

At the time, Chatham was described as being "crammed with wounded and dying covering all available space of every room and even, (as Miss Barton never forgot) "the floors of the frigid porches."

In his book, "The Wound Dresser," Whitman described the scene at Chatham: "It (the house) is used as a hospital since the battle, and it seems to have received only the worst cases. Outdoors, at the foot of a catalpa tree, within ten yards of the front of the house, I noticed a heap of amputated feet, legs, arms, hands, etc. — about a load for a one-horse cart. Several dead bodies lie nearby, each covered with its brown woolen blanket. In the dooryard, toward the river, are some graves, mostly of officers, their names on crosses of barrel staves or broken board, stuck in the dirt.

"The house is quite crowded, everything impromptu, no system, all bad enough, but I have no doubt the best that can be done; all the wounds pretty bad, some frightful, the men in their old clothes, unclean and bloody. . .Some of the men are dying."

Following the war, the 12,000-square-foot mansion was carefully restored to its former elegance, and regained its status as one of the most beautiful 18th century homes in the state. The last private owner, industrialist John Lee Pratt decreed in his will that Chatham be preserved for the "enjoyment of this and future generations," and deeded the house and grounds to the National Park Service.

Oddly, the ghostly legend at Chatham is not associated with the Civil War, although so much agony and death pervaded the house and grounds in the 1860s. One hundred and thirty three Union soldiers once lay buried under the front lawn, although 130 of these bodies were later reinterred. Psychics who have visited the house immediately sensed "blood" when they walked into the right wing room where so many amputations took place.

The ghost, instead, is a lady who lived in George Washington's day, although she did not make her haunting presence known until the 20th century. The National Park Service says Chatham "has been granted a Lady-in-White who first materialized in this century. A lonely periodic walker, she has not been seen for some time. Other ghosts, however, abound at all times. Though these spirits

Chatham

have not a body like man (or woman), a perceptive soul can sense their permeation of house and grounds."

Tammy Cross, a National Park Service employee at Chatham, tells visitors this version of the story of "the Lady in White": "One of the first persons to see the lady was Mrs. Randolph Howard. She lived in the house from 1909 to 1914. She reported seeing the apparition while looking out from one of the front windows on the west side. The date was June 21st. She said she just saw a flowing white figure walking up and down the front lawn, actually in the colonial carriage lane. The place where she saw the lady came to be known as the 'ghost walk.'

"Mrs. Howard was apprehensive about mentioning what she saw to the servants and to her family members. She was afraid it might scare the servants, and that her family might think she was 'seeing things.' She was the only one to have seen this and it was in the afternoon. But she was intrigued and wanted to find out more about it.

"Years later, a woman magazine writer researching some material in a library in Newark, New Jersey, came across a book about ghosts written in French in the early 19th century. She found references to a Lady in White at Chatham. She then wrote an article about the references, which Mrs. Howard read. She then invited the writer to visit her in Fredericksburg, and they discussed the ghost over tea or lunch."

(Author's note: It should be mentioned that while Tammy says it was a woman writer who found the reference to the Lady in White at Chatham, other versions say it was: a man writer; a French scholar and/or a friend of Mrs. Howard. Whatever, Tammy continues the story.)

"Apparently, the Frenchman who wrote the book had been told the story of the Lady in White while he had been visiting Chatham sometime early in the 1800s." Tammy Cross didn't say it, but Mrs. Howard must have been delighted to find some confirmation of her sighting. Tammy did say that when she began work at the house, she was instructed not to bring the subject up unless asked directly about it, because there had been no reoccurrences of the apparition since the Park Service took over the house in 1976.

But there have been others who claim to have seen her this century — always on the same date, June 21st, and always in seven year intervals. There also have been a number of articles written about the Lady in White over the past 80 years.

The legend goes that sometime in the last quarter of the 18th

century, an Englishman who has been described only as "a distinguished man of letters," came to this country and brought his
beautiful young daughter with him. One of the reasons for his
travel to America was to disengage his daughter from a flaming
romance she was carrying on in England with a drysalter — a
dealer in dry chemicals, dyes and salted food products. She had
met him when her beloved pet, a talking parrot had died, and he
was called in to preserve the bird. Her father, however, felt the
young man was unworthy of the family's prominent social status.

So the father and disconsolate daughter made the rounds,
visiting many friends in this country. At some point, they were
invited by William Fitzhugh to stay at Chatham. Unbeknownst to
the father, the drysalter had somehow managed to follow his love
across the ocean, and, with the help of a servant, he managed to get
a message to his sweetheart at the mansion. They exchanged notes,
and had a secret meeting. They planned an elopement.

Alas, the father got word of the plan and locked the girl in her
room nightly. But the determined young man got a message to her
that he would call for her on a specific night. She was to lower herself from her room by means of a rope ladder. Word of this plan
was passed around the servants' quarters, and someone told it to
the man-servant of George Washington, who happened to also be a
guest of Fitzhugh at the time. He told the general, who had the
drysalter detained by his men.

And, at the appointed hour, when the girl descended the rope
ladder, she landed in the arms not of her lover but of George
Washington! It is said he bore her with a "stout grip" into her
father's room.

This was enough for the Englishman. He hurried her back to
England and arranged her marriage with someone more suitable to
her status. Resigned to her fate, she had ten children, but she never
forgot her lost love at Chatham. She vowed on her deathbed that
she would return to the great house on the Rappahannock on the
anniversary of her death to walk up and down the garden path
and search for the young man.

It is the vision of this love-struck young woman who Mrs.
Howard allegedly saw early in the 1900s, and who others have
claimed to have seen in the years since — always on the same date,
June 21st. Her last "scheduled" visit, since she has been reported
seen only once every seven years, was in 1986. Tammy Cross says
several Park Service employees held a vigil at the house on that
date that year until midnight, but no one saw anything.

Three questions come to mind. Tammy asks one of them. "Why didn't the lady have a name? I've always wondered that. It kind of adds an air of mystery."

The second question is why did the lady not reappear on the expected date in 1986? One day a year or so ago, a group of Fredericksburg third graders visited the house and Tammy told them the ghost story. A nine-year-old girl piped up: "Maybe she hasn't returned because she finally found who she was looking for." Adds Tammy: "I don't know why I had never thought of that. It seems so simple."

And, lastly, what was the significance of June 21st? Here, there may be a plausible explanation. That was the precise date, in 1790, on which the Lady in White died!

(Author's note: There is a postscript to Chatham. In October 1993, I received a letter from Merry Kelley of Leonardtown, Maryland. Here is what she wrote: "A friend of mine sent me a copy of your book 'The Ghosts of Fredericksburg' a few years ago, directing my attention to 'The Lady in White at Chatham.' I read it with great interest as I am a metaphysic and psychic, and visited Chatham (not knowing the story connected to it at all) this past June 21st at the suggestion of another friend in Virginia.

"I don't know if she (the Lady in White) appeared in 1986, but I do know she did appear this past June 21st, as I saw her, and several other manifestation there! The Free Lance Star and the Potomac News, Stafford edition, both carried the story and picture of me on their front page. Just thought that perhaps you might like to know that she did appear there this year."

* * * * *

"POOR LITTLE SARAH"
(Alexandria)

he home which once stood at the southeast corner of Duke and Washington Streets has long since fallen victim to the concrete sprawl of urban development. It was a relic of either the late 18th or early 19th century, and was not distinguished with an inclusion in the Virginia Landmarks Register, or any other book on the notable houses of the commonwealth. In fact, it has been described as having been "rather bleak in appearance."

This was in sharp contrast to the young lady who lived there in the 1860s. Her name was Sarah, and Ruth Lincoln Kaye, in her interesting little book on "Legends and Folk Tales of Old Alexandria," wrote, she was "of legendary beauty with a talent for writing poetry." During the Civil War, she was introduced by her brother to a "dashing" young Federal officer, "with whom she fell madly in love." Although the family expressed some reluctance to the romance, they knew scarcely little about the young man, they nevertheless consented to Sarah's wishes to be married. Because of the vagaries of war, he moved into the house and shared with Sarah her bedroom in the northeast corner of the second floor.

Alas, she had chosen unwisely. Sarah awoke one morning, "turning on her left side to see an empty place in the bed beside her." Her lover had fled in the dark of night, stealing her clothes and her jewelry in the process. Subsequent inquiries led to the sad discovery that the officer had a wife in the North.

Devastation is too weak a word to describe the impact this had on the beautiful young lady. It is said that, "overcome by shame and grief, "she never left the house again — for the next *50 years*! And, she refused to enter her bedroom again. When she died in 1910, her body left, but "her spirit remained till the house was torn down in the 1950s!"

Author Kaye interviewed an elderly resident in the city for her book, published in 1975. The woman had grown up in the house during the period after Sarah's death. As a child, she told of running into the kitchen one day after school and asking her mother who the visitor on the sofa was. When her mother told her she had not been expecting anyone, she responded, "There is a very pretty lady, sitting on the sofa and she has a beautiful storybook dress." However, when her mother went with her into the drawing room, there was no one there!

The woman, as a child, said she saw the vision of the woman many times after that in all parts of the house except in her own bedroom, the same room Sarah had occupied on the northeast corner. The woman also recalled that once she awoke in her bed "experiencing an overpowering sense of gloom and fright." She said she tried to turn on her left side, and "a tremendous force kept her from doing so!"

* * * * *

THE LAST DANCE AT CARTER'S TAVERN
(Halifax County)

arter's Tavern on River Road (Halifax County Highway 659) is, says the Virginia Landmarks Register, "a handsomely restored example of an early southern Virginia ordinary." The capacious frame building provides a rare picture of the "character and arrangement of a once-common Virginia institution." Among its most interesting features, says the Register, "is the great quantity of original graining and marbleizing on the woodwork, most of it well preserved and unusually ornate."

Records indicate the old ordinary began operations around 1802 and continued until 1843. Then, after the owner died, the building stood "derelict and decaying" for 130 years. It then was thoroughly restored and made available for tours and special events by a Mrs. Robert H. Edmunds.

Many stories or traditions have lingered around the inn. In its glory days, it was a much-appreciated rest stop for travellers from New York to New Orleans. It was told that the drivers of stage coaches would ring a bell when approaching about five miles away, one toll for each traveller, and by that means the cook at the inn would know how many meals to prepare. Most journeyers spent the night at Carter's Tavern.

The building has three stories, and the third was said to have been used for a ball room, and that, as long-time resident Mrs. J. S. Barnes once wrote, "many gay balls were given there to entertain the travellers and, of course, the neighborhood young folk." Julia Carrington, of the Halifax County-South Boston Regional Library, says, "The tavern was the hub of the community. The men gathered nightly for the news of the outside world.

"Dances were held on the third floor ballroom. A legend goes that one night the husband of a local woman became enraged when his wife danced with another man, and he shot him at the top of the stairs." Julia adds that the blood stains are still visible, and that the ghost of the woman still "roams the ball room and hangs out of the window gazing up the road."

* * * * *

THE SAD SPECTER AT BLACK WALNUT
(Halifax County)

t one time, in the period between the Revolutionary and Civil Wars, Black Walnut, complete with manor house, nearly a dozen out buildings, and more than 2,000 acres of land in Halifax County at the bottom middle of the commonwealth, was a lively, thriving plantation. There are conflicting reports as to when the first part of this clapboard house was built, the dates vary between 1765 and 1776. A large addition was made about 1850.

In its heyday, Black Walnut featured a huge silver tea service, so large that the sugar dish held five pounds of sugar. It is said that one of the owners of the plantation brought $500 in Mexican silver dollars from the Mexican War and had these melted down and made into the service by a Philadelphia silversmith.

Today, Dr. William Wadkins owns the estate, which still includes about 400 to 500 acres, several of the original outbuildings, and an old family cemetery. He uses it as a summer home. In recent years, Black Walnut has been listed on both the Virginia and National Registries of Historic Places.

It was on part of the plantation property on June 25, 1864, that the Battle of Staunton River Bridge was fought. This was the only fight of any consequence in Halifax County, and although historians have largely passed it over, it was of significance because had the Union won the bridge and destroyed the railroad beyond it, a key supply line to General Robert E. Lee would have been cut off. The battle also was of more than usual interest because of the ages of the combatants. To set the scene, by 1864, the county was suffering severely from the draining effects of the war. All the young men of age had long since left their homes to fight for the Southern cause. Consequently, once-thriving plantations and large farms, once lush with healthy crops, were barren and neglected. Even the horses had been drafted; thoroughbreds had been sent to General Jeb Stuart's cavalry forces, and workhorses were used to haul supplies and artillery.

When word came that Federal troops were heading toward the Staunton River Bridge, the Confederates had only about 250 reserves ready to defend. A call was made for volunteers. Most of them came from the Halifax County "home guard." They included middle teenage students from a boys' academy, and a batch of grizzled men in their 60s and 70s. They formed the now legendary "Old Men and Young Boys" brigade, and marched off to the bridge, carrying whatever leftover weapons that were available. Two companies of regular troops were positioned at the right of the bridge, and the old timers and young boys occupied the left entrenchment. They dug into position and waited. On the afternoon of the 25th, the attack began. Four times that day, the Union soldiers charged across the fields trying to take the bridge, and four times the heavily outnumbered home guard repulsed them. The north lost 300 men, killed or wounded, that afternoon; the south suffered but 35 casualties, and held the bridge. One officer later remarked, "Each man (and boy) was actuated by a feeling of his own responsibility for the successful termination of the fight, and no army that ever trod the earth had produced a braver band than the 300 who saved the day at Staunton River."

John Thrift, III, grandson of the present owners of Black Walnut writes of the resident ghost there: "It was a regular plantation, it being like most in its day. It raised tobacco and other crops that would bring quick as well as easy money for the owner. Money was even of greater importance to the owner during the mid-1800s being that he saw war approaching. He had to do everything possible to ensure the future of his family. That meant to him working hard and avoiding all issues of the war.

"When his young, determined daughter fell deeply in love with a Confederate officer, he was very distressed and forbid her to see her lover anymore. It practically broke her heart. Nevertheless, she met the officer still, in secret places, keeping the romance alive, and still hoping that one day her father would 'come around.' During one of these visits, the officer told her of a battle that was to take place on plantation land at the Staunton River Bridge the next day. He seemed very excited as he rode off after their meeting. It was the last time she saw him.

"He died in the fighting. This sent the young woman into a dark depression. She became ill, and with little will to live, died within a year." Since that time, Thrift says, the spirit of the saddened young woman has never left the plantation grounds. She roams the house at night, her softened footsteps and rustled skirt, have been heard by many over the years. She also has been heard wandering through the lawns and gardens outside, crying, and calling out the name of her fallen hero. Thrift says, too, that visitors to the house "are always thoroughly checked out in their sleep by the ghost. She seems determined," he concludes, "to find her lost love."

* * * * *

LOST LOVE AT EDGEWOOD
(Charles City County)

he gentle, romantic spirit of a young woman, Miss Elizabeth "Lizzie" Rowland, still searches vainly for her lost lover at an historic house in Charles City County. Located just a quarter of a mile from Berkeley, directly on Route 5, Edgewood is a three story Gothic home with 12 rooms, 10 fireplaces and five chimneys. Inside is a beautiful winding three story stairway, original lustrous wide pine floors, original Gothic windows and a large country kitchen.

The house was built about 1849 by Spencer Rowland, Lizzie's father. It was also referred to as Roland's Mill. About 80 yards from the house, still standing, is an old mill which was part of the Berkeley Plantation, dating back to the early 1800s. Here, one may see massive hand-hewn timbers, huge mill stones and the canal, or mill race, which was dug by slave labor and extends to Harrison Lake a mile away. It is said that Confederate General Jeb Stuart stopped at Edgewood on June 15, 1862, for a cup of coffee before continuing on his famous ride around McClellan's forces.

Lizzie was Spencer Rowland's only daughter, and her tombstone can be found today in nearby Westover church-yard. The inscription reads: "Elizabeth Rowland, born May 20, 1823 ... died Feb. 6, 1870 ... Dear Sister How We Loved Thee."

The details of Lizzie's love affair have grown faint through the years. Little is known of her gentleman admirer except that he apparently lived on an adjacent plantation, perhaps Berkeley, and often could be heard approaching Edgewood on what has been described as his "spirited horse." Lizzie would rush to a front bedroom window whenever she heard the hoof beats. Then her lover left her to go off to battle during the Civil War, never to return.

Thus Lizzie died a few years later, a saddened maiden. But her spirit apparently lives on at Edgewood, still hoping for her lover to come back. A number of witnesses have declared seeing the frail specter of Lizzie peering from behind the curtains of an upstairs window. She usually is dressed in white and holds a candle. To those who have watched in revered silence, it appears that the apparition passes from window to window. Subsequent searches of the house, however, reveal no trace of anyone.

335

Edgewood

"Oh, her presence definitely still is in the house," says Dot Boulware, current owner of Edgewood. "I've experienced her a number of times personally, and so have many visitors. When my husband and I first bought the house in 1978, we heard a legend that Lizzie had etched her name in a bedroom window, but previous owners had never been able to find it. One day my son was cleaning the windows in the bedroom where she had died — the windows were so filthy you could hardly see out of them — when he screamed at me. There, in the upper left hand corner of the bottom pane, we saw her name delicately etched in the glass."

A number of eerie incidents have happened to Dot at Edgewood. "We've had pictures fall off the walls, and once a heavy ornamental cannon fell off a mantel. There is no way it could have fallen on its own. We think Lizzie was upset at something and knocked it off. Another time a fire started in one of the upstairs rooms without apparent cause. Even the insurance man couldn't figure out what started it. At other times we've found the front door wide open after it had been locked."

Dot says once an old woman came to tour through the house and when they got to the second floor, she stopped cold at the entrance to Lizzie's bedroom. "She turned to me and said, 'honey, do you know this house is haunted?' She said she had a strong extra-sensory perception and she felt strong vibrations. When I told her about the pictures and the cannon falling, she said it was because when Lizzie's boyfriend went off to war he went by sailing ship, one that had cannon on its decks. But she also told me Lizzie's spirit likes me and I am in no danger.

"Another time," Dot continues, "a psychic came to visit after she had heard about the ghost of Edgewood. She took a candle in a bowl when she explored the rooms, and wherever she said she felt the presence of Lizzie, the flame grew brighter, her hands got very cold and the room became frigid. This woman had never seen the house before, but she went right to the window pane where Lizzie had sketched her name."

Occasionally, Dot and her husband host weddings at Edgewood. In fact, the house was used for church services during the Civil War when nearby Westover Church was stabling Union horses. After one such wedding, Dot and some friends were looking over the photographs taken of the occasion, when someone exclaimed, "look at the upper window." There, it appeared a frail woman was looking out.

"There is no way anyone could have been in that room at the time," Dot says, "because when we have a wedding we store all the parlor furniture in that room, and it's wall to wall. No human being could have gotten through it all to that window. It must have been Lizzie!"

But of all the incidents which have happened at Edgewood since Dot has owned it, the most frightening occurred one evening when she and her husband were hosting a dinner party for 12 couples. "After dinner the men all went into another room and we all stayed in the dining room, chatting. The talk got around to Lizzie and I began telling them about her, when one of the women said, 'that's all a lot of baloney. There are no ghosts.' Just then a brass plate that had been atop a cabinet suddenly fell off and hit the woman on the head. Everyone was stunned into silence, and within a few minutes everyone had left. They were all visibly shaken."

And so, it seems, according to Dot Boulware and many others, Lizzie continues to stand her lonely vigil, in the never-dying hope that she will once again glimpse the sight of her lost beau bounding across the grounds on his robust steed, coming at last to claim the love that was lost in life.

* * * * *

THE DISAPPOINTED BELLE AT BRIGHTLY
(Goochland County)

he details are a little sketchy, but the gist of the story is that in 1838 a young man named Walter Pleasants, then just 22-year-old, was soon to marry a Goochland County belle named Charlotte. For some reason, it has not been specified exactly why, although it appears to have been a case of jealousy, a Dr. Isaac Vaughan was distressed at the thought of the pending wedding. Perhaps distressed is too weak a word; obsessively distraught might be better. Anyway, Dr. Vaughan, who was described in a diary as being a "ruthless savage," followed young Pleasants to Richmond one day, entered his hotel room with a revolver in hand, and shot him dead.

Pleasants allegedly came back to a house called Brightly "in search of his betrothed," but, according to legend, she pined away and died a recluse. What is confusing about all this is that the young man was killed in 1838, yet Brightly wasn't built until four years later in 1842. Possibly, Charlotte was living in the house and that's why his spirit moved there.

Or at least that's what Robin Hauser thinks. She lived in a two-story tenant's house on the Brightly property in the early 1980s, and after experiencing a series of strange things, began to do some local research on the place. That's when she discovered the tragic past of Walter and Charlotte.

"I was never one to believe in ghosts," Robin said. "But I do now. Yet when 'he' was around, I was never scared. I always had a really good and peaceful feeling with 'him.' It was like 'he' made me feel safe."

Considering some of the manifestations that occurred, this seems like a questionable statement. At first it was banging in the kitchen. "I'd be upstairs in bed," Robin remembers, and I'd hear all my cookware rattling loudly. It was like someone was banging it on the counter. Whenever I walked downstairs into the kitchen, though, the noise would stop. I'd go back upstairs, and it would start again."

Robin said one thing that was unusual about all this was that her dog would never come downstairs with her. "It was like my dog, Damien, sensed there was something in the kitchen. He would stay at the top of the stairs and whine and whimper." To get away from the clanging racket, Robin took Damien with her to visit her parents in Roanoke for a weekend. "I just know that Walter followed me up there," she says.

She and her mother decided to go shopping, so they locked the dog in a large coal bin in the basement. Then, in case he got out, they put a large vacuum cleaner and a wicker basket as a barricade against the door to the basement, locked the door from the outside, and hung the key in the kitchen. When they returned to the house, Damien met them at the front door! The basement door was still locked, the barricade still in place, and the key just where they had left it. There was no other way for the dog to have gotten out!

One other odd phenomenon was reported at Brightly, during her stay. There was a small glass bottle suspended by string in an airless corner of a room. It was called a "witch bottle," and was said to be a means for capturing haunting wayward spirits. The bottle at times would swing wildly, although there were no windows or air currents in the room.

In her research into the past, Robin Hauser pored over records at the Goochland County courthouse. There, she apparently found an old picture of Charlotte. She expressed surprise, because the girl looked a lot like her. Each had long blonde curls.

Could it be that the ghost of Walter Pleasants had mistaken Robin for his long lost love?

* * * * *

REVIVAL OF A SPIRIT AT THE SPRINGS
(Bedford County)

ore than 150 years ago historian Samuel Kercheval wrote: "The great reputation which the Mineral Springs of Virginia has of late years acquired, causes them to be resorted to, in great numbers, not only by invalids from every section of the United States and foreign parts, but also by individuals of leisure and fashion, whose principal object is to pass the summer in an agreeable manner. The properties of the Warm, Hot, Sweet, White Sulphur, Salt Sulphur, and Red Sulphur Springs are generally known."

One of the lesser known spas was the now-defunct Bedford Springs, located a few miles south of Lynchburg, and therein lies an oft-repeated legend of the area. It seems there was a young man who returned, "tired and weary" from Yorktown after the end of the Revolutionary War, only to discover that his beloved had wed another in his absence. In despair, he rode off and soon arrived at Bedford Springs, where he allegedly "lay down beside the spring to die."

It is said that a young girl from a neighboring farm saw him and brought him a cup of "the renewing water" from the spring. His will to live was restored. Little is known of what happened to the heart-broken young man during the rest of his life, but the incident at the spring and the kindness of the girl there must have deeply affected him.

For there are still today accounts of sightings of his apparition. He is seen, occasionally at midnight, "arriving on horseback, dismounting and partaking of the water. He then disappears, fading into the night around the spring."

CHAPTER 59

Bizarre Happenings at Berkeley

(Charles City County)

But for an ironic quirk of fate, the U.S. may have lost two future presidents and one signer of the Declaration of Independence, and thus the course of American history might have been dramatically altered — all in the flash of a single lightning bolt. And therein lies a tale of interest, intrigue and psychic phenomena that remains unexplained to this day.

It happened on a dark rainy night in 1744. As the storm gathered fury sweeping up the James River, Benjamin Harrison, IV, master of Berkeley Plantation in Charles City County, halfway between Richmond and Williamsburg, dashed through the house closing windows and locking shutters. In an upstairs bedroom overlooking the river, he apparently had trouble with a particular window which seemed to be stuck. He called for help, and two of his daughters, one carrying his infant son, Benjamin Harrison, V, came to the aid.

As they stood silhouetted in the window, a terrific flash of lightning struck them, killing all but the infant instantly. Luckily, there was a doctor in the mansion, a dinner guest. As was the medical custom in that day, he "bled" the baby, and Benjamin Harrison, V, survived. Perhaps he would have anyway, but that is what happened. This Harrison, in turn, grew to become a leader of the American Colonies, signed the Declaration of Independence, and sired William Henry Harrison, who distinguished himself as an

Indian fighter, earning the name "Tippecanoe," and later was elected ninth President of the United States. His grandson, another Benjamin Harrison, became 23rd President of the United States.

It is said that the ghosts of Benjamin Harrison, IV, and at least one of his daughters have never left Berkeley; that their "presence," in the form of peculiar manifestations, is still regularly felt by the residents, staff members and even visitors to the plantation. More on this later.

First, it is noteworthy to consider the rich historical lore that surrounds Berkeley, which has been described as the finest mansion among the many that dot historic Route 5 linking Richmond and Williamsburg. In fact, there is so much history and color here, it is difficult to know where to begin.

The plantation land itself was part of a grant made in 1619 by King James I to the Berkeley Company and was designated "Berkeley Hundred." There is controversy surrounding the arrival of the first settlers to this area. In contrast to what many history books report, Virginians are adamant in believing that the first actual observance of Thanksgiving was, in fact, held at Berkeley in 1619, two years before the Pilgrims celebrated in New England.

According to Dr. Samuel E. Burr, Jr., a retired university history professor, Captain John Woodlief left Bristol, England on September 15, 1619, and reached Berkeley Plantation early in December. "On December 4, 1619," says Dr. Burr, "the crew held a Thanksgiving observance.

"These English settlers were joined by about 90 American Indians, led by their Chief Massasoit," notes Dr. Burr. "There were religious services — also military drills, games of skill, singing and sumptuous feast." He says the menu consisted of turkeys, venison, bear meat, greens, herbs, ducks, geese, shellfish, eels, codfish, flounder, wild fruit and berries and a variety of wines and "home brew." He adds that cranberries and pumpkin pies were not added until years later.

It is likely such services, as an annual event, did not last long, however, for it was at Berkeley, on Good Friday, 1622, that a band of marauding Indians stormed the fragile settlement and killed nine people. For years afterward, the 8,000 or so acres of Berkeley Hundred were abandoned.

The site was not reclaimed until 1636. It eventually became the property of John Bland, a merchant of London. His son, Giles Bland, was a favored lieutenant of the rebellion leader, Nathanial Bacon, and when Bacon's insurrection collapsed in 1676,

Bland was ordered hanged by, coincidentally, Governor Sir William Berkeley.

The property then came into the possession of Benjamin Harrison III, whose ancestors were from Wakefield. His son, Benjamin, IV, built the Georgian style, three-story brick mansion in 1726.

Incidentally, in addition to claiming the first official Thanksgiving, Berkeley also is listed as being the site of the first commercial shipyard, and, in 1621, of having the first bourbon whiskey distilled there. Further distinctions include the fact that every United States President from George Washington through James Buchanan (the 15th) was entertained by the gracious hospitality of the plantation's hosts. Washington, a close friend of Benjamin Harrison, V, often visited.

Both William Henry Harrison, and Benjamin Harrison were born at Berkeley, sharing this singular honor as the ancestral home of two U.S. presidents with only the Adams House in Massachusetts.

There are dubious glories associated with the plantation, too. It was ransacked during the Revolutionary War by Benedict Arnold. During the early years of the Civil War, General McClelland used the house as headquarters for his Army of the Potomac as he battled with Robert E. Lee in his attempts to march on Richmond. Lincoln visited his general there, and at one time there were as many as 140,000 Union troops in the area. It is said the cellar once was used as a prison for Confederate soldiers.

Today, visitors can see Civil War bullets with toothmarks in them where soldiers bit while being operated on. The house was converted to a hospital. And, it was at Berkeley, in July 1862, that Union General Daniel Butterfield composed the classic military strains of "Taps."

It was also during the Civil War that a 14-year-old drummer boy first saw Berkeley. His name was John Jamieson. In the latter years of the war, the house was abused badly, at one point being turned into an animal barn. It lay in disrepair for decades. Jamieson subsequently became a successful engineer, and, 50 years after he had first been there, he came back to buy the ruined plantation. His son, Malcolm "Mac" Jamieson moved to Berkeley in 1930, and he and his wife, Grace, have devoted their lives to restoring the place to its original grandeur.

Thus, today, Berkeley is a lovely place to visit. From the front of the house, five terraces, dug during the Revolutionary War, lead to the James River. Boxwood gardens flank the path, which meets with a ladies winter garden of roses and other flowers. Inside, the restored rooms are furnished with Queen Anne secretaries, English Hepplewhite clocks, a 1725 gentleman's chest, and a 1690 William and Mary chest from Scotland, in addition to fine paintings and portraits. The house is open to the public and expert guides retell its rich history daily.

Ah, but what of the ghosts?

Mac Jamieson says one of the most common manifestations is that the balky bedroom window, where Benjamin Harrison, IV, and his daughters stood when they were struck by lightning, periodically slams shut by itself, as if closed by spiritual hands.

"For no apparent reason that window sometimes will close by itself," Jamieson says. "I was in the room one day and was telling a friend about the legend, when the window began to come down while we were looking at it. Now," he laughs, "everybody accuses me of having a button that I push to make the window close, which I haven't, of course."

Others have reported sighting the apparition of a young girl with an infant in her arms at the window late at night. Investigations have revealed no one upstairs at the time.

Berkeley

Mac also tells of the legend of the "ghost in the bottom." He says there is a dip in the road leading into the mansion, and for centuries it has been believed to be haunted by a young child who cries at night. Jamieson is skeptical of this story, however. "Personally, I think it probably was an owl, but the plantation owners didn't discourage the story because it tended to keep the slaves in their quarters at night rather than out partying. The owners felt this kept the slaves fresh for a day's work the next morning so they let the tale perpetuate itself."

There is no logical explanation, however, for the plight of a poor photographer who once visited the plantation. First, he took still pictures. One was of the portrait of Mrs. Jamieson's great grandmother, Elizabeth Burford, in the south parlor. But when he got his film developed, the picture was of another person entirely. He accused the staff of shifting the portraits, but no one had moved anything. Then, he rented a television camera and when he set up in the house to shoot film for a proposed documentary, the camera wouldn't work. When he took it back to the camera shop it worked perfectly. Was some spirit guarding the privacy of the house?

Tour guide Vickey Hoover has had a number of experiences with the "presence" in the house, although she is not in the least afraid of it. She feels it is the ghost of Benjamin Harrison. "He just has ways of letting us know he's around at times," she says. She wasn't a believer when she first joined the staff but she soon changed her mind.

"I guess he thought I was being disrespectful and he wanted to show me," she recalls. "Anyway, I was standing in the front hall beside the linen press door when it burst open and hit me in the shoulder." This has happened to her three or four times since. "Once I was explaining the phenomenon to a group of tourists, and the door swung open again. I had to tell them I wasn't pressing any secret lever hidden under the carpet." Another time while she stood by the large piece of furniture the door opened and began swinging back and fourth. Once, she returned after two months off on maternity leave. "I kidded with the other hostesses that Benjamin must not know I'm back, one day as I stood in front of the press. Almost as if on signal, I heard three knocks, turned, and saw the door swing open."

Both Vickey and Jennifer Hess also have heard mysterious rattles from time to time. "I was in the laundry room one day," Vickey says, "when I heard the sound. It was like a door rattling in the dining room, but no one was there. There is a candelabra in the front parlor and when anyone walks across the floor in there, you can hear the glass in it tinkling. I have heard this more than once, but each time when I checked no one was in the parlor."

Vickey also has heard a baby crying, when there was no infant in the house. "I heard it crying in the basement. I went down to look but saw nothing, and when I went back up to the breakfast room, it stopped altogether. We're really not afraid of him. He just likes to play tricks on everyone."

One day during the summer of 1984, Mrs. Jamieson called from the main house to the tour guides in an adjacent building and wanted to know who was in her attic. "We told her we didn't know of anyone," says Jan Wycoff, "but she was adamant that she heard distinct footsteps up there. She said she knew it wasn't squirrels or anything like that. It definitely was a human being's footsteps. I checked the attic and the door was bolted shut like it always is. Then I went outside to see if any workmen had any ladders against the house and were working around the attic area. I didn't see anyone."

But it is in the Berkeley dining room where most of the psychic phenomena occurs. "We don't even have to tell tourists we have a ghost," says Virginia Anders, tour guide leader. "Many of them say they feel a presence the minute they walk into the dining room. We just smile. There is something there, but we can't explain it." Other guides nod in agreement. "I took a group into the dining room one day," says Jan Wycoff, "and the minute we entered the room a woman told me, 'you have a ghost in here. I can feel it.'"

Most of these manifestations are centered in a fruit bowl on the dining room table. Anders, for example, carefully placed a fresh apple in the bowl one morning, then before she left the room she heard it drop. She turned around and saw the apple sail through the air and go over a Chinese screen. "I got out of there real fast," she says. "I was frightened." Later, she went back. No one else had been in the room, but the apple now rested comfortably in the bowl where she had first placed it.

Such a scary experience has happened to others on the staff. Wycoff says the apples "come out on their own and fall to the floor without hitting the wide table." Once, she adds, an artificial lemon, fixed to a nail in the bowl, came out and rolled across the table on its own. Curiously, most of the fruit movements seem to occur in the winter months of January, February, and March when there are relatively few tourists afoot.

Another time Wycoff came in before the first tour one morning and found peanuts scattered across the table. "Where did they come from and how did they get there?" she asks. She told fellow guide Vickey Hoover about it, asking her to clean up the mess when she went through. Hoover saw her later and inquired, "what peanuts were you talking about. I didn't see any." They had mysteriously vanished.

"I feel the explanation of the fruit bowl in the dining room lies with Benjamin Harrison, IV," says Anders. "Maybe he didn't like the arrangement at certain times. I don't know what else to think. We know none of us do it."

CHAPTER 60

The Fearful Force
at Croaker

(Croaker, James City County)

(Author's note: One of the more interesting letters I have received in the past year was from a young man named John Deusebio, Jr., who lives in Castlewood, and works as chief geologist for the Wellmore Coal Corporation in Grundy, in the southwestern end of Virginia. He said he had enjoyed reading my ghost books, and added, "Although some individuals might consider your work as 'light' reading, I, however, have a great deal of respect for your efforts to preserve pieces of our oral history and cultural heritage for future generations." How could I resist including such a letter?)

 ohn went on to say that he had just read a short piece I did on "The Photographic Spirit of Croaker" (near Williamsburg). "My family has owned a house and property near Croaker since the 1920s, and I lived there during the mid to late 1970s while attending William & Mary. I did not know the people of which you wrote, nor have I ever heard that story before reading it in your book, but I had very similar experiences! Perhaps we have two spirits in that area, or just one that wanders about."

Naturally, as you might imagine, John's letter intrigued me. First, I had to go back to reread about the "Photographic Spirit." It involved some William & Mary students who were renting a 125-

year-old farmhouse in Croaker in the mid-1970s, at about the same time that John was there. At first, the two young women and a young man who were living there heard "heavy, booted footsteps and doors slamming in the middle of the night. Then the young man, who slept upstairs, was strangely "afflicted with a series of seizures." Visitors to the house also heard the unexplained noises. One day, a photo was taken of some students sitting on a couch in the house. When the pictures were developed one showed, behind the students, "an ethereal, wispy white mass." One of the coeds had a friend in the Central Intelligence Agency. She gave him the photo and asked him if he would have it examined.

Later, he told her that the "thing" in the picture was a "massive living matter, but not human." He said the agency's past experience with such photos was that ghosts never show up unless "standing directly behind a male human being" (which it was). That mystery was never solved, but after I talked with John Deusebio, following his letter to me, one wonders if John's experiences are not related, somehow, to the photogenic specter. Following is an account, in John's words, of the extraordinary chain of events which happened to him at the same time, in the same location, and perhaps even in the same house!

"During the summers in those years, I did odd jobs, repair work, to help pay my college expenses. There are a number of seasonal cottages in the area, near or on the York River, and I used to fix them up for the owners, most of whom only came there for the summer season. Well, I had been asked to repair some light switches by the front door. So one day, it was about five or six in the evening, but it was in July so there still was plenty of daylight left, I went over to the house, which was adjacent to where I was staying.

"I entered the house through the back door and proceeded past the hall stairway to the front of the house, where I started to work. I kept getting the overwhelming feeling that someone or something was standing behind me, looking over my left shoulder. I can't really describe it. I kept looking around, and even looked out the front door, but there was no one there. In time, the feeling passed.

"When I finished, I had also been asked to do something on the second floor, so I started up the stairway. I had one foot on the second step and was about to advance to the third step, when a blast — and that's the best way I can define it — a blast of icy cold air hit me. It was like a freezer door opened in your face. It totally

'Force' House at Croaker

enveloped me. I could not move forward. It was like I hit a brick wall. I decided to get the hell out of there as fast as I could.

"I went back to my house and tried to figure what in the world that was. Finally, I decided that it was ridiculous, and that I would go back across the street and try again. This time the frigid blast hit me as I walked out onto my porch. I literally could not move forward. I could move backwards or sideways, but I could not go forward. It was some kind of force. I don't know how else to explain it. Something didn't want me to go over there. So I went back into my house and turned on every light and appliance there.

"Now, let me say here that I don't scare easily. I had done some part-time work in a funeral home in Williamsburg, and I thought I had seen just about everything. I saw murder victims, suicide victims, drowning victims, there wasn't much I hadn't seen, but that force did scare me. I just couldn't understand it.

"Anyway, the next evening I was coming home about 10 at night after having spent some time in Williamsburg. I had an old 1955 Willys Jeep and it was a clear night as I drove down state road 607 to get home. Just as I got abreast of the old farmhouse, the electrical system in the vehicle went crazy. At first, I thought something had shorted out. You can expect that in an old car. But this time it was different. All the arrows on the gauges were dancing back and forth as fast as they could go. The headlights flashed on and off by themselves, and then went out. The ignition went out and the engine died.

"I looked up and froze at what I saw. Right over the hood of the jeep was a wispy, white, cloud-like image. It was about six feet long, two feet wide, and was semi-opaque. It appeared to be just hovering there right in front of me. I thought at first it just must be a patch of low-hanging fog. But then I wondered. I don't remember how long it stayed there, probably just a few seconds, and then it moved off and headed straight towards the old farmhouse where I had met 'the force.'

"As soon as it lifted, the car started right up and everything in the electrical system seemed to be working perfectly. I then drove the couple of hundred yards to my house. Later, I had a real chilling thought as I tried to sort things out. If that cloud or whatever it was had actually been a patch of fog, then it would have moved in the opposite direction from what it did, because the wind off the river was blowing *the other way.*

CHAPTER 61

"Mad Lucy" of Ludwell — Paradise House
(Williamsburg)

ome called her, perhaps too generously, eccentric, capricious, whimsical or odd. Others just said she was crazy. Whatever, it is certain that she was one of a kind, and her curious behavior caused excited titters of whispered gossip in the upper strata of 18th century social circles on two continents.

It is probable that had she not been from a well-to-do family, she might have been committed to a mental institution early on in her life. As it was, her actions were covered up, embarrassingly laughed off, or otherwise explained away as those of a high strung young lady with a flair for mischief.

She was Lucy Ludwell, second daughter of Philip Ludwell, III. She married John Paradise, a scholar and linguist and an accepted member of the intellectual set which, in those days, surrounded the eminent Dr. Samuel Johnson. Lucy lived much of her life in London, and, according to one published account, "startled London society by such exploits as dashing boiling water from her tea urn on a too garrulous gentleman who annoyed her."

Earlier in the 18th century her grandfather had built a town residence in Williamsburg — a handsome brick mansion that was called "architecturally sophisticated" for its day. Surrounding the main house are stables, a paddock, a well, smokehouse, "necessary" house, and a woodhouse close to the kitchen. A garden features a prized dwarf boxwood collection.

Property Lucy inherited in Virginia was confiscated by the commonwealth during the Revolutionary War, because the politics espoused by her husband were alien to the cause of the colonists fighting for their freedom. In 1805, however, 10 years after her husband died, Lucy set sail for America and was allowed to take up residence in what has become known as Ludwell-Paradise House.

It was here, as she grew older, that she again became the talk of the town with her peculiar habits. For openers, Lucy, because of her social position in London, considered herself "above" her friends and neighbors in Virginia. She had a haughty attitude which she made no effort to disguise. It is said she "held court" at her house, and didn't object in the least to being called "Madame."

She also was impulsive and obsessive. Once when the future fifth President of the United States, James Monroe, and his family came to Williamsburg, Lucy startled him by rushing up and declaring, "Sir, we have determined to make you president."

Another of Lucy's quirks was her penchant for borrowing the new clothes of her lady friends, especially hats. She viewed herself as a fashion plate of the times and seemed oblivious to the fact that everyone in town knew when she was donning loaned clothing. On Sundays the congregation at her church always got a chuckle because Lucy regularly had her "little black boy" — a servant's son — carry her prayer book into church ahead of her, as if to announce her imminent entrance.

Mad Lucy is probably best remembered for entertaining guests on weird carriage rides. They were weird in that they never went anywhere. She had a favorite coach reassembled on the back porch of her house. When callers dropped by she would invite them into the coach and then have it rolled back and forth across the porch on imaginary trips by a servant.

Her fantasy carriage rides became so frequent and her other peculiarities so pronounced that Lucy began having difficulty differentiating between the worlds of make-believe and reality. Eventually, in 1812, she was committed to the state asylum.

While Lucy died two years later, her spirit apparently remains entranced in the Ludwell-Paradise House. A number of occupants have reported hearing strange sounds there unattributable to any known physical source. Most notable of the witnesses are Mr. and Mrs. Rudolph Bares. Bares is a retired vice president of Colonial Williamsburg who lived in the house for several years in the 1960s and 1970s.

"Oh, we never heard any ghostly voices, saw any levitations or

Ludwell-Paradise House

anything like that," Bare says. "But my wife and I each experienced the same odd phenomenon on several different occasions, maybe eight, 10 or 12 separate times. And that is we would be downstairs when we would hear the water running in a second floor bathtub. Then we would hear a splashing sound in the tub, as if someone were taking a bath.

"The first few times we heard it, we went up the stairs to take a look, but there was never anything or anyone there, and no water was running in the tub. So after a while we wouldn't even check when we heard it. We'd just laugh and say it must be Lucy pouring a bath for herself."

Cleanliness, it should be noted, was another of Mad Lucy's idiosyncrasies. She was known to often have taken several baths a day.

The Missing Vault at Bruton Parish Church

(Williamsburg)

o mystic spirits haunt the old cemetery at historic Bruton Parish Church in Williamsburg?

If not, then how else would one explain the unbelievably bizarre activities which took place in this otherwise quiet community in the summer and fall of 1991; events which shook townspeople to their core for a period of several months and created international media attention.

The strangeness seemed to peak in the early morning hours of November 27, 1991, when a Colonial Williamsburg security officer, patrolling the famous Duke of Gloucester Street at 4:30 in the morning, heard some noise coming from the Bruton Parish Church graveyard. He then shined his flashlight on an eerie scene: two men, pick and shovels in hand, were digging a huge hole amidst the centuries-old tombstones. The instant the beam of light hit them, the men dropped their tools, leaped over a brick wall, and escaped in the darkness. The officer then walked to the site of their activity and stared into the bottom of a seven-and-a-half- foot deep pit!

The mystery was not quite as deep as the pit, however, because this was the second attempt at an illegal entry into the sacred grounds of the church in two months. A previous surreptitious excavation had taken place during the pre-dawn hours of September 9, and it, too, had been interrupted by authorities. The perpetrators were then identified as being a trio of New Age activists from Santa Fe, New Mexico: 39-year-old Marsha Middleton, her husband, Frank Flint, and Doug Moore.

They were not your everyday ordinary grave robbers. Quite the contrary. They were driven in their nocturnal quests by a profound belief that a secret vault lay buried deep in a corner of the cemetery — a vault which they felt held invaluable papers that would provide the guidance to a "new world order." So possessed were they in their quest to uncover the subterranean vault, that even after they had been caught and identified in the September

Bruton Parish Church

dig, and threatened with prosecution if they ever returned, they came back to search again in November anyway. Mrs. Middleton said at the time that they "were guided" to come back by a Biblical passage in the book of Revelations: "We have to stand up for what we believe and know is true."

What they believed was that the mystical vault, which they said was buried secretly in early colonial days, contained copper cylinders holding the lost manuscripts of Sir Francis Bacon, a brilliant philosopher and scientist who was born in England in 1561 and died in 1626. Further, these papers were said to hold the key for a "new united world, and would be a precursor to the second coming of Jesus Christ." It was also speculated that the manuscripts would prove that Bacon was actually the author of the great works that have been attributed to William Shakespeare!

Such an extraordinary assertion was not new with Mrs. Middleton and her tunneling associates. In fact, the feeling that such a vault existed was first raised more than 55 years ago by a California woman named Marie Bauer Hall. She had done extensive research on the subject and came to Williamsburg in 1938 to sponsor an authorized search at Bruton Parish church.

Mrs. Hall became convinced that Bacon's long-lost manuscripts had not really been lost at all — they had been hidden. She said that by deciphering complex codes contained in Bacon's published works, in Shakespeare's plays, and on ancient church tombstones, she had discovered that one of Bacon's descendents had brought the invaluable papers to America and buried them at the Williamsburg site in 1676.

The current church was built in 1715, but a previous church existed there before, dating into the 17th century. Armed with her research studies and properly financed, Mrs. Hall somehow convinced vestry officials to allow her to dig for the vault. Excavations began on June 9, 1938, at the base of the bell tower. At a depth of nine feet, workers came upon a "tomb-like structure." Mrs. Hall said this was not the vault, and that they had been digging in the wrong place. She then began to decipher directions from other tombstones in the cemetery, and felt the actual location would be nearer the site of the original church foundation.

Records indicated the first building had been completed in 1683. By translating dates on the stones into feet she determined where they should next dig. For example, one grave marker date of 1711 was measured off at 1,711 feet from a point on the nearby College of William and Mary campus, which she said she had decoded as being the point from which to start.

On August 26, 1938, they began again, and this time they uncovered "bricks laid in the form of an old foundation." Three days later the entire foundation was laid bare, 65 feet by 28 feet, which is exactly what Mrs. Hall had predicted. The dig stirred considerable excitement in the then-sleepy town. College students and visitors crowded the scene and created a circus-like atmosphere. Eventually, at a depth of nearly 20 feet, "a body of about 10 feet square, partially filled and much larger than an ordinary tomb," was found.

At this point, for a reason that remains unexplained to this day, church officials abruptly ordered the massive hole filled. Mrs. Hall said she was never told why the effort was discontinued. So the mystery remained unsolved, and largely forgotten, for nearly 50 years.

In 1985, Mrs. Hall, who apparently had never lost faith in her belief that the vault existed, arranged for some scientific testing at the site. This included ground penetrating radar, magnetometric readings and electrical resistivity measurements. The first results were unsuccessful because they didn't go deep enough. However, subsequent tests turned up tantalizing clues. One of the investigators, Dr. Billy Hibbard, a chemist, said, "Absolutely, there is a chance something is there because we got a basic difference in resistance measurements in the area they believe the vault is located."

Again, strangely, the testing was halted, and the parish grounds were left undisturbed until Mrs. Middleton and the two men arrived on the scene in 1991. Amidst a swirl of publicity generated by their two nocturnal diggings, church officials finally relented and authorized a team of Colonial Williamsburg archeological experts and a geology professor to try and answer once and for all the question of whether or not there was a vault there.

In the summer of 1992 they began work, drilling core borings straight down and at diagonal angles under the grave site of Anna Graham. They again found the foundations of the original church, and a portion of a casket made of wood with straps of leather around it. This was believed to be the grave of a child. The experts drilled deeply into the ground and said they found only soil which had been "undisturbed for thousands of years."

This seemed to satisfy all but the most die-hard Bacon enthusiasts, including Mrs. Middleton and her team. They still believed the vault existed somewhere in the Bruton Parish church yard, and that the archeologists had bored in the wrong place.

And so, to some at least, the mystery remains. Is there a vault? Does it contain the missing Bacon papers? Would such papers prove that Bacon had written Shakespeare's plays? Would the papers also lay the groundwork for a New World Order?

Such puzzlers may never be answered. There are a couple of intriguing footnotes to this whole incredible episode, one psychically related. Ivor Noel-Hume is the much respected, retired head of archeology at Colonial Williamsburg. He is an expert of international renown, and has written a number of books and articles on colonial era discoveries. At the height of the controversy, in October 1991, at a public meeting on the subject of the vault, he told a crowd of townspeople, curiosity seekers, and media representatives that he had in his possession a tape of a psychic reading made in Canada in 1974. The reading indicated that a "mysterious vault" was buried in a churchyard. The psychic said it contained "a box with maps and papers," and she identified the owner of the box as ... Sir Francis Bacon!

And then, one wonders why church authorities so abruptly halted the 1938 excavations, just when it appeared they were about to discover something which might unveil the mystery. One of those who questioned this peculiar action is Marshall Allen, a retired mechanical engineer now living in Pennsylvania. He had been a student at William and Mary in 1938, and had witnessed the diggings then. He was interviewed by Richmond Times Dispatch writer Wilford Kale in September 1991. Kale wrote that "something was found about 10 feet under the Bruton Parish Church yard in November 1938. Some people said it was a burial vault. Indeed, church vestry minutes cryptically suggested it was a coffin."

Allen disagreed. "It looked too wide to be a coffin," he said. Kale noted that Allen "believes something was found that caused either Bruton vestry leaders or Colonial Williamsburg officials to suddenly end the excavations." Allen added that "had the vault ever been buried on the site it would have been easy to find by digging down to the undisturbed earth, but in the manner in which it was performed, there can be no conclusive evidence given.

"I know they found a very large box," Allen continued. "It was about four-and-a-half feet wide and they didn't know how long it was because it was never uncovered. They never finished digging it out. It was between nine and 10 feet deep. . . When the box was found, photographers climbed over the wall and jumped inside of the hole and began taking pictures. Everyone got excited and they (the officials) cleared out the whole mess. Then the church people said that's a coffin and we can't have any more digging and everything was stopped. They could have found out what it was. But the way it was handled left a bad taste and is the reason why the story has continued until this day."

It thus seems somehow appropriate that a nightly ghost tour, based on the author's book, "The Ghosts of Williamsburg," wends it way from the campus of William and Mary, past several historic houses in Colonial Williamsburg, and winds up in the Bruton Parish Church cemetery. There, tourists are told of some of the legendary haunts of the area, unaware that they are standing on sacred grounds that may contain the answer to one of the most enigmatic mysteries of all!

* * * * *

THE MYSTICAL NEW AGE

ew Age religion has been described as encompassing a myriad of beliefs, which, for the most part, deal with the mystical side of religion, ranging from pyramid power and astrology to out-of- body experiences. It is said to be a religion "with a vision" to create a "new world order" that would allow drawing on other unusual beliefs for the development of personal faith. Mrs. Hall's late husband, Manly P. Hall, was reported to be one of the founders of New Age, and the Los Angeles Times once called him, before his death in 1990, "the last remaining Western mystic." Many New Agers believed that Sir Francis Bacon set a course for the new world order in the papers he wrote; papers that have been missing for nearly four centuries.

The Jealous Barkeep of Yorktown

(Yorktown)

ittle did Margaret Thompson know what lay ahead of her when she moved into the old medical shop in Yorktown in 1981. After all, she was excited, and justifiably so. She was now to reside in the heart of the town's historic section, and she was within easy walking distance of her office at the National Park Service. She loved her job as a park officer, and everything appeared to be going her way. Margaret, for the moment at least, was at peace with the world.

The serenity lasted only a few months. Then all hell broke loose. "It started with the flowers," the attractive, effervescent Margaret says today. "I love flowers. I had put all kinds of flowers in the house, most of them in glass jars, and I had placed them on the deep window sills. Well, I came home from work one evening, and the flowers, jars and all, were thrown at me. They were literally thrown at me. And there was no one else in the house. Needless to day, it unnerved me. I have a degree in science — biology — so I was looking for a rational explanation. There had to be one. But I couldn't find it.

"That was the first experience I had with the presence that came to be an intimate if not always welcome part of my life for the next four years," Margaret says. Whatever it was, it made itself known in a number of different ways. "I would hear footsteps in the attic late at night, yet I knew no one was there," she adds. "I had a double dead-bolt lock on the front and back doors. There was no way for anyone to get in, yet the footsteps were very distinct. And every time I would search for the source, I found nothing.

I would leave some lights on when I went to sleep and when I woke up the entire house would be in darkness. The lights had all been turned out. And then there were the cold spots. Usually they were around the fireplace, or by my bed, or in the bathroom. You could move just a few feet, from one spot to another, and the temperature seemed to drop 10 to 20 degrees. Then if you took a few steps to the other side, you would be out of it. It was weird."

Perplexed, Margaret told some co-workers about her experiences, and some stayed with her in the house. Nothing ever happened while they were there, and they began giving Margaret strange looks. "People kept telling me I was just nervous and imagining things," she remembers. "Hell, I don't have a nervous bone in my body. They began to think I was crazy, so I stopped telling anybody about it."

The occurrences continued. The ghost seemed to be playful at times, and would hide or misplace Margaret's clothes and personal items. She would search for days for things only to find them out in the open in places where they hadn't been before. Once her mother, Elizabeth Thompson of Richmond, came over for a visit. "She always wore a special pair of flat shoes when she drove," Margaret says. "So when she arrived we placed the shoes on the attic steps. A few days later when she was ready to leave, the shoes were gone. We looked everywhere, but we couldn't find them. They had disappeared. She drove back to Richmond and I followed her in my car. When we got there, we walked into the kitchen, and there were her driving shoes, sitting on top of the kitchen table!"

Margaret's mother had two other brushes with the presence while she was visiting her daughter at Yorktown. On one occasion, she clearly heard the sounds of heavy breathing coming from the fireplace area. On another, a camera's flash attachment exploded on a table near the fireplace. Mrs. Thompson couldn't explain such happenings, but she refused to believe they had anything to do with the supernatural.

At times Margaret would see her rocking chair rock by itself. Her kitten would sometimes slap a paw and leap at an imaginary string, as if it was being dangled by an unseen hand. And there were the odors; powerful odors. "There were three distinct ones," Margaret says. One was wintergreen, and one was Resonil, which is an old-time salve used for such things as scraped knees.

Margaret described the third smell as that of a musty old vacuum cleaner bag, which she says is a "standard other world odor." These smells would come and go, as if they were directly associated with the ghost.

As time went on, Margaret began to sense that it was a male spirit and "he" was jealous. It seemed that every time she had a date, if he didn't like the date, he would make his displeasure known. Light fuses would blow inexplicably. Keys would be lost. Items of clothing would be missing, and when there was real irritation, dishes would be smashed and the whole house would be torn apart.

"He" particularly didn't like Margaret's square dance partner. "In square dancing you have matching costumes, down to the handkerchief," she explains. "It's a very precise ensemble, and on nights when I was supposed to go dancing, I couldn't find certain parts of the outfit. So I couldn't go on those nights. Usually, the next day they would surface. It was very frustrating."

Even more bothersome were the times when Margaret would come home from a date to find her house ransacked. "Dishes were all over the floor, and it looked like every drawer in the house had been turned upside down and the contents dumped out," she says. "I really got mad. I cussed at 'him.' I told him I was tired of cleaning up after him." It got so bad, she bought a set of plastic dishes. On one or two occasions she even witnessed objects rising off tables and sailing through the air.

Twice, Margaret caught fleeting glimpses of her spirit. Once, she saw a "flash of white" in the kitchen. The other time, on Yorktown Day, she caught the reflection of a man's shoulder in her mirror. He was clothed in white and had a "blousy-type" sleeve reminiscent of colonial garb. "I thought someone had gotten into the house and I yelled at him to get out," Margaret says. "But when I turned around to face the mirror there was no one there. I was told later that he wouldn't fully materialize in front of me because there was not enough positive kinetic energy. Since I was not a true believer, there were some 'unfavorable vibes' which held him back."

After a period of several months of intermittent occurrences, the combination of curiosity and frustration got to Margaret. If she were going to continue to be haunted, she wanted to know something about who was doing the haunting and why. Friends suggested she contact an area medium who had a reputation for contacting spirits from "the other world." A seance was set up in

Margaret's house. The attendees were Margaret, the medium, and two "friendlies," who were described as people with positive vibes which help bring out spirits.

The seance proved both informative and eventful. "We heard pacing in the attic," Margaret recalls. "There were the sounds of someone going up and down the stairs, and doors being scratched. There was a big-leafed plant in the room and the leaves bent as if they were being blown by a high wind. The place where the medium sat got as cold as ice, although I was sitting just across the room from her and I was hot.

"The medium said the spirit was in the room with us. She said he was a white male of British lineage from a noble family. He was the second or third son, who had been sent to America more than 200 years ago in disgrace. He was in his 30s, over six feet tall and had dark hair and dark eyes and a full beard. He spoke with a French accent, and he had a badly healed duel wound on his right palm. This possibly explained the odors of wintergreen and Resonil."

The medium said his name was Robert Queasly Baker and that he was very romantic and considered himself a poet. She said he worked in Yorktown during the time of the Revolutionary War in a tavern. "That fit perfectly," Margaret says, "because the medical shop where I lived had been built over the foundation of an old tavern of that period."

The woman said Robert had fought in the battle of Yorktown and had later become destitute, fell ill and died from a disease and was buried in an unmarked grave in the pauper's cemetery in Yorktown. "There was a pauper's cemetery just as she described it," Margaret says, "but the medium had been in town for just a week or two, and I am sure she had no way of knowing about it."

The medium went on. The reason Robert was "with" Margaret was the fact that they had been lovers in the 18th century. He had been a barkeep and she had been a bar maid, a wench "of loose morals." He retained a romantic interest in her and was very protective. This explained his jealous rages when she went out on dates.

The medium then talked about the cold spots in the house. This was Robert. Whenever he was present there would be a cold spot, generally by Margaret's bed, in her bathroom, or by the fireplace with which, the woman said, he was somehow associated. At the end of the seance, the medium asked Robert to leave the house, and within minutes there was a sharp slamming of the front door.

Margaret Thompson

Afterwards, Margaret did some detective work. She verified that there had been an old tavern on the site, and that there was a pauper's cemetery on Read Street, now hidden under a paved parking lot. She found the name Robert Queasly Baker in colonial records. His appearance was substantiated some time later by the Yorktown visit of a 300-pound psychic who told her that Robert did indeed have piercing black eyes, with flaming dark red hair and beard, "Like that of a Viking." The psychic was in town to investigate a ghost in the Moore House, and nearly died in the effort. While walking up the stairs in the house he collapsed and said he was suffocating, he couldn't breathe. Margaret helped revive him.

After the seance, Robert's activities diminished somewhat, although he still kicked up a fuss when he became upset. For example, in October 1982, Margaret agreed to be interviewed for a newspaper article about her ghost if the writer would not reveal her name or where she lived. When she met the reporter, Margaret told her, "I had a hard time getting out of the house this morning. All the fuses were blowing, my appliances wouldn't work, and my clothes were out of place. He's not very happy about this story."

On at least two occasions Robert, who Margaret says often travelled with her, was inadvertently left behind when she returned home. Uncomfortable in strange surroundings, he created mild forms of havoc which brought pleas to Margaret to "get him out of here." Once, for example, she visited her mother in Richmond during the year-end holiday season, and then returned home. Hardly had she arrived when her mother, irate, called. Why, she wanted to know, had Margaret stuffed Christmas cookies deep down into the recesses of her sofa?

"You have to understand that nobody goes into my mother's living room unless she is having special guests," Margaret says. "I told her I hadn't been near the room and that I certainly wouldn't cram cookies in the couch. I said it must be Robert. He must have gotten left behind. She nearly panicked. She wanted me to get him out of there, so I yelled through the phone for Robert to leave. Mother told me later that night after she hung up, she heard the front door slam. I guess Robert didn't want to stay where he wasn't wanted."

On the other occasion, Robert got left behind at the volunteer fire station on Hubbard Lane in Williamsburg. Margaret served as an emergency medical technician, certified in CPR, at the station a few years ago, and sometimes, it seemed, Robert went with her. They even "talked" to him through a Ouija board. This particular time, Margaret left the station to go home and the firemen put a big pot of water on the stove to make a batch of spaghetti, only the water wouldn't boil. They called Margaret and she ordered Robert to leave. Within minutes the firemen heard one of their exterior doors slam shut, and simultaneously, the water on the stove began to boil.

As a sidelight, Margaret says that through Robert during an Ouija session, the volunteers found out their station was built on or very close to an old Indian graveyard. In fact, Robert told them about one of the Indians, an old squaw named Severette. It was she, the firemen believed, who once left a woman's footprints in the dust of the loft in the station house. That the place had spirits of its own became more certain in Margaret's mind one night when she came in to pull her shift. She found that a Bible had been placed on every bunk in the building, but no one would tell her why.

"I couldn't get anyone to talk," she recalls. "They all were as white as sheets. Something had obviously scared them." Finally, the truth came out. The volunteers had been playing with the Ouija board when they "conjured up the Devil." They said they looked at one of the windows, which was set up high off the ground, and they saw the image of Satan himself looking down upon them. That's when they had gotten out the Bibles and that's all Margaret could get out of them. No one wanted to talk any more about it.

As time wore on, Robert's appearances became less frequent. In 1984, Margaret left the National Park Service and moved to Williamsburg. Since then he has not thrown any tantrums. In fact, he has been eerily silent. "I feel he is still there. He's still protecting me," Margaret says. "I know he'll never harm me. Now, he doesn't feel I need him as much."

Recently, Margaret went to another psychic and had more readings. From these she was told that she and Robert actually had been together in three different lifetimes. One in Yorktown, one during Christ's time on earth, and one in ancient Egyptian times. Perhaps that explains why Margaret, when asked the question if she would be relieved if Robert ever left for good, answered, "I'd never believe he was really gone. I've got him for life."

The Terrible Crash That Wasn't

(Newport News)

(Author's note: As I have often said, I am continually amazed at the great variety of ghostly psychic phenomena which I have encountered in my travels across the state. One, of course, hears more than his share of footsteps in the attic and moans in the basement, and after a while you have to fight the feeling that you have "heard it all." But the reality is, you never have. There seems always to be something new in the way of spiritual manifestations in this rich and beautiful state.

I have to admit, one of the most unusual cases I ever heard came to me in October 1993, when I was telling ghost stories to children as part of the annual Newport News Fall Festival. A recently retired Hampton Police Department officer came up to me, and said, "I've got a story to tell you, but you'd never believe it." "Try me," I countered with a smile. But he was genuinely reluctant. He said I would think he was crazy. I told him I had heard just about everything regarding ghosts, and that I deeply believed in the sincerity of the people I interviewed, regardless of how extreme their experiences were. After several more minutes of talking back and forth, the former officer finally told me. His name is Richard Rohrbaugh, and what happened to him one night about 10 or 12 years ago, he has forgotten the exact date, speaks for itself. All I could add after hearing it, was that "incredible" was far too weak a word to describe it.)

e were on detective duty, in plain clothes and in an unmarked car," Rohrbaugh remembers. "There were three of us, myself, Wayne Pendergrass, and Richard Martin. Wayne is still with the Hampton Police Department, and Richard is with the Newport News police. We were working the four to midnight shift, and I remember we had just completed investigating a case, it was midnight or possibly one or two in the morning, and we were on our way back to the station to call it a night."

Rohrbaugh continues: "We were going down Mercury Boulevard when Richard spotted a pickup truck in the used car lot at Holloman Pontiac. He asked if we could swing by the lot to take a look at it, as he was in the market for a truck. We said sure. We pulled into the lot and were looking at the truck, when a car came roaring by on Mercury going the wrong way. It was going east in the west bound lane at an excessively high rate of speed. All three of us saw it at once. We couldn't tell what model it was because it was so dark. All we could see were the headlights. Richard or Wayne, I can't remember who, said, 'look at that. Where do you think he's going?'

"We all kind of craned our necks to follow the car down the street. Then we saw another car's headlights, heading west in the lane, at the intersection of Mercury and Armistead, and in an instant they smashed head-on into each other. It was a terrible crash, at high speed. There was an awful sound of metal colliding and glass breaking. Glass and metal were strewn everywhere, all over the intersection, and a big cloud of steam rose up from the busted radiators.

"Richard ran over to our car and immediately radioed to our dispatcher that there was a horrible accident at the intersection of Mercury and Armistead and there were undoubtedly serious injuries and possibly fatalities. He asked the dispatcher to send an ambulance and a marked car (with uniformed patrolmen) to handle the accident.

"We then jumped into our car and sped to the scene, which was only about a half block away. It couldn't have taken us more than a minute or two to get there.

"When we got to the site, there was nothing there! I mean nothing! There were no cars. There was no twisted metal, no broken glass, no injured or killed people, no blood, nothing! It was almost as if someone had taken a vacuum cleaner and sucked up the place. We just looked at each other in utter amazement."

"That's true," confirms Wayne Pendergrass, a seasoned veteran with more than 20 years as a member of the Hampton Police Department. "We all saw the same thing — the car speeding the wrong way up Mercury, and the collision at the intersection. Yet there was nothing there. There was a small pool of water, and some steam rising, but that was it. Not even an oil slick."

Both Rohrbaugh and Pendergrass adamantly state that there was no way either of the cars could have driven off. First, the crash was so destructive, the cars wouldn't have been in any condition to move, much less the people inside them. Second, as they raced to the scene, taking no more than 90 or 120 seconds, they saw no other cars on the road in either direction!

"You explain it," Rohrbaugh says. "I can't. In all my years on the force I never saw anything like it. We all three saw the same thing at the same time. We all three know there is no way either of the cars could have driven off. Yet there was nothing there!"

Within minutes the marked patrol car and the ambulance arrived, and the uniformed officers asked the detectives where the accident was. "When we told them, right here, they just looked at us in bewilderment," Rohrbaugh says. "They asked us if we had been on the sauce, and I have to admit, at that point it was kind of embarrassing. I'm sure they thought we were crazy. I think now that if I had been by myself and come upon the scene I probably never would have called it in. I couldn't explain it and I didn't even want to talk about it for a long time afterwards."

There may be sort of a psychic precedence for the bizarre accident the three officers witnessed. There are, for example, a number of curious reported incidents of vanishing hitchhikers. A typical one occurred a few years ago to a young man driving between Greensboro and Lexington, North Carolina. It was on a foggy summer night, and as he neared a tunnel that went under some train tracks he slowed down. Many bad wrecks had taken place at this spot.

Halfway through the tunnel he saw what he described as "an indistinct white figure with arm raised in a gesture of distress." He slammed on his brakes. It was, he said, "a girl, young, beautiful, resplendent in a long white evening dress. Her troubled eyes were glaring straight toward him." Obviously, she was in need. he asked if he could help her and she replied, in a strange low voice, "yes. I want to go home. I live in High Point." She got in his car and they drove off. She said she had been at a dance and had gotten into a quarrel with her boyfriend. She had gotten out of his car at the spot where the young man saw her. She didn't speak again until they arrived in High Point, then she pointed out where she lived. He parked and got out of the car to go around and open the door for her.

But when he opened the door there was no one there! She had disappeared. Totally confused, he went up to the house they had pulled in front of and knocked on the door. A white-haired woman in a night robe opened the door. He told her he had just brought a girl to this house. He had picked her up on the highway, but she had vanished.

The woman didn't seem surprised. She merely asked where he had picked her up. At the Jamestown underpass he told the woman.

"Yes, I know," she responded. "That was my daughter. She was killed in a wreck at that tunnel five years ago tonight. And every year since, on this very night, she signals a young man like you to pick her up. She is still trying to get home."

Thus could it be possible that the terrible crash the officers Rohrbaugh, Pendergrass and Martin saw take place on Mercury Boulevard actually have happened, only at another time?

When asked if there had been any history of bad accidents occurring at the intersection of Mercury and Armistead, Rohrbaugh quickly responded, "oh yes. There have been a number of bad accidents there over the past few years, including some fatalities."

CHAPTER 6 5

The Ghosts of Edgar Cayce

(Virginia Beach)

I t would seem almost sacrilegious to write a book on Virginia ghosts and not include at least some mention — if not a chapter or entire section — on the extraordinary man from Virginia Beach who is widely recognized as perhaps the greatest psychic of the 20 century — Edgar Cayce.

He was also known as the "Sleeping Prophet," the "Psychic Diagnostician," and the "Miracle Worker of Virginia Beach." For more than 40 years, Cayce helped save lives, lengthen lives, cure ailments, and heal the sick through detailed "readings" he gave while in a trance-like state. Two-thirds of his more than 14,000 readings were medically related. Though he had no more than an eighth grade education, Cayce, while asleep, somehow had the ability to envision and diagnose the ailments, no matter how complicated, of people all over the country. Then, in precise, meticulous, and sophisticated detail, he would prescribe the medicines and/or treatments essential to the patient's return to full health. Often, such prescriptions included lengthy, and complex medical terminology, and, at times, obscure or long forgotten remedies of which Cayce had no knowledge when awake.

Astoundingly, of those cases verified by patients' reports, 85 percent of the diagnoses were found to be completely accurate, and those who followed the prescribed treatments got the results predicted in the readings.

Consider, for example, a couple of sample case studies. In one instance, he gave a reading for a man who had been confined to an insane asylum for three years following a nervous breakdown caused, it had been suspected, by nervous tension. In the reading, Cayce said "through pressures upon nerve energies in the coccyx area and the ileum plexus, as well as that pressure upon the lumbar axis, there had been a deflection of coordination between the sympathetic and the cerebrospinal nervous system." He further diagnosed that the man's condition had actually been caused by a spinal injury incurred by a fall. He didn't need psychotherapy. Instead, Cayce advised osteopathic adjustment and a mild, specially outlined electrotherapy to normalize the disrupted nerve forces. The treatment was followed and the results were dramatically successful. The man regained excellent health within six months and returned to a normal life.

Cayce's wife, Gertrude, once suffered from what doctors had diagnosed as incurable tuberculosis. He gave her a reading and prescribed a diet, some simple drugs, and an unheard of treatment: inhaling apple brandy fumes from a charred oak keg. Remarkably, it worked, and Mrs. Cayce recovered from her "incurable" tuberculosis.

One of the most amazing cures effected by the readings involved a young girl who had suddenly gone insane. Her condition did not respond to any of the treatments administered at the hospital. In desperation, her parents turned to Cayce for help. In his sleep-state, he described the trouble as an impacted wisdom tooth which was disrupting nerve and brain function. He said when the tooth was removed, the trouble would disappear. He had never seen the girl — he was 400 miles away from the hospital where she was staying — yet when a dentist examined her, the impaction was found exactly as outlined. The dentist removed the tooth. Four hours later the girl had regained her normal state of mind and never again showed any symptoms of mental disturbance.

To further his work for the benefit of mankind — Cayce never really profited in a material sense from his psychic powers — he founded, in 1931, the Association for Research and Enlightenment at 67th Street and Atlantic Avenue in Virginia Beach. Today, the A.R.E., headed by his grandson, Charles Thomas Cayce, has 100,000 members worldwide, and is dedicated to physical, mental and spiritual self-improvement programs through researching and applying the information in Edgar Cayce's psychic readings.

Eventually, in addition to medical diagnoses, the scope of his readings expanded to include information and advice on approximately 10,000 different subjects. These included such topics as world religions, philosophy, psychology, dreams, history, reincarnation, soul growth, diet and nutrition, spiritual development, and the fabled lost continent of Atlantis, among others.

When he died in 1945, Edgar Cayce left behind a legacy of readings which have stood the test of decades of intensive research and study. He remains the most documented psychic of all times.

Did Edgar Cayce ever have any experiences with ghosts? The answer, says Charles Thomas, is yes. "I was only three when my grandfather died, so I can only tell you what I heard from members of the family and friends," he adds. "My father (Hugh Lynn Cayce, now dead) and my uncle (Edgar Evans Cayce, still living in Virginia Beach) mentioned stories about my grandfather communicating with ghosts. Are there such things as ghosts? The answer is yes. Some people are talented or gifted in ways of communicating with spirits. They are psychically talented in the same way a person may be musically or athletically talented."

Vada F. Carlson, in a short composition on the early life of Edgar Cayce titled, "The Vision of the Promise," said that Edgar saw and played with a whole group of ghostly playmates, both boys and girls. "It was disappointing to Edgar," Carlson wrote, "that the grownups could not see the 'play people' with whom he had so much fun, but Anna Seay, a small girl who lived nearby and sometimes came over to play with him, saw them as well as he did. She and Edgar played happily with them in woodsy places and in the cool shade of the barn. Edgar's mother believed him when he told her about the invisible children. . . His mother was the one person in the world who completely understood him. . . One day she glanced out the window and saw them waiting in the yard for him. 'Go play with your friends,' she told him. 'They're waiting.' It made Edgar very happy to know that she, too, could see the children."

Cayce, Carlson reported, seemed amazed that his spectral friends could run in the rain without getting wet, and he wondered why they always disappeared whenever grownups came near. Once Edgar was talking and laughing in the field when his father came by and asked him who he was talking to. "My friends," he told him. "Where are they?" asked his father. "Right here," the boy said, pointing. But his father saw no one.

There are two specific references in Edgar Cayce's authorized biography — written by his long-time friend Thomas Sugrue during Cayce's lifetime — relating to ghosts. One involved the death of his grandfather when Edgar was a small boy of five or six. They had been out horseback riding together, Grandpa in front, little Edgar behind him, holding on. They stopped in a pond to water the horse, and the boy slid off. Suddenly, the horse threw up its head, reared, and plunged into deeper water. "We don't really know what happened," says Charles Thomas Cayce today. "Perhaps it was frightened by a snake." The horse swam to the other side of the pond and raced to a fence, failed to jump it, and galloped back to the pond, with Grandpa hanging on.

This time the horse stumbled as it entered the water, and Grandpa was thrown over its head, landing on his back. The horse got to its feet, reared again, and brought the full force of its forefeet down on the old man's chest. Then it ran off. Grandpa's head was under water. Young Edgar called to him and when there was no answer, frightened, he ran for help. But by then it was too late and his grandfather was dead. Edgar said that even at that moment, he could still talk with his grandfather, but in the excitement and the grief, no one listened to him.

Later, Sugrue said in his biography that Edgar would see his grandfather "sometimes in the barns, usually when the tobacco was being fired. Of course, Grandpa wasn't really there. You could see through him if you looked real hard." Edgar would only tell his mother and grandmother about the apparitions, because he knew

Association for Research and Enlightenment

that at that time it would have angered his father. But his grand-mother liked him to tell her about seeing Grandpa.

Once when Edgar came into the house his mother asked him what he had been doing. He told her he was visiting with Grandpa in the tobacco barn. His mother seemed unconcerned, but one of his aunts who was visiting, told him he was a wicked boy. "How can you tell such wicked lies, when you know your grandfather is dead and buried?" she chided. "But I saw him," Edgar pleaded. "I talked to him, and he talked to me." When the aunt scolded Edgar's mother, she merely replied that Edgar was a truthful boy, and that if he said he saw his grandfather, she did not doubt him.

The second reference in the biography to his seeing a presence occurred when Edgar was 12 years old. "When he was young, my grandfather spent a lot of time alone in the fields," says Charles Thomas. He would go out often to read his Bible. One afternoon in May as he sat alone in the woods, reading the story of Manoah, he became aware of the presence of someone else."

Edgar looked up and saw a woman standing before him. At first, peering into the sun after reading, he thought it was his mother. But then she spoke and he realized it was someone he did not know. "Her voice," wrote Sugrue, "was soft and very clear; it reminded him of music." The woman told him his prayers had been answered and she asked him what he would like most of all, so that she might give it to him.

At first, he could not speak. He was frightened, especially when he noticed that she had shadows on her back "shaped like wings." She reassured him by smiling. Finally, he managed to say that, "most of all, I would like to be helpful to others, and espe-cially to children when they are sick." Then, suddenly, the woman was gone.

Edgar ran home and told his mother of the ethereal experience. He told her that maybe he had been reading the Bible too much and was losing his sanity. She reassured him by quoting from the Gospel of St. John. ". . . Verily, verily, I say unto you, Whatsoever ye shall ask the Father in my name, he will give it (to) you. Hitherto have ye asked nothing in my name: ask, and ye shall receive, that your joy may be full." Then she told her son that because he was a good boy and wanted to help others, "why shouldn't your prayers be heard?"

They talked about the meaning of the apparitional visit. It might mean, she told Edgar, that he was destined to become a doc-tor, or a preacher, or possibly a missionary. Only later, when he became fully aware of his psychic powers, did he realize the true meaning of his experience. It meant that he was to use those powers in a positive way to help others.

And the first true clue to his great gift came the next evening. He had done miserably at school that day, particularly in his spelling lessons. When he couldn't correctly spell the word "cabin," his teacher made him stay after school and write "cabin" 500 times on the blackboard. His father heard about the incident and that night he told Edgar he was a disgrace to the family. After supper the boy and his father sat for hours, poring over the lesson book, and Edgar's answers were all wrong. Twice Squire Cayce had become so exasperated, he had knocked the boy out of his chair.

Then, tired and sleepy, Edgar heard the voice of the woman he had seen the day before. She told him if he could sleep a little, "we can help you." He begged his father to let him rest. He reluctantly agreed, telling him it would be his last chance. The Squire then went into the kitchen for a few minutes and Edgar, almost instantly, nodded off.

When he father came back, Edgar woke up and told him he knew his lessons. And he did. He got every word right. Not only that, he knew the assignment for the next day. In fact, by sleeping on his book, he had, somehow, inexplicably, memorized every word and picture on every page in the book. He could envision the word, where it was on the page, and what the illustrations were. When he spelled "synthesis" perfectly, the Squire lost his temper and struck him again.

When Edgar told his mother about the episode the next day, and still knew every word on every page of the book, she said to him that she was sure the lady was "keeping her promise." After that Edgar would take other school books to bed, put them under his pillow and sleep on them, and the next day he would know everything in the book. When his befuddled father asked him how he did it, he told him he didn't know. But it worked!

Was the lady angel an apparition or a dream? "I'm not sure," says Charles Thomas. "But I was told that it was something he experienced while he was awake, so I don't think it was a dream."

Cayce apparently had a number of encounters with ghosts during his adult years as well, and although this is not specifically addressed in his readings, Charles Thomas says his father, Hugh Lynn Cayce, remembered Edgar talking about such incidents at times. Hugh Lynn, in fact, in a lecture series, told of the gentle tapping one evening at a downstairs window. Edgar rose from his bed to go down and see what it was. Apparently, it was an apparition, because Hugh Lynn wrote: "It seemed to him (Edgar) perfectly natural procedure to get up, go downstairs, unlock the front door and let in a rather diffident young woman who had been quite dead a few years!"

The woman told Cayce in so many words that she had died (of toxic throat infection) without fully realizing she was dead, and she was having a terrible time adjusting to "the other side." In this confused state, she had haunted Cayce's former photographic studio in Selma, Alabama, but then, when she found out he had moved to Virginia Beach, she had travelled there to see if he could help her. He did. Hugh Lynn said he taught her how to release herself from what some people call the "earthbound condition," and to move forward in her path of development.

"Edgar Cayce both saw and heard this girl," Hugh Lynn said. "Actually he saw *through* her, because she wasn't exactly solid, but she was solid enough to ask for his help, and to tap on the window loud enough to attract his attention." Hugh Lynn said this was a combination of clairvoyance and clairaudience.

Hugh Lynn himself, along with other members of his family, experienced ghostly visitations once in their house at Virginia Beach shortly after Squire Cayce, Hugh Lynn's grandfather, had died. They heard "puttering around" upstairs, mostly in a bedroom, when there was no one upstairs. Edgar told everyone not to worry, that it was just his father "returning" to straighten out some papers before he "left." Edgar said to just leave him alone and he would be gone pretty soon.

But Hugh Lynn couldn't resist the temptation. "I heard the noise so clearly at lunch," he said later, "that I insisted on running upstairs to check." As he reached the landing before getting to the top of the stairs, he felt a presence which he described as "a cold area ... a feeling like cobwebs." Hugh Lynn said "every hair stood at attention."

One evening in the fall of 1933, Edgar was alone downstairs in his Virginia Beach house, listening to the radio, when suddenly the room got icy cold, and he felt something "uncanny or unusual" taking place. When Edgar looked toward the radio, he realized that a friend of his who had been dead for several months, was sitting in front of the radio!

Cayce said, "he turned and smiled at me, saying 'There is the survival of personality. I know! And a life of service and prayer is the only one to live.' I was shaking all over. He said nothing more and he just seemed to disappear. I turned off the radio. It still appeared as if the room was full of some presence. As I switched off the light and climbed the stairs, I could hear many voices coming from the darkened room.

'Jumping in bed and shivering from cold, I aroused my wife. She asked me why I hadn't turned off the radio. I assured her that I had. She opened the door and said, 'I hear it. I hear voices.' We both did."

Cayce wrote of the experience in a short monograph. He noted in it that this particular friend had been an executive of the Western Union Telegraph Company in Chicago, and that when the two of them had gotten together, they often discussed whether or not there was a survival of personality after death. Cayce said the friend would usually close the talk by saying, "Well, whoever one goes first will communicate with the other."

Perhaps the most frightening manifestation occurred in June 1936, on a bright sunny day, when Edgar was hoeing in his garden. He heard a noise he described like "a swarming of bees." Startled, he looked up and saw in the sky a chariot drawn by four white horses. Then he heard a voice saying "look behind you." When he did, he saw a man with a shield and helmet, kneeguards and a cape, clad in burnished silver. The phantom raised his hand in salute and said, "the chariot of the Lord and the horsemen thereof." With that, the vision vanished. Cayce was so upset, he bolted into the house and locked himself in his study. Hours later, when he emerged, he said what he saw signalled the approach of World War II and the death of millions.

There were several other incidents involving ghostly visitations. Cayce seemed to attract them, but many were not officially recorded, and have been lost to memory lapses over the years. Others now are but fragmentary remembrances. Gerry McDowell, a spry septuagenarian who works in the library of the Association for Research and Enlightenment, says she recalls one such occasion, hidden somewhere in the A.R.E.'s voluminous files. Edgar was on a train travelling from Virginia Beach to Hopkinsville, Kentucky, his birthplace. A man sat down next to him and they carried on a conversation for some time. Then the man told Edgar that he had recently drowned at Virginia Beach!

Edgar, who died in 1945, is said to have reappeared at least once, coincidentally to the same Gerry McDowell. It happened in 1976. Gerry at the time was a volunteer worker at A.R.E. She had finished a shift at her full time job, and not feeling tired, had gone out to the old building at 67th and Atlantic Avenue in Virginia Beach to do some work there. But when she kept nodding off, she was told to go outside in the hallway and lie down on the couch. It was the same couch that Edgar had used to sleep on for many of his readings.

"I guess I slept for about an hour," Gerry says. "When I awoke, there, standing over me, was a man. I had never seen Edgar Cayce in life, but I recognized him immediately from his photographs. He was wearing a blue suit, a blue tie and a white shirt. He smiled at me and I smiled at him. He pointed a finger at me, and then he disappeared. I went in and told the others in the office what had happened, and they said it meant he wanted me to stay; that I would never get away from here now." Two years later Gerry joined the full time staff at A.R.E. and has worked there faithfully ever since.

* * * * *

 ertainly, one of the strangest cases Edgar Cayce ever encountered in life occurred on April 18, 1938, when he gave a reading for a troubled woman in Norfolk who believed she was possessed by a devilish "power." By the time she had come to Cayce, as a last resort, she had exhausted normal medical channels and even been to "witchcraft" doctors, to no avail. Her condition, described by her as unbearable, was apparently worsening. She said she felt like a "power" took possession of her, and she was bothered "with tiny images like tiny dwarfs crawling all over her." She added that she had a terrible time sleeping, and even when she fell asleep, she had the "perfectly awful" experience of feeling that she was a man and she wandered in search of someone "with whom to gratify sex association." She pleaded for Cayce to "dispossess" her.

In his trance-like state, Cayce envisioned the woman's "disturbing conditions," and said they become very acute because of activities produced upon the "imaginative or sympathetic nervous system." He saw toxic forces at work in her body, combined with pressures on the nervous system which produced "convulsions in the activities when the body attempts to rest." For relief from her torment, he prescribed use of an electrically driven vibrator, a "hand machine violet ray, application of oils and enemas, and a diet free of any fried foods, hog meat and white bread."

Edgar Cayce

In response to the woman's question, Cayce said the "burning sensation" which came over her — the "power" — was actually caused by the incoordination between the cerebrospinal and the sympathetic nervous system. This, he said, produced the toxic forces in her body, the burning, and the "effect of possession!"

Apparently, Cayce took a personal interest in the woman's problems, because it appears that either he or one of his top associates (it is not clear as to just who it was) stopped by to see her during a trip to Norfolk over two years later. They said the woman wouldn't invite him into the house and that they had to talk to her through a screened door. She had not followed Cayce's suggested treatment and still reported having some trouble, but she had stopped eating meat, and it was believed she felt better overall. This must have been the case for she outlived Edgar Cayce by nine years!

* * * * *

hough Charles Thomas Cayce does not profess to have psychic abilities like his grandfather did, he nevertheless has had his share of psychic experiences. For example, he once dreamed that a plane would crash on its way from Norfolk to Atlanta — and it did! Cayce has a degree in psychology, and when he has the time, he likes to work with and counsel psychically-gifted people.

One of the most unusual cases he ever encountered occurred several years ago, involving a 14-year-old school girl and her "ghostly friend." "Her name was Phyllis, and she said her unseen friend's name was Phil," Cayce remembers. She told him Phil was with her most of the time and that he had blond hair in a crew cut and had died suddenly. The girl's mother had arranged the appointment because she was understandably concerned about her daughter communicating with a dead person.

Cayce asked to speak with "Phil" but Phyllis told him he couldn't. She was the only one he would "talk" to, and he did it in a strange manner — by writing on her kneecap. Next, Cayce set up an impromptu test. He walked down the hall to another room, opened an 800-page dictionary at random, and then went back and asked Phyllis to ask Phil what page he had opened the book to. Phil wrote the page number on her knee and it was correct. Cayce was amazed. He repeated the test several times, the last time opening the dictionary without looking at the page number, possibly to preclude Phil from reading his mind. The page number was called out accurately every time!

"Whether this was a psychic ability of hers, or there really was the ghost of a person around her, I don't know," Cayce said. "In either event, it was an impressive demonstration. I did learn that Phil had only 'appeared' to her shortly after the death of her grandmother. Phyllis also said she often still saw her grandmother rocking in her favorite rocking chair, but she didn't talk about it because she knew it would upset her father."

Cayce sensed Phyllis was a little uncomfortable about the situation, so he arranged for her to meet some other teenage girls who had psychic sensitivities. After that she felt better about things. Eventually, she lost touch with Phil, which Cayce says is quite common because teens have a great desire to conform. They often try to block out their intuitive abilities.

* * * * *

nother memorable case involved a Virginia Beach teenager who appeared to be haunted by a poltergeist. Objects fell and moved around her with no apparent cause. Her mother brought her to see Cayce after a particularly disturbing incident. The girl and her mother had argued about how late she could stay out at night. As the teenager passed through the kitchen while her mother was preparing dinner, soup jumped out of the pot and all over the mother's clothes, according to the account Cayce heard. Fortunately, the soup was not hot enough to burn her, but the mother was extremely frightened. Cayce believed there was no poltergeist involved. Rather, he suspected, the girl was deeply psychic and was able to move inanimate objects without even being aware she was doing it.

* * * * *

he question is often asked: why did Edgar Cayce choose to live and work in Virginia Beach. The answer, or answers came in a reading he gave more than 65 years ago in Dayton, Ohio. "Actually, there were a couple reasons given in his reading," says Charles Thomas Cayce. "First, he envisioned, correctly, that the east coast of the United States would become a major population center, from New England to Miami. The location on the coast between New York City and Washington in the north, and the large population of Florida in the south, would mean lots of traffic back and forth, and a tremendous increase in the population in this area itself that would be helpful to his work.

"The second reason was a kind of metaphysical condition. Virginia Beach was near two large bodies of water — the Chesapeake Bay and the Atlantic Ocean, and the sand of the beach had special energy in it. There was an implication about the energies of the area being particularly conducive to psychic forces. This would be helpful in his giving of readings, sort of like good transmission."

About the Author

L. B. Taylor, Jr. — a Scorpio — is a native Virginian. He was born in Lynchburg and has a BS degree in Journalism from Florida State University. He wrote about America's space programs for 16 years, for NASA and aerospace contractors, before moving to Williamsburg, Virginia, in 1974, as public affairs director for BASF Corporation. He retired in 1993. Taylor is the author of more than 300 national magazine articles and 30 non-fiction books. His research for the book "Haunted Houses," published by Simon and Schuster in 1983, stimulated his interest in area psychic phenomena and led to the publication of five regional Virginia ghost books preceding "The Ghosts of Virginia," and "The Ghosts of Virginia, Volume II."

(Personally autographed copies of: "The Ghosts of Williamsburg" — 84 pages, illustrated, $6; "The Ghosts of Richmond" — 172 pages, illustrated, $10; "The Ghosts of Tidewater" — 232 pages, illustrated, $10; "The Ghosts of Fredericksburg" — 177 pages, illustrated, $10; and "The Ghosts of Charlottesville and Lynchburg" — 188 pages, illustrated, $10; ($40 for all five); and "The Ghosts of Virginia" (Volume I) — 400 pages, illustrated, $14 (Volumes I and II together, $25); are available from L. B. Taylor, Jr., 248 Archers Mead, Williamsburg, VA, 23185 (804-253-2636). Please add $2 for postage and handling, $4 for multiple book orders. Also, please specify to whom you wish the book(s) signed.

L. B. Taylor, Jr., is available (depending upon his schedule) to speak on the subject of Virginia ghosts to civic, social, fraternal, business, school, library and other groups. Call or write about dates and details.

OTHER BOOKS BY L. B. TAYLOR, JR.

PIECES OF EIGHT: Recovering the Riches of a Lost
                       Spanish Treasure Fleet

THAT OTHERS MAY LIVE (AIR FORCE RESCUE & RECOVERY
SERVICE)

LIFTOFF: THE STORY OF AMERICA'S SPACEPORT

FOR ALL MANKIND

GIFTS FROM SPACE (SPINOFF BENEFITS FROM SPACE RESEARCH)

CHEMISTRY CAREERS

SPACE SHUTTLE

RESCUE (TRUE STORIES OF TEENAGE HEROISM)

THE DRAFT

SHOPLIFTING

SPACE: BATTLEGROUND OF THE FUTURE

THE NUCLEAR ARMS RACE

THE NEW RIGHT

THE GHOSTS OF WILLIAMSBURG

SPOTLIGHT ON ... (FOUR TEENAGE IDOLS)

EMERGENCY SQUADS

SOUTHEAST AFRICA

DRIVING HIGH (EFFECTS OF ALCOHOL AND DRUGS ON DRIVING)

CHEMICAL AND BIOLOGICAL WARFARE

HAUNTED HOUSES

THE GHOSTS OF RICHMOND

THE COMMERCIALIZATION OF SPACE

ELECTRONIC SURVEILLANCE

HOSTAGE

THE GHOSTS OF TIDEWATER

THE GHOSTS OF FREDERICKSBURG

THE GHOSTS OF CHARLOTTESVILLE AND LYNCHBURG

THE GHOSTS OF VIRGINIA – VOLUME I